Churchill as
Home Secretary

With loving memories of
Anthony Charles 'Tony' Evans (ACE)
8 October 1942 (Higher Bebington, Wirral)
to 9 October 2018 (Christchurch, New Zealand)

I have laid aside business, and gone a-fishing

Churchill as Home Secretary

Suffragettes, Strikes and Social Reform, 1910–1911

Charles Stephenson

PEN & SWORD
HISTORY

First published in Great Britain in 2023 by
PEN & SWORD HISTORY
an imprint of Pen & Sword Books Ltd
Yorkshire – Philadelphia

ISBN 978-1-39906-261-9

A CIP catalogue record for this book is available from the British Library.

Typeset by Concept, Huddersfield, West Yorkshire, HD4 5JL.
Printed and bound in England by CPI Group (UK) Ltd, Croydon CR0 4YY.

Pen & Sword Books Ltd incorporates the imprints of Aviation, Atlas,
Family History, Fiction, Maritime, Military, Discovery, Politics, History,
Archaeology, Select, Wharncliffe Local History, Wharncliffe True Crime,
Military Classics, Wharncliffe Transport, Leo Cooper, The Praetorian Press,
Remember When, White Owl, Seaforth Publishing and Frontline Books.

For a complete list of Pen & Sword titles please contact
PEN & SWORD BOOKS LTD
47 Church Street, Barnsley, South Yorkshire, S70 2AS, England
E-mail: enquiries@pen-and-sword.co.uk
Website: www.pen-and-sword.co.uk
or
PEN & SWORD BOOKS
1950 Lawrence Rd, Havertown, PA 19083, USA
E-mail: uspen-and-sword@casematepublishers.com
Website: www.penandswordbooks.com

Contents

Contents

Introduction

'It has ... been, consistently, my experience that there is no more flawed source for recalling the events of yesterday than human recollection.'[1]

* * *

The Golden Glow of Memory

There can be few statesmen whose lives and careers have received as much investigation and literary attention as Winston Churchill. The centrepiece of this vast body of work is undoubtedly the eight-volume official biography (plus multitudinous companion volumes) by Randolph Churchill and Martin Gilbert. Thus huge endeavour, to steal a line from John Charmley, constitutes 'a "quarry" from which much of the stone for any other monument must be taken'.[2] In addition there have been innumerable biographies, and other works that have focused on specific aspects of the long Churchillian career.

Relatively little, however, has appeared which deals specifically or holistically with his first senior ministerial role: that of Secretary of State for the Home Office. This may be due to the fact that, of the three Great Offices of State[3] which he was to occupy over the course of his long political life, his tenure as Home Secretary was the briefest: aged 35, he was appointed by Liberal Prime Minister Herbert Asquith on 14 February 1910, relinquishing the position on 25 October 1911. Apart from his sinecure as Chancellor of the Duchy of Lancaster (May–November 1915) and his stewardship of the Colonial Office under Lloyd George (February 1921–October 1922), it was his shortest ministerial appointment and the one he liked least of all.

As one of his successors as Prime Minister has put it, 'Home Secretaries never do have an easy time', and Churchill's tenure was certainly marked by a huge degree of political and social turbulence. The Liberal Government elected in 1906 was bent on social and political reform, which was viewed by many conservatives as heralding the death of a once great society. This perception was encapsulated in a 1909 poem by Rudyard Kipling, 'The City of Brass': 'a fiercely patriotic defence of Britain's age-old values and traditions and a denunciation of their potential destruction by the tax-raising, social-reforming Liberal government'.[4] Indeed, even Churchill's son and biographer noted, with respect to House of Lords reform, that 'The proposed swamping of the Upper House was to appear even to many objective people as an act of constitutional indecency.'[5]

Though Churchill was one of those at the forefront of the push for constitutional change, his responsibility for domestic affairs led to him facing other, major, challenges departmentally. This was a time of substantial commotion on the social front, with widespread industrial and civil strife. Not only that but he had a plethora of other matters to absorb his energies; as Sir Edward Troup, permanent secretary throughout Churchill's tenure, was to describe it: the Home Office was 'responsible for all matters of domestic administration not specifically assigned to any other department'.[6]

It is, though, not proposed to delve into each and every matter with which Home Secretary Churchill involved himself or had to deal, such as, for example, the 1911 Shops Act, which improved conditions for retail workers, and his connection with attempts to achieve Welsh Disestablishment. These and similar matters are, it is submitted, of mainly academic interest and this book is in no way intended to be an academic work. Rather it is an attempt at narrative history, which is targeted at the general reader rather than the professional historian or, indeed, the Churchill aficionado; there is very little to be found here which hasn't already been covered somewhere else, though not necessarily all in one place.

In writing it I have, however, chosen to transgress one of the truisms enunciated by the subject: 'chronology is the key to narrative'. My doing so is justified, I would argue, and even supported by his qualification of the point: 'Yet where a throng of events are marching abreast, it is inevitable that their progress should be modified by selection and classification.'[7] During the period in question there were indeed a throng of events marching abreast, and so several chapters are mainly thematic with consequent disruption to chronology. I have also taken some space to place the various matters discussed into their contexts, and can only hope all this will meet with the general approval of the reader. If not, then *mea culpa*.

A word needs to be said concerning sources. Churchill's political career had several peaks and troughs with, of course, his 1940–1945 premiership elevating him to international recognition and worldwide renown as the man who led Britain to victory. One consequence is that post-1945 memories of him, because they are recollected or viewed through a distorting lens suffused with the 'golden glow' (see below) of his wartime apotheosis, risk being warped. An example concerns the 1965 book published by Violet Bonham-Carter née Asquith, *Winston Churchill as I Knew Him*. She certainly knew him very well, and did so for several decades: 'I have had the supreme good fortune to know Winston Churchill for the best part of my life.'[8]

Her account of their first meeting in the 'early summer of 1906' is often quoted as being an excellent example of how he regarded himself and was seen by her at that time. This was the occasion when, she recalled, he spoke 'in a torrent of magnificent language which appeared to be both effortless and inexhaustible', concluding with the wonderful aphorism – 'the words I shall always remember' –

that: 'We are all worms. But I do believe that I am a glow-worm.' Her account continues:

> Until the end of dinner I listened to him spellbound. I can remember thinking: *This* is what people mean when they talk of 'seeing stars' – this is what I am doing now ... I knew only that I had seen a 'great light'. I recognised it as the light of genius.[9]

A fascinating vignette of a near sixty-year-old occasion. However, when Violet Bonham-Carter's diaries were published in 1996 there was no mention of this occasion, nor of Churchill's enrapturing of her 19-year-old self in 1906. Indeed, the following year she wrote that she was 'quite amused [by] and liked Winston (whom I'd never properly spoken to before) very much'.[10] Roy Jenkins, in his introduction to the book, commented on the 'glow-worm' passage:

> What is distinctly odd is that there is no diary reference to the Churchill encounter to which she herself was to give great prominence in the book she wrote about him . . . This was a wonderfully descriptive passage, but was it true at the time or did it require a combination of the golden glow of memory and Churchill's subsequent rise to fame to burnish the exchange to brilliance?[11]

This is, of course, a diplomatically phrased way of saying that she had, in modern parlance, 'misremembered'. It is a common problem; the distinguished newspaperman and writer Antony Howard once remarked that 'It has ... been, consistently, my experience that there is no more flawed source for recalling the events of yesterday than human recollection.'[12]

There is another side to it. Violet Bonham-Carter's published letters and diaries are based on contemporary documents which she produced or received. However, this cannot be said for every similar account. By way of illustrating this point, consider the book by Churchill's doctor, Charles McMoran Wilson, later Lord Moran, which appeared in 1966.[13] This purported to be based on diaries kept between 1940 and 1965, the period when he was Churchill's personal physician. However, as Sir Martin Gilbert, Churchill's official biographer following the death of Randolph Churchill in 1968, later discovered, this was not so:

> Perhaps the most disturbing discovery I have made on sources for Churchill's life came after I had finished the eighth and final volume of the biography, in which a major source, for me as for all historians of his last twenty years, was the voluminous diary kept by Churchill's doctor, Lord Moran. Throughout the period of my researches the diary was closed to historians. Then, after the completion of an authorized life of Moran, it was brought to a leading medical library. I asked for the diary entry for a single date ... To my dismay, not merely for myself but for historical truth, I was told by the custodian of the papers that there was no entry for that day at all,

even though an entry under that exact date appears in the published book. Even the entries that did exist, I was told, were 'not a diary in the accepted sense of the word'. The mind boggles at how much misinformation may have crept into the history books, mine included, by such routes. As in the marketplace for fruit and vegetables, so for diaries, *caveat emptor*, let the purchaser beware.[14]

Beware indeed, and as Douglas Jeffrey plainly put it: 'much of what Moran wrote was not in his diary at the time. It could only have been made up later.'[15]

Conversely, Churchill's wilderness years in the 1930s were a time when he was widely thought of as a has-been, a man with a controversial past but without a political future. Consequently, in recollections dating from this period the glow of memory is considerably less golden. However, though neither Moran nor his diary directly feature in this work, the caveat alluded to by Gilbert certainly applies to all those diaries, memoirs and recollections which do, and this is mentioned and, if necessary, discussed at appropriate points in the text.

An examination of Churchill's first major political role is, I think, informative. It was the first time that he was empowered to wield the considerable executive authority inherent in the role of one of His Majesty's Principal Secretaries of State, and he certainly did not shrink from doing so. There were, of course, commensurate responsibilities, and how he shouldered them is also worth examination. The reader will be left to judge how effective, or otherwise, he was in discharging the duties and applying the powers entrusted to him.

Finally it remains for me to thank those who have been of great assistance in putting this work together. Once again I am grateful to Michael Perratt and Charles Blackwood for their invaluable advice and help. I am also deeply grateful to Sarah Cook for again deploying her superlative copy editing skills on my behalf. As always, though, any errors or defects that may be perceived are my responsibility, and mine alone.

Charles Stephenson
June 2022

Chapter One

The City of Brass

They unwound and flung from them with rage, as a rag that defied them,
The imperial gains of the age which their forefathers piled them.
They ran panting in haste to lay waste and embitter for ever
The wellsprings of Wisdom and Strengths which are Faith and Endeavour.
They nosed out and digged up and dragged forth and exposed to derision
All doctrine of purpose and worth and restraint and prevision:
And it ceased, and God granted them all things for which they had striven,
And the heart of a beast in the place of a man's heart was given ...

[Rudyard Kipling, 'The City of Brass', 1909.]

* * *

The trajectory that culminated in Churchill's elevation to the 'top table' as Home Secretary was somewhat convoluted, and in briefly tracing it and its context an outline of the troubled and turbulent times within which it occurred emerges. As a candidate for the Conservative Party, he had fought and lost a by-election at Oldham in 1899 before venturing to South Africa as a war correspondent to cover the Anglo-Boer War (also known as the Second Boer War or just the Boer War). Already an established author with three books under his belt,[1] his subsequent capture by the Boers, incarceration as a prisoner of war and successful escape to Portuguese East Africa (Mozambique) meant that he returned to Britain as an acknowledged 'Hero of the Empire' in 1900.

The Empire indeed seemed triumphant; Bloemfontein, the capital of the Orange Free State (*Oranje-Vrystaat*) had been occupied on 13 March and Pretoria, the capital of the South African Republic (*Zuid-Afrikaansche Republiek* or *Transvaal*), fell to Field Marshal Lord Roberts' forces on 5 June; the Boers appeared to have been defeated. This success of British arms, particularly when contrasted with the inauspicious beginnings of the war, led the Prime Minister, Robert Gascoyne-Cecil, 3rd Marquess of Salisbury (Lord Salisbury), to dissolve parliament in September and call a general election. As Churchill was to recall it some thirty years later: 'The Conservative leaders determined to appeal to the country before the enthusiasm of victory died down. They had already been in office five years. A General Election must come in eighteen months, and the opportunity was too good to be thrown away.'[2]

The political strategy behind this so-called 'Khaki Election' – with Joseph Chamberlain, the Colonial Secretary, famously arguing that 'every vote given against the government is a vote given to the Boers'[3] – proved successful. Despite securing only 5.6 per cent more votes than Sir Henry Campbell-Bannerman's Liberals on a relatively low turnout – more than a million fewer went to the polls than had done so in the previous election of 1895 (2,133,622 as against 3,409,711)[4] – the Unionist Party[5] was returned to power with a majority of over 130 seats in the House of Commons.[6] The Prime Minister was not amongst them, of course, being a member of the House of Lords, but was represented in the lower chamber by his nephew, Arthur Balfour, who was both Leader of the House of Commons and First Lord of the Treasury.

Churchill had again stood in Oldham, which returned two MPs to Parliament, and this time was elected as a Conservative member along with the Liberal Alfred Emmott. He wrote to Lord Salisbury following his success, stating that 'it is clear to me from the figures that nothing but personal popularity arising out of the late South African War, carried me in …'.[7] In fact the South African War was far from being 'late'. It had instead segued into a different kind of conflict, into guerrilla warfare. Ultimately it cost the UK more than £200 million, nearly 22,000 lives (out of a deployed force numbering just under 450,000), and some three-and-a-half years to subdue their largely irregular foe, some 87,365 strong; peace finally came with the Treaty of Vereeniging signed on 31 May 1902. Furthermore, in order to win the conflict the British had famously resorted to 'methods of barbarism'[8] and 'extermination'.[9] According to one of its chroniclers, it was 'the most humiliating war for Britain between 1815 and 1914'.[10] Even before it had ended none other than Kipling had declared that 'we have had no end of a lesson: it will do us no end of good'.[11]

Whether it did any good or not, the inquiry into this lesson certainly raised some troubling points. Chamberlain had from the beginning framed the conflict in ultra-patriotic terms. The Boers, he said, would never again 'be able to treat an Englishman as if he belonged to an inferior race'.[12] The possibility that English-men might, though, be turning, be degenerating, into an 'inferior race', was mooted by the subsequent investigation. The four volumes compiled by the Royal Commission on the South African War came out in 1903 and produced, according to contemporary journalistic accounts, a 'profound sensation'.[13] For those disinclined to peruse such weighty tomes, the *Daily Mail* helpfully pro-duced a condensed, 43 page, guide which it sold for three pence. Many of the 'ghastly blunders' pertaining to the conflict were rooted in administrative and organisational failures, but, as the guide informed its readership, there were prob-lems with the raw material too:

> The soldiers themselves were not the pick of the nation. Their mental capacity was low, as they were drawn from the humblest class; personally brave, they were not intelligent; they entered [the army], in many cases … because they could not obtain work outside it. In the field they displayed magnificent qualities, endurance, and contempt for dangers; but in intellect they were no match for the Boers. […] Their health was not good; and the

enormous losses from enteric [typhoid] were due, in the opinion of many witnesses, in great part to the defective physique of the men, who suffered far more than the stronger and healthier officers.[14]

For humblest read poorest, and with officers being overwhelmingly drawn from moneyed and propertied classes, this account outlined the dichotomy that encapsulated the social problem pertaining in the UK. It also raised a deeper question. If these soldiers – adjudged to be 'in physique and intelligence ... inferior to the Continental soldier'[15] – were amongst those who had passed the requisite recruitment tests, then what sort of condition were those who had failed likely to be in?

These were troublesome points and have been explored somewhat here because the issues raised, centring on and around the perception of national decline and degeneration, will feature later. This decline was more than just a perception in the economic sphere; it was grounded in harsh reality. Though there are differences of opinion as regards the reasons, there is little argument that the UK's former industrial and commercial domination had been seriously eroded by the first decade of the twentieth century. This 'Descent from Hegemony' between 1870 and 1913,[16] when British growth rates for industrial productivity trailed those in Germany and the USA, left the country in third place behind its international competitors.[17] One proposed political remedy for this situation, for preserving and indeed enhancing the UK's great power status and to also bind the various territories comprising the British Empire more closely to the 'mother country', was tariff reform.[18]

This was an intensely divisive subject. Churchill, representing a Lancashire constituency whose wealth was built on 'King Cotton' and free trade, was both politically and personally against tariff reform. Indeed, the principle had largely underpinned Britain's economic policy since the repeal of the Corn Laws in 1846.[19] The chief proponent of tariff reform was the Colonial Secretary Joseph Chamberlain, and in order to wage a campaign for it he resigned from the cabinet on 14 September 1903. Put in simple terms, the reformers sought to transform the Empire into a worldwide, single, trading bloc that would be of a size better able to deal with its competitors. Under the scheme, tariffs would be levelled on imports, making them more expensive and thus preventing any undercutting of British products. Opponents, however, argued that protectionism would mean dearer food, especially bread.[20] The issue threatened to split the Conservatives and smash their coalition with the Liberal Unionists.[21] Indeed Chamberlain, no doubt unwittingly but with unerring precision, had alighted on the one and only issue that was guaranteed to disrupt his own party whilst uniting that of his opponents.

Lord Salisbury had resigned in May 1902 to be succeeded by Balfour, who was then forced to tread a precariously narrow line between the factions. One of the most intellectually gifted of men, he was able to successfully paper over most of the cracks most of the time. It was no easy task, even for someone of his ability.

Churchill had, however, found himself at odds with his party leaders and the government even before the question of protectionism arose. Perhaps the most prominent example was his opposition to the proposed reforms of the Army as set out by St John Brodrick, the Secretary of State for War from 12 November 1900 to 12 October 1903. A set of six speeches he made on the subject were published in a short book of 102 pages in 1903.[22] According to his son and official biographer, Churchill was even in 1902 finding the Liberal Party 'increasingly sympathetic to his rapidly maturing political conceptions'.[23] This sympathy grew; a speech he gave on 22 April 1904 in favour of Trade Unions was reported by the *Daily Mail* as espousing 'Radicalism of the reddest type'.[24] There is no doubt that Churchill's differences with the government and with his party were genuine, especially when he perceived that Balfour might be moving towards protectionism. This is revealed by his private correspondence with many individuals and his public utterances in relation to Free Trade; in a series of his speeches published in 1906, but made between 1902 and 1905 and numbering nine in total, his exhortation of Free Trade was consistent.[25] Of this number, seven were made whilst he was still a Conservative MP. The final two came after 31 May 1904, the day he 'crossed the floor' and became a member of the Liberal Party in the House of Commons.[26] He was neither the first nor the last to do so; nine other Conservative or Liberal Unionist MPs decamped to the Liberals between 1900 and 1906, whilst one went in the other direction.[27]

Churchill's defection wasn't spontaneous; the Conservative whip had been withdrawn from him in January 1904,[28] and the ground vis-à-vis his new political home was well prepared. He had met with David Lloyd George by appointment on 31 December 1903, their 'first political meeting' according to W.R.P. George. On this occasion, as Lloyd George's contemporary account records, Churchill informed him that:

> He is willing to come over to our side and thinks 30 other Unionists will accompany him. I told him that on Education and Temperance we were inexorable. He is willing to meet us on these. In fact, he is willing to play the Progressive game all round ...[29]

The 'package' offered to the defector, which he accepted, included running as a Liberal candidate in the Manchester North West constituency at the next General Election.[30] His erstwhile colleagues were, of course, furious, dubbing him 'the Blenheim Rat'; Blenheim being both the palace where he was born and the home of his ancestors and family. As Roy Jenkins was to phrase it in terms of the party he joined: he 'brought no experience of government, but he brought a famous name, an ebullient personality and a sense, not entirely complimentary, that he was unlikely to join a losing side'.[31]

Churchill's first foray against his former party came with the Government's introduction of the 1904 Aliens Bill. Drafted following the report of a Royal Commission on Alien Immigration, which commenced its investigations on 24 April 1902 and produced its report on 10 August 1903, it proposed to give the Home Secretary considerable powers of discretion and control over immigration, or at least in respect of certain categories of immigrant.[32] Churchill, along with the Liberal leadership, wholeheartedly opposed the Bill. His publicly expressed, and extremely powerful, disapproval appeared in a two-page leaflet, entitled *Mr Winston Churchill on the Aliens Bill: A Letter Addressed to a Manchester Correspondent*, which reproduced a 30 May 1904 missive sent to Nathan Laski of Manchester, the 'uncrowned king' of the Jewish community. The text, which also appeared in *The Times* of 31 May 1904 and was widely syndicated in provincial newspapers, excoriated the Government in no uncertain terms, arguing that 'we can only wonder that an English gentleman should make such proposals to the House of Commons in the 20th century'. He went on to state that:

> The whole Bill looks like an attempt on the part of the Government to gratify a small but noisy section of their own supporters and to purchase a little popularity in the constituencies by dealing harshly with a number of unfortunate aliens who have no votes. It will commend itself to those who like patriotism at other people's expense and admire Imperialism on the Russian model. It is expected to appeal to insular prejudice against foreigners, to racial prejudice against Jews, and to labour prejudice against competition; and it will no doubt supply a variety of rhetorical phrases for the approaching election. The same men who are obstinate opponents of trade unionism will declaim about 'the rights of British labour'. Those who champion the interests of slum landlords will dilate on the evils of overcrowding. Those who have been most forward in bringing Chinese into Africa will pose as champions of racial purity at home.[33]

The Bill failed to make it onto the Statute Book, largely because it became bogged-down by being referred to a Grand Committee, to which Churchill was appointed. This body eventually found, in July 1904, that it was 'useless' to proceed further with the Bill 'in view of the large number of Amendments' that were put down against it. Churchill had a large hand in this outcome, establishing a reputation as a defender of minority rights. The Government did not abandon the matter entirely, however, and eventually got a much watered-down version into law on 11 August 1905. This was, however, 'a highly unsuccessful piece of legislation ... enacted by an enfeebled Conservative government at the very end of its period of office ...'.[34]

That Balfour's Government was indeed reaching the end of its term had become obvious, if not rapidly then certainly by degrees, in 1905, an example being their loss of a vote in the House of Commons on 20 July.[35] Though he did not resign then, the end finally came for the Prime Minister on 21 November 1905 when Chamberlain made a widely reported speech to the Liberal Unionist Council, this being an assembly which he dominated. Though uttered in coded terms, it was perceived as being highly critical of Balfour and his leadership, or rather lack thereof.[36] The Prime Minister's resignation came on 5 December but, in a move seen as demonstrating his 'surpassing subtlety',[37] he did not dissolve Parliament and call an election. Ignoring established constitutional practice,[38] he handed power directly to Campbell-Bannerman, a decision which was viewed contemporaneously as a 'smart stroke in the game of tactics'.[39]

This was so because many, perhaps most, Conservatives believed that any administration led by Campbell-Bannerman would prove both difficult to assemble, given the competing egos amongst the leading lights, and in any event unpopular. There would have to be an election within two years, and during the intervening period the electorate would see in power 'the man who had defamed the British Army and set himself against the nation in its time of peril'.[40] This brief interlude of Liberal rule, as they foresaw it being, would also allow space for Balfour to recover the initiative by joining hands with Chamberlain against the new Government. Unionists were, according to Spender, all but unanimous that Balfour had acted wisely.[41]

Whether he had or not remained to be seen, but that he might have miscalculated on one factor became evident when the Liberal leader put together a cabinet with little or no difficulty. That Churchill had acted wisely became evident on 9 December 1905; Campbell-Bannerman elevated him to a Junior Ministerial position as Under-Secretary of State for the Colonies.[42] This followed him turning down the post he was first offered, Financial Secretary to the Treasury, despite it being a more senior position. It was, as Rose notes, 'generally accepted that Churchill's preference of the Colonial Office sprang from dubious motives'.[43] These alleged 'motives' revolved around the fact that, despite the position being a subordinate one, it actually provided him with an excellent platform in the House of Commons. His superior as Colonial Secretary, Victor Bruce, the 9th Earl of Elgin, was confined to the House of Lords, thus leaving Churchill to be the spokesman on colonial matters where it mattered most. It was undoubtedly presumptuous that a man who, to reiterate Jenkins' point, had no experience of government and moreover had only been a Liberal for about eighteen months, should attempt to dictate what promotion he might take. He got away with it, because, as Campbell-Bannerman's biographer put it, the Prime Minister had decided his Ministry 'should be well salted with new and vigorous young men'. The names of two such stand out: David Lloyd George and Winston Churchill.[44]

Churchill and Elgin made what, on the face of it, seemed an odd team. The two had met previously when the former, as a junior officer, was stationed in India whilst Elgin was Viceroy. It seems highly unlikely that the latter would have remembered one out of the many undistinguished officers he came into fleeting contact with. He did, though, as he revealed some three years after the event, have initial misgivings about working with his new junior, though also related that these proved groundless:

> When I accepted Churchill as my Under Sec[retar]y I knew I should have no easy task. I resolved to give him access to all business – but to keep control (& my temper). I think I may say I succeeded. Certainly we have had no quarrel during the 2½ years, on the contrary he has again and again thanked me for what he had learned and for our pleasant personal relations.[45]

Churchill's Private Secretary, Edward Marsh, a Civil Service clerk appointed in 1905 and who subsequently became a lifelong friend, described the relationship between the Colonial Secretary and his deputy as being one of 'qualified esteem'.[46] At any rate there was much pressing business for Elgin and Churchill to attend to, the most obvious being the requirement for settling how the former Boer Republics in South Africa, now the Transvaal Colony and Orange River Colony, would be governed within the British Empire. First, though, there was a General Election to fight; the King formally dissolved Parliament on 8 January 1906 but the campaign was well under way before it had been announced.[47]

The election itself was held over the period 12 January to 8 February and one of its predominant motifs, as mentioned in Churchill's letter to Nathan Laski, was the question of indentured Chinese labourers imported on three-year contracts to South Africa to work in the gold-mining industry. By 1906 some 50,000 were so employed and their living conditions – they were kept in compounds and subject to corporal punishment – excited vigorous protests at this 'Chinese slavery'. As J.B. Priestley, born in 1894, recalled many years later: 'I can remember staring, as a small boy, at the cartoons and posters with their Chinese faces and caricatures of bloated capitalists using slave labour.'[48]

The effect this had on the outcome is unknown, but the results of the election demonstrated beyond doubt that Balfour's supposed 'smart stroke' had, in fact, gone horribly awry. Not only did the former Prime Minister lose his own seat of twenty years at Manchester East, whilst Churchill won his at the neighbouring constituency of Manchester North West, but the Unionist Party was crushed across the board.[49] The Liberals emerged with 399 MPs whilst the Unionists could only muster 156. Balfour had remained leader of the Unionist Party, and secured his return to the House of Commons by winning a by-election on 27 February held in the City of London. The vacancy had been created by the newly re-elected Conservative member, Alban Gibbs, resigning to allow his party leader to stand in a safe seat. Balfour thus returned to the House of Commons as Leader of the Opposition on 12 March.[50] He thereby missed Churchill's response to an Opposition amendment on the question of the Chinese in South Africa. This deprecated the Government bringing 'the reputation of this country into contempt by describing the employment of Chinese indentured labour as slavery ... whilst contemplating no effectual method of bringing it to an end'. In his response Churchill coined a famous phrase:

> I took occasion during the elections to say, and I repeat it now, that the conditions ... under which Chinese labour is now being carried on ... cannot ... be classified as slavery in the extreme acceptance of the word without some risk of terminological inexactitude.[51]

Aside from his election victory and continuation in post, 1906 was a notable year in Churchill's literary life. His first biographical work, his father Lord Randolph Churchill being the subject, was published in two volumes in the middle of the year.[52] Though it attracted both acclaim and criticism, there is no doubt that, in the words of a contemporary reviewer, the author displayed 'great literary talent'.[53] One later assessment of this 'filial monument' dubbed it 'an immense, whitewashed shrine erected ... out of carefully selected materials ...'.[54] Coincidentally, the only 'tangible or enduring record' of Lord Randolph's political life and labours was considered by his son to have been in much the same field as the one he now occupied: the 1 January 1886 annexation of 'the Burma province'.[55] This had been achieved at the end of Lord Randolph's brief period as Secretary of State for India (June 1885–January 1886).

Colonial matters continued to engross Churchill and Elgin, who had gone back to work after the election. In fact the new Government changed policy in respect of the former Boer republics on 8 February 1906, when the Prime Minister persuaded the cabinet to grant them self, or responsible, government. This measure, which overturned and superseded the less democratic 'Lyttleton Constitution' put forward in 1903 by the previous administration, was vehemently condemned by the Opposition as 'a dangerous and reckless experiment'.[56] These denunciations continued until December 1906, when Letters Patent granting the new constitution for the Transvaal were issued.[57]

The availability of this methodology was fortuitous, inasmuch as passing legislation through parliament on the matter would have likely proved impossible. This was so because even though Campbell-Bannerman could command a huge majority in the House of Commons, the situation was very different in respect of the UK Parliament's second chamber, the House of Lords. The problem this engendered was far from novel and had been well, and arguably best, expressed by a former leader of the Liberal Party, Archibald Primrose, the 5th Earl of Rosebery (Lord Rosebery), who had served as Prime Minister from March 1894 to June 1895. He explained it thus to Queen Victoria in 1894:

> When the Conservative Party is in power, there is practically no House of Lords: it takes whatever the Conservative Government brings it from the House of Commons without question or dispute; but the moment a Liberal Government is formed, this harmless body assumes an active life, and its activity is entirely exercised in opposition to the Government ... the determined hostility of this body ... is in fact a permanent barrier raised against the Liberal party.[58]

As Herbert Asquith later phrased it: 'the History of Parliament from 1906 to 1911 is the record of a protracted and persistent struggle between the representative and the non-representative Chambers'.[59] This struggle manifested itself from the very start; the Lords effectively destroyed a number of Bills sent up to them by the Commons though, by constitutional convention, they did not impede finance bills. Unsurprisingly then, reform of the House of Lords became a matter that exercised the Government and a number of schemes were discussed.

Churchill was kept busy during the first months of 1907 preparing for the month-long Colonial Conference, a meeting of Prime Ministers from the self-governing British colonies, scheduled for 15 April–14 May.[60] Even so, he managed to find time to opine on other matters; he did not take the, then conventional, view that Under-Secretaries confined 'their oratory to the work of their own departments'.[61]

Still perforce making a living from his pen as Members of Parliament below ministerial (Cabinet) level were unwaged,[62] he wrote a piece on the House of Lords issue for a new magazine, *The Nation*, which appeared on 9 March 1907. Entitled 'A Smooth Way with the Peers', it appeared alongside commentary probably contributed by the editor, the radical journalist Henry William Massingham. Though fairly unremarkable in itself, an example of the reaction it elicited, and where, is perhaps instructive:

> Mr Winston Churchill is the extreme example of the danger to the British Empire of entrusting power to a leaderless party. It would be absurd to call Sir Henry Campbell-Bannerman the leader of the present British government in any but a purely technical sense. [...]
>
> His scheme for a new House of Lords is funny – funnier even than Sir Henry's threats to the clouds. The title, 'A Smooth Way with the Peers,' is characteristic.
>
> The smooth way is simple: the government of the day shall dictate to the sovereign what peers and other privy councillors shall sit for the life of each parliament – that is that the second chamber shall be merely the endorser and registrar of the acts of the Commons.
>
> The suggestion that a certain custom should be established at once is delicious and very Winstonian.[63]

Though the tone of the piece is obviously mocking and critical of Churchill's views, it does surely serve to demonstrate that he, and those views, had gained a certain currency, notoriety even, given that his name had been adjectivised. Indeed, according to Massingham, he was 'the most observed of Ministers after the head of the Government. Here at least every man discovers a star whose course he cannot predict with certainty, while it attracts him by its light.'[64]

For the moment, though, Churchill had to play a minor role, certainly in terms of the Colonial Conference which had originally been scheduled, by the previous Government, for 1906 but had been delayed by circumstances in Australia and New Zealand.[65] Given the postponement and the granting of the Transvaal Constitution in the meantime, one of the attendees was 'General The Honourable Louis Botha, Prime Minister of the Transvaal'.[66] Churchill and Botha met often and seemingly 'got along famously'.[67] The former was to later write that 'Botha always felt he had a special call upon my attention. Whenever he visited Europe we saw each other many times ...'.[68] One premier who was perhaps less enamoured of Churchill was the Australian federal Prime Minister, Alfred Deakin, who has been described as 'the bete noire of the Liberals'.[69] Indeed, during a debate on 7 May 1907 around the subject of Preferential Trade, Deakin joshed Churchill (who was not present), contending that his arguments had been 'magnified and exaggerated so beyond all measure – that they temporarily hypnotised the Under Secretary, as he with his eloquence was hypnotising us'.[70] He was, of course, not the last person to make claims in that vein; his official biographer opined that 'While he was a backbencher, Churchill had spoken as if he were an Under-Secretary; now, as an Under-Secretary, as if a member of the Cabinet ...'.[71]

Notwithstanding his position as Under-Secretary, he continued to pronounce on domestic matters, and did so with more than a hint of radicalism. His June 1907 speech during a debate on the House of Lords evidences this:

> I say that to dispute the authority of a newly-elected Parliament is something very like an incitement to violence on the part of the other House. [...] What steps do they suggest that we should take in order to bring home to them the earnestness of our plea? What steps do they suggest that the people should take in order to assert their wishes? I hold entirely by what I said that to dispute the authority of an elected body fresh from its constituents is a deliberate incitement to the adoption of lawless and unconstitutional methods.[72]

He further characterised the struggle between the two Houses as being a fight between wealth and poverty, between the rich and the poor.[73] He predicted victory for the latter: 'we shall wrest from the hands of privilege and wealth the evil and ugly and sinister weapon of the Peers' veto, which they have used so ill so long.'[74] Inflammatory language of this kind was expected from, say, Lloyd George but coming from Churchill it was particularly resented:

> He [Churchill] had been born into the English aristocracy at a time when British noblemen were considered (and certainly considered themselves) little less than godlike. His grandfather, the Duke of Marlborough, was Viceroy of Ireland;[75] his nursery, in the Viceregal Palace.[76]

Such 'Winstonian' utterances certainly helped to cement his reputation amongst Conservatives as 'a Judas, a turncoat, a renegade, a class traitor ...'.[77] Though obviously not all aristocrats thought so; earlier in June Churchill had discussed with his chief the taking of an extended, roughly four-month, trip to East Africa later that year.

Despite being accompanied by his Private Secretary Edward Marsh, a civil servant, this was not an official visit and was undertaken at Churchill's expense. Lord Elgin approved: 'if it is convenient & appeals to you to undertake that expedition, it will I am sure be of the greatest advantage that you should have seen the country – where we have so many difficult problems to deal with. I can only hope that it will be a pleasant as well as an interesting trip.'[78] Campbell-Bannerman dubbed the proposed trip a 'pilgrimage' in a letter to Churchill thanking him for his work on the two South African constitutions. The Prime Minister deemed them the 'greatest achievement of this Government' and 'the finest & noblest work of the British power in modern times'. He told Churchill that he had 'so identified' himself with the policy, and 'so greatly contributed to its successful enforcement that a large part of the credit of it must be always attributed to you'. The missive concluded by urging him to 'take a good holiday' and not to 'overdo it'.[79]

Any illusion Elgin may have entertained that his lieutenant had departed on 'a purely sporting and private expedition'[80] was soon shattered. Churchill travelled to East Africa via France and Italy, then took ship across the Mediterranean. He broke his voyage at Malta and Cyprus, arriving at the former on the evening of 2 October 1907. The following day 'a lengthy address' appeared in the *Daily Malta Chronicle* entitled 'Malta Lacks a Constitution', which posed a rhetorical question:

> Can anyone believe that same England which … had given an autonomous government to conquered South Africa, should obstinately refuse to grant the management of its domestic affairs to our Malta … which entered the British Empire of its own free will, relying on the honour and good faith of the British Nation?[81]

This theme was expanded upon the following day when the Under-Secretary met with the 'elected Members and representatives of the nobility, the Malta bar, and the Chamber of Commerce …'. By way of reply he informed them that 'the door is not closed on the constitutional question'. He followed up his words by sending a lengthy letter to Elgin on that and other matters, with the promise of 'making some modest proposals which will relieve the local situation' in a memo yet to be drawn up.[82]

Something along the same lines occurred after his 'five busy days' in Cyprus (8–13 October), with Elgin receiving a confidential telegram letting him know 'I am writing to you fully upon numerous important questions which require attention.'[83] The subsequent memorandum, entitled 'Condition of Cyprus', was sent to both Elgin and Sir Francis Hopwood, the Permanent Under-Secretary at the Colonial Office. It ran to four pages when printed and began 'I am concerned about the condition of Cyprus, which I have just left, after a short but crowded visit', before moving on to recount a litany of errors relating to British Imperial rule, mainly in the financial field. 'Things cannot go on as they are,' he stated, before arguing that 'It is futile for British visitors to go about complaining of Cypriot "ingratitude". Look behind the symptom, touch the cause.'[84]

It has to be said that Churchill raised some valid points in these communications but they, and several others on various subjects that he subsequently sent from East Africa, annoyed his colleagues back in London. Hopwood, a civil servant it should be remembered, wrote to Elgin on the matter:

> He is most tiresome to deal with & will I fear give trouble – as his father did – in any position to which he may be called. The restless energy, uncontrollable desire for notoriety & the lack of moral perception make him an anxiety indeed! Churchill should have reserved his points until he

returned home … he can never understand that there is a better way of enforcing an argument.[85]

Such observations from an adviser to his political superior, on that superior's deputy, were deemed 'mischief' and 'wholly unsuitable' by Randolph Churchill.[86] That may be so, but there is no doubt that Lord Elgin was entirely in accord with the general tone of the sentiments expressed. He was to write to his successor that the course of the East African trip was 'strewn with memoranda' and that he believed 'most of them hopelessly to be impracticable at least as they stand'.[87] This was another portent of the future: Elgin and Hopwood were certainly not the last to be troubled by Churchill's 'restless energy' and resultant epistolary productivity. Indeed Edward Marsh, who had joined the party at Malta and may have thought he was going on a holiday, was apparently kept busy for '14 hours work on one day upon these memoranda in the heat & discomfort of the Red Sea'.[88]

Neither was Churchill's literary output confined to official matters. He wrote nine articles on the excursion for *The Strand Magazine*, which were published monthly from March to November 1908, sharing the September edition with a new Sherlock Holmes story.[89] Randolph Churchill, who noted only five, states that he was paid £750 for these pieces, which would 'definitely liquidate all possible expenses' involved in the trip.[90] The adventure became a distinctly profitable enterprise in the financial sense when the *Strand* articles, along with an additional two chapters, were republished in book form in December 1908 as *My African Journey*, the source material having been 'written mainly in long hot Uganda afternoons, after the day's march was done,.[91] The first of the additional chapters, however, entitled 'Down The White Nile' and which narrated the initial stages of the journey home, related a tragedy. Marsh also recounted it:

> At Khartoum we suffered our one calamity. Winston had brought out from England his valet George Scrivings, who had been a steward in his mother's hospital-ship *Maine* in the South African war, and ever since his stand-by and faithful friend. He was a man of decided character, quite undaunted by his formidable master … He seemed full of health and vigour, but the tropics found a chink in his defences, and he died after a few days' illness. This was a great sorrow to us all, and most of all to Winston, who had brought him away from his home and his wife and children to die in his service …[92]

Churchill wrote a heartfelt letter to Mrs Scrivings, dated 24 December 1907, which only came into the public domain in 2016. It included the lines: 'My heart bleeds for you and your poor children. It will be my duty to make adequate provision for your future and theirs; and you need not worry on these matters.'[93]

A further death, or at least an imminent one, was shortly to make its mark on Churchill, but this time in political terms. As Asquith's wife recounted it: 'On the 27th of March, 1908, Henry [Herbert Henry Asquith] came into my room at 7.30 p.m. and told me that Sir Henry Campbell-Bannerman had sent for him that day to tell him that he was dying.'[94] The Prime Minister was indeed very ill, and had been for some time, and he and Asquith, as his designated and acknowledged successor, began to ponder and discuss the structure of his forthcoming administration. Churchill's future came under consideration, with several missives on the subject passing between the two men. Subsequent to Campbell-Bannerman's resignation on 3 April 1908, and Asquith becoming Prime Minister five days later, the new premier offered Churchill the cabinet-level position of President of the Board of Trade.[95] He thus stepped into Lloyd George's former position, with the latter elevated to Asquith's former role as Chancellor of the Exchequer. With these 'heavenly twins of social reform' in the Cabinet, the tempo of reform dramatically quickened.[96]

But before he could do anything politically, and because he would now be paid a ministerial salary, under the rules then applying Churchill had to fight a by-election. During the late nineteenth century it had become unusual for oppositions to put up opposing candidates, particularly if the contest occurred immediately following a general election.[97] This was not, of course, the case in this instance and furthermore, as Otte and Readman have noted, such contests 'offered useful opportunities for the opposition to challenge governments and their policy, particularly policy associated with the ministers in question'.[98] Perhaps even more pertinently, 'in 1908 the Tories were in no mood to allow the renegade and venomous Churchill to accept preferment to a Liberal Cabinet without a fight'.[99]

It was indeed a hard-fought, and ill-tempered, campaign. Furthermore, if the Conservative candidate William Joynson-Hicks suffered, as he remarked that he did, from vociferous Jews who were very difficult to 'shout down' at his meetings, then his opponent had a similar problem, though with different culprits.[100] Annoyed that Asquith, who was opposed to female suffrage, had succeeded Campbell-Bannerman, who had been in favour, Christabel Pankhurst despatched her 'lieutenants' to Manchester. Some forty in number, they organised a campaign so that when Churchill arrived, the operation to secure his rejection at the polls, and thus damage Asquith's government, was already in place.[101] Christabel herself masterminded the venture, which involved organising up to twelve meetings a day in various venues.[102]

Churchill stated that he was on their side. When asked, at a public meeting, what he would do to help women to get the Parliamentary suffrage, he said he would 'try my best as and when occasion offers'. He further offered that he sincerely thought 'that the women have always had a logical case, and they have now got behind them a great popular demand among women'.

Christabel Pankhurst was having none of it, responding in an open letter that 'we attach no value to Mr Churchill's assertion that he will use his influence with the Government in the interests of women's suffrage. [...] Unless this official Government pledge is made to us we shall continue our opposition to the candidature of Mr Churchill and other Government candidates.'[103]

Lloyd George later, and rather waspishly, joked that whilst 'we all hate the suffragettes for spoiling our speeches', they made Churchill 'very bitter because they ruin his perorations ... His perorations, prepared with the utmost care, are completely wrecked and spoiled by squeaky voices calling out, "Mr. Churchill! What about votes for women?"'[104]

Whether or not the ruination of his perorations played any part in it must remain unknown. However, when the votes were counted after the election on 24 April 1908 he had come second, following a 6.4 per cent swing to the Conservatives.[105] The latter were, of course, exultant; apocryphally, the witticism 'What is the use of a WC without a seat?' did the rounds. Even the 'normally staid' *Daily Telegraph* became 'delirious':

> Churchill out – language fails us just when it is most needed. We have all been yearning for this to happen with a yearning beyond utterance. Figures – oh, yes, there are figures, but who cares for figures today. Winston Churchill is out, OUT, OUT![106]

Churchill informed his recently acquired significant other, Clementine Hozier, that 'but for those sulky Irish Catholics changing sides at the last moment under priestly pressure, the result would have been different'.[107] Whatever the reasons for his defeat, it was a personal and political setback but, as Jenkins observed, a far from fatal one; he was now a 'famous figure whose rumbustious politics appealed to Liberal activists'.[108] The Liberal Association at Dundee was quickest off the mark; immediately after the result he received a telegram from them inviting him to be their candidate in a pending by-election caused by the incumbent's elevation to the House of Lords. Dundee was a dual-member constituency and the vacancy was considered safe for a Liberal; his predecessor had first been elected there in 1885.[109] After thinking about it for a few days, and in preference to the other 'eight or nine safe seats' which had been placed at his disposal,[110] Churchill decided to accept the Dundee offer:

> On the strong advice of the Chief Whips in Scotland and England and with the recommendation of the PM I have accepted ... They all seem to think it is a certainty ... It is a life seat and cheap and easy beyond all experience.[111]

He was wrong about one factor; the campaign, though very different from that at Manchester, proved far from easy. Not in the political sense; he made free trade the key issue of his appeal to the voters, despite the fact that the vital Dundee jute industry was in something of a depression at that time. Rather it was because his speeches on the matter,[112] and not just the perorations, were severely disrupted by suffragettes; 'on his accepting the invitation, the Suffragettes' armies hastened North to oppose him ...'.[113] One particular disruptrix, whom Randolph Churchill dubbed, with what was probably unwitting drollness, the 'ring-leader', was Mary Maloney, *aka* 'la Belle Maloney'.[114] As a press report put it under the headline 'A Speech Spoiled: Miss Molony's [*sic*] Successful Interruption of the Liberal Candidate':

> On Monday [3 May], when Mr Churchill was addressing a meeting of workmen during dinner-time at a large factory, Miss Molony, an Irish Suffragist,

appeared on the scene in a carriage, and began to drown the speaker's voice with a hand-bell. [...] For some time Mr Churchill struggled good-humouredly against the bell, but at last he gave up the effort in despair, saying, 'If she thinks that is a reasonable argument she may use it. I don't care. I bid you good afternoon.'[115]

Locally, and even further afield, the by-election was long-remembered for Mary Moloney's bell, and Churchill took these 'ding-dong exchanges' in good part, even though they forced the cancellation of several meetings. Despite these annoyances, when the results of the election were announced on 9 May, Churchill, notwithstanding a last-minute exhibition of palpable apprehension, had received the most votes.[116] Thus, alongside Labour's Alexander Wilkie, he became one of Dundee's two parliamentary representatives and was back in the House of Commons.[117] His victory was viewed as a serious check to the Labour cause, but his 'aggressive radicalism and talk of social reconstruction paid handsome dividends'.[118]

Churchill's anxiety over the result as noted above was likely due to his fear that George Stuart, his Labour opponent, would beat him; that 'the labouring classes' might choose one of their own to represent them. Unlike in England and Wales, there was no Liberal-Labour alliance in Scotland to ensure the progressive vote didn't split, and Randolph Churchill noted his worry that Stuart was making 'sizeable inroads into the Liberal vote'.[119] This concern was far from groundless; the election of Wilkie in 1906 had demonstrated that Liberal domination of Dundee was slipping.[120]

Attempts to prevent further slippage had been evident in a (bell free) speech he made to a packed audience in the Kinnaird Hall in Dundee's Bank Street, which had an official capacity of about 2,000, on 4 May.[121] Here Churchill trod a fine line in wooing potential Labour voters whilst disavowing what he termed 'the revolutionary Socialist'.[122] He warned his audience not to 'underrate the growing strength of the Tory reaction now in progress in many of the constituencies in England'. He went on:

> I say it earnestly to those who are members of the Labour Party here to-day – do not underrate the storm which is gathering over your heads as well as ours. I am not afraid of the forces which are against us. With your support we shall overwhelm them – with your support we shall bear them down. Ah, but we must have that support.[123]

These sentiments largely echoed those he had previously expressed in public on the issue. On that earlier occasion Churchill had, however, declined to 'plunge into a discussion of the philosophical divergences between Socialism and Liberalism.[124] Now he did so, whilst arguing that Labour supporters came in two types, only one of which he was appealing to. Of those whom he deemed to possess 'violent and extreme views who call themselves Socialists', he was dismissive:

'I recognise that they are perfectly right in voting against me and voting against the Liberals, because Liberalism is not Socialism, and never will be ...'.[125]

Though he was obviously highlighting the difference between 'moderate' and 'militant' socialists, as he perceived them, it is difficult to ascertain quite whom Churchill's group of 'violent and extreme' socialists actually were in the Dundee context. It is true that outside the 'official' Labour Party, the party with which the Liberals had an electoral pact in England and Wales, there existed a group called the Socialist Labour Party (SLP). Founded in Scotland, they regarded the Labour Party as being capitalist-embracing, liberal, social democrats. They were, however, a miniscule organisation of virtually no political significance, and there was no SLP candidate at Dundee in 1908. In any case, he was obviously attempting to influence the, relatively small, number of voters; out of a total population of between 161,000 and 165,000,[126] those Dundonians holding the franchise totalled only a little under 19,000.[127] Of that electorate, about 60 per cent were categorised as working class,[128] with the remainder being of the middling variety.[129] Perhaps it was to that smaller contingent that his comments were aimed, Liberalism being, even in its 'New' guise of the early 1900s, a 'middle-class philosophy',[130] albeit with 'considerable common ground' in relation to the 'essentially gradualist, evolutionary socialism espoused by most of the Labour party's political theorists'.[131]

In any event, and fortified by his renewed democratic mandate, the new President of the Board of Trade returned to London to put into practice concrete policies pursuant to industry and the other matters within the purview of his department. In addition, and more generally, there was the social reform agenda. Randolph Churchill argues, in relation to that subject, that Winston Churchill was actually pursuing a version of 'Tory Democracy' as supposedly expounded by Lord Randolph.[132] No doubt he was; however, as Quinault has comprehensively demonstrated, 'Tory Democracy', if it existed at all, was an exceedingly ill-defined doctrine.[133] Indeed, Lord Randolph himself admitted that its chief characteristic was opportunism.[134] Perhaps Addison put it best when he spoke of 'the myth of his father's career' which ran in Churchill's head.[135]

Interestingly perhaps, one of Lloyd George's biographers posits that Lord Randolph's style, as distinct to any philosophy he might have espoused, influenced his subject.[136] That may be so, but there is little doubt that whomever might have influenced Lloyd George, Lloyd George certainly influenced Winston Churchill, and to a large degree at that. Violet Bonham Carter, Asquith's daughter and confidante, and Churchill's close friend, was to retrospectively observe that 'the most curious and surprising feature' of the Lloyd George-Churchill partnership was 'that while it exercised no influence whatsoever on Lloyd George, politically or otherwise, it directed, shaped and coloured Winston Churchill's mental attitude and his political course during the next few years'.[137] There is other evidence concerning this perception. Robert Boothby, Parliamentary Private Secretary to Churchill from 1926 to 1929, when the latter was Chancellor of the Exchequer in the Baldwin administration, also commented on the nature of the relationship. He claimed to have arranged a meeting, which he doesn't date specifically, between the two men:

> They were alone together for about an hour. After that I heard Lloyd George leave by the outside door, down the corridor. I sat alone in the secretary's room. Nothing happened. No bell rang. After about ten minutes curiosity overcame me and I went in to find the Chancellor sitting in an armchair, gazing into the fire, in a kind of brown study. I said to him: 'How did it go?' He looked up and replied: 'You will be glad to hear that it could not have gone better. He answered all my questions.' Then a hard look came into his face and he went on: 'Within five minutes the old relationship between us was completely re-established. The relationship between Master and Servant. And I was the servant.'[138]

Toye's judgement of the matter pre-1914 is similar. He records that 'the relationship between the two men was not yet one of equals. Churchill was Lloyd George's partner, but a junior one, and he was often a supplicant for advice.'[139] It is undoubtedly the case that, with their huge differences in background, they might have seemed an incongruous pair.[140] Nevertheless Lloyd George's son Richard considered that 'In many ways, both men were remarkably alike.' They were, he remembered, 'both dominant, independent, immensely dangerous in Opposition and capable of daring flights of imagination. Both men had ideals; Winston had scruples, too – father hadn't.'[141] Grigg identified one 'all important characteristic' they had in common: 'a driving, unlimited ambition to rule, which was just as strong in the cottage-bred as in the palace-born boy'.[142]

In respect of Churchill, this was not just a view arrived at retrospectively. A commentator in 1907 had opined that: 'He is a soldier of fortune who has never pretended to be animated by any motive beyond a desire for his own advancement. He has no principles and no enthusiasm except egoism.'[143] Shannon assigns rather more noble motivations, pointing out that neither Lloyd George nor Churchill was an 'easily definable species of Liberal. They were statesmen of genius in search of great roles to play in politics.'[144] There was, though, no conspicuously 'great' role to play at the Board of Trade; his position, whilst entirely worthwhile, was essentially mundane.

It was also demanding, inasmuch as he had to deal with industrial strife, which was on the increase. Prior to the Liberal victory of 1906, the Unionist government had involved itself in attempts to mediate and conciliate in disputes between unions and employers under the auspices of the 1896 Conciliation Act.[145] Official strikes, though, were greatly constrained by the infamous 1901 Taff Vale legal judgment, which rendered trades unions liable for any loss of profits to employers that were thus caused.[146] The Trade Disputes Act of 1906, a measure promoted by Campbell-Bannerman personally, reversed the effects and, perhaps surprisingly, survived its passage through the House of Lords intact: 'It was apparently part of the Opposition strategy in these days not to throw a challenge to organised Labour ...'[147] Whatever the rationale, this legislation meant that employers' efforts to resist unionisation thus lacked the 'extra crucial dimension of state leverage' and the balance of overall advantage swung to the workers.[148] It was an advantage that was taken. Randolph Churchill calculated that whilst Lloyd George was at the Board of Trade in 1906-1907, fifty-nine industrial conciliation cases were undertaken, whilst in 1908 as many cases arose as in the two previous years combined.[149] Indeed, 1908 was the worst year since 1894 in terms of the number of workers who downed tools across Britain's industries.[150]

Churchill did not, of course, intervene personally in all the disputes but he was certainly kept busy. There was also a raft of legislation to translate into practice. One example was the establishment of trade boards, later dubbed wages councils, pertaining to the sweated trades where there was little or no trade unionism.[151] The Trade Boards Act of 1909 initially covered 200,000 of these workers, many of them female, and introduced a statutory minimum wage.[152] Of perhaps even greater importance was his appointment of William Beveridge, later to gain fame as the author of the 1942 Beveridge Report, to devise a nationwide system of state-run labour exchanges to assist the unemployed in finding work. In addition, the creation of a system of compulsory, contributory, insurance against sickness and unemployment covering over two million working people in specific industries was formulated.[153] Lloyd George was to absorb this scheme into what became the 1911 National Insurance Act.[154]

The inspiration for these programmes lay, in the main, with the example of Germany. As Massingham phrased it in introducing a volume of Churchill's speeches:

> In the main [these speeches] preach a gospel – that of national 'efficiency' – common to all reformers, and accepted by Bismarck, the modern archetype of 'Empire-makers', as necessary to the consolidation of the great German nation.[155]

The German model, a comprehensive system of social support originally introduced by Otto von Bismarck in the nineteenth century, particularly impressed itself on Lloyd George.[156] He travelled to Germany in the late summer of 1908, traversing the country by motor-car 'from west to east and from south to north' as a guest of Liberal MP Charles Henry. He arrived back in time to witness a matter which, in personal terms, had an immense impact on Winston Churchill; he had, on 11 August, proposed to Clementine Hozier and been accepted. The engagement was short. The marriage took place on 12 September, the lack of notice meaning the absence of many potential guests who found themselves unavoidably occupied elsewhere. Lloyd George was, though, able to attend, and appended his signature to the register.[157]

Though he had not discussed 'international questions' whilst in Germany, they were to have a major impact on his work as Chancellor. The various schemes he and Churchill were pushing involved significant expense, as of course did constructing dreadnought battleships. In that context the 'Navy Scare' early the following year created an unexpected political crisis which was solved, in Churchill's famous phraseology, as follows: 'The Admiralty had demanded six ships: the economists offered four: and we finally compromised on eight.'[158] Churchill and Lloyd George were, of course, the chief 'economists' but they were eventually overruled. It inevitably followed that in 1909 Lloyd George was faced with an enormous financial shortfall, and needed to find new revenue to fund the social programmes as well as the increase in naval expenditure. There were two other issues of concern to Asquith, his government and the Liberal Party more generally. They appeared to be losing support in the country, as had been evidenced by a number of by-election losses,[159] and the House of Lords' veto continued to create great difficulties with any legislation which the Opposition disliked.[160]

The new Chancellor of the Exchequer attempted, with his first budget, to cut this political Gordian Knot. Whether from the start he also sought to provoke the House of Lords and thus a constitutional crisis is a matter of debate, though that was, of course, what happened. As is well known, the proposals he unveiled on 29 April 1909 in furtherance of what he called his 'war budget' for 'raising money to wage implacable warfare against poverty and squalidness'[161] caused huge controversy and opposition. The measures that aroused the most ire amongst conservatives and aristocrats related to the introduction of increased death duties on the estates of the rich, combined with proposals for the valuation and taxation of land.[162]

The Budget was fought by every possible device and measure the Opposition could muster in the House of Commons, and was discussed and debated widely throughout the country. As Charmley points out, whilst it may be overly cynical to say that the Budget was a device for 'pulling the Liberal Government back together', that was certainly one of its effects.[163] On the other hand, an indication of how it was viewed by those opposing it may be discerned by studying the reaction of Lord Rosebery. He regarded it as pure socialism, 'the end of all, the negation of faith, of family, of property, of Monarchy, of Empire'.[164] Given that Rosebery was a Liberal, indeed a former leader of the party, then the reaction of Conservatives can be imagined. Their views on the issue were arguably akin to those Shaw gave Britannus in *Caesar and Cleopatra*: 'that the customs of his tribe and island are the laws of nature'.[165] One who seemingly considered that Lloyd George and his ilk were transgressing those laws was Shaw's literary contemporary, Rudyard Kipling. His poem 'The City of Brass' was published in the *Morning Post* on 28 June 1909. Described as 'a fiercely patriotic defence of Britain's age-old values and traditions', it denounced their 'potential destruction by the tax-raising, social-reforming Liberal government'.[166] The final four lines were apocalyptic:

> The eaters of other men's bread, the exempted from hardship,
> The excusers of impotence fled, abdicating their wardship,
> For the hate they had taught through the State brought the State no
>   defender,
> And it passed from the roll of the Nations in headlong surrender![167]

Vituperation, albeit rather less poetic, was poured on the heads of the two fore-most proponents of the Budget. The classically educated dubbed them Cleon and Alcibiades, the demagogue shoemaker and the renegade aristocrat as depicted in Thucydides' *History of the Peloponnesian War*, whilst those less cultured resorted to the 'terrible twins' and worse.[168]

A Budget Protest League was formed and the Irish Unionist MP for the South County Dublin constituency, Walter Long, accepted its presidency.[169] On the opposite side of the political fence sat the Budget League with Churchill as its president.[170] Though it is Lloyd Georges' speeches, and most particularly the address he gave at the Edinburgh Castle, Limehouse, on 30 July 1909, that are remembered, Churchill also expounded on the matter. He did so with much the same passion, as is evidenced by the oration he gave at Leicester in September on the Lords' veto. He was forthright on the matter:

> the issue will be whether the British people ... are going to be ruled through a representative Assembly ... or whether they are going to allow themselves to be dictated to and domineered over by a minute minority of titled persons, who represent nobody, who are answerable to nobody, and who only scurry up to London to vote in their party interests, in their class interests, and in their own interests. These will be the issues, and I am content that the responsibility for such a struggle, if it should come, should rest with the House of Lords themselves. But if it is to come ... We will engage in it with all our hearts and with all our might, it being always clearly understood that the fight will be a fight to the finish, and that the fullest forfeits, which are in accordance with the national welfare, shall be exacted from the defeated foe.[171]

This was, of course, viewed as highly provocative and there is evidence that Churchill, seeing political advantage in the matter, wanted the House of Lords to exercise its veto and provoke a showdown. He and Clementine were part of a 'shooting party' staying with the poet and writer Wilfrid Scawen Blunt over the weekend of 2–3 October 1909, and the latter recorded a discussion held on the Budget question:[172]

> Winston gave us a very full account of what his policy in the Budget dispute with the Lords would be. He began by saying that his hope and prayer was that they would throw out the Bill, as it would save the Government from a certain defeat if the Elections were put off. The Budget, once it became law, would be immensely unpopular, and everybody would be against it. It was therefore to the interest of the Opposition to let it pass.[173]

The 'Opposition' neglected to follow this line of reasoning. On 30 November 1909, and to use the language of the time and place, the question put to the House of Lords 'that the Bill be read a Second Time' was voted down by a large majority who were 'not content'.[174] On 2 December Asquith proposed a motion in the House of Commons 'That the action of the House of Lords in refusing to pass into law the financial provision made by this house ... is a breach of the constitution and a usurpation of the rights of the Commons.'[175] The motion was carried and Parliament was dissolved. The question would now be put to the people in a General Election.

An interesting pen-portrait of Churchill at an Edwardian country-house week-end in December 1909 has come down to us via the journal of T.J. Cobden-Sanderson, the author and owner of the Doves Press. His wife, Anne Cobden-Sanderson, was the daughter of famous Liberal politician and free-trader Richard Cobden, an outspoken suffragette and a friend of Clementine Churchill. She and her husband had attended the Churchill-Hozier wedding in 1908 as guests of the bride.[176]

> He is not as ugly as his photos, and he is, or appears to be, absolutely *naif*, frankly confessing his ignorance where he is ignorant, and of things which, common to others, seem to be quite new to him – as for example, what is the meaning of *sine qua non*, what is the meaning of pragmatism – and confessing that he had never learnt any Latin. He has not an agreeable voice, nor does he speak well in conversation; and I daresay he can be rude on occasion. To me he has been rather specially polite, but at tea on Sunday, after per-haps Clementine had reported our conversation together, in which I had explained to her the election policy of the Women's Social and Political Union, he was incidentally impertinent, and raised a smothered laugh which seemed to envelope me as his object ... I let the laugh be smothered and sub-side, and then I asked him if he thought it unreasonable that women should strive by means of the cry 'Votes for Women', and otherwise, to cast off the restriction imposed upon their sex, and to take their share in the develop-ment and conduct of the world's history; and whether, admitting their right, he should be led to deny it by any 'tactics' which they might be led to adopt in support of it?[177]

If he received an answer it was not recorded. The election campaign gave rise to some emotion on both sides; the *Daily Mail* accused the government of 'surrendering to socialism' and claimed that it was the patriotic duty of the British people to vote for the Conservative Party.[178] Consequently, and as the statistician Simon Rosenbaum put it, 'the intensity of political feeling, as manifested by the proportions of the electorates proceeding to the polls [between 15 January and 10 February 1910] was exceptionally great. This is shown by the fact that in all the contested seats of Great Britain 87 per cent of the electorate voted.'[179]

The proportion of those who were enfranchised and had exercised their voting rights was indeed large, but the registered electorate formed only a small pro-portion of the population as a whole. The 1884 Representation of the People, or Third Reform, Act, had established a standardised, property-based, exclusively male, landowning, household, and lodger franchise across the United Kingdom. It rationalised differences which had previously existed between voters in boroughs, basically urban areas, and those in counties. According to Charles

Seymour, 'the main effect of the bill was ... simply to extend the borough franchise to counties'.[180] The borough franchise in question had been established by the Second Reform Act, which became law in England and Wales in 1867 and in the following year in Scotland. Applied UK wide, those who now qualified after 1884 were: Those with lands or tenements worth £10 a year; Householders, subject to a one-year residential qualification and payment of rates; and Lodgers who occupied lodgings worth £10 a year, subject to a one-year residential quali-fication.[181] There were disqualifications for some of those who met those criteria. These included 'alienage' (holding foreign citizenship) and 'conviction for corrupt practices'. Voting rights were also forfeit if an individual fell on hard times; those who 'within 12 months preceding 15 July received parochial [poor] relief (other than medical relief) or other disqualifying alms' were debarred.[182]

Nor was getting onto the register a seamless process. For householders, and for some property owners, the main obstacle to enfranchisement was the lengthy residence requirement. Because the register did not come into effect until six months after it was compiled, it meant the minimum qualifying period was effec-tively eighteen months.[183] Lodgers had an even more difficult time, particularly in regard to calculating the value of their lodgings, and it was claimed that 'no clause of any Representation Act has been interpreted in so many ways'.[184] That was so because the arbiter of the electoral register in England, Wales and Ireland was the revising barrister, appointed annually by the senior Assize Judge for the county.[185] He adjudicated all arguments pertaining to who qualified for inclusion on it or not: 'People could claim to be put on, and people could object to others being put on, and the claims and objections could be investigated by the Revising Barrister.'[186] Agents of political parties could, and did, appeal to the registration courts in order to minimise the registration of those they deemed political opponents and, of course, to maximise the number of their supporters:[187]

> The party agents devote all the resources of their professional knowledge to multiplying [disputed points] in order to deprive as many persons on the other side as possible of the right to vote. They leave no stone unturned. Nothing is more common for them than to object to the spelling of a proper name.[188]

The revising barrister possessed considerable powers of interpretation in respect of the matter.[189] Further, since each registration court covered, on average, five constituencies, any decisions made affected a large number of people.[190]

The census taken in 1911 enumerated the total UK population, including Ireland, to be 45,221,000.[191] Only some 25 per cent of that total, 11,900,000, were adult males of 21 years or over, of whom, in 1910, 7,250,000 were electors who, because of the plural voting system then in operation, could poll 7,700,000 votes. Some 4,665,000 adult males were not qualified to vote at all, nor, of course, any females whatsoever.[192] The system, particularly as it applied in relation to registration, was biased towards the Conservatives and though there were fewer plural voters in Wales and Scotland than in England, and virtually none in

Ireland, it was reckoned contemporaneously that 80 per cent of such votes went to the Conservative party.[193]

Despite these disadvantages the Liberal Party won, inasmuch as Asquith remained Prime Minister, but their majority of 125 seats over all other parties in the House of Commons crumbled, the end result being 274 Liberal MPS to 272 Conservative and Liberal Unionists. Reduced thus to near parity with the opposition, the Liberals were forced to rely on the 71 Irish Parliamentary Party MPs, led by John Redmond, and the 40 seats won by the Labour Party.[194]

Both main parties were disappointed with these results. As William D. Rubinstein points out, 'the Liberals expected their popular anti-House of Lords cry to be echoed by the electorate, while the Unionists expected to win back the ascendancy with the electorate that they had enjoyed before the abnormality of 1906'.[195] It seems likely that the Conservatives were the more disappointed, inasmuch as Asquith's reliance on Redmond meant that the issue of Irish Home Rule, which was anathema to Unionist politicians and a prerequisite for Irish support, was now bound to come to the fore. Achieving this would, however, involve removing the veto power of the House of Lords, where there was a permanent Conservative majority.

Churchill, returned at Dundee with an increased majority, had participated fully in the election campaign and several of his speeches given between 3 and 11 December were edited and published in book form in January 1910.[196] These were adjudged to have been of high quality; Asquith wrote to him on 1 February 1910 offering his 'warmest thanks & best congratulations' on the work he had done during the election. 'Your speeches', he went on to say, 'have reached high-water mark, and will live in history.'[197] He also offered Churchill promotion to the position of Chief Secretary for Ireland, the government minister with responsibility for governing 'John Bull's Other Island'.[198] Churchill's reply was, in Randolph Churchill's words, 'forthright, guileful and masterly'. He effectively turned down the offer, bidding instead to go either to the Admiralty or to the Home Office.[199] Asquith decided to make him Home Secretary.

This was a significant promotion by any standards; he was now one of the principal figures in the Cabinet. Only Lloyd George and Sir Edward Grey, the Foreign Secretary, were ahead of him in the pecking order should Asquith resign or otherwise cease to be Prime Minister, and he was 12 and 13 years younger than them respectively.[200] He was also the youngest man to hold the position since Robert Peel in 1822, and being 'hyperactively ambitious and publicity-seeking' he could by no means be considered a safe pair of hands.[201] Indeed, given the febrile political climate in the country, plus the several social tensions manifesting themselves, he had grasped one of the most glittering of prizes at an extremely testing time.

Chapter Two

South Wales Strife (1): Newport

'The state of things at Newport is serious, and Mr Churchill, before he left, had considered the possibility of their applying for troops. He is most anxious to avoid their being used, and is doing all he can by offering to supply Metropolitan Police and otherwise to avoid the necessity; but of course if the Mayor or Magistrates requisition them, they must be ready to go. Mr Churchill asked me specially to impress on the War Office that *mounted troops* should be sent. They are far more effective than infantry in dealing with a riot, and the risk of their employment leading to loss of life is much less.'[1]

'... in the Argentine they managed these things better; they would send artillery and machine guns, and give proper protection to their subjects.'[2]

* * *

It has been said that Churchill's role in the Tonypandy riots of November 1910, and after, affected his reputation for the rest of his life. The Welsh historian Dai Smith recalled that when Rhondda cinemas showed films of Churchill in the 1950s, 'we booed and booed and booed' at his appearance.[3] It is still the case that 'in Wales the resentment lingers today'.[4] Furthermore the phrase attributed to him –'if the Welsh are striking over hunger, we must fill their bellies with lead' – endures even further afield.[5] He never said it, of course, but the myth, as myths do, persists. In fact his approach to, and policy regarding, riot and civil disorder arising from industrial disputes had been portended earlier in the year in a location not far removed from Tonypandy and the Rhondda.

The May 1910 Newport Dock Strike grew out of the decision by one of the users of the port, the Empire Transport Company (a subsidiary of Houlder Brothers Company), to unilaterally alter a formerly agreed payment system pertaining to dock workers. Industrial relations at Newport, and indeed the wider south Wales waterfront, had generally been placid largely because of the 'unbelligerence' of various local concerns.[6] That situation dramatically changed on 14 May when the vessel *Indian Transport* arrived and Houlder's announced that it would be loaded by men paid by the day rather than on a piece-work system. This directly affected around a hundred dockers who refused to work under the terms offered, but their action was supported by the rest of the workforce who feared that the change was merely the thin end of a wedge.

Houlder's, having 'upset the well-established relations between unions and employers on the docks at Newport,' refused to compromise and arranged for so called 'free labour' (non-union dockers) to be sent from London.[7] When these, fifty-two in number, arrived, a dock-wide unofficial strike was called on 18 May and some 300 Newport dockers prevented this blackleg labour from working the wharfs. Violence broke out and unsuccessful attempts were made to board *Indian Transport*. These culminated in the ship's captain inviting two of the strikers on-board to address the blacklegs, who were offered their train fares back to London and guaranteed safe passage to the station, if they immediately left the ship. This offer was accepted.[8]

The next day, a procession of some 2,000 dockers, led by a band, paraded through Newport in an effort to gain support for their actions whilst, rather less publicly, negotiations commenced to settle the issue. These involved not only union officials and the management of the Alexandra (Newport and South Wales) Docks and Railway Company[9] but also the Mayor of Newport, all of whom were anxious to resolve the matter quickly.[10] This aspiration, though, was not shared by Houlder Brothers, who arranged for further blacklegs to be brought to Newport by ship under the auspices of the Shipping Federation. Founded as 'a fighting machine to counter strikes',[11] it had formed a Labour Department in the 1890s, one of the main functions of which was to supply blackleg labour.[12] They asked the Home Office for assistance on 19 May:

> Men employed by owners to load steamer Indian Transport at Newport Monmouthshire have been attacked, assaulted and grossly intimidated by other labourers on strike and are consequently unable [to] work. Owners are suffering great loss from detention of vessels. Local authorities are unable provide police protection without strong reinforcements from out-side. Respectfully request that you will take necessary steps maintain law and order and afford such protection as will enable men engaged to pursue their lawful occupation: matter is urgent. Trust that immediate action be taken.[13]

Churchill wasn't there. Prior to journeying to Switzerland and northern Italy for a holiday, he was at the Dorset estate of the Welsh industrialist Ivor Guest, Baron Wimborne, who was his uncle by marriage.[14] The Permanent Under-Secretary of State at the Home Office, Sir Edward Troup,[15] telegraphed him there follow-ing receipt of the above telegram and after a visit in person from 'three repre-sentatives of the Empire Transport Company' who had called 'to represent that':

> in connection with [a] strike of stevedores ... serious disturbances have occurred, [and] that police have failed to give adequate protection and that their free workmen have been assaulted and intimidated. They ask Home Secretary to intervene. I have told them local police are entirely responsible, and if numbers insufficient should obtain assistance from other forces. I have also communicated with Board of Trade who had not heard of dispute but Mitchell[16] is now communicating with firm and they will watch the case and

give help if possible. Meantime may I telegraph to local police to remind them of their responsibility to maintain order and prevent outrage or intimidation?[17]

Churchill's reply of that day authorised Troup to telegraph in the vein indicated, and stated that any public announcement should mention the intervention by Mitchell and the Board of Trade. He continued:

The Empire Transport Company should be made to realise that employing large droves of men from London to break the strike is a very strong order. Do not on any account give them or the public the impression that we approve their action.[18]

Troup then telegraphed Councillor William Blackburn, the Mayor of Newport,[19] explaining the Home Secretary's position:

He desires to remind you that police and magistrates are responsible for maintenance of order and prevention of outrage or intimidation and that if local police are insufficient immediate steps should be taken to obtain assistance from other police forces.[20]

Blackburn replied that the Watch Committee, the local government body which oversaw policing, had authorised the Head Constable[21] of the Newport Borough Police to take 'all necessary steps for the preservation of peace' and that the Committee would meet the following day to further consider the matter.[22] The manpower immediately at the disposal of Head Constable Allan Inderwick Sinclair was, however, limited; the Newport Borough Police Force numbered 106 personnel all told.[23] This was, quite obviously, hopelessly inadequate given the number of strikers they were likely to encounter. Sinclair reported his difficulties in this regard on 20 May:

[The] Watch Committee [are] alive to [the] situation and will require 500 men and 20 mounted officers to afford adequate protection if any further labour [is] imported. Can only get 250 from neighbouring forces. Do not propose to provide additional assistance until informed further importation of labour [is] certain and date. Can [the Watch] Committee obtain adequate notice of this and what men can be sent?[24]

Troup telegraphed this information to Churchill the next day, adding that Sir Edward Richard Henry, the Commissioner of the London Metropolitan Police, had been contacted and would send the required reinforcements, of 250 foot and 50 mounted police, if necessary. Churchill replied approving this, also stating that 'if they want more they must have more'. He also informed Troup that 'from tomorrow' (i.e. Sunday, 22 May) he could be reached at the Hotel du Palais, Lucerne.[25] Churchill, as Home Secretary, was the legal police authority for the Metropolitan Police and the Commissioner, equivalent to the Chief or Head Constable in other forces, was subject to his general direction.[26] Some

17,000 strong, the Metropolitan Police was the only force that had duties of national rather than merely local importance, and could be used as a kind of strategic reserve to be deployed as necessary at the Government's behest. In so doing it formed a, comparatively weak, substitute for those centralised police forces, or gendarmeries, such as for example existed in France, Italy and Spain.

The multi-polar communication over the 'Victorian Internet'[27] continued, with Troup passing on Churchill's consent to Councillor Blackburn on Saturday, 21 May. He also pointed out that 'only in the last resort' and in a situation of 'grave emergency' should the application to the Metropolitan Police be actually made.[28] That the 'last resort' might well have been upon them was communicated in turn that day by Head Constable Sinclair, who complained that his telegram of 20 May, asking for information concerning reinforcements, remained unanswered. He also imparted the news that the 'imported labour' was due to arrive the very next day and thus it was 'essential we should have 250 Metropolitan Police to reach here by two o'clock Sunday afternoon [22 May]' and that the request had been made to the Commissioner.[29]

A telegram from the Shipping Federation also arrived at the Home Office, confirming the urgency as related by Sinclair and indeed attempting to up the ante:

> Fifty-five labourers for *Indian Transport* will arrive Newport Sunday evening nine o'clock. Owners have warned [the] Mayor [of the] necessity for *military protection* as [the] attitude and large numbers of strikers threaten very serious danger to persons carrying on work at this steamer. Trust you will take all possible steps [to] assist [the] owners to obtain protection from violence.[30]

This came amongst a flurry of telegraphic messages that Saturday, in which Troup assured the Head Constable and the Mayor that the police reinforcements had been sanctioned. On the other hand, the Mayor informed Troup that 'severe riots [were] anticipated here in connection with the dock strikes' and confirmed that the warning from the Shipping Federation in terms of 'military protection' had been acted upon:

> At meeting of borough magistrates here this morning it was unanimously resolved that the War Office be requested to hold in readiness two hundred infantrymen and one hundred mounted men to assist the local police and five hundred imported police. Duplicate of this telegram sent [to the] Secretary of State for War.[31]

Troup attempted to contact his opposite number at the War Office, the Permanent Under-Secretary Sir Edward Ward, and through him the Minister for War Richard Haldane:

> The state of things at Newport is serious, and Mr Churchill, before he left, had considered the possibility of their applying for troops. He is most anxious to avoid their being used, and is doing all he can by offering to

supply Metropolitan Police and otherwise to avoid the necessity; but of course if the Mayor or Magistrates requisition them, they must be ready to go. Mr Churchill asked me specially to impress on the War Office that *mounted troops* should be sent. They are far more effective than infantry in dealing with a riot, and the risk of their employment leading to loss of life is much less.[32]

He sent copies of these communications to Churchill, adding that he had been unable to reach anyone at the War Office either by telephone or messenger; he quipped that if any 'possible invader' chose to land on a Saturday afternoon the War Office would only discover it the following Monday. The import of his message to Sir Edward Ward was also conveyed: '[I] explained your views about mounted troops, and of course said that you were doing all you could to avoid the necessity of [them] being there at all.'[33] Nevertheless, the Mayor of Newport was informed by Ward that the General Officer Commanding-in-Chief at Chester[34] 'has been communicated with and will comply with such requisition as may be found necessary'.[35] There were small military forces available locally: a cavalry/artillery barracks (now Raglan Barracks) was located at Allt-yr-yn, Newport, and the 1st Battalion of the Monmouthshire Regiment was based at Stow Hill, Newport. However, and as several authors have noted, army policy was to avoid using troops who may have had local affiliations: 'when detailing troops for duty in strike areas care was always taken not to send any units with territorial connections in those particular localities.'[36] The reasoning behind this was straightforward; they might have sympathised with the strikers. Furthermore, if called on to apply deadly force then they may well have baulked at doing so against family and friends.

Troup also received a further message from Councillor Blackburn, telling him that all local police resources were exhausted, but that he had been promised 'sixty men from Bristol and forty from Merthyr' on Sunday, 22 May, and was hoping to get forty each from the Glamorgan County and Monmouthshire County forces. These latter eighty were, however, doubtful. He reiterated that the imported labour was arriving 'in two sections tomorrow, one by rail, the other by water' and that the reinforcements from London were required.[37]

The situation on the evening of Saturday, 21 May looked grim; the blackleg labour was due to arrive the following evening and would undoubtedly provoke a violent reaction. Efforts to contain this involved the despatch of 300 Metropolitan Police, including 50 mounted officers, plus the circa 180-strong contingent assembled locally. In addition, military forces from the Army's Western Command could be called into play as a last resort.

Two events occurred overnight. At 10.45pm Frank Houlder, the chairman of Houlder Brothers, called at Troup's house to air his concerns about the situation. According to Troup's report of the incident compiled shortly afterwards, the shipping magnate 'seemed to have dined and was much excited'.[38] It went on to relate that Houlder had become convinced that '500 strikers were assembled on the dock; that there were only three police on duty; and that his men were trying to save the vessel from attack by getting her off to a buoy in the river'. He further claimed that forty of his men were being murdered 'at that moment' and that Troup, and by extension the Government which he held responsible, should 'instantly take steps to save them'.

Efforts to calm Houlder by explaining that the local authorities, and not the Government, were responsible for maintaining order, but that the Government were sending 300 police by special train tomorrow to help in that regard, were seemingly unsuccessful. Troup records that the response to this was that 'in the Argentine they managed these things better; they would send artillery and machine guns, and give proper protection to their subjects'. To add to Troup's woes, Houlder's secretary arrived and 'assumed the same offensive and bullying manner as his chief'. The two eventually left, stating that they would visit the Admiralty and demand assistance there. Troup telegraphed Sinclair in Newport to enquire if there were any truth in Houlder's assertions, and received 'in an hour or two' the assurance that all was calm. He was also informed that a conference was then in progress which the Head Constable hoped would lead to a settlement of the dispute.[39]

That Sinclair was not hoping in vain became apparent to Troup when a telegram arrived at 'between 2 and 3 o'clock this [Sunday, 22 May] morning'. The sender was Councillor Blackburn who had, in company with several others, also been burning the midnight oil:

> Further to telegrams of today, [the] Newport labour dispute [has] just been settled in [a] conference with [the] Mayor and representatives of [the] masters and men, and with [the] assistance of the Board of Trade. Police and military assistance not now required. Have communicated direct with Scotland Yard and officer commanding troops at Chester to this effect.[40]

A further communication from Isaac Mitchell followed some ten hours later. This informed Troup that his arrival had been 'opportune' and that 'Both parties [had] agreed to Board of Trade arbitration. All men resume work tomorrow morning [Monday, 23 May].'[41] These latest developments were communicated to Churchill at Lucerne, with Troup remarking that he felt 'sure that the satisfactory result comes directly from your policy of supporting the authorities on the one hand and on the other insisting on conciliation'. He added that, in relation to his interview with Houlder, if he 'bullied his stevedores as he tried to bully me, it is no wonder there was a strike' and informed the Home Secretary that he had, at 3 o'clock that morning, stopped the movement of the Metropolitan Police reinforcements.[42]

Churchill's reply stated that he was 'very pleased' with the settlement and asked that formal thanks be sent to the Board of Trade in terms of Isaac Mitchell's 'excellent work'. Thanks in the form of 'civil letters' were also to be written to Councillor Blackburn and Head Constable Sinclair, with the caveat that they should not be sent 'if you see any serious reason not known to me'. He also transmitted the text of a telegram that he wanted despatching to Houlder Brothers:

Begins. I desire to thank you personally for the assistance you have rendered in the friendly settlement of a dangerous dispute and for the consideration with which you have treated me throughout. I trust your difficulties will not recur. CHURCHILL. Ends.[43]

As stated, the terms of the settlement brokered by Mitchell meant that work at Newport Docks would resume. The formerly agreed payment system pertaining to piece work would apply, and the question of alteration to it would be submitted to arbitration.[44] There was, though, to be a coda to the affair, which threatened major trouble.

The employers' representative at the meetings which reached the settlement was John Macauley, the General Manager of the Alexandra Docks. For his part in it, and his 'conciliatory spirit' during the negotiations, he received one of the letters Churchill had asked to be sent.[45] However, Houlder Brothers and the Shipping Federation, and there was 'no other employer's organisation quite as aggressive and as unscrupulous as the Shipping Federation,'[46] disavowed the agreement and upended the 'friendly settlement' upon which they had just been congratulated. The Federation telegraphed the Home Office on the afternoon of Monday, 23 May informing them not only of this repudiation but also that further blackleg labour was due to land at eight o'clock that very evening:

At [the] request of Houlder Brothers, [the] Shipping Federation have engaged fifty men [to] load their vessel ... These men are now on their way ... [The] Chairman [of the] Watch Committee and Mayor were advised [of] this proceeding yesterday and this afternoon and requested [to] provide protection. Reply has been received ... [and] protection will not be granted ... Request [that] you will point out to [the] Local Authorities their duty. Their refusal [to] provide protection is based upon [the] result of some negotiations between certain officials of [the] Union and [the] General Manager of [the] Dock Company to which [the] owners of [the] vessel were not parties and by which they decline to be bound.[47]

The men referred to were already at Newport aboard the *Lady Jocelyn*, a sailing ship (with auxiliary steam propulsion) owned by the Shipping Federation and used specifically for conveying blacklegs to wherever they were required.[48] It was obvious to all concerned that if they were landed, which they would have to be in order to load the *Indian Transport*, then serious disorder would ensue. Troup replied to the Shipping Federation, stating that Churchill 'thinks that you should at once stop the sending to Newport of [the] men mentioned ... you will incur grave responsibility if, in disregard of agreement by representatives you import unnecessary labour into Newport'.[49]

The Shipping Federation replied that evening, stating that the 'Secretary of State is misinformed' and that Houlder Brothers had 'no representatives' at the meeting where the appeal to arbitration was agreed. They complained that the vessel was still 'blocked and suffering ruinous delay'. The nub of the matter from the Federation's perspective was outlined as follows:

> Position apparently is that local authorities are averse from giving protection and are seeking [a] pretext for disregarding their duty. Too late now [to] stop [the] men. Respectfully submit they are entitled to be safeguarded in pursuit of their lawful calling. Beg you will do what lies in your power to save them from the violence of Trade Unionists at Newport.[50]

This was a transparent attempt to force the Home Office, and Government more generally, into action. In the severely practical sense, inasmuch as the Metropolitan Police and military reinforcements had been stood down, it was an impossible demand to satisfy in the postulated timeframe. Troup's reply reiterated his earlier point: 'if you land men at Newport or bring them into [the] docks in present circumstances you will incur [a] very grave responsibility'.[51] Indeed, such action would have entirely invalidated the tactics employed by Head Constable Sinclair, and endorsed by the Watch Committee, for keeping the situation under control. Given the limited police manpower, these tactics devolved on avoiding a situation where conflict and violence would likely occur. This, in turn, meant preventing the dockers and blacklegs from coming into contact with one another, which was a simple enough proposition provided the latter remained aboard the *Lady Jocelyn*.[52] Until such time as Sinclair and the Watch Committee were prepared to guarantee their safety, there they would remain. This was, of course, not at all to the satisfaction of the Shipping Federation, which replied stating that they had 'been able to arrange [to] stop men en route'. They went on, 'but you will understand they cannot be indefinitely held back in this way. [The] local authorities have refused protection pending an interview with you tomorrow.'[53]

Meanwhile a meeting had been held that afternoon, 23 May, at Houlder Brothers' offices at 146 Leadenhall Street, London. In attendance on the one hand were the Board of Trade's Isaac Mitchell, who had brokered the 22 May settlement, John Macauley of Alexandra Docks, and William Blackburn, the Mayor of Newport. On the other were Frank and Maurice Houlder, plus Cuthbert Laws, the General Manager of the Shipping Federation.

Laws had been the Shipping Federation's first Secretary before succeeding his father, George Laws, as General Manager in 1901, and he is an interesting character. Described as having a 'powerful personality', he is credited, if that is the correct term, with relishing conflict. The author of the Shipping Federation's official history put it thus: 'He never shirked – sometimes, indeed, he seemed to seek – a fight, but unlike so many fighters, he knew well when the time had come for peace and reconstruction.'[54] Those who opposed him had a slightly different perspective: 'Mr Cuthbert Laws and his colleagues hate trade unionism as the devil hates holy water, and would do anything in their power to thwart and destroy it.'[55] Evidently the time for 'peace and reconstruction' was not yet nigh, and consequently thwarting and destruction still held sway. According to

Mitchell's account, they were told that the Shipping Federation had held a meeting earlier and decided not to recognise the agreement. It was, he said:

> evident that the firm [Houlder Brothers] had put itself entirely under the control of Mr Laws, who made no secret of his intentions to import men ... on his conditions. He demanded police protection from the Mayor and altogether made any prospect of settlement impossible.
>
> The position now is that a recurrence of all the trouble is threatened by the actions of this one firm, all the men being employed by the other firms being back at work. A ship's general cargo is lying at the docks ready to be loaded into one of Messrs Houlder's ships which is alongside. If this could be got away Mr Macauley would, if he had power, decline to accept cargo at the dock for this firm and so save further trouble.
>
> Mr Macauley and the Mayor of Newport will call today [24 May 1910] at Gwydyr House [the location of the Board of Trade's Labour Department] at 12 noon. The Dock Board meets in London at 2 pm.
>
> Mr Laws is meanwhile pressing the Mayor for police protection for the new men he intends sending to Newport. If they are sent a general upheaval seems inevitable.[56]

Troup forwarded updates on the situation to Churchill, who was then at Lugano, Switzerland, adding a note to Mitchell's report. In this he argued that Houlder Brothers were 'behaving very badly. On Sunday they or their agents so far accepted the agreement ... and it was only on Monday [that] they decided to repudiate.' Further evidence of Houlder's intransigence as perceived by Troup was provided. He noted that Macauley had offered to make up any financial loss Houlder's might incur if they would agree to their vessel being loaded under the agreed, piece work, system. 'But,' he said, 'they would have none of it' and their hostility towards Macauley became so strong that it was feared they would resort to physical violence. Troup also reported that he had seen Councillor Blackburn that day [24 May], and that the Mayor was 'very much disturbed' at Houlder Brothers' conduct. Troup reassured him:

> I told him that it was his duty to do his utmost to maintain order; but that he was clearly entitled to tell Messrs Houlder that he could not perform impossibilities, [and] that if they imported 'free labour' in [circumstances] which must necessarily give rise to uncontrollable disorder, their responsibility would be very grave.[57]

In fact both the Shipping Federation and Houlder Brothers had been warned on the evening of Monday, 23 May by Mark Mordey JP, the Chairman of Newport Watch Committee, that they could not undertake the responsibility of protecting any 'imported men':

> Five hundred additional police and mounted men would have been in town yesterday had we not been informed by all parties concerned that police and

military arrangements might be cancelled. To now import free labour would, in my opinion, be little short of madness after the settlement has been announced. All other workmen [have] gone back to work on [the] faith of it and the town [is] settling down quietly. Instead of 500, it would require at least double that number to give protection, having regard to fearful results all through the town. Cannot now undertake [the] responsibility of protecting imported men.[58]

To reinforce the last point, a 'special meeting' of the Watch Committee was convened on the afternoon of Tuesday, 24 May, following which their deliberations were published:

Having heard the telegrams passed between the chief-constable, the chairman of the watch committee, Messrs Houlder Bros, and the Shipping Federation ... this committee are not prepared to provide additional protection, which would be necessary if labour is imported, until commanded to do so by the Home Office, and that any labourers proposing to come to Newport be warned that it is unsafe to do so in existing circumstances.[59]

The unnamed author of the article which included both the above communications, and was published in the Cardiff-based *Evening Express and Evening Mail* as well as being syndicated more widely, also drew a highly pertinent conclusion: 'The whole contention has now been changed to one of not the employers versus the men, but the Shipping Federation on the one side and the watch committee of Newport on the other.' However, given that the Committee had effectively handed the decision over protection for the blacklegs over, or perhaps up, to the Home Office, then that department became in effect one of the contenders in its place. Be that as it may, negotiations continued between Houlder Brothers and the Shipping Federation on the one hand, and the Mayor of Newport and the Trade Unions on the other, but to no avail; the former continued to refuse to accept the 22 May settlement.

Churchill was kept abreast of these developments. However, in the formal context, the responsibilities of the Home Secretary had been placed in the hands of another Secretary of State, Richard Haldane, Minister for War, during his absence. It was then to Haldane that Councillor Blackburn, in the absence of any impending resolution to the matter, wrote on Thursday, 26 May calling his attention to the 'appalling state of things' if the blacklegs were allowed to land:

We confidently expect that ... there will be a great strike throughout the town and docks, involving possibly a stoppage of collieries in the Monmouthshire district in consequence of their being unable to ship their coal at the docks, and quite possibly an extension of the strike to other ports in the Bristol Channel. In our town the corporation employés have already passed a resolution to cease work if free labour be imported ... To adequately protect the free labourers ... from the violence of the enormous crowds ... would require a police force which is estimated by the Head Constable at

500 additional men at least, and having regard to the necessity of relieving the constables so engaged it means double the number to be brought into the town.

The letter continued by stating that the local authorites were 'most seriously apprehensive' should Houlder Brothers be 'permitted to carry out their intentions' and that there would 'be serious riot and bloodshed'. Councillor Blackburn laid the blame for the entire issue on the shipping company:

It is only fair to state that the men honourably and faithfully carried out the terms of the agreement which was entered into by their leaders on their behalf (although many dissented from its terms), by returning to their work on Monday morning, and it is the indignation which will arise when they think that it has been departed from by one section of employers which will produce the stormy passions which we apprehend.

It concluded by re-emphasising his, and the local authorities', 'anxious fear for the peace and order of the town if the importation of free labour is allowed'.[60]

Haldane held a meeting with Houlder Brothers that same day with Troup in attendance. The Home Office position, covering four points as determined by the opinion of the Government's legal advisers, the Solicitor General, Sir Rufus Isaacs, and the counsel to the Inland Revenue and the Treasury, Sidney Rowlatt,[61] was put 'plainly and courteously' to the shipowners. This was that whilst it was the duty of the local authorities to provide sufficient force 'to suppress disorder, riot or outrage', it was also their duty to use all legal means to prevent occasions for such conflicts.

In the context under discussion, this would firstly involve attempting to prevent crowds from assembling on the docks. Secondly, they should attempt to 'dissuade' Houlder Brothers and their agents from landing the imported labour, and also 'dissuade' that labour from landing. The third point involved the local authorities supporting the dock company 'in any action they may be advised to take' to exclude both imported labour and/or strikers from the docks. The final point was the most important and controversial: in the 'last extremity' they may 'forbid and prevent' the imported labour from actually landing. This point, which 'would mean preventing Houlders from exercise of what, in ordinary circumstances, would be their legal rights', would only be taken if the local authority can show that landing imported labour 'would inevitably cause riot and bloodshed, and would lead to a general and disastrous strike'.[62] Given Councillor Blackburn's opinion as noted above, it was obvious that the 'last extremity' had already been arrived at so far as the local authorities were concerned. Accordingly, the Newport Borough Police would indeed 'forbid and prevent' the blacklegs from landing. Houlder Brothers and the Shipping Federation, which Churchill later opined 'had not made things as easy as they could throughout the matter, and who seemed to think that any moment an unlimited supply of horse, foot, and artillery would be at their disposal', now had little option. They accordingly agreed to submit the matter to arbitration as per the agreement reached some six days earlier. Thus, as the Home Secretary put it, 'the second of the two crises passed peacefully away'.[63]

Churchill's explanation of the matter came after the event and during a debate in the House of Commons, on 22 June 1910, over the role of the Board of Trade and the Home Office in the dispute. The opposition sought to censure these departments for preventing, as it was put by Sir Frederick Banbury, Conservative MP for the City of London, an employer (Houlder Brothers) from employing labour as they liked and for being 'forced into arbitration by threats that the forces of the Crown will be used to compel him to arbitrate'.[64] The Home Secretary was able to justify the conduct of his department, and that of the local authorities, arguing that it provided a temporary solution specific to that time and place. It did not herald the establishment of a general principle. Indeed as Haldane, who was the man on the spot, as it were, at the time, phrased it: 'what would otherwise be legal action on the part of Messrs Houlder would be illegal if persisted in, in the then circumstance.'[65]

Although Haldane had, temporarily and nominally, been in charge whilst Churchill was away, there is no doubt that the policy adopted by the Home Office during the course of the dispute was Churchill's. There is a caveat, however, to the latter statement. The prime mover behind developing a plan for centrally directed responses to local unrest, since his appointment in 1908, had been Troup.[66] Be that as it may, the responsibility for it was Churchill's and, even if not actually initiated by him, the correspondence quoted has shown that he approved it.

Also demonstrated therein is that his approach from the start was conciliatory and de-escalatory. The offer to send Metropolitan Police as reinforcements, in the stead of military aid, can also be viewed in terms of a desire to lower the temperature and prevent bloodshed. Using the Metropolitan Police, as already noted the only force under central Government control, as a strategic reserve was not novel. Home Secretaries of the day had despatched several hundred Metropolitan officers to trouble spots during disturbances relating to the New Poor Law and Chartist protests in the 1830s and 1840s.[67] Indeed Asquith, as Home Secretary under William Ewart Gladstone in 1893, had despatched 400 Metropolitan Police to Yorkshire to assist with the widespread unrest there occasioned by a miners' strike.[68] What was rather more innovatory, however, as argued by Jane Morgan for example,[69] was that in taking the approach it did, Churchill's Home Office arrogated to itself an expanded, supervisory, role with the no doubt grateful acquiescence of Newport Watch Committee. This was something of a constitutional novelty. Asquith, in the case above mentioned, had entirely disclaimed Home Office responsibility for the preservation of public order (outside London). The responsibility for the prevention and suppression of local disorder lay, he said, where it had always lain 'from the earliest period of our history, with the Local Authority'. He did, though, acknowledge that the Home Secretary was the 'channel through which the demands of a Local Authority for assistance, when their own police resources are insufficient ... may be made'.[70] That responsibility, as the several communications from the Home Office quoted have made plain, had not changed in 1910, though the duties of the Home Secretary had been clarified somewhat by a Select Committee report of 1908.[71] In any event under Churchill, and at Newport, the Home Secretarial 'channel' had flowed in both directions. Indeed, whilst he had yet to completely overturn the 'existing procedure'[72] for dealing with industrial strife and disorder, he had shown that he was quite prepared to do so.

Chapter Three

South Wales Strife (2): Tonypandy

'I never for a moment believed that the British working man would sink to the level of Irishmen or foreigners, by the use of lethal weapons against unarmed police.'[1]

* * *

The aphorism that trade unionism and the wider labour movement in Britain owes more to Methodism than to Marx has several claimants in terms of authorship.[2] Whatever the general truth of it, there is probably no better example than that of William Abraham, the first President of the South Wales Miners' Federation. The 'Fed' was formed in 1898 by an amalgamation of the multitudinous small trade unions, including Abraham's own Cambrian Miners' Association, pertaining to the mining industry in the region.[3] Universally known by his *enw barddol* (bardic name) of Mabon, he was a staunch Liberal and a deacon of Nazareth Methodist Chapel in the Rhondda village of Pentre, close to Treorchy, and thus 'a characteristic product of industrial non-conformity'.[4] As such, he was viewed as a 'responsible leader' who was known to start a union meeting with a word of prayer.[5] Mabon was also MP for the area, being first elected on the Liberal-Labour ticket for Rhondda in 1885. He retained his seat at every subsequent General Election, though omitted the word 'Labour' entirely in his election addresses[6] and argued in 1903 that whilst he was 'pledged to vote for Labour reform, whatever Government brings in the Bill ... as an individual in politics I am a Liberal'.[7] His gifts, according to one biographical study of him, were 'those of oratory and leadership rather than the ability to think out difficult problems of union structure and policy', whilst his social philosophy was based 'on the simple truths of the New Testament and not on the tortuous canon of Karl Marx'.[8] 'His ideas,' says Kenneth O. Morgan, 'seemed outdated during his own lifetime.'[9]

That this might have been so was a reflection of the immense changes that manifested themselves in the South Wales coalfields during that lifetime. Between 1881 and 1911 the population of the Rhondda almost tripled, from 55,000 to 152,000, with most of the increase being made up of workers moving from England to seek employment.[10] This influx naturally had an effect on the character of the local communities, many of which were pit villages whose very existence depended on coal-mining, with a large degree of Anglicisation in the cultural and linguistic contexts.[11] Such demographic change was probably responsible for a cultural shift amongst South Wales' trade unionists; they moved away from Methodism and headed instead in the general direction of Marx. Indeed, in 1909 John Vyrnwy Morgan, a clergyman of distinctly conservative bent, wrote in respect of the 1904–1905 Welsh religious revival that 'working men have recently reverted to the old belief that their salvation is not to come by the way of the pulpit … but by way of the Labour Party and Westminster'.[12] He likely had in mind the 1900 election of Keir Hardie as MP for the Merthyr Tydfil and Aberdare constituency.[13] Another man of the cloth, though of a very different political persuasion to Morgan, perceived much the same phenomenon. Rex Barker, a Methodist minister in Tonypandy, albeit writing in the period after the First World War, opined that in the Rhondda Valleys 'more men know the writings of Karl Marx and the philosophy of Dietzgen[14] than in any other working-class community in the country'.[15] What this meant in practical terms was that, from about 1902 onwards, there was an increasing rejection of Mabon's belief in 'the identity of interest between capital and labour'.[16] Rather, the enthusiasm of his 'younger colleagues … for action which he reckoned to be too militant' came to the fore.[17]

The Rhondda mine-owners were embodied by, and amalgamated within, the Cambrian Trust, also known as the Cambrian Combine. The 'moving spirit' behind this body was David Alfred Thomas, 'one of the greatest coal-owners in the United Kingdom'.[18] The son and heir of a coal-owner, he had translated his inheritance from private ownership into Cambrian Collieries Ltd in 1895 before, in 1907, forming the Cambrian Trust under whose auspices a large number of other collieries and associated businesses were combined. By 1910 the Combine, which operated as a single unit under one management headed by Thomas as managing director, employed some 12,000 miners and produced almost 3 million tons of coal per annum. It was, in the words of one of Rhondda's literary sons, the 'largest and most profitable of our underground kingdom'.[19]

D.A. Thomas was also a Liberal MP, having first been elected at Merthyr Tydfil in 1888. He shared that dual-member constituency with Keir Hardie until January 1910 when, in the latter election, he successfully fought the single-member constituency of Cardiff.[20] Given his political interests, Thomas left the day-to-day running of the Combine to his general manager, Leonard Wilkinson Llewelyn.[21] Llewelyn was described by a neutral, though diplomatic, source who had dealings with him contemporaneously as 'a forceful autocratic man' who was admired by the miners in several respects. However 'by his rough-and-ready methods' he was 'apt to drive those working for him to a state of desperation'.[22]

A dispute arose in 1909 between some 80 men and the management of the Ely pit of the Naval Colliery Company, part of the Cambrian Combine, over a failure to agree a price list, a price per ton, that the miners would be paid for working a new seam: 'the opening out of the Upper Five Feet [or Bute] Seam under piece-rate labour conditions'.[23] Such disagreements were common, the management believing that when attempting to appraise a new seam the men worked 'ca canny' in order to show that it was 'difficult' and thus deserving of a high rate during normal production.[24] There was a procedure for arbitrating such differences via a Conciliation Board, but though this first considered the question in December 1909 it failed to secure an agreement, and 'the two parties adhered to their respective positions'. Deadlock was reached in June 1910 and on 1 August, after announcing that the pit 'could not be worked at a profit unless he got a reasonable cutting price fixed for the new seam', Llewelyn gave notice that the mine was to close.[25] This, from the trade union perspective, was a lockout, and whilst the Upper Five Feet seam affected only 80 colliers directly, the entire Ely workforce was now involved. Efforts to submit the matter of payment to arbitration were 'obviated by the objection of the coal-owners to the application of the principle of arbitration to such a dispute'. The lockout took effect and the mine closed on 1 September; thus '900 workpeople were thrown out of employment'.[26]

Lloyd George is supposed to have once remarked that he had never met such stupid men as the mine-workers – until he met the mine-owners.[27] Indeed, the decision to shut the mine over a dispute involving less than 10 per cent of the workforce would, on the face of it, appear to be a distinct overreaction. However, those affected perceived a more calculating and distinctly sinister motive. This was explained in a manifesto that sought support from the rest of the coalfield. It was claimed that the Bute seam extended to, and was ready for working at, adjacent collieries in the Combine, and that from it alone millions of tons of coal would ultimately be extracted. Yet nowhere had a price been fixed for working the seam. It followed that if the 'despotic attempt' to force upon Ely a 'starvation price list' succeeded, then that 'list once settled will undoubtedly be a price list for the whole of the Cambrian Combine'.[28] There may well have been something in this, particularly given that the Naval Colliery owners claimed to have worked their pits at a loss from the start.[29]

Two of the Naval pits came out in sympathy on 5 September, whilst the workforce in other collieries decided to do so following meetings held on 7 September. The entire matter was discussed at a meeting of delegates from some forty pits held on 9 September with Mabon present. According to Robin Page Arnot, who provides no source, Mabon 'pleaded' with the meeting not to decide to come out on strike. His justification was that his 'friend D.A. Thomas ... has been suffering from poor health: and I feel sure that on his holiday in France he will not benefit in health if he were to hear of such a strike as this. I beg you, I beg you to hold your hand.'[30] Anthony Mór O'Brien comments that this statement was 'remarkable', which is beyond question, and that it 'speaks volumes for the way in which he regarded the owners, and for the way in which the workers must increasingly have regarded Mabon'.[31]

According to Arnot, this statement elicited a response along the lines of Thomas being no friend of the rank and file, but that they would call off the strike if he, Mabon, agreed to call a coalfield conference of all the south Wales miners. He did so, and a meeting at Cory Hall, Cardiff, on 17 September was attended by 248 delegates representing 147,430 union members. The decision was taken to hold a coalfield-wide ballot, the question to be put being whether the Cambrian Combine workforce, who would give a month's notice of strike action on 1 October, should be sustained financially by way of a levy in aid, or whether their action should be escalated to encompass the entire membership of the South Wales Miners' Federation? The result announced on 25 September was, by a large margin, for financial support and thus against widening the strike.[32] The situation had, though, become unstable, and was far from being under the control of the union leaders. As an example, a mass meeting of the Combine workmen at Tonypandy on 18 September decided to bring forward their strike to the same day as the ballot result was announced.[33]

Nevertheless, negotiations led by Mabon continued in October and an increased price for working the Upper Five Feet seam was conceded by the Combine's management. This was deemed insufficient and rejected accordingly by the rank and file. Arnot argues that the atmosphere throughout the coalfield was becoming 'more and more tense and critical' with 'widespread feeling that the owners were in an unreasonable mood' – a feeling that was fully reciprocated.[34]

This tension manifested itself in, and was exacerbated by, unofficial strike action that broke out in the Cynon, or Aberdare, Valley, where the miners had voted 3,301–2,432 in favour of a general stoppage in September.[35] The pre-eminent employer in the Cynon was the Powell Dyffryn Steam Coal Company, the general manager of which was Edmund Mills Hann.[36] There seems little doubt that Hann deliberately provoked his workforce and wanted a showdown with the unions, though it has to be said that given the fractious state of industrial relations a rupture was probably inevitable anyway.[37] In any event, on 20 October several Powell Dyffryn pits and some 6,600 men came out on unofficial strike.[38] The official strike by the employees of the Cambrian Combine began ten days later on 1 November, whereupon some 11,500 Rhondda men struck. By that time over 11,000 were on strike in the Cynon Valley. Arnot estimates that with these numbers, plus those taking action in other regions such as around Maesteg in the Llynfi Valley and in Monmouthshire's Western Valley, there were some 27,000 to 33,000 men out. This meant that around 15 per cent of the 213,000 employed across the south Wales and Monmouthshire coalfields were out on strike.[39] It was in order to persuade and indeed prevent those still working from continuing to do so, particularly in the Cynon Valley, that large-scale picketing began. This soon turned violent, with incidents at Aberaman, a village some 4 miles to the south of Aberdare, assuming the status of 'riots':

> Matters have become very serious in Aberaman, the strikers having assumed a very threatening attitude. Attacks have been made upon the houses occupied by minor officials of the various 'PD' [Powell Dyffryn] collieries whom the men allege are not officials but workmen in receipt of percentages.
>
> An extraordinary feeling has engendered against these officials, and on Wednesday night [2 November] their houses ... were visited and their windows smashed to atoms.

A very serious row occurred last night [4 November] in an attempt to get at some workmen in the workmen's train ... a number of strikers rushed on the platform, smashing the windows ... and pulling out some of the men. The remainder ... got frightened and jumped out ... Rushing down the line ... they were followed by a hooting crowd, which grew in numbers as it went along. Several of the men were somewhat badly mauled, while others had their clothes ripped off their backs.[40]

Now it is unarguable that press reports were, and indeed are, often sensational-ised. It is also the case that what is printed often serves the interest of those who put it there rather than bearing any resemblance to the truth. Furthermore the coal-owners, and particularly D.A. Thomas, controlled or could influence certain sections of the local press.[41] Nevertheless there is no doubt that the above report is, in its essentials, accurate. The incident, and others of a similar nature, also made national headlines and, more importantly, drew the attention of the Home Office. A telegram was sent to Captain Lionel Arthur Lindsay, Chief Constable of the Glamorgan Constabulary, seeking further details.[42] Lindsay is a character of interest. Appointed Chief Constable in succession to his father, Lieutenant Colonel Henry Gore Lindsay, his early career had been spent policing in Egypt as an officer in the gendarmerie. This 'military model' of policing was adopted in Egypt in order to 'aid in political repression and to hold costs down' whilst the local elite, who cooperated with the occupiers, viewed it 'as a means to keep the lower classes in line'.[43]

Lindsay's appointment as Police Superintendent for Merthyr in 1889 caused a proverbial 'question in the House' to be asked by one D.A. Thomas MP.[44] Promotion to the top job two years later has been styled as 'a typical example' of county magnates appointing 'county men, usually with military backgrounds' who 'had a social outlook similar to their own'. Indeed, Morgan calculates that eight out of twelve Chief Constables of Welsh counties were ex-military men.[45] Despite Lindsay's background being para-military rather than strictly military, he has been characterised as having 'marked right wing views' and of regarding himself as 'the voice of the employers, the coal-owners and their allies'.[46] These characteristics, combined with his background, arguably lend credence to Robin Page Arnot's lampoon which branded the Chief Constable as being unable to disabuse himself of 'the notion that he was part of a Coalmasters' Army of Occupation in South Wales'.[47]

Faced with the large scale of the strikes, and at the urging of the coal-owners if Page Arnot is correct, Lindsay approached his colleagues in adjacent forces for reinforcements on 5 November. He received these promptly, with thirty arriving from Swansea, fifty from Cardiff and a further sixty-three from Bristol; these, added to the roughly 115 men under his command, more than doubled the man-power available to him. These were more-or-less equally distributed between the two valleys. He did not request any further assistance, police or military, at that time.[48]

That situation, however, changed following incidents at the Glamorgan Colliery, Llwynypia, near Tonypandy on the night of 7/8 November where, according to Page Arnot, Leonard Llewelyn had erected a 'fortress against trade union action'.[49] Inside the surface installations and particularly the power station, the output of which drove pumps that kept the underground workings from flooding, were the general manager himself plus between fifty and sixty colliery officials. Also present was Chief Constable Lindsay commanding ninety-nine foot and mounted policemen.[50]

According to Evans, the 'miners who had been successful in their assaults on the other collieries ... posted themselves in large numbers around the ... Colliery, and from 10.30 p.m. till 12.30 a.m. (Tuesday) maintained a frenzied and desperate attack on the property'. Had they succeeded, and the boiler fires been extinguished with the consequent stopping of the ventilating and pumping machinery, then, he reckoned, the 'safety of the colliery and the lives of the 300 horses entombed in the workings' would have been imperilled.[51]

The miners were, however, unsuccessful, being driven off by the baton-wielding police. Evans' account of the incident paints it in quasi-military terms: 'Mr Leonard Llewelyn, the general manager, whose determination and courage against such heavy odds had excited the admiration of the whole country, and had drawn messages of congratulation from almost every quarter of the globe, had held successfully his Fort Chabrol, and he was pledged to see the "thing through" in his own way.'[52] Indeed, Weinberger argues that Llewelyn and Lindsay sought the confrontation at Llwynypia and were keen on confrontation leading to, as they hoped, a decisive victory.[53]

Evans' bracketing of the situation at Llwynypia with that of 'Fort Chabrol', and thus Llewelyn with a virulently anti-Semitic *putschist*, seems a curious comparison to make.[54] This is particularly so given that his perspective was synonymous with that of the coal-owners.[55] He probably used it in the context of the place,

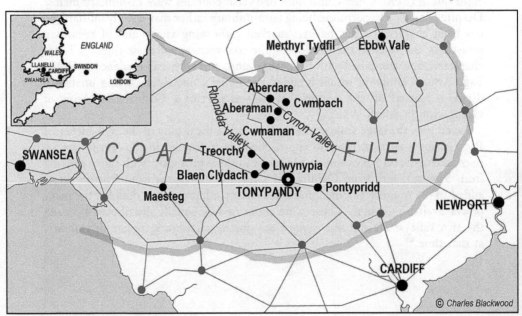

and its defenders, resisting an attempted assault.[56] If so then he was, according to the later testimony from a rather more impartial source, who decried 'the inclination on the part of the colliery managers to send in highly coloured and alarmist reports', certainly guilty of overstatement.[57]

Whether or not the scale and potential dangers of the clashes at Llwynypia were exaggerated, they and their aftermath, with fighting taking place between police and strikers in Tonypandy centre itself in the early hours of 8 November, stimulated Lindsay into calling for military aid. Having pre-warned the various military authorities that assistance was likely to be required, at 1am on 8 November he telegraphed to Shrewsbury (Shropshire), Chester (Cheshire) and Tidworth (Salisbury Plain, Wiltshire) for troops to be sent. This is noteworthy because army barracks existed in Brecon, Cardiff and Newport which, geographically, were closer.[58] However, and as previously noted, the army was averse to utilising troops with local affiliations in suppressing civil disorder.

In any event, a reply was received from Tidworth at 3am to the effect that both infantry and cavalry had been despatched. These were scheduled to arrive at Pontypridd at about 9am but, to the apparent surprise of Lindsay, they failed to arrive.[59] At 10am he telegraphed the Home Office:

> All the Cambrian collieries menaced last night. The Llwynypia Colliery savagely attacked by large crowd of strikers. Many casualties on both sides. Am expecting two companies of infantry and 200 cavalry to-day. Very little accommodation for police or soldiers. Position grave. Will wire again.[60]

The non-arrival of the contingent from Tidworth was due to Government intervention. As Churchill later explained it:

> The cavalry and infantry, sent for by the Chief Constable on Monday night, were not asked for from the Secretary of State for War or from me. But they were sent, pending instructions by the General Officer commanding the Southern Command, and it was not until ten the next day that I was informed of what was taking place.

His account also related how a meeting was subsequently convened at the Home Office with Haldane, the Secretary of State for War, and Sir John Spencer Ewart, the Adjutant-General. Following 'a long discussion' it was decided that 'definitely' and 'as a matter of public policy' the matter should be dealt with 'by police in the first instance and not by soldiers'. Furthermore, 'if soldiers should be used at all they should only be used in support of the police, and every precaution should be taken not to bring the military into direct collision with the crowd of strikers'.[61] Accordingly, the military contingent on its way from Wiltshire by train had been halted at Swindon.[62]

Lindsay had followed up his telegram by telephoning the Home Office and speaking directly to Churchill. According to Evans, he 'represented to the Home Secretary his fear that owing to the hilly character of the district at and about the Glamorgan Colliery he would not be able with police alone to prevent another night attack on the pit'. Consequently 'disappointment ... was expressed at the delay in the arrival of the military'.[63]

The potential for further disappointment was high; not only had Churchill interfered with Lindsay's arrangements, but he was taking steps to remove responsibility for the matter from his hands altogether, or at least in so far as he could. According to Major General Sir Nevil Macready, the man chosen to assume that mantle:

> About noon I received a message to go to the Home Office. It appeared that Mr Churchill was anxious to send at once a special officer, to whom he could give personal directions, to command the troops which were being despatched. The first intention was to send an officer from Salisbury, but as Mr Churchill wished to see him there would necessarily be delay. So when I walked into the room I found that my fate was fixed, and Mr Winston Churchill in his usual impetuous way asked if I could catch a train at about 1 p.m. Having to collect a toothbrush and other necessaries at my house, I compromised for a train at 3:15 that afternoon by which I started on my first venture to deal with labour trouble.[64]

Despite what Macready said about the 'first intention' for the role being 'an officer from Salisbury', Churchill was to tell the House of Commons that: 'We did not leave it to the chance of whatever officer happened to be summoned ... We picked a special officer ...'[65] He was, of course, speaking with the benefit of hindsight and in an attempt at vindicating his policy, so quite what made that particular officer 'special' before the event is unknown. Macready's behaviour during his tenure as what became, in effect, Home Office commissioner to the Welsh valleys responsible for law and order, demonstrated that he did not conform to the reactionary stereotype often associated with senior British military men of the period. He did have some experience of policing, albeit with the Military Police, both in Egypt and from having been Provost Marshal at Port Elizabeth in South Africa following the Boer War. Otherwise there seems nothing in his background, whether on active service or in staff positions, to suggest that he was especially qualified for such a role. Churchill and Haldane obviously thought differently. As Macready put it: 'The two Ministers, while promising to supply all reasonable assistance in the way of police and military, were insistent that firearms should not be made use of except as a very last resort. From the time I started from London I came under the direct authority of the Home Office, except as regards purely military matters connected with the troops.'[66]

Churchill's intervention, and certainly the manner of it, was of dubious validity in legal and constitutional terms. Firstly, the Home Secretary didn't feature in the chain of command and so had no prerogative in respect of military deployments. That he was able to impose his will was purely down to a 'private arrangement' with Haldane, which allowed him to issue instructions via the War Office.[67] O'Brien discusses the possible reasons why Haldane 'took a back seat' in the manner he did. Amongst these he offers that the War Secretary, who was not in good health, may not have relished a confrontation with his younger, highly pugnacious, colleague. He also posits that, as had been demonstrated during the earlier situation concerning the trouble at Newport, he agreed with the policy of developing centrally directed responses to local unrest.[68] So long as Churchill and Haldane remained in accord, then there would be no difficulties in that regard.

There was, though, a greater barrier to the Home Office policy of intervention, particularly as it developed; the responsibility for the prevention and suppression of local disorder lay with the Chief Constable, supported as necessary by magistrates and the Watch Committee. In other words, Lindsay might well refuse to accept that Macready, although he would obviously command the troops, had any additional authority over him or his role in enforcing the law. That Churchill had a larger part in mind for the general was, however, not immediately apparent, nor communicated, to the Chief Constable.

Following his meeting with Macready, Churchill telegraphed further information to Lindsay at 1.30pm, telling him that 'Infantry should not be used till all other means have failed' and that they would, meanwhile, remain at Swindon. In their stead, however, he was sending 300 Metropolitan Police, a third being mounted officers, by special train. These were expected to arrive at Pontypridd at 8pm that evening whilst, as a further precautionary measure, 200 cavalry would also be 'moved into the district and remain there pending cessation of trouble'. In fact the cavalry contingent consisted of 14 officers and 200 NCOs and men of the 18th (Queen Mary's Own) Royal Hussars commanded by Major C.K. Burnett.[69] Churchill was later to explain that he made the distinction between infantry and cavalry 'because cavalry can use their horses, but infantry can only fire or charge with their weapons'.[70]

Also imparted was the news that Macready had been chosen to command the military and that he would 'act in conjunction with the civil authorities as circumstances may require'. Military assistance, however, would not be provided unless it became 'clear that police reinforcements are unable to cope with the situation'. To exactly whom it would have to become 'clear', and therefore who would decide that the military should indeed intervene, wasn't specified, but Lindsay was asked to reply stating whether or not the arrangements were sufficient.[71]

He responded by telephone an hour later. Churchill phrased it curiously when recounting the conversation to the House of Commons, stating that he had been 'fortunate enough to establish clear telephonic communication with the Chief Constable'.[72] Did this imply that their previous telephone conversation had not been 'clear'? An unanswerable question and, be that as it may, the two now definitely reached agreement as to what would happen next. Lindsay reckoned that the Metropolitan Police contingent would be sufficient for his needs provided they arrived that evening and therefore the cavalry squadron, for which there was little in the way of accommodation, could be delayed. Accordingly orders were sent via the War Office for the Hussars to detrain at Cardiff.

Macready, who was of course on his way to south Wales, was also contacted and informed of these developments, and told further that if it was found necessary he could, at his discretion, remobilise the cavalry. The latter seemed to Churchill a remote contingency: 'What the cavalry could have done in the night was never very clear.'[73] Nevertheless a telegram confirming the arrangements was despatched to Lindsay at 6.30pm, informing him that the general would be in command of the cavalry and, if an 'emergency arises so serious that [the] police cannot cope with it you should communicate with him'.[74]

The situation had indeed become more serious. A mass-meeting of the strikers and those locked out took place in the early afternoon at 'The Mid' (the Mid Rhondda football ground),[75] during the course of which a message from Churchill was read out. Whilst stating that moves were afoot to involve the Board of Trade in conciliation efforts, and that the government, the miners' 'best friends', would do its utmost in the interests of 'fair treatment' for them, it warned that 'rioting must cease at once'. The final sentence read stated that: 'Confiding in the good sense of the Cambrian Combine workmen we are holding back the soldiers for the present, and sending police instead.'[76]

This message was widely condemned; as Mrs Stuart Menzies rather sardonically phrased it: 'No doubt this was considered a very masterly stroke on the part of the genius who compiled it but it did not improve matters.'[77] That was a retrospective judgement, but there was broad agreement with it more or less contemporaneously. For example, John St Loe Strachey, editor and proprietor of *The Spectator*, at that time deemed 'the most influential of all the London weeklies',[78] was condemnatory:

> Surely this is a model of what a message from the Home Office ought not to be. What right has the Home Secretary to take up the position of a partisan, and assume that the men have been unfairly treated? ... His words are a foolish bribe to law-breakers to cease their criminal acts, and it is astonishing to us that Mr Churchill did not see the impropriety of using them.[79]

Evans was also censorious, pointing out that the message 'with its faintly disguised innuendo against the employers was resented by the general body of the coal-owners'. He also implied that, having been 'assured officially that no troops would arrive that evening', the strikers were thus emboldened to make another attempt at completely shutting down the Glamorgan Colliery at Llwynypia. In support of this he argues that 'Strikers were heard to say that it would be "their last chance, as the soldiers would be arriving tomorrow".'[80] On the other hand, Dai Smith reckons that it 'could be seen as a veiled threat more than a promise'.[81]

Whatever the veracity of Evans' points, or the propriety or otherwise of Churchill's message and whether or not it was a threat, what can be said for sure is that there was some serious disorder later. Following the close of the meeting the miners moved in 'a huge procession' from the football ground to Llwynypia, gathering outside the colliery at about 4pm.[82] Attempts were made by a contingent of mounted police, drafted in from Bristol, to disperse the crowd, which by

Evans' account had become 'truculent'. These were unsuccessful and a violent hand-to-hand conflict then developed which lasted up until about 7.30pm.[83]

Evans claimed that this fighting was 'unparalleled' for 'the grim fierceness with which it was fought and in the bloodshed which it entailed'. The object of 'the mob' in his account was the gaining of access to, and the capture of, Leonard Llewelyn's 'Fort Chabrol', as had been attempted the previous day. Once again he paints the action in brilliant military colours, describing how the defenders, who were becoming exhausted, made 'one last desperate effort to crush the spirit of the mob' by charging at them. The police, 'with a dervish yell and batons drawn ... dashed out between 80 and 90 strong from the colliery yard and cut a way clean through the densely packed mob'.[84] This last-ditch effort was effective, inasmuch as it drove the majority of the strikers away from the colliery, many of whom retreated in the direction of Tonypandy. Whilst investigations over the next day or so concluded that the reports upon which Evans based his account had been much exaggerated, there was no doubt that some nasty fighting had indeed taken place around the Glamorgan Colliery. Indeed, it seems likely that Samuel Rhys (sometimes rendered as Rays) of Tonypandy, the only person to perish during the course of the coalfield troubles, received during these clashes the blows from which he died three days later. However, as the inquest found, the evidence was not sufficiently clear about how he received his injuries.[85]

Other violent incidents apart from Llwynypia were also occurring on that November evening. In the Cynon Valley 'serious riots' occurred when a group of some 2,000 strikers accompanied by 'many hundreds of women' concentrated on attacking the Powell Dyffryn-owned coal washery, which was sited between Cwmbach and Aberaman around 1½ miles from Aberdare. Their objective was as at Llwynypia, and in Evans' words, 'the intimidation into abstention from work of those servants of the Company who had resisted the efforts of the strikers to bring them out and had remained faithful to their employers'.[86]

Some thirty police officers were guarding the installation, around which had been erected an apparently extemporised 'live wire' (electric) fence. This method-ology, using 'wires charged with electric current to exclude persons from the mine premises' was later dubbed illegal and the mine managers were forbidden to utilise it.[87] Whether there was any connection between the electrified fence and the tactic of attempting to drive the crowd back from it by playing a water hose on them is unknown. In any event, when both methods proved ineffectual, the police were 'compelled to charge the crowd with drawn truncheons', where-upon they 'dispersed in all directions, hundreds running along the railway line and others down the canal bank'. Many were jostled into the canal, but none drowned. However, some sixty strikers were injured, one having a seriously burned hand from contact with the live electric wire, and another a fractured leg. An unquantifiable number of policemen were also injured, two constables being 'seriously hurt', and the following day 'dozens of men and boys could be seen walking about with bandaged heads' at Cwmbach, providing 'unmistakeable evidence of the severe encounter with the police on the night previous'.[88]

Small wonder then that Macready 'came upon a scene of administrative panic which doubtless lost nothing in his later re-telling' as he arrived in the locality.[89] The general remembered being met at Cardiff

> by various military and police officials who struck me as being unduly per-turbed by reports that were coming in from Tonypandy. It was pouring with rain, I had no Staff officer or servant with me, and the few officials I managed to get in touch with at Pontypridd seemed to have lost all sense of propor-tion, and to be obsessed with but one idea: to flood the valleys with troops.[90]

Indeed, the stipendiary magistrate for Pontypridd and Rhondda, Daniel Lleufer Thomas, had despatched an urgent telegram to Churchill at 7:45pm:[91]

> Police cannot cope with rioters at Llwynypia, Rhondda Valley. Troops at Cardiff absolutely necessary. Will you order them forthwith. Am ready to accompany them.[92]

That a magistrate was proposing to accompany troops could only mean one thing: that he would read the Riot Act. That act dated from 1715 and under it, and by virtue of a magistrate or other official reading the relevant portion aloud, any gathering of twelve or more people was obliged to disperse. If they failed to do so within an hour, then force could be used to compel their compliance, and anyone thus injured forfeited any compensatory rights. Indeed, refusing to scatter after the Riot Act had been read was a felony with a maximum sentence of death.[93] According to Evans, that the Riot Act would indeed be read was 'con-sidered almost inevitable',[94] and there is evidence that preparations were made for magistrates in Aberdare to do so.[95]

In fact there was to be no reading of the Riot Act, though there was most certainly a riot or something very like one. This culminated in, as Evans and elements of the press termed it, 'The Sack of Tonypandy.'[96] The precursor was the movement of the strikers driven away from Llwynypia following the police charge. Many of them moved towards Tonypandy where, because they were otherwise engaged guarding the coal-owners' property, there was little or no police presence. There is general consensus on what happened, and the following newspaper account is typical:

> From eight o'clock onwards the town was entirely in the hands of the strikers, who smashed nearly all the windows of the business premises from the Square at Tonypandy to Penygraig, a distance of a quarter of a mile. With loud shouts the strikers rushed along, hurling huge stones at the large plate glass windows and belabouring them with sticks. Terror-stricken, the shop owners rushed into their premises and left the contents of the windows to the mercy of the looters, who in many instances threw the articles in the roadway.[97]

By the time the Metropolitan Police reinforcements despatched by Churchill arrived on the scene, at approximately 10pm after their train was delayed by a minor accident, the disturbances were over.[98] The press reports the next day were lurid. A 'Special Correspondent' of the *Evening Express and Evening Mail* wrote, under banner headlines proclaiming 'RIOTS, ROBBERY, RUIN' and "Pandy Plundered', that

> Mid-Rhondda was in a state of anarchy last night. Such scenes as those witnessed are almost, if not completely, without parallel in any civilised country. It was pandemonium let loose. The strikers seemed like men possessed, and were obsessed with only one purpose – destruction.[99]

The *South Wales Daily Post* announced 'CIVIL WAR IN THE RHONDDA' and 'TONYPANDY LOOTED BY THE STRIKERS'.[100] At a national level, the arguably more sober *Manchester Guardian* reported that following the violence: 'All night long men were boarding up the shattered shop fronts and carts were going round for the sweepings of plate glass that littered the main street for three quarters of a mile.' More ominously it added that 'The few shops that escaped damage yesterday are being barricaded today, and the night is awaited with dread.'[101] This window smashing and looting was undoubtedly severe, though perhaps not quite as brutal as Captain Wyndham Childs, whom Macready drafted into the area as his Chief Intelligence Officer, recalled some years later.[102] According to his memoirs:

> I can honestly say that in France I saw towns and villages evacuated by the Germans which were in better condition than those that the rioters had wrecked. All the shops had been looted, and not only their contents, but the actual fittings such as gas-brackets, shelves, etc., had been carried off. There was hardly an unbroken pane of glass in the place.[103]

Hyperbole no doubt; nothing in or about Tonypandy was burned down, blown up or otherwise subjected to anything resembling Prussian frightfulness. Indeed, the window-smashers and looters were curiously selective. For example, they famously left untouched a chemist's shop owned by a local celebrity, the former Welsh rugby international Willie Llewellyn.[104] They also spared Royal Stores at Blaenclydach, a village adjoining Tonypandy, the shop being a grocery business owned by Thomas and Sarah Davies, the parents of the writer Rhys Davies, who was then a schoolboy. The Davies were believed to be sympathetic to the miners; they allowed credit and helped less literate customers with their correspondence and legal affairs.[105]

This selectivity as regards targets, and indeed the violence as a whole, has been seen by some scholars as evidence of deeper issues than an industrial dispute that simply 'got out of hand'. Barclay characterises it as a 'temporary assertion' of a community's rights 'to exercise control over their work and lives' which created a 'serious social upheaval'. This, he argues, was 'the product of a process of social and industrial change which went on to engulf the whole coalfield and shape its post-war history'.[106] Smith posits that the riots 'should be seen as evidence of social fracture as much as of industrial dispute',[107] and indeed that the dispute served as a catalyst for the riots.[108] The crowd, he argues, chose targets that were 'symbolic of their discontent with a community which was supposedly their own natural focus of being'.[109] This discontent manifested itself in an attack on those perceived as being higher up the social scale:

> The social elite of the township of Tonypandy was, above all others, the shop-owning class. The angry, wealth-producing crowd turned against the symbol of social attainment, the conspicuous, wealth-making shops. And they did so in a manner that expressed contempt and resentment rather than greed and fear. The shops were smashed systematically but not indiscriminately.[110]

There was also a 'portent of greater mischief than ever', according to one newspaper account. This reported, though without great fanfare, that 'another shop raided was that of a pawnbroker who happened to have stocked a large number of rifles'.[111] The implications of that were clear. It is, though, arguable that the trouble in general can be contextualised within, as Porter puts it, the 'pent-up general fears' that had been steadily rising in Britain for several years and which 'suddenly took on specific and tangible forms'.[112] Not having the benefit of hindsight, and unlikely to have been impressed with such arguments in any event, Chief Constable Lindsay saw merely 'a lawless mob who could only be restrained by force'.[113] The headlines in the local newspapers have already been quoted. There could only be one response:

> The following communication was issued from the Home Office late on Tuesday night [8 November 1910]:-
>
> > Information was received by the Home Office early in the evening that ... disturbances began as soon as it was dark. In these circumstances authority was at once given to General Macready ... to move the cavalry into the district by the morning and an infantry detachment will be moved to Newport on Wednesday.[114]

Churchill now drew fire from both sides. Conservative opinion was particularly forthright. As one local newspaper had it: 'The general opinion in the Rhondda Valley is that Mr Winston Churchill, in stopping the military yesterday, made THE BLUNDER OF HIS LIFE.'[115] *The Times* agreed: 'The Chief Constable knows the local conditions ... and he is responsible for order in the district. If he asked for troops it was no doubt because he was convinced they were needed.'[116] The Monmouthshire and South Wales Coal-owners' Association also complained. They protested 'very strongly ... against the delay which occurred in the sending of the troops into the district'. The 'serious rioting which has occurred both in the Rhondda and Aberdare Valleys' they attributed to 'the lack of a sufficiently protective force'.[117]

Churchill defended himself, the reply to the above message stating that he was 'unable to accept the view that a premature display of military force would have had the effect of preventing the rioting which occurred on Tuesday last. It is not unlikely that it might have had precisely the opposite effect.'[118] That was to be his position throughout the affair and afterwards.

On the other hand, if there were those who deprecated the, as they saw it, late deployment of the military then there were others, mainly represented by the Labour Party and Trades Unions, who criticised the fact they had been employed at all. Churchill records that in the House of Commons on 15 November 'Mr Keir Hardie raised the Tonypandy riots, the impropriety of sending [the] military [and the] harsh methods of the police ...'.[119] His letter to the king reporting the exchange, and referring to himself in the third person, concluded: 'Mr Churchill's conduct was not challenged in any quarter of the House [of Commons] except from the Labour benches.'[120]

Even before the event there had been disapproval. Enoch Edwards, the Labour MP for Hanley and leader of the Miners' Federation of Great Britain, had argued on 6 November 1910 that 'the military are organised for the purpose of killing, and South Wales is no place for them to go and kill.'[121]

They did go; two squadrons of the 18th Hussars were accommodated at Pontypridd, whilst three companies of infantry drawn from the Lancashire Fusiliers, the Royal Munster Fusiliers and the Duke of Wellington's (West Riding) Regiment went to Llwynypia, Aberaman and Pontypridd. A further two companies were retained at Newport as a reserve.[122] There was, however, to be no killing. Indeed General Macready is widely acknowledged to have handled what was undoubtedly a potentially fraught situation with tact. Despite the fact that the Chief Constable was legally responsible, Churchill wanted his man in charge. A telegram he sent to Macready evidences this point:

> Am telegraphing Chief Constable to act in consultation with you in all matters affecting distribution of police forces, especially London police and military forces. You should therefore make your views prevail so if possible [the] Chief Constable will not be offended. I am confident he will act in deference to you [.] [I]f difficulties arise and you desire more definite authority I will secure it to you with regard to London police. However, it will be easiest to me in [explaining it to] Parliament if it can be avoided.[123]

As Jane Morgan put it: 'rather than leave the direction of public order in the hands of local magistrates, Churchill placed constitutional power in the safe keeping of General Macready'.[124] The latter, according to his memoirs, records that the coal-owners and their attitude singularly failed to impress him and his officers. For example, when the strikers offered to help bring up the horses from underground this was refused by Leonard Llewelyn. As Macready noted:

> The incident of the horses created considerable stir in the press at the time, and was a clever journalistic move on the part of the management of the colliery with the object of enlisting sympathy against the strikers ... As a matter of fact the horses were fed and watered daily and were quite unaffected by the strike, nor was there at any time any question of their safety

from the moment that the Metropolitan Police and soldiers arrived at Tonypandy ...[125]

Such 'journalistic moves' were behind the general's threat to 'deport from the area' the secretary to one of the principal mine managers. This person, a former newspaper reporter who might possibly have been David Evans, was 'the instigator of much of the highly coloured propaganda that was being scattered broadcast to prejudice the public mind'. The appearance of this material in the local press 'contributed towards maintaining and developing the atmosphere of tension and excitement in the strike area'.[126] Quite how this 'deportation' might have been squared legally was never put to the test, but the fact that Macready assumed 'constitutional power' and used it in other areas was undoubtedly a factor in minimising disorder. Had the Chief Constable been in that position then it is reasonable to assume that he would have been far from a calming force. John Moylan, a civil servant whom Churchill sent down 'as a sort of liaison officer' to Macready and who reported directly to the Home Office,[127] wrote on 10 November that 'Lindsay has got the fighting spirit in him and is rather hoping, I think, to take on the rioters again now that he has a stronger force and [to] teach them a lesson.'[128]

Teaching the strikers a lesson, of one sort or another, was undeniably in the minds of the coal-owners. Indeed, on 12 November they informed George Askwith and Isaac Mitchell of the Board of Trade, who were attempting to broker a settlement, that mediation was not possible until after a return to work. Further, those employed by the Cambrian Combine would have to accept the price for working the Upper Five Feet seam that had been negotiated with Mabon in October.[129] Macready, from discussions he had with Leonard Llewelyn in December 1910, concluded that a prolonged strike was 'desired from the owner's point of view', their rationale being that 'if the men were reduced to great straits, they would not be likely to come out again for some ten years or so. Whereas if they return to work without feeling the pinch of striking, they may possibly come out again on small provocation.'[130] Llewelyn was thinking in terms of three or four months but the dispute continued until October 1911.

One factor little mentioned in most accounts of the strike and associated events is the possibility of them segueing from 'social fracture' into something resembling an insurrection.[131] Macready's memoirs reference 'some wild talk about arming the strikers with revolvers' before going on to state that 'I never for a moment believed that the British working man would sink to the level of Irishmen or foreigners, by the use of lethal weapons against unarmed police.'[132] He had been a little more expansive at the time, at least according to a report, dated 16 November 1910, sent to Churchill. This detailed a meeting held with 'local leaders in the Cambrian strike' at the Thistle Hotel, Tonypandy, where he told them that he had 'in the last few days heard a great deal about the purchase of revolvers and the preparation of bombs made out of boxes filled with explosives and fired by a fuse'. He explained that whilst his forces were there to support the police only if necessary, if 'anything in the shape of revolver shooting or bomb throwing were attempted' then military intervention would be immediate. The results could only 'be disastrous to the strikers'. The strike leaders responded by stating that they had urged their followers to abstain from violence, but did not have absolute control over them. The 'theft of explosives' as had been reported in the newspapers was put down to 'a clever journalistic move on the owners' side', and they were convinced that none had been taken by any of the strikers.[133]

This example of an alleged 'clever journalistic move' might have some connection with Macready's threat of journalistic deportation mentioned above. In any event, there were to be no bombs thrown nor revolver shooting. Lindsay's deputy did, however, produce a report showing that in the period 4–12 November seven revolvers had been sold in Tonypandy. Sales had, though, been refused in another 118 cases because the applicants failed to produce the necessary licence.[134] Whatever the reasons for their purchase, these weapons were not discharged during the course of the strike.

No more was heard of the 'large number of rifles' supposedly stolen from the pawnbrokers either. This incident may, of course, have been merely another example of creative journalism. What does seem to be grounded rather more in fact was the removal from drill halls of the rifles and ammunition which had been issued to the local Territorial forces.[135] This led to a correspondent to the *Industrial Worker*, an American journal self-described as 'The Voice of Revolutionary Industrial Unionism', to opine that 'the plain suggestion ... that the militia [*sic*] is not only not to be depended on for use against the strikers, but is even likely to use its arms in the strikers' defense, has opened the country's eyes to the possibility of what looks like the dangers of civil war'.[136] Had it been printed in Cwmaman rather than Chicago, Macready would likely have had the writer deported. Or tried to, at least.

Even if there had ever been a danger of the conflict assuming anything like 'civil war' proportions, then the presence of the military would have suppressed it. Macready wrote to Churchill on 25 November telling him that in his opinion the strikers recognised that 'a mob has little chance against disciplined Police, and that the intervention of even a small force of soldiers would be disastrous to them'.[137] As it was, there was hardly any direct antagonistic contact between the soldiers and the strikers. The author of the 18th Hussars' history recorded that whilst those involved found deployment 'in aid of the civil power' an 'unpleasant duty', they 'never actually came to loggerheads with the miners'. He adds, 'in fact, when not actually engaged in guarding pit-heads and power stations, many friendly games of football were played with our quondam opponents'.[138]

The police drafted into the area were less well regarded, particularly the Metropolitans who were by far the most numerous.[139] Indeed, out of a total of 1,499 police sent into the Rhondda and Aberdare Valleys at different times during the strike from eleven different forces, 902 were Metropolitan policemen. Of that overall total, the highest number engaged on duty at any one time, on 15 and 16 November 1910, was 1,301. By the middle of February 1911 the number of imported police had reduced to 312.[140] Macready had departed a month or so earlier, handing command over to Major George Freeth of the Lancashire Fusiliers on 5 January.[141]

There can be no doubt that the November deployment of Metropolitan Police and military units under Macready's direct, and Churchill's indirect, control was instrumental in maintaining law and order in the south Wales valleys. The appointment of Macready as, effectively, Home Office commissioner to the Welsh valleys, and the dubious constitutional validity of subordinating Chief Constable Lionel Lindsay to him, is surely an early illustration of the Churchillian propensity to push boundaries. Randolph Churchill's comment about how, as a backbencher, Churchill had spoken as if he were an Under-Secretary and, as an Under-Secretary, as if he were a member of the Cabinet, has already been noted. That observation went further, noting that 'when he reached the Cabinet he was apt to speak as if he were Prime Minister'.[142] One might add, 'and act like one too', even if, and according to one of his more recent biographers, Asquith was 'privately sympathetic' to the strikers.[143] What can be said is that the Prime Minister must have, at least tacitly, approved of his Home Secretary's actions whilst Haldane at the War Office actively cooperated.

This was, at bottom, an extension of state power. The despatch of centrally directed reinforcements, as had been the case at Newport earlier, represented a further, and larger, example of the Home Office arrogating to itself an expanded, supervisory, role when it came to dealing with civil disorder on a significant, and therefore politically sensitive, scale. As Weinberger put it: 'At one stroke the local police were thereby catapulted into the twentieth century and forced to rethink the whole basis on which their previous strategy had been based.'[144] In that context then, Churchill was an expansionist and interventionist Secretary of State, unafraid of pushing the boundaries of Home Office responsibility, and involving himself and his department in areas previously considered beyond their purview. These can be viewed as early manifestations of tendencies that were to become pronounced throughout his life and career.

There were others. Churchill is often credited, if that is the correct term, with the phrase 'history will be kind to me, for I intend to write it'. It is another apocryphal quote. He did, though, write, or had a large hand in compiling, the Government's official Blue Book on the south Wales disturbances in 1911.[145] The correspondence in this official account was, however, as O'Brien has demonstrated by comparing the contents with original documents only released decades later, subjected to a weeding and editing process:

> Apart from excluding sensitive passages, the editors – under Churchill's direction – seem on occasions to have engineered a subtle re-writing of the documents released with such remarkable rapidity to the general public in March 1911; a correlation between the wording of the originals and of the published documents does not always emerge.[146]

This 'polishing' of the record, as it might be termed, was another practice that was periodically reprised during Churchill's later career.

Nevertheless, an objective assessment of Churchill's role and actions during November 1910 and after, as they pertained to the south Wales coalfield strikes, cannot but conclude that his performance was, all in all, both prudent and wise. That he came in for criticism from both ends of the political spectrum is, arguably, evidence of this. But concrete testimony to the delicate but successful handling of a volatile situation can surely be found in the fact that it was accomplished without incurring fatalities, if not entirely peacefully.

The two main sufferers arising from the dispute were Churchill's reputation and the south Wales miners, the first being contingent on the second. As noted, the dispute ground on until October 1911 before the strikers were effectively starved back to work, and obliged to accept the employers' terms as laid down more than a year earlier. 'With no hope of active support in the form of a [national] strike, the Cambrian Combine committee was forced to acknowledge defeat.'[147] It was a grim and dismal prospect. According to Rhys Davies, 'Half the people remained for ever in bad debt because of the long Cambrian strike.'[148]

Though Churchill did not have any miners shot, and was arguably instrumental in preventing any such thing occurring, his actions were nevertheless bitterly resented by those on the losing side of the dispute. One of the duties of a Home Secretary was, of course, the maintenance of law and order which, as his official biographer noted, could be 'unpopular'.[149] Indeed, law and order, in the context of the time and place under discussion, might be compared with Wodehouse's witticism about the fascination of shooting as a sport: 'It depends almost wholly on whether you are at the right or wrong end of the gun.'[150] The strikers were on the wrong end of law and order. As David Maddox, joint author of a book on the Tonypandy Riots,[151] explained during a TV programme marking their centenary:

> The bitterness towards Churchill, which has been passed down the years, stems from the fact that the troops' presence made picketing impossible, and effectively broke the strike.[152] It stuck in the craw of the miners that a Liberal government would use the army to side with pit owners over the workers.[153]

Indeed it did and, as has been noted, it is still the case that 'in Wales the resentment lingers today'.[154] Indeed the south Wales' coalfield dispute of 1910–1911, and Churchill's part in it, became encapsulated in a single word: 'Tonypandy.' Whether fairly or otherwise, and of course dependent upon perspective, until greater events supervened to claim the title, Tonypandy became Churchill's albatross.[155]

Chapter Four

Cutting off 'this stream of madness'

'After World War II, nobody was a eugenicist, and nobody had ever been a eugenicist. Biographers of the celebrated and the powerful did not dwell on the attractions of this philosophy to their subjects, and sometimes did not mention it at all.'[1]

'Winston is ... a strong eugenist. He told us he had himself drafted the Bill which is to give power of shutting up people of weak intellect and so prevent their breeding. He thought it might be arranged to sterilize them.'[2]

* * *

The fears of national decline and degeneration brought into focus by the investigations following the Boer War dovetailed, and represented a continuum, with earlier and ongoing concerns in that area. The original source of these was the work of Charles Darwin, as interpreted and extrapolated by his polymathic cousin, Francis Galton.[3] As the latter phrased it in his autobiography:

> The publication in 1859 of the *Origin of Species* ... made a marked epoch in my own mental development, as it did in that of human thought generally. Its effect was to demolish a multitude of dogmatic barriers by a single stroke, and to arouse a spirit of rebellion against all ancient authorities whose positive and unauthenticated statements were contradicted by modern science.[4]

Galton said that he 'devoured' the *Origin of Species* and assimilated its contents 'as fast as they were devoured'.[5] In June and August of 1865 the results of this assimilation led to two articles in *Macmillan's Magazine*. These were entitled 'Hereditary Character and Talent: Part I' and 'Hereditary Character and Talent: Second Paper' respectively.[6] The ideas propounded were expanded upon in 1869 in a subsequent book entitled *Hereditary Genius*,[7] which is claimed to be 'the first serious study of the inheritance of intelligence'.[8] In that context, Galton popularised, though did not coin, the term 'nature versus nurture' and was convinced of the predominance of the former. In an example given in one of his later works he claimed that 'the child had developed into manhood, along a predestined course laid out in his nature'.[9]

There were to be many such sentiments expressed in many such works, the recurring theme being the claim that psychological abilities, tendencies and intelligence were inherited just as with physical characteristics, and were thus equally subject to the laws of natural selection – or rather that they would be had not 'civilised men' intervened to 'check the process'. The implications of this had been delineated by Charles Darwin in 1872:

> With savages, the weak in body or mind are soon eliminated; and those that survive commonly exhibit a vigorous state of health. We civilised men, on the other hand, do our utmost to check the process of elimination ... excepting in the case of man himself, hardly any one is so ignorant as to allow his worst animals to breed.[10]

The end result of this was obvious: 'the reckless, degraded, and often vicious members of society tend to increase at a quicker rate than the provident and generally virtuous members'.[11] The check to this otherwise apparently inexorable process of degradation was to be found in what Galton, in 1883, dubbed 'eugenics'. Eugenics encompassed two main principles: the positive kind, seeking to ensure that the 'best people' bred, and the negative, 'intended to encourage the socially disadvantaged to breed less – or better yet, not at all'.[12] Positive eugenics amounted to little more than a pipe dream, whilst negative eugenics had a darker, and conceivably more concrete, side. Indeed, whilst it might have been *practically* difficult, if not impossible, to mate people like domestic animals, a programme of incarceration and sterilisation was in no way unfeasible. Indeed, attempts to have such a programme enacted politically formed a central plank of the eugenist movement's aims. Taking both positive and negative notions to their extreme conclusions, George Bernard Shaw scandalised the central branch of the British Eugenics Society in 1910 by invoking, albeit in a 'tongue-in-cheek manner', the use of the 'lethal chamber' and the 'methods of the stud farm'.[13]

Shaw might have been jesting, he was of course famous for it, but he wasn't the first to postulate such notions. The eminent scientist Sir William Cecil Dampier Whetham and the writer Catherine Durning Whetham co-authored a work which had appeared the year before. In this they submit that whilst it is 'impossible to say' exactly what causes contribute to the 'decadence of nations', nevertheless 'present knowledge ... suggests more and more that, in the survival and reproduction of the unfittest, we have discovered the most important clue to the true theory of the subject'. They continue:

> Indeed, as one looks back through the volume of ancient history most familiar to the average Englishman, one cannot help wondering whether Pharaoh's celebrated decree ordering the extermination of the male children of the Hebrews was not an effort to right the effects of what he deemed a misdirected selective birth-rate. He may have found it easier to destroy the children of the prolific alien population than to persuade the better classes of his native-born Egyptians to keep the balance even.[14]

There was, of course, no such presumption in the aims of the Eugenics Society, which had been founded in 1907 as the Eugenics Education Society.[15] Nominal membership of the society never exceeded 1,700 but made up for the lack of numbers by what was described as 'excellent patronage'[16] The problem of the 'unfittest' and what to do with them was a perennial preoccupation of the society; indeed, it was their *raison d'être*. The 'unfit', however, from a eugenist perspective, could be and were classified according to their economic status. Galton stated it thus in 1909:

> The aim of Eugenics is to bring as many influences as can be reasonably employed, to cause the more useful classes in the community to contribute *more* than their proportion to the next generation.[17]

He also compared his own 'natural divisions' of society with those into which Charles Booth had divided the population of London, and found a high correlation between the two.[18] There have been suggestions that this comparative process was 'gerrymandered'.[19] (See diagram below.)

Be that as it may, there was, of course, a further difficulty. Defining terms such as 'civic worth' and 'the unfit', and identifying 'the more useful classes', is quite

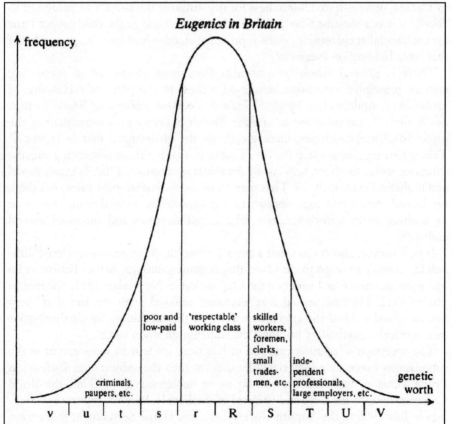

Eugenics in Britain

Social categories mapped. Sir Francis Galton's 1901 correlation of heritable 'civic worth' with social category, the latter as determined in Charles Booth's *Life and Labour of the People in London*. (*Source*: Donald MacKenzie, 'Eugenics in Britain', *Social Studies of Science*, September 1976, 6(3/4): 514)

obviously a subjective process and a matter of perspective. That being so, most scholars who have studied the matter are agreed that eugenic nostrums had political underpinnings. Dorothy Porter, for example, has argued for the correctness of Searle's view that 'the political appeal of eugenics in Britain before the First World War lay in the opportunities it afforded to the "radical right" to mount an ideological challenge to traditional liberalism and welfare socialism'.[20] There is something of a scholarly consensus on this. Mazumdar, for instance, argues persuasively that 'British eugenics … [concentrated] … on applying the laws of inheritance to the social problems of poverty and pauperism'.[21] Greta Jones has a similar position: 'eugenics was a means … of managing the health, moral and social condition of the poor'.[22]

However, by no means all promoters of eugenic principles could be dubbed 'radical right' conservatives. For instance, Karl Pearson, one of the founders of modern statistical methodology and Galton's first biographer – who, according to Blacker, demonstrated 'boundless loyalty' towards the subject he professed to 'love'[23] – was a socialist who 'held up scientific method as the only proper basis for true, socialist citizenship, since it provided standards of knowledge and belief that were binding on everyone'.[24]

There is general scholarly consensus that those concerned in promoting eugenic principles were overwhelmingly, almost to the point of exclusivity, of professional, middle-class, origin.[25] Indeed, a reviewer of one of Searle's works has it thus: 'it makes sense to analyse British eugenics as a movement *of* the professional middle classes, ideologically *for* the professional middle classes'.[26] Taking that argument a step further, Tanner posits that those advocating eugenic solutions were, in effect, seeking to demonstrate their own 'intellectual, moral and biological superiority'.[27] That may be so, or at least in some cases, but there can be little doubt that eugenics particularly appealed to a social group that owed its position to its knowledge, educational qualifications and supposed mental ability.[28]

It is, however, also certain that a single, coherent, position was rendered difficult by disunity amongst those advocating eugenic solutions. Arthur Balfour, who had been succeeded as Leader of the Opposition in November 1911, referred to this in 1912. He commented that 'eugenics suffered from the fact that every faddist seized hold of the eugenic problem as the machinery for furthering his own particular method of bringing the millennium upon earth'.[29]

The spectrum of opinion referred to had been evident to some extent in the submissions made to a formal public inquiry into the subject that Balfour, as Prime Minister, had caused to be set up in September 1904. This, the Royal Commission into the Care and Control of the Feeble-Minded, reported its findings in July 1908 to the Asquith Government, the Home Secretary at that period being Herbert Gladstone.[30] Also known as the 'Radnor Report',[31] it stated that there was 'well-nigh universal agreement among witnesses … that the greater number of these "feeble-minded" persons are mentally deficient from birth, though often the fact that mental defect exists is not discovered until later'. It also pointed out that 'in a very large proportion these persons are the offspring of mentally defective parents or are members of families in which other nearly related members are mentally defective'.[32]

This near universal agreement did not endure in respect of causes. The report continues: there was a 'marked difference of opinion in regard to the relative importance to be assigned to "heredity" as against what may be termed the influence of environment'.[33] There was, though, a large majority 'who attach[ed] supreme importance to the fact that in a very large proportion of cases of mental defect there is a history of mental defect in the parents or near ancestors'.[34] This majority was quantified as twenty-five out of thirty-five, with the testimony of sixteen of them being cited. Amongst them, that of the distinguished neurologist and psychiatrist, and 'Physician to the Littleton Home for Defective Children', Dr Alfred Frank Tredgold.[35]

The solution to the problem of exactly how to define a mentally defective person was addressed, and a table of categories drawn up. Also calculated were numbers. The report assessed that in England and Wales (Scotland and Ireland were dealt with separately) there were '149,628 mentally defective persons', a figure which equated to 0.46 per cent of the population. Of that total, which did not include certified lunatics, '66,509 or 44.45 per cent' were estimated to be 'at the present time urgently in need of provision, either: (1) in their own interest; or (2) for the public safety'. The total number of mentally defective persons, including certified lunatics, was projected as being 271,607 persons, or 0.83 per cent, of the population.[36] The nature of the 'provision' referred to, and which over 66,000 people were apparently in urgent need of, was also laid out:

> the State should have authority to segregate and to detain mentally defective persons under proper conditions and limitations and on their behalf to compel the payment of contributions from relations who are able to pay for their support; or should itself provide such care and accommodation as may be necessary, either directly or through the local authority. This, subject to many variations and adjustments, is an extension to the whole class of the mentally defective of advantages now given to lunatics and idiots only.[37]

This report was just about all that the most fervent eugenicist could have asked for. Galton certainly thought so: 'The Royal Commission on the Feeble-Minded have attacked a Eugenic problem of the first order of magnitude with thoroughness and remarkable success.' This opinion appeared in an abstract comprising the most important points of the report.[38]

It was, though, one thing to have recommendations, but quite another to have them translated into parliamentary action. It was in pursuit of the latter that on 31 August 1909 the Liberal MP for St Pancras North, Willoughby Dickinson, introduced a twenty-strong deputation to Herbert Gladstone, the Home

Secretary. The object of the exercise was to urge the necessity for early legislation in order to carry out the recommendations contained in the report:

> The deputation was very anxious that the Government should legislate on the subject as early as possible, and suggested that, as the matter was one involving social welfare, there would be no difficulty in the way.[39]

Among those in attendance were the Reverend William Inge, Lady Margaret's Professor of Divinity at Cambridge and a future Dean of St Paul's Cathedral. He had contributed a short piece to the abstract of the Royal Commission report which had argued, amongst other things, that 'The laws of heredity are divine laws, and if we are allowed to know them, it is in order that we may use them.'[40] Also included were two Liberal MPs, Charles Mallet (Plymouth) and Charles Nicholson (Doncaster), the latter discoursing on the case of a 'half-witted woman who passed in and out of the workhouse, and gave birth to no less than seven illegitimate children'.[41] Perhaps curiously, no Conservative MPs appear to have been present.

Gladstone's response was anodyne. He had 'listened with very great interest to the speeches which had been made on a most important subject'. The 'present lunacy law was in many respects very good, but in other respects it was archaic'. He went on to emphasise the complications – 'the matter, of course, was one of great difficulty: its difficulties were in proportion to its scope, which, unfortunately, was very widespread' – before stating that he had 'regretfully, abandoned the hope that it would be possible to introduce a bill in the present session'.[42]

However, when Churchill took Gladstone's place it became apparent that his view on eugenics in general, and the findings of the Royal Commission in particular, were far more forceful. Indeed, several documents and memoranda were circulated to the Prime Minister and his Cabinet colleagues, and within the Home Office, under his aegis. Asquith received an imprecisely dated letter in 1910 laying out the Home Secretary's perspective on the matter:

> The unnatural and increasingly rapid growth of the feeble-minded and insane classes, coupled as it is with a steady restriction among all the thrifty, energetic and superior stocks, constitutes a national and race danger which it is impossible to exaggerate ... I feel that the source from which this stream of madness is fed should be cut off and sealed up before another year has passed.[43]

He also transmitted a document, 'Treatment of weakminded prisoners. Proposals by the Secretary of State (Mr Winston Churchill)', for the consideration of the Cabinet.[44] This, again, is dated with no more precision than '1910', so we do not know exactly when it was actually laid before his colleagues. The title is also misleading, as the thirty-page paper covers a far greater range than merely relates to prisoners and is in fact a copy of parts of the report of the Royal Commission on the Care and Control of the Feeble-Minded; specifically Part IV *Mental Defect and Crime* and Part VI *Causation of Mental Defect; Definitions of Classes of Mental Defect; and Investigations of the Numbers of Mentally Defective Persons.*

That this was a matter which had impressed itself deeply upon him is plain. Indeed, he found the time in December 1910, a period of intense political activity relating to the second General Election of the year it should be borne in mind, to again address Asquith on the subject:

> I am convinced that the multiplication of the Feeble-Minded, which is proceeding now at an artificial rate, unchecked by any of the old constraints of nature and actually fostered by civilized conditions, is a very terrible danger to the race. The number of children in feebleminded families is calculated at 7.4; whereas in normal families, it is but 4.2 ... [There are] 12,000 feebleminded and defective children in the Special Schools; many others are in residential homes ... The girls come out by the thousand at 16, are the mothers of imbeciles at 17 and thereafter, with surprising regularity, they frequent our workhouse lying-in wards year by year. The males contribute an ever-broadening streak to the insane or half-insane crime which darkens the life of our towns and fills the convict prisons.[45]

What the Prime Minister made of it is unknown. Yet another imprecisely dated paper entitled 'The Feeble Minded – A Social Danger',[46] which is described as being 'signed in 1911', was circulated to the Cabinet. It was a typescript of an address given by 'A.F. Tredgold ... Medical Expert to the Royal Commission on the Feeble Minded, &c. &c.' to the 'National Association for the Welfare of the Feeble-minded' at the Mansion House on 13 May 1909. This paper was accompanied by an (equally undated) cover note from Churchill:

> I think the Cabinet may like to see this report of an address delivered in May 1909 by Dr Tredgold on the subject of the Feeble-Minded. Dr Tredgold speaks from wide experience and with special authority, since as one of the medical investigators employed by the Royal Commission on the Feeble-Minded, he carried out an elaborate enquiry in Somerset. This address gives a concise and, I am informed, not exaggerated statement of the serious problem to be faced. The Government is pledged to legislation, and a Bill is being drafted to carry out the recommendations of the Royal Commission.[47]

As discussed, the Royal Commission report had estimated that the numbers of mentally defective persons in England and Wales amounted to 149,628.[48] Tredgold amended this by excluding 'sane' epileptics, and thus arrived at a lower figure of 138,529.[49] Despite this, it presented an apocalyptic picture: 'we find that in this country there is *one* person out of every 180 who suffers from severe disease of mind'.[50] The problem was, however, much greater than this:

> we now know that mental deficiency is the result, not of chance, but of law, and due to certain definite antecedent conditions. These conditions are

many and varied, but they are all such as induce nervous and physical debility, and amongst the chief of them are alcoholism and consumption ...

... the feeble-minded and their relations form a very considerable proportion, if not the whole, of the social failures – the degenerates of a nation. [...] There is, however, another fact regarding these persons which is so startling and important that it cannot be too strongly emphasised, and that is the rate at which they increase. [...]

According to the registrar-general the average number of births to a marriage in the whole population of this country is 4.63. I have ascertained that the average number of births in these degenerate families is no less than 7.3. It is obvious that if this alarming propagation is not checked, the time must inevitably come, if it has not already come, when our nation will contain a preponderance of citizens lacking that intellectual and physical vigour which is absolutely essential to progress [...]

Now I have given a good deal of attention to this subject, and I have come to the conclusion that ... there is one measure, and one measure only that will fulfil ... [the requirements of removing the feeble-minded from society and reducing their financial burden on society] ... and which is at the same time practically possible, namely the establishment of suitable farm and industrial colonies. In such institutions the feeble-minded would not only be happy, far happier in fact amid companions like themselves than in the outside world, but they would also contribute to their own support.[51]

Detailed analysis of this document is unnecessary within the current context, but clearly Tredgold blames nearly all the ills of society, including perhaps surprisingly the scourge of pulmonary tuberculosis, on the 'feeble-minded'. It is also apparent that the looming apocalypse foreseen by the author will only be avoided by resort to his remedy: compulsory, sexually segregated, work camps. It is perhaps worth reiterating that this document was circulated to the Cabinet with a cover note signed by the Home Secretary.

The question of interning sections of the population was touched upon by Churchill on 10 February 1911 in a letter to the King, the task of reporting, on a daily basis, the business of the House of Commons to the sovereign being one that Asquith had delegated to him. His official biographer considers that it was 'a tribute both to his sense of the House of Commons and to his literary style that the job came his way'.[52]

On this occasion, however, Churchill's phraseology, in one portion, affronted royal sensibilities:

As for tramps and wastrels there ought to be proper Labour Colonies where they could be sent for considerable periods and made to realise their duty to the State. Such institutions are now being considered at the Home Office. It must not, however, be forgotten that there are idlers and wastrels at both ends of the social scale.[53]

This was, whether unconsciously or not, rather echoing Lloyd George's biting comment made in 1909 about the membership of the House of Lords being composed of those 'chosen accidentally from among the unemployed'.[54] In any event, and whatever might have inspired these words, they offended George V. This resulted in a letter to the Prime Minister's private secretary, Vaughan Nash, from his royal counterpart, Francis Knollys (Lord Knollys):

> The King thinks that Mr Churchill's views ... are very socialistic. What he advocates is nothing more than workshops which have been tried in France & have turned out a complete failure. ... H[is] M[ajesty] considers it quite superfluous for Churchill in a letter of the description he was writing to him, to bring in about 'idlers and wastrels at both ends of the social ladder'.[55]

Churchill's reply to this, when he learned of it, is of interest because it contains his considered views of the matter. As with all his correspondence to the king, it was written in the third person:

> Mr Churchill cannot understand why this should be thought to be Socialistic in its character. The Government contemplate measures to deal with vagrancy and the punishment and reform of tramps and incorrigible loafers by means of labour colonies on the continental system, and the Home Office is already studying the subject with a view to drafting a bill. It is a national difficulty which stands in the way of such measures that the reproach may be uttered that even-handed justice would require that all persons should render some service to the State whether rich or poor. To say this is not to attack the wealthy classes, most of whom as Mr Churchill knows well have done their duty in many ways: but only to point to those particular persons whose idle and frivolous conduct and lack of public spirit brings a reproach to the meritorious class to which they belong. Mr Churchill therefore adheres most respectfully to the truth and sincerity of the opinion which he expressed in endeavouring in a few sentences to give Your Majesty a correct impression of the issue in the House of Commons on Friday last.[56]

The epistolic tiff between the King and his Secretary of State rumbled on for a little while, with Knollys writing on 14 February:

> You ... implied that a comparison could be fairly drawn between 'Tramps and Wastrels' whom you would relegate to 'Labour Colonies' and 'idlers and wastrels' at the other end of the social scale.
>
> I cannot conceal from you that the King would have preferred it, had you seen your way to suppress this remark, to which moreover an obvious answer might be offered that the cost of support in one case falls on the State and does not do so on the other.[57]

By 17 February peace had been declared, even though the conciliatory approach Churchill took was reckoned to be akin to 'A Bull in a China Shop' by Knollys.[58] Nevertheless he was able to write to the Home Secretary, telling him that the

King 'desires me to thank you for continuing your "House of Commons letters" which are always very interesting'.[59] It is singularly unfortunate that the identity of those 'whose idle and frivolous conduct and lack of public spirit' was worthy of reproach remains unrevealed. In the absence of evidence, then just who amongst the 'wealthy classes' the Home Secretary thought deserving of incarceration in 'Labour Colonies' must remain a matter of speculation. Indeed, it may have just been a throwaway remark by the author, rather than any manifestation of an impulse to expand the pool of potential detainees. Where the Home Secretary had indisputably pushed at a boundary, however, was in relation to the treatment of those with whom the Royal Commission had sought to deal. This is evidenced by his circulating within his department a document, published in the United States of America, that advocated a measure specifically disavowed in the Commission's report: compulsory sterilisation.

The document in question was an annotated pamphlet authored by Dr Harry C. Sharp, 'physician to the Indiana State Reformatory at Jeffersonville, who in 1899 pioneered the sterilisation of criminals by vasectomy'.[60] Indiana had become, in 1907, the first state to introduce compulsory sterilisation for those considered, for whatever reason, unfit to reproduce.[61] Sharp's pamphlet was entitled 'Sterilization of the Mentally Degenerate' and Churchill circulated it in mid-May 1910. Again we see the use of apocalyptical terms, but of greater interest are the Home Secretary's annotations which appeared as highlighted sections. In the following extracts these are indicated *thus*:

There is no longer any questioning of the fact that the degenerate class is increasing out of all proportion to the increase of the general population. [...] Restricting propagation seems to be universally agreed upon as necessary for the relief of this condition. The difficulty lies in deciding upon the proper method to bring about this restriction. [...] Castration is ... [a] ... means that has been suggested for the purpose of preventing procreation in the unfit. *A superintendent of the Kansas Feeble Minded Institution thus operated upon forty-eight boys in that institution about the year 1898.* This ... causes entirely too much mental and nervous disturbance to ever become popular or justifiable as a medical measure, but there is one operation that I heartily endorse as an additional punishment in certain offenses.

Since October, 1899, I have been performing an operation known as a vasectomy ... This operation is indeed very simple and easy to perform, I do it without administering an anaesthetic either general or local. It requires about three minutes' time to perform the operation and the subject returns to his work immediately, suffers no inconvenience, and is in no way impaired for his pursuit of life, liberty, and happiness, but is effectively sterilized. I have been doing this operation for nine full years. I have two-hundred and thirty-six cases that have afforded splendid opportunity for post operative observation *and I have never seen any unfavorable symptom* [...] the patient becomes of a more sunny disposition, brighter of intellect, ceases excessive masturbation, and advises his fellows to submit to the operation for their own good. And here is where this method of preventing procreation is so infinitely superior to all others proposed – that it is endorsed by the subjected persons [...] There is a law providing for the sterilization of defectives in effect in Indiana and it is being carried out at the Indiana Reformatory. [...] This law reads as follows:

A Bill for an Act, entitled an act to prevent procreation of confirmed criminals, idiots, imbeciles, and rapists;[62] providing that superintendents and boards of managers of institutions where such persons are confined shall have the authority and are empowered to appoint a committee of experts, consisting of two (2) physicians to examine into the mental condition of such inmates.

Whereas, Heredity plays a most important part in the transmission of crime, idiocy and imbecility;

Therefore, Be it enacted by the General Assembly of the State of Indiana, That on and after the passage of this act it shall be compulsory for each and every institution in the State, entrusted with the care of confirmed criminals, idiots, rapists, and imbeciles to appoint upon its staff, in addition to the regular institutional physician, two (2) skilled surgeons of recognized ability, whose duty it shall be, in conjunction with the chief physician of the Institution, to examine the mental and physical condition of such inmates as are recommended by the institutional physician and board of managers. If, in the judgement of this committee of experts and the board of managers, procreation is inadvisable and there is no probability of improvement of the mental and physical condition of the inmate, it shall be lawful for the surgeons to perform such operation for the prevention of procreation as shall be decided safest and most effective. But this operation shall not be performed except in cases that have been pronounced unimprovable: Provided, That in no case shall the consultation fee be more than three (3) dollars to each expert, to be paid out of the funds appropriated for the maintenance of such institution.[63]

This is indeed a very long step in the right direction and will never be rescinded for the simple reason that it is right, just to all, and humane.

Under the provision of the above quoted law women may be subjected to sterilization methods as well as men. The operation on women is almost as simple for it consists of simply ligating the fallopian tube.[64]

As in previous documents quoted at some length, it is not proposed to engage in a critique or rebuttal of the contents, but to allow it to speak for itself, as it were, in making the case for Churchill attempting to go beyond contemporary British eugenist desiderata as contained in the Royal Commission report. His covering note to Sir Edward Troup asked that the feasibility of putting the 'Indiana Law' into practice should be investigated, and that information on 'the best surgical operation' be obtained.

Sharp's pamphlet was forwarded to the Director of Convict Prisons, Dr Bryan Donkin. A former Commissioner of Prisons, and a member of the Royal Commission on the Care and Control of the Feeble Minded, Donkin was knighted in 1911 after a long and distinguished career. He was an authority on mental illness, and noted as a man who 'readily engaged in controversy' and for whom 'the joy of strenuous mental combat was his'.[65] An example of this trait may perhaps be noted in his 1880 lecture, delivered at the Westminster Hospital Medical School, entitled 'Thoughts on Ignorance and Quackery'.[66] He was also credited by the famous escapologist Houdini as being jointly responsible, along with the zoologist and evolutionary biologist Ray Lankester, for debunking and exposing 'fraud mediums'.[67] He seemingly thought much along the same lines about Sharp's work: 'The real fact is that no one hardly who tries to propagate doctrine or stimulate action in the matter of sterilization has informed his or herself of the elementary grammar of heredity.' Therefore the pamphlet, and those like it, comprised 'an arrogation of scientific knowledge by persons who had no claim to it' and the particular paper in question was 'a monument of ignorance and hopeless mental confusion'.[68]

Despite this rebuff, the famously persistent Home Secretary did not give up. Indeed, he found what he considered to be a specific case where sterilisation was applicable. This was detailed in a memorandum drawn up at his request into the case of a 'typical example of the village fool with dangerous sexual tendencies'. Dated 7 January 1911, it outlines the case of Alfred Oxtoby, described as a 'lad' but whose age is not given, who presented the 'physical and mental characteristics of a low grade imbecile'. Oxtoby had been charged at Beverley, Yorkshire, on 28 June 1910 with attempted 'bestiality with mare'. Having been found 'insane on arraignment', he had then been committed to the Broadmoor Asylum for the criminally insane. Churchill argued, undoubtedly after reading Sharp's pamphlet, that here was a case where sterilisation might provide an answer: 'This seems to be a case where a complete cure might be at once effected by sterilization.' Once again it fell to Donkin to disabuse him of these notions:

> there does not appear to be any prospect of cure by sterilization in the case. Certainly the procreative power would cease, but its effect in lessening the sexual appetite is extremely problematical, – probably it would have no effect at all.[69]

There was, of course, also the question of consent, such being necessary in the absence of Indiana-style laws. However, given that Oxtoby had been found legally insane, then he was incapable of giving consent, though of course his parents or guardians might have.

Despite these rebuffs, Churchill did not quickly abandon eugenics or their solutions, as they were posited, even after he had left the Home Office. He was one of the thirty-six vice-presidents named in the programme of the First International Eugenics Congress, held from 24 to 29 July 1912 in London. He was also one of only two Members of Parliament on that list, the other being his successor as Home Secretary, Reginald McKenna.[70] Though the issue was no longer his concern departmentally, he continued to hold to, and argue for, eugenic solutions.

Wilfrid Scawen Blunt recorded one example, dating from October 1912, when Churchill was visiting him:

Winston is ... a strong eugenist. He told us he had himself drafted the Bill which is to give power of shutting up people of weak intellect and so prevent their breeding. He thought it might be arranged to sterilize them. It was possible by the use of Rontgen rays, both for men and women, though for women some operation might also be necessary. ... Without something of the sort the race must decay. It was rapidly decaying, but would be stopped by some such means.[71]

The Bill in question, the 68-clause Mental Deficiency and Lunacy Bill, had been introduced to the House of Commons on 16 May 1912 by Churchill's successor. Lack of parliamentary time meant that it had to be sacrificed, but his reintroduced bill of 25 March 1913, the Mental Deficiency Act, was successful.[72] During the debate on the legislation, McKenna argued that the Government had 'omitted any reference to what might be regarded as the Eugenic idea' and that 'as the measure now stands, it exists for the protection of individual sufferers'.[73] This was disputed by the MP for Newcastle-under-Lyme, Josiah Wedgwood, who accused the Government of following up 'the suggestions of eugenic cranks in regard to this Bill ...'.[74] However, and despite these 'suggestions', there was not a word about sterilisation in the legislation.

Nevertheless, there can be no question that the Mental Deficiency Act represented a significant increase in state power vis-à-vis the individual. Allowing, as it did, incarceration of those deemed unfit and their non-consensual treatment, it required local authorities to provide places for, and make arrangements to supervise, those deemed to be 'idiots', 'imbeciles' and 'feeble-minded'. The latter category especially cast the net of control extremely wide, catching many whom later generations would view as having only mild learning difficulties.[75] As has been shown, had Churchill had his way it would have encompassed the even more drastic measure of enforced sterilisation.

The 1913 Act, with slight amendment in 1927, remained on the statute book until 1959, when it was superseded and replaced by the Mental Health Act of that year. At that point there were 65,000 people with 'intellectual disabilities' in state-operated institutions in England and Wales.[76]

Despite his fervent arguments for, and championing of, eugenic solutions whilst Home Secretary, it seems Churchill largely forgot the matter afterwards. At least there is no evidence that, other than involvement with the First International Eugenics Congress as noted, he publicly promoted eugenic ideals after leaving the Home Office in October 1911, despite his private views seemingly remaining unchanged in 1912. This may have been because even though he held high political positions, albeit not continuously, until 1929 he was never again in a department concerned with 'social policy' as such. Also, and given the difficult and trying circumstances surrounding the periods when he filled these later offices, he would have been more-than-fully occupied with departmental matters.

In addition to this heavy workload, any 'spare' time that he might have been able to find was undoubtedly taken up in authoring the five substantial volumes, in six separate books, that comprised his account of the First World War. Entitled *The World Crisis*, all but the final volume appeared whilst he held Cabinet-level positions. Even given his 'cottage industry' authorship technique of employing assistants to do the research and dictating the text to secretaries, the resultant 2,500 pages (with a further 400 pages appearing in 1931) represented a formidable literary achievement.

By that time, the very concept of eugenics, particularly its supposed correlation with social status, had been significantly undermined by the Great Depression. The General Secretary of the Eugenics Society noted that, in those years, the 'chronic unemployables' which formed the focus of their attention necessarily formed only a small fraction of the workless.[77] The aims of the Eugenics Society had also morphed into what was now a campaign for voluntary sterilisation: 'By the late 1920s, voluntary sterilization had become the ideological leading edge of the eugenics movement.'[78] There is, though, evidence that this was envisaged as being merely a step in a process leading to coercive sterilisation. Indeed, given the difficult-to-refute point that a person who was truly mentally defective could not provide legally valid consent to the operation, coercive measures would seem, logically, to provide the only answer.[79] Some saw this as being a necessity; Lord Riddell, proprietor of the *News of the World* and President of the Medico-Legal Society, warned in 1929 that 'it looks as if we are going to be eaten out of house and home by lunatics and mental deficients' due to the difficulty of ascertaining who they were and then segregating them. He went on, with no apparent sense of irony, to argue that this was so because 'mental defectives are extremely persistent and clever in eluding observation'.[80]

The years of the Great Depression coincided with Churchill's 'wilderness years', but even though time was now his to arrange, he did not return to the subject. Perhaps being occupied with finishing the final volume of *The World Crisis*,[81] he neither spoke nor voted during a debate in the House of Commons of 21 July 1931 on a motion pertaining: 'That leave be given to bring in a Bill to enable mental defectives to undergo sterilizing operations or sterilizing treatment upon their own application, or that of their spouses or parents or guardians; and for purposes connected therewith.'

The Labour MP for Camberwell North West, Dr Hyacinth Morgan, eviscerated the arguments in favour, ridiculing his opponents along the way: 'Some when inebriated see beetles; the eugenist, intoxicated, sees defectives.' He also raised a point that has been touched on previously: 'I submit that this is class legislation. In Europe there are Monarchies and dynasties riddled with haemophilia ... I have never yet heard one expert speak of the advantage of sterilisation in the case of these royalties.'[82] The motion was defeated.

Churchill's evident abandonment of eugenics was undoubtedly fortunate in terms of his future reputation; his period in the political wilderness more or less coincided with the rise of Hitler. The latter had been appointed Chancellor on

30 January 1933 and ascended to the role of Führer of the German Reich and People on 2 August 1934. Within a very few months of him coming to power the dangers implicit in Hitler's policies in respect of the British eugenics movement became apparent. Writing in December 1933, one member of the Eugenics Society council, Michael Pease of Cambridge University,[83] opined that 'Hitler ... has made eugenics stink in the nostrils of any decent folk'.[84] The reason for this 'stink' was 'The Law for the Prevention of Hereditarily Diseased Offspring'. Enacted in July 1933, this made sterilisation compulsory for any citizen whom a 'Court of Genetic Health' determined to be suffering from a genetic disorder.[85] This was 'mere pseudo-science', wrote Professor Julian Huxley to Blacker, 'and it would be a great pity if we were tarred with that same brush!'[86]

Churchill, in a 1935 treatment of Hitler, made no mention of this law but remarked that the German dictator's 'triumphant career has been borne onwards, not only by a passionate love of Germany, but by currents of hatred so intense as to sear the souls of those who swim upon them'. He was, of course, referring to the 'Jews of Germany', who had, he wrote, been declared 'a foul and odious race'.[87] On 18 June 1940, in a speech to the House of Commons, Churchill as recently elevated Prime Minister spoke of Hitler's regime as threatening the world with 'the abyss of a new dark age made more sinister, and perhaps more prolonged, by the lights of a perverted science'.[88] He never expanded on quite what branch of science he meant and speculation is unhelpful.

However, when the full horrors of Hitler's rule became apparent, it was clear that George Bernard Shaw's quip of some thirty-five years earlier concerning the use of the 'lethal chamber' and the 'methods of the stud farm' had demonstrated remarkable prescience. Heinrich Himmler was an ex-farmer who had been 'fascinated by the principles of and methods of breeding in agriculture, which he had studied at Munich's *Technische Hochschule*'.[89] As *Reichsführer-SS* he was to introduce to Germany the methods of the stud-farm through his *Lebensborn* policy.[90] Nazi activities with regard to the negative side of the eugenic equation, the use of the 'lethal chamber', are too well known to require repetition here.

Small wonder then that: 'After World War II, nobody was a eugenicist, and nobody had ever been a eugenicist. Biographers of the celebrated and the powerful did not dwell on the attractions of this philosophy to their subjects, and sometimes did not mention it at all.'[91]

Quite so!

Chapter Five

Crime, Punishment, and the 'Prisoners' Friend'

'His own experience of captivity had made him the prisoners' friend, and his mind was seething with plans for lightening their lot by earned remissions of sentence and, while 'in durance vile',[1] by libraries and entertainment. 'They must have food for thought – plenty of books – that's what I missed most – except of course the chance of breaking bounds and getting out of the damned place – and I suppose I mustn't give them that!'[2]

'By maintaining certain institutions we might alter, we perpetuate certain evils we might cure.'[3]

* * *

Herbert Gladstone had been a significant prison reformer and was, in part at least, responsible for the creation of the penal system as it existed in 1910. Some years earlier, and as Under-Secretary of State to the Home Office under Asquith, he had chaired a Departmental Committee on Prisons that reported in 1895. This had been set up due to public disquiet with the prison administration of that time.[4] The report of the 'Gladstone Committee', which largely translated into the Prison Act of 1898, laid then the foundations of the prison system for which Churchill now found himself responsible.

Prior to 1898 there had been two separately administered penal systems in England and Wales with two types of prison. The first, dubbed convict prisons, housed inmates sentenced to penal servitude – 'the successor of transportation'[5] – for two years or more.[6] These had 'emerged as a complement to transportation in the 1840s rather than as a substitute for it'. However, following the last convict-ship sailing for Van Diemen's Land in 1852, the Penal Servitude Acts provided for long-term imprisonment as a substitute, though some 300 a year were still sent to Western Australia until 1867. The second type were local prisons, so called because until 1878 local authorities owned and controlled them. Within their walls were prisoners serving sentences of less than two years, which were, in many cases, often very short: days or weeks rather than months.[7]

Any implied distinction by the use of the term 'imprisonment', denoting sentences of two years and under, and 'penal servitude' for longer sentences had ceased to have any significance by 1885, or at least according to Sir Edmund Du Cane, the then Chairman of Prison Commissioners. As he put it: 'both classes of prisoners are undergoing "imprisonment", and are equally in a condition of "penal servitude"'. He also noted that, in effect, those in question were undergoing 'hard labour', 'for any prisoner sentenced to imprisonment should be, and is by law, required to labour, under specified conditions'. Therefore differences in terminology as regards penal servitude, imprisonment and imprisonment with hard labour were meaningless in fact.[8] That they nevertheless remained in existence legally until 1948 is, as Professor Rupert Cross pointed out, 'by no means the sole illustration of the snail's pace with which penal reform proceeds'.[9]

Evidence of a slightly increased pace was, though, surely evidenced in 1898. The Act of that year united these two systems under a single governing body called the Prison Commission, under the overall control of the Home Office, as well as making several changes to the regime enforced on the inmates.[10] The Gladstone Committee also proposed the removal of those aged below 21 from adult prisons and their placing in separate, training, establishments. This was given force in the 1908 Prevention of Crime Act under which such institutions were set up; one, a development of an experimental scheme housed in a special wing of Borstal Prison, Kent, gave its name to the whole system.[11] Churchill was thus ultimately responsible for over three-score penal institutions of various types: six convict prisons, fifty-six local prisons and three borstals.[12] The overall number of persons incarcerated within these institutions between 1 April 1909 and 31 March 1910 totalled 200,265, with a daily average of 21,926, the vast majority of them, around 87 per cent, being male.[13]

A substantial proportion of this population were incarcerated for non-payment of fines and drunkenness; Randolph Churchill calculated that prisoners in those categories amounted to 'over half' and 'a third' of the population respectively for the period 1908–9. 'Clearly,' he goes on to argue, 'too many people were being sent to prison' and 'here were areas where reform was necessary and urgent'.[14]

Winston Churchill's zeal for reforming the penal system overall – and in addition to reducing the number of those committed to prison, he was to push for shorter sentences and better treatment of those who were – is unarguable. Opinion as to his motivation in the matter is virtually unanimous; he had suffered incarceration himself, albeit as a prisoner of war. Some thirty years later he was to describe this as being 'the least unfortunate kind of prisoner to be, but it is nevertheless a melancholy state'. Indeed, he claimed that 'I certainly hated every minute of my captivity more than I have ever hated any other period in my whole life.'[15] His hatred did not long endure; he entered the *Staats Model School* in Pretoria on 18 November 1899 and went over the wall never to return on 12 December.[16] If both his own account and those by others concerning what he told them are to be believed, the experience lent him an enduring interest in the welfare of prisoners. Violet Bonham Carter's recollection is often cited in support of this:

His own experience of captivity had made him the prisoners' friend, and his mind was seething with plans for lightening their lot by earned remissions of sentence and, while 'in durance vile',[17] by libraries and entertainment. 'They must have food for thought – plenty of books – that's what I missed most – except of course the chance of breaking bounds and getting out of the damned place – and I suppose I mustn't give them that!'[18]

Augmenting his general inclination was advice which he sought, and took, from those outside the Home Office bureaucracy. His social milieu included Wilfrid Scawen Blunt, an ardent proponent of reform having first-hand experience of the matter, and he knew and corresponded with the similarly inclined author and playwright John Galsworthy. The latter's 1910 play *Justice: A Tragedy in Four Acts*, the first-night audience of which included both the new Home Secretary and the Chairman of the Prison Commission Sir Evelyn Ruggles-Brise, is acknowledged as 'having had a small but direct impact on penal decision making' at that time.[19] According to Galsworthy, who is of course hardly an objective source, it actually had a large impact on the Home Secretary and his companion: 'Winston Churchill . . . and Ruggles-Brise . . . both witnessed it, the first with sympathy, the second with a sinking sensation. His eyes were observed to start out of his head, according to an eyewitness.'[20]

Written with the intent of supporting the campaign for improving conditions in British prisons, one of the most memorable portions is Act III Scene III when the play's main protagonist, William Falder, is driven insane by being in 'separate confinement'.[21] This was the practice whereby all newly committed convicts underwent an initial period of solitary confinement, the length being dependent upon their classification.

There were three classes of prisoner, the first being 'stars' or 'star men', who were first offenders and identified by red star-shaped patches sewn to the front of their caps and both sleeves of their jackets. This practice, which dated from 1879, was to ensure that they were kept 'quite separate' from other prisoners during exercise periods and the like.[22] It was, as Ruggles-Brise was to put it, 'the first and most practical attempt to introduce the principle of segregation of the better from the worse'.[23] The second classification, introduced in 1905, was 'intermediates', who comprised that 'large body on the borderland between those not previously convicted of crime, and those who have made crime a profession'.[24] Scarlet chevrons sewn on their sleeves and caps identified prisoners in this class. Lastly there were the recidivists, 'whose record shows that [they have] been guilty of grave or persistent crime', or had previously served sentences of penal servitude.[25]

For all three classes of offender imprisonment began with a period of solitary or separate confinement; they were shut inside their cell for twenty-three hours per day in strict silence, and forbidden to communicate with other prisoners at any time.[26] Between 1898 and 1909 this period had been set at three months for star men and six for intermediates, whilst for the recidivists it was nine months. It was decided in 1909, under Gladstone's auspices and with the decision to take effect on 1 April 1910, that it would be standardised thereafter at three months in all cases, though, as proponents of the system were keen to emphasise, 'in all cases subject to a medical report upon [their] mental and physical condition'.[27]

This particular facet of the penal system was the one that Galsworthy and other reformers railed against most. They regarded it as the infliction of gratuitous, or 'superfluous', suffering. Indeed, though he confessed himself 'loth to ask you, while you are picking up the reins of office', Galsworthy contacted Churchill about that very matter in February 1910 (no date otherwise), requesting him 'to devote some little of your attention' to it:

> I want especially to draw your attention to the late Home Secretary's deliberate opinion, stated in the minute confirming this new order and repeated to myself, that separate confinement must be held to have broken down as a deterrent ... and to the fact that he would have done away with it altogether ... but for *administrative* difficulties.
>
> I feel certain that you will come to the same conclusion. And I would urge you to consider ... whether difficulty or expense ... should be allowed by the most civilised State in the world to be responsible for what is seen to be a really appalling amount of unnecessary suffering ...[28]

Churchill replied on 24 February 1910, saying that he greatly admired 'the keen and vigorous way in which you are driving forward a good cause' and explaining that he was 'in entire sympathy with your general mood'. Not having had time to examine the question specifically, he had 'given instructions for it to be brought before me with the least possible delay'. Once he had grasped the facts then he would welcome the opportunity to discuss them further: 'My time may be short, so that if action is practically possible, it is essential that it should be prompt.'[29]

Promptness was certainly apparent in the Home Secretary's 'instruction' to Ruggles-Brise of the same date. In this he asked him to supply 'the main arguments against the total and immediate abolition of separate confinement as part of our ordinary Penal Code', and required it within a week.[30] Despite the fact that, in the words of his memoirist, Ruggles-Brise found 'Galsworthy's propaganda ... vexatious',[31] promptitude was also much in evidence once again: the response was dated 25 February. As requested, arguments, numbering seven in total, as to why separate confinement should not be totally and immediately abolished were provided:

(1) It was a requirement under the 1905 Prison Rules;
(2) It provided for a period of *recueillement* – recollection and contemplation – on the part of those who had lived a criminal life;
(3) It was preferred by first offenders and disliked by recidivists;
(4) Given the safeguards that were in place, it was not damaging; Galsworthy's theatrical depiction was inaccurate;
(5) It accentuated the penal aspect of the sentence and had both a reformatory and deterrent effect;
(6) From the disciplinary point of view, it was unwise to mix fresh prisoners with those already inside; and
(7) It increased the rigour of imprisonment.[32]

This message reached Churchill via Troup, the latter adding his own take on the subject by emphasising points three and five of the list. He also warned the Home Secretary that abandoning Gladstone's soon-to-be-introduced change to the system without giving it a fair trial would be tantamount to admitting Galsworthy's impact: 'Everyone would imagine that the Secretary of State had been influenced by Mr Galsworthy's play and that we admitted the truth of his representation of "solitary confinement".'[33] Rather than being deterred by this, Churchill initiated a search for more information on separate confinement and indeed all aspects of the prison system. Ruggles-Brise and Troup were tasked with providing what Baxendale termed a 'formidable volume of information about convict crime'.[34]

Thus began a significant exchange of facts, figures, opinions and ideas, into which it is not proposed to delve, but which highlighted in no uncertain terms the difficulties inherent in making changes within a large and established bureaucracy. This was not solely, or even mainly, due to obstructive practices on the part of senior officials such as Troup and Ruggles-Brise, both of whom were reform-minded in any event. Rather it owed more to the sheer intrinsic inertia in any such system. Having said that, Harold Butler, a junior Home Office civil servant in 1910, who went on to achieve internationally recognised eminence and a knighthood, was to later record the human reaction to Churchill's methods of doing business. According to his recollection: 'The old hands in the department were rather dismayed by the temerity with which he challenged principles and practices which had remained sacrosanct for many years ...'.[35]

Despite being an observation susceptible to distortion via the 'golden glow', this has the ring of truth about it. In any event, and dismayed or not, the senior officials worked to accommodate Churchill's desires and a manageable compromise was reached. The new policy was unveiled during the Home Secretary's notable speech to the House of Commons on 20 July 1910. He was fulsome in publicly praising his predecessor:

> I come to the question of separate confinement. My Noble Friend Lord Gladstone made all his preparations ready for effecting a substantial reduction in the period of solitary confinement. That subject has been brought before our notice by various able writers in the Press, and exponents of the drama, who have with force and feeling brought home to the general public the pangs which the prisoner may suffer in long months of solitude. I have decided that my Noble Friend's proposal to reduce solitary confinement to three months in all cases shall be carried one step further, and that it shall be reduced to one month in all cases, except in the case of convicts who return again and again to penal servitude, and who are called recidivists.[36]

It was during the peroration of this speech, which included a number of other matters pertaining to prison reform, that Churchill made a general comment summing up his whole approach to the question. This, over a century later, is still considered valid:[37] 'The mood and temper of the public in regard to the treatment of crime and criminals is one of the most unfailing tests of the civilisation of any country.'[38]

Though Churchill had tried to give due credit to his predecessor, Troup's warning about the assignment of responsibility proved prescient. Galsworthy's diary records a luncheon engagement he attended nine days after the speech with several senior politicians; the Prime Minister and Foreign Secretary were present. He sat between Mrs Asquith and his fellow writer Maurice Baring, later recording that the latter was of the opinion that the 'prison reforms were all due to me'.[39] This belief was reflected in many press reports, leading the playwright to offer apologies to the Home Secretary. Churchill was magnanimous:

> There can be no question that your admirable play bore a most important part in creating that atmosphere of sympathy and interest which is so noticeable upon this subject at the present time. So far from feeling the slightest irritation at newspaper comments assigning to you the credit of prison reform, I have always felt uncomfortable at receiving the easily-won applauses which come to the heads of great departments whenever they have ploughed with borrowed oxen and reaped where they have not sown. In this case I can only claim a personal interest which has led me to seek the knowledge of others.[40]

This was not the only step Churchill took in respect of reforming, or 'humanizing' as Baxendale terms it, the prison regime. Initiatives in this regard included: improvements in the treatment of aged convicts; an 'incentive labour scheme' involving more meaningful employment; aid to discharged inmates; lectures and concerts for prisoners; and an expansion of provision with regards to prison libraries.[41] He was undoubtedly projecting his own views in respect of the latter; a large proportion of the prison population was illiterate or effectively so.[42]

Churchill could also affect the lives of the prison population in a more direct manner. As Home Secretary, he wielded the authority to pardon convicted criminals or commute their sentence; reduce the length of sentences imposed, or the amount of fines levied, via a process known as remission; and postpone the implementation of a sentence pending further consideration. Officially vested in the person of the monarch, and termed the Royal Prerogative of Mercy, these powers were in practice exercised on the advice of the Secretary of State. Blunt records him stating that as Home Secretary he had been able to 'go into any prison and on his sole authority ... order a release, which if once notified to a prisoner cannot be changed afterwards by any power in England'. He went on to assert that he had used this power on several occasions 'notwithstanding the protests of the judges'.[43]

The most portentous exercise of the Home Secretary's prerogative was in relation to capital sentences. In this matter, he stood between the condemned and the gallows with, literally, the power of life or death: 'It is his duty to decide in every case of murder whether the capital sentence should be carried out.'[44]

Roy Jenkins, who is unique amongst Churchill's biographers in having held the position himself, described how a Home Secretary was reminded of this duty on a daily basis:

> it was the practice to keep in an alcove to the right of the Home Secretary's desk a chart, somewhat in the form of a billiard marker, on which a disc for each sentenced man (or occasionally woman) was moved from day to day along a track beginning with the sentence and ending with the date of projected execution. The Home Secretary was thus daily reminded of how long still remained for his decision. The device avoided the danger of a hanging taking place inadvertently through his preoccupation with other matters. It also cast a constant sombre pall over the room ... as well as weighing heavily on the mind of any sensitive holder of the office. Nor was there any respite, for the pattern of an average of one death sentence every two weeks almost guaranteed that, as each case was disposed of, in one way or another, the macabre board was always reinforced.[45]

Whether or not Churchill can be dubbed 'sensitive' is a moot point. Nor is it known if he found the 'macabre board' a dismal fixture. What has, though, been claimed, largely based on a number of articles he wrote for the *News of the World* in the mid- and late 1930s and a later statement he made in the House of Commons, is that he felt the burden of deciding these matters 'especially acutely'.[46] In fact a year or so after leaving the Home Office he and Clementine were weekend guests of Wilfred Scawen Blunt, the latter noting that 'he is in more vigorous health now that he has left the Home Office for the Admiralty'.[47] On the second day of the visit, one possible reason for this improvement was divulged: 'Winston told us admirable stories of his experience as Home Secretary and of how it had become a nightmare to him the having to exercise his power of life and death in the case of condemned criminals, on an average of one case a fortnight ...'[48]

These experiences remained in his mind, and were personally related again some forty years later:

> I found it very distressing ... to be at the Home Office. There is no post that I have occupied in Governments which I was more glad to leave. It was not so much taking the decisions in capital cases that oppressed me, although that was a painful duty. I used to read the letters of appeal written by convicts undergoing long or life sentences begging to be let out. This was for me an even more harassing task.[49]

Apropos of his appearing in better health after leaving the Home Office, and Jenkins' remark about decisions on capital punishment 'weighing heavily on the mind of any sensitive holder of the office', it has been argued that Churchill suffered from 'his most severe bout of depression' whilst Home Secretary.[50] This, if true, could well have been related to the 'nightmare' and 'painful' duties, plus the 'harassing tasks', mentioned. However, whilst the subject of Churchill's mental health has attracted several studies over recent years with varying retrospective diagnoses, the notion that he was suffering from depression in any serious sense around 1910–1911 has been thoroughly debunked. As Vale and Scadding argue: 'Specifically, it is preposterous to suppose that Churchill was depressed in any serious sense during a tumultuous time in British politics during which he was President of the Board of Trade ... or Home Secretary ...'[51]

Whilst Harold Butler remembered no sign of depression, he did recall that decisions pertaining to capital punishment 'often caused him real anguish'. He also reported that Churchill 'was never content with any opinion but his own. He would read every document for himself and arrive at his decision after consulting everybody who could throw any light upon the crime.'[52] The final decision on whether or not someone should hang was, in most cases, not announced until three days before the date fixed for the execution.[53] There were no procedures or protocols to follow in these matters. As Herbert Gladstone had stated it: 'It would be neither desirable nor possible to lay down hard and fast rules as to the exercise of the prerogative of mercy.'[54]

The most famous, or infamous, man hanged during Churchill's tenure was Hawley Harvey 'Dr' Crippen. Though subsequent research has cast some doubt on the safety of his conviction, which depended to a large degree upon the evidence given at his trial by pathologists concerning the identity of human remains, neither Churchill nor anyone else knew this at the time. Consequently, the Home Secretary annotated Crippen's file with the standard, dread, phrase used on these occasions: 'The law must take its course.' In accordance with that law, Crippen 'crossed the threshold to the next world' on the morning of 23 November 1910, 'without a word or a sign'.[55]

If there was little doubt at the time about the guilt of Dr Crippen, the same cannot be said in the earlier case of John Alexander Dickman, who stood trial at Newcastle from 4–6 July 1910, charged with the murder of John Innes Nisbet. The victim had been shot five times on 18 March 1910 whilst aboard a train travelling from Newcastle to Alnmouth, and the motive was undoubtedly robbery. It was a Friday and Nisbet, a colliery clerk and bookkeeper, was carrying the miners' wage bag containing a little over £370. All the evidence against Dickman was purely circumstantial. Nevertheless, the jury returned a verdict of guilty and thereby gave the judge no option: 'in passing sentence I only do that duty which the law commands'. That command was, of course, that Dickman be 'hanged by the neck until you be dead'.[56]

Churchill was troubled by the case initially, and took the rare step of referring it to the recently set up Court of Appeal.[57] Despite some new evidence, particularly concerning irregularities in respect of witnesses, the appeal failed. The Home Secretary discussed and argued the matter with Troup and other senior officials, before concluding that the original verdict should be upheld and that 'The law must take its course'. It actually fell to Sir Edward Grey, the Foreign Secretary, to publicise this as Churchill was away on holiday at the relevant time. In any event, Dickman's early morning appointment with John Ellis, the Home Office's 'number one' hangman,[58] took place on 9 August 1910 at Newcastle

Gaol.[59] Documents pertaining to the case, used as examples of Churchill's thoroughness in these matters, are included in his official biography and relevant companion volume.[60] Whilst they do indeed demonstrate diligence, Dickman nevertheless seems a curious choice of subject to use as an example inasmuch as the question of his guilt was, and remains, very much arguable.[61]

Also controversial contemporaneously was a decision Churchill made in the opposite direction: to exercise mercy. This was the case of Stinie, or Steinie, Morrison, and it opened a window onto a world that most could only have otherwise glimpsed through the works of Charles Dickens, Arthur Morrison, Arthur Conan Doyle and the like.[62] Indeed, it involved a policeman, Detective Inspector Frederick Porter Wensley, dubbed, after Doyle's most famous literary creation, 'Whitechapel's Sherlock Holmes'.[63]

Morrison too appears as something of a character straight out of detective fiction:

> If ever a man in this world started off with all the advantages that Nature could endow him, it was Stinie Morrison. He was tall, extremely handsome, easy and fascinating in his manner, and, for a man who had received little or no education, a more than passable linguist.[64]

Known to have adopted several aliases, including Alex Petropavloff, Moses Tagger, Morris Stein and Morris Steinaud, he also claimed at different times to have been born in Russia and Australia.[65] Butler says he was a Russian Jew and that 'constitutionally he was a natural criminal'.[66] He was certainly well known to the authorities and had served several gaol sentences. Wensley claimed that in 1910 his 'record as a burglar and thief went back for twelve years, when he would have been about seventeen or eighteen years old'.[67]

His latest brush with the law saw him accused of the murder of Leon Beron, a Russian Jew living in Whitechapel. Having been stabbed and battered to death, Beron's corpse was discovered under some bushes on Clapham Common on 1 January 1911. 'Whitechapel's Sherlock Holmes' investigated the matter, resulting in Morrison being, on 6 March 1911, put on trial for his life at the Old Bailey. Hugh Fletcher Moulton, a barrister and the author/editor of a book dealing with the case, described it thus:

> the action unrolls itself in a milieu, which not only suggests the theatre, but seems hardly conceivable as existing in modern London. The apparent irresponsibility of all the characters and their strange *far niente*[68] lives [were] conducted according to rules and motives utterly strange to the average Briton ...[69]

As with the Dickman case referred to above, the evidence against Morrison was circumstantial, and whether or not the exoticism of the witnesses was such as to bewilder the honest British jury is unknown.[70] The recent Houndsditch Murders, followed by the Siege of Sidney Street (also dubbed the Battle of Stepney), may have influenced their outlook with respect to alien immigrants and their perceived activities; as a distinguished judge wrote some forty years later: 'The jury is not really representative of the nation as a whole. It is predominantly male, middle-aged, middle-minded and middle-class.'[71] Such matters must, however, remain in the realm of speculation. In any event, they returned a verdict of guilty after only thirty-five minutes' deliberation, giving the judge no option but to pass the death sentence. After a somewhat peremptory hearing, the Court of Appeal upheld the conviction, leaving the matter in the hands of Churchill.[72]

Whether justice had been done was dependant on perspective. Wensley, perhaps predictably, thought it had. He was to write in his memoirs that 'I am, I think, the only living person who knows every circumstance of that case, and after twenty years I am still convinced that Stinie Morrison was convicted as justly as any murderer I have ever known.'[73] Morrison's defence counsel was Edward Abinger, whom Wensley termed 'a gentleman of excitable and emotional temperament, who, with a fervid belief in his client's innocence, stuck at little in his attempts to secure an acquittal'.[74] It was indeed the case that Abinger went well beyond the call of duty in his efforts on Morrison's behalf:

> It will always be open to the gravest possible doubt whether or not Stinie Morrison was guilty of actually murdering Leon Beron. It would be idle for me to deny that he was a man of extremely bad character, and the only reason why I made such strenuous efforts to save his life was that I considered it to be an infringement of the cardinal principles of justice that he should go to the gallows upon some of the flimsiest and most unreliable evidence I have ever known.[75]

These strenuous efforts included contacting Churchill following the failure of the appeal, and providing him with new evidence that had not been presented at that tribunal nor at the original trial. This tended to eliminate robbery as a motive from the equation.[76] The Home Secretary was swayed. The writer Sidney Theodore Felstead offered an opinion as to why: 'Maybe Mr Churchill thought what many other people were thinking in England just then – that this sensational case had not been fought out in the calm, judicial atmosphere that English justice demanded.'[77] Anyhow, on 12 April the Home Office informed Abinger that Morrison's sentence had been commuted to life imprisonment.[78]

Given that 'London' had been 'stirred to its vitals' over the problem of 'whether or not we should hang one Stinie Morrison for the killing of an aged Jew on Clapham Common',[79] this was inevitably a decision which led to much debate and criticism. According to Moulton: 'The leader-writer, and the man who fills the correspondence columns, had a full opportunity of indulging in that cheap and usually fallacious logic so dear to a portion of the reading public.'[80]

Churchill was, and remained all of his life, a supporter of capital punishment. Indeed, he considered that 'To most men – including all the best – a life sentence is worse than a death sentence.'[81] This is no doubt an easy principle to enunciate in general terms, and particularly when it applies to others. During his tenure as Home Secretary, Churchill had to take decisions of life or death in forty-three cases, twenty-one of which received mercy under the Royal Prerogative.[82] Proportionally, this was broadly in line with decisions made by his predecessors; in other words he set no precedents, nor was otherwise remarkable, in that regard. Nor was there any great manifestation of abolitionist sentiment in regards to the death penalty during his time as Secretary of State, though there had been previous attempts at doing away with it. Consequently, controversies around the application of capital punishment, or not, came and went dependent upon the individual in question. These were particularly fierce when it came to the question of hanging women and, though none was hanged whilst Churchill was in office,[83] he did intervene in respect of one who had been previously sentenced to death and then reprieved: the curious case of Edith Carew.

Edith Carew was an Englishwoman married to an Englishman, Walter Hallowell Carew, and living in Yokohama, Japan. In 1897 she was convicted of poisoning her husband with arsenic and sentenced to death; not, however, by a Japanese court. Rather, and because of the system of extra-territoriality then in force, she was tried before a consular court, the British Court for Japan.[84] This consisted of 'a Colonial judge who had probably never before tried a difficult murder case, and a jury of five men selected from the small British community, in which the dead man and his wife were well-known figures'.[85]

Fortunately for Mrs Carew, and arguably the reputation of British justice, the senior British official in Japan, Envoy Extraordinary and Minister Plenipotentiary Sir Ernest Satow, had to confirm the verdict – or not. Satow found, to his 'great relief', a way out 'of issuing a warrant for execution'.[86] Accordingly, he commuted the sentence to one of life imprisonment. Thus, and by way of a spell in Victoria Prison, Hong Kong, Edith Carew found herself incarcerated in the adult women's prison at Aylesbury, Buckinghamshire. Another six years went by before the 'fat file' on Edith Carew's case passed 'in the ordinary routine' across a desk in the Home Office where it was scrutinised by the young Harold Butler. According to his account:

> With Oxford lectures on the theory of punishment fresh in mind, I proceeded to argue that on no theory could her further detention be justified. Retribution had been exacted. Prolonged confinement might reasonably be supposed to have exercised all the deterrent and all the reformatory effects of which it was capable. There was moreover a possible doubt as to the justice of the sentence imposed by a court inadequately equipped to deal with a case full of odd and perplexing features. This seemed to be eminently an instance in which leniency was justified. Several weeks later it returned with a neatly written minute over the initials WSC directing the release of the prisoner.[87]

Churchill's freeing of Edith Carew drew attention internationally and allowed a retelling of her story.[88] Such tales were popular; lady-poisoners, particularly if they were also adulteresses, scandalised Victorian and Edwardian imagination to an inordinately large extent. Public opinion, insofar as it can be measured by press coverage, was especially outraged when the 'hidden underbelly' of 'respectable' domestic life was publicised.[89] These instances, perhaps, underlined Macaulay's 1831 observation that there is 'no spectacle so ridiculous as the British public in one of its periodical fits of morality'.[90]

The British public, or the Tory-leaning portion of it anyway, was undoubtedly exercised in the instance of one freed prisoner: David Davies, the 'Dartmoor Shepherd'. Davies' case first attracted the attention of the Home Secretary in April 1910. The previous year, aged 68, he had been found guilty of stealing two shillings from a church offertory box and sentenced to three years' penal servitude. On top of that, however, he had received a further ten years 'preventive detention'.

'Preventive Detention', or the 'Detention of Habitual Criminals', had been introduced in 1908 by Herbert Gladstone as Part II of that year's Prevention of Crime Act.[91] The purpose, as he defined it on 12 June 1908 to the House of Commons, was to deal with professional, rather than just habitual, criminals, the distinction between the two types being 'well known to criminologists'.[92] Despite the distinction being well known to criminologists it was seemingly less so to others. This was perhaps to some extent the fault of the legal draughtsmen; the text of the Act consistently used the term 'habitual'. Under its provisions, those who were 'found by a jury to be a habitual criminal', which was defined as, since the age of 16, having been convicted on three previous occasions or 'leading persistently a dishonest or criminal life', could receive a further sentence in addition to that for any particular crime. This would be 'for such period not exceeding ten nor less than five years, as the court may determine'.[93] A special prison for those undergoing preventive detention was built at Camp Hill in the Isle of Wight, neighbouring Parkhurst Prison, which opened fully in 1912.[94]

A Welshman from Montgomeryshire, David Davies was certainly a habitual criminal; between 1870 and 1909 he had been incarcerated on ten separate occasions for periods of between one month and fifteen years.[95] He was, though, hardly a 'professional'. As noted, his last conviction was for stealing two shillings[96] and his previous criminal activity had been petty in the extreme: 'All the sentences were for minor burglaries or – his speciality – robbing church poor boxes.'[97] In that context, an announcement concerning him, which appeared in an 1899 edition of the *Police Gazette*, stated that David Davies, alias Dai Penllys-Bach,[98] was wanted for committing 'sacrilege' in the Shropshire villages of Leaton and Myddle. He was described as a 'tramp' who 'may seek employment at farmhouses'.[99]

Churchill could see neither sense nor justice in the relationship between Davies' crime and the sentence it had attracted. The contrast, he said, was 'grotesque'; it was 'impossible to balance the offence and the penalty against each other'.[100] Davies, it seems, thought along similar lines and had petitioned the Home Secretary on 9 October 1909 stating that, given his age, he had effectively been handed a life sentence. On the other hand the governor of Dartmoor Prison, where Davies was held and where he tended to the institution's flock of sheep, reckoned that 'he used to commit burglaries as a means for getting back to his sheep'.[101]

Churchill, according to his later account, had already determined on his early release before deciding to visit Dartmoor Prison.[102] He travelled to Exeter on the evening of 23 October 1910 and stayed the night at Coffins, the intriguingly named home of the Local Liberal MP George Lambert, in the village of Sprey-ton. The Chancellor of the Exchequer was also in the vicinity as he and Margaret Lloyd George, plus daughter Megan, were visiting the area.[103] In any event, on the morning of 24 October the two ministers were driven the 20 or so miles to Princetown, the location of the forbidding prison.[104] Quite why he took Lloyd George along is unknown, but Jenkins suggests he may have been 'trying to get more prison money out of him'.[105] Whatever the rationale behind it, Lloyd George, who must have discussed the matter with Churchill, asked to see Davies. They obviously conversed in their native tongue; Basil Thomson, the prison governor, later reckoned that the Chancellor did so in order 'to show off his proficiency in Welsh to the gentlemen of his party'.[106] This was Anglo-centric nonsense; Welsh was Lloyd George's first language, as it was Davies'. The occasion obviously stuck in the Chancellor's mind, however.

On 21 November 1910 he addressed a mostly working-class meeting at Mile End in east London. Given that a general election revolving around the power of the House of Lords was in the offing, the theme of his speech came as no surprise. Indeed, during the course of his oration the following memorable exchange was recorded: 'Aristocracy is like cheese; the older it is (A voice: "The more it stinks" (loud laughter) – the higher it becomes (laughter).' He also mentioned his visit to Dartmoor:

> You and I are now paying rates in order to make up the revenue appropriated by those noble people who rejected the budget. The Home Secretary and I the other day paid a visit to Dartmoor. On that bleak, mist-sodden upland I saw an old man of sixty-five in the convict garb. He had been sentenced to thirteen years penal servitude because under the influence of drink he had broken into a church poor-box and stolen two shillings. The next time I am called a thief and a robber by one of the descendants of those noblemen, because I propose a tax upon the wealthy, I will say, 'You are living upon the proceeds of the church poor-box your ancestors robbed.'[107]

Conservative opinion, particularly of the aristocratic variety, was predictably outraged. David Lindsay, heir to the Earldoms of Crawford and Balcarres, wrote in his diary the next day that 'Lloyd George's utterance in Mile End leaves one with a feeling of nauseous impotence. His scurrility is beyond competition...'.[108] Lloyd George had, according to one of his biographers, learned his oratory 'beneath the pulpit of the Shoemaker of Llanystumdwy' and had never forgotten its purpose: 'not to please men or lull them, but to move them'.[109]

Others took a less sophisticated view of his undoubted brilliance at speechifying, dubbing such rhetorical flights as 'Lloyd Georgeisms'. This particular example took the Davies case out of the Home Office and thrust it into the public eye where, under scrutiny, the facts emerged. The reaction of the Tory supporting press was as might have been expected:

> That novel electioneering trick, 'The poor Dartmoor prisoner' or 'How to exploit a convict for political purposes', which has been successfully performed this week by Messrs Lloyd George and Churchill, was exposed in the House of Commons yesterday [...] The facts as disclosed by the Home Secretary in Parliament on Thursday are:-
>
> (1) The sentence was three (not 13) years' penal servitude.
> (2) That the old man was an old gaolbird, and had been many times convicted in the last forty years.
> (3) That he pleaded guilty to being a habitual criminal, and was sentenced to be detained for a further ten years under the Prevention of Crimes Act.
>
> Mr Hilaire Belloc completed the exposure by pointing out that the Prevention of Crimes Act under which the man had been sentenced to ten years' detention was introduced by Mr Herbert Gladstone and carried with the approval of Mr Lloyd George and Mr Churchill.[110]

Belloc was the Liberal MP for Salford South and had 'energetically resisted' the introduction of preventive detention, largely on the grounds that it would be misused, and persistent petty criminals would end up receiving disproportionate sentences.[111] Though Churchill had voted for the Act in 1908, as Home Secretary he manifested distinct reservations. Shortly after assuming offices in February 1910, he had written that 'I have serious misgivings lest the institution of preventive detention should lead to a reversion to the ferocious sentences of the last generation.' He went on to add that 'preventive detention is penal servitude in all essentials, but it soothes the consciences of judges and of the public'.[112] He made much the same point that summer to Parliament:

> Preventive detention is penal servitude in all its aspects [...] The House will agree that such a system of preventive detention must be closely watched and that it cannot stand alone. We cannot impose these serious penalties upon individuals unless we make a great effort and a new effort to rehabilitate men who have been in prison and secure their having a chance to resume their places in the ranks of honourable industry.[113]

Despite the undoubted embarrassment caused by the 'Lloyd Georgeism', he moved, once reappointed following the December general election, to give the Dartmoor Shepherd a chance to take his place 'in the ranks of honourable industry'. He remitted Davies' sentence, thus releasing him on licence, with gainful employment found for him on a farm at Ruthin, Denbighshire, by the Royal Society for the Assistance of Discharged Prisoners.[114]

That the Home Secretary had left himself a hostage to fortune was amply demonstrated when, after two days, Davies disappeared. As Randolph Churchill noted: 'Great were the derision and the sarcasm with which the episode of the Shepherd was discussed in the Press and in the House.'[115] The 'High Tory' commentator, Charles Whibley, had a field day:

the Chancellor of the Exchequer and the Home Secretary ... were determined that the gentle shepherd should again breathe the free air of heaven. They brought him out of his comfortable jail, and they found him a situation upon a Welsh farm. The Welsh farm was not to his mind. Two days of well-ordered freedom were enough for the old man, who disappeared with disconcerting suddenness, and is now mourned by two great departments of State. What happens to the old shepherd is immaterial. He has electrified Mile End and served his turn. Perhaps he has returned to the comfort of Dartmoor, perhaps he has taken up again his profession of quiet pilfering in the hills of Wales ... For the present he has been raised from martyrdom to mystery, and we eagerly await the opening of Parliament for news of him. The whole episode is ludicrous. In vain you will search the annals of the Commons for a parallel.[116]

Thus Churchill was embarrassed for a second time, and then a third when he was unable to offer any evidence to support his suggestion that Davies had been 'enticed away' from the farm 'for political purposes'; that 'the Unionists had spirited the old man away'.[117] They hadn't. Davies had indeed 'taken up again his profession' and, despite being imprisoned on more than one occasion subsequently, kept on with it whenever he could.[118]

Despite the discomfiture caused by the case, Churchill nevertheless continued with attempts to thwart the system of preventive detention as it was being applied. In doing so he faced the difficulty that the provision existed as a matter of law as interpreted and applied by an independent judiciary. Thus this effort, legal experts argued, 'practically amounts to this, that in the face of judges and juries the present Home Secretary – certainly in cases where violent danger to the public does not exist – may make the salutary provisions of the Act of 1908 a dead letter'.[119] In fact 'may make' became 'did make': according to Radzinowicz and Hood: 'The whole movement toward indeterminate sentencing was put into abeyance. In 1910, 177 men had been sentenced to preventive detention; the following year there were fifty-three. The momentum was lost, and forever.'[120]

In addition to abating preventive detention for non-violent and petty criminals like Davies, Churchill had proposed to reduce the number of those committed to prison overall. In his own memorable phraseology to Parliament on 20 July 1910: 'the first real principle which should guide anyone trying to establish a good system of prisons should be to prevent as many people as possible getting there at all ... every care, consistent with the maintenance of law and order, must be taken constantly to minimise the number of persons who are committed to gaol.'[121]

This was continuing a policy promoted by his predecessor, one that was embodied in the Probation of Offenders Act of 1907, the purpose of which:

> was to enable Courts of Justice to appoint probation officers ... so that certain offenders whom the Court did not think fit to imprison, on account of their age, character, or antecedents, might be placed on probation under the supervision of these officers, whose duty it would be to guide, admonish, and befriend them.'[122]

One of those so appointed, Henry Edgar Norman, was to write that the Act was 'an expression of the community's will to win back an offender from his evil ways rather than to seek satisfaction in his sufferings under legal punishment'.[123] Churchill considered it 'an admirable Act' that had in 1910 'already made its effect manifest upon our criminal statistics'.[124] He did, though, identify one problem, and a large one at that from his perspective:

> There were 90,000 persons committed to prison last year in default of the payment of fines, and of those 13,000 or 14,000 paid the fine in whole or in part after they had been committed to prison. I think a much larger proportion would have paid the fine if they had had a reasonable period of time to get the money either by earning it or obtaining it from their friends and relations.[125]

Having studied the statistics for the previous year, he discovered that 61 per cent of all sentences passed during that period had involved locking people up for less than a fortnight. He composed a memorandum, pointing out that this equated to 'nearly 125,000 perfectly purposeless short sentences' of which more than half had been imposed upon 'first offenders'. This was addressed to Ruggles Brise and Charles Masterman, his deputy, with the directive that they should 'consider and advise' him as to how this 'gigantic number of useless and often pernicious committals can be abolished, or, at least, vastly abated'.[126] There was much more in Churchill's memorandum, including proposals for greater use of 'suspensory' (what a later generation would term 'suspended') sentences, and a thorough rationalisation of the entire prison system:

> If the prisons were cleared of all the enormous burdens of purposeless congestion for petty offences, a far greater specialization in the treatment offered by each prison would become possible. Instead of having a lot of prisons of substantially the same type and reproducing the same features, scattered about all over the country, we should have a regular series of scientifically graded institutions which would gradually and increasingly become adapted to the treatment of every variety of human weakness.[127]

The various reforms the Home Secretary enunciated and proposed, and the consideration they required, constituted a formidable workload for officials in his department. This was recognised with the creation of the Abatement of Imprisonment Committee on 29 December 1910, which was tasked with examining

Churchill's desiderata and, where possible, translating them into legislative form. Chaired by Ernley Blackwell, the Assistant Secretary at the Home Department and thus Troup's deputy, the members included two Home Office officials, two senior officers of the Metropolitan Police plus a London magistrate from the metropolis, and the Clerk to the Liverpool Justices (magistrates). The findings of the Blackwell Committee, which endorsed many but by no means all of Churchill's ideas and proposals, were embodied in the draft of a Bill, the Administration of Justice Bill (1911), which was published on 8 April 1911. It failed to progress further, however, and fell by the wayside completely after Churchill left the Home Office.[128]

That Churchill was a hard taskmaster, imposing considerable burdens upon his departmental officials, is undoubted. He was, though, no desk-bound dictator. Butler remarked upon the 'appalling energy with which he conducted a lightning personal survey of the gaols of the country'. One such visit merited elaboration:

> One day I happened to be temporarily acting as his private secretary, when he had gone off to Dartmoor to inspect the convict settlement. Calculating that he could not possibly get back until after lunch, I was settling down comfortably to a leisurely morning, when I was startled by the furious buzzing of his bell soon after eleven o'clock. There he was spruce and debonair in his grey frock-coat with a sheaf of minutes and directions dictated in the train, all on fire to translate the impressions of his trip into action. When I had time to look round, I resorted to Bradshaw and found that he had taken the milk train from Devonshire by rising in the small hours.[129]

He could also display similar levels of energy in other directions and did so in respect of the curious case of Edward Frederick Mylius, a man whom he was determined should be locked up. The case arose following the death of King Edward VII on 6 May 1910 and the accession of George V. As Prince George, he had not been in the direct line of succession until January 1892 when his elder brother Albert Victor, the Duke of Clarence, who was expected to succeed in due course, became ill and perished. This was an event that effectively ended George's promising naval career,[130] but gained him a wife. Albert Victor had been affianced to Princess Victoria Mary (known universally as May) of Teck. With such arrangements considered dynastical matters, Queen Victoria being the ultimate arbiter, the bereaved Princess soon found herself engaged to George, who had in the meantime become Duke of York. Their wedding took place on 6 July 1893. There was, though, a conspiracy theory, which, at least to its devotees, made the union controversial:

> When his Majesty [King George V], as Duke of York, was married to Princess May, there were rumours afloat that he had contracted a morganatic alliance with a daughter of Admiral Seymour, then commanding the Naval Squadron at Malta. Our readers will remember how prevalent were these

rumours. We have good reason to remember them, for at the time of the royal marriage, letters of protest poured in upon us ...[131]

There was no truth in the 'prevalent rumours' that the Duke was committing bigamy when he married, no matter how many letters of protest poured in but the rumours persisted. Only outside the mainstream, though; no newspaper, the only mass media then in existence, with any pretention to respectability would, of course, touch such a story and no action was taken to publicly deny it. The King, it has been claimed, was amused by the tale, or at least until 'in 1910 a journalist named Edward Mylius resurrected the legend in a seditious Parisian publication, *The Liberator*'. He now determined to put an end once and for all to what he termed 'a damnable lie'.[132]

The 'seditious Parisian publication' was a Republican broadsheet published by Edward Holden James, an American and a nephew of the novelist Henry James. Appearing monthly, its circulation would have undoubtedly been minimal, but free copies were sent to every MP as a matter of course.[133] Mylius, Belgian by birth but a British citizen, was its London distributor and correspondent and the November 1910 edition contained an article written by him titled 'Sanctified Bigamy':

> In the year 1890, in the island of Malta, the present King of England con-
> tracted a lawful marriage with the daughter of Sir Michael Culme-Seymour,
> a British admiral. Children were born of this marriage. At the time the Duke
> of Clarence, who subsequently died, was heir to the throne [...]
>
>   The daughter of Sir Michael Culme-Seymour, if she still lives, is by the
> unchangeable law of the Christian Church, as well as by the common law of
> England, the rightful Queen of England, and her children are the only
> rightful heirs to the English throne.[134]

This, under English law, constituted criminal libel for which the author could be prosecuted. The publication of a libel known to be false had become a separate statutory offence under the Libel Act 1843, though to succeed any such prose-cution would have to demonstrate that it was serious enough to vilify the subject, or victim, and have the tendency to bring that person into hatred, contempt and ridicule.[135]

HM Customs and Excise intercepted and detained approximately a thousand copies of *The Liberator* containing the article in question at Newhaven, East Sussex, on 17 November 1910. It was, though, pointed out in a letter to the Director of Public Prosecutions, Sir Charles Matthews, that there was 'no statu-tory power under which this particular publication can be detained unless it can be described as being indecent or obscene'.[136]

Though the matter was not discussed by the Cabinet, the Government's senior law officers, Attorney General Sir Rufus Isaacs and Solicitor General Sir John Simon, were in the process of compiling a Joint Opinion on the viability of prose-cuting Mylius for, as mentioned, criminal libel. Apart from the legal aspect, though, there was also a political perspective to take into account and Churchill, ultimately, was the arbiter of that. As Troup explained it:

> The Home Secretary has ... always been the authority who, in consultation with the Law Officers of the Crown and the Director of Public Prosecutions, settles whether a prosecution in the nature of a political prosecution should be undertaken ... the question of policy – whether in the existing circumstances it will best serve the public interests to prosecute a man who has been guilty (for instance) of using seditious language, or to ignore the offence and avoid giving an advertisement to the offender – is one which the Home Secretary must either himself decide or, if the matter be of first importance, bring before the Prime Minister or the Cabinet.[137]

Churchill kept Asquith informed but, as stated, the rest of the Cabinet remained in the dark as regards the whole issue. There was one other person who had to be consulted, however, and that was the King. The Home Secretary wrote to George V on 24 November enclosing the opinion of the Law Officers, which was that if Mylius was charged with criminal libel, the King could not be required to give evidence at the trial.[138] On 26 November Churchill sent the Prime Minister a note outlining 'the present position' in respect of the case, and the rationale behind the proposed course of action against Mylius:

> The Law Officers of the Crown have given their opinion as follows: The paper undoubtedly contains a criminal libel on the King. An action by the Culme-Seymour family would demonstrate the falsity of the libel, but would probably fail to secure a conviction in the face of a defence that it was the King and not the Culme-Seymour family who was attacked. A prosecution for seditious libel on the other hand would secure a conviction, but would afford no occasion for demonstrating the falsity of the libel. Both these courses are therefore unsuitable. Procedure by a criminal information [a formal charge which begins court proceedings] for criminal libel on the King in the Court of King's Bench would, however, not only secure a conviction, but enable the falsity of the libel to be demonstrated. It would not be necessary for the King to appear as witness. Action could be taken on his behalf by the Attorney General ... It is this third course therefore which alone is suitable.[139]

He was to report to the King on 18 December that Asquith was in favour of proceeding, and that he thought the Home Secretary 'would do well to take the opportunity of crushing this thing out'.[140] The 'crushing' was being well choreographed legally whilst Mylius, obviously unaware of what was planned, returned to the subject in the 19 December issue of *The Liberator*: 'The Daily News of London tells us that the King plans to visit India with his wife. Would the newspaper kindly tell us which wife?'[141]

The dénouement began on 26 December when, following the filing of an indictment (in legal terminology, 'ex officio criminal information'), Mylius was arrested.[142] A remand hearing was held on 28 December where the Attorney-General suggested that bail terms for Mylius should be set at £10,000 in his own recognizance, plus two sureties of £5,000 each, with a remand in custody if the specified terms could not be met. These were colossal sums, equivalent a century later to more than two million pounds in total,[143] which resulted in Mylius being remanded in Brixton prison until his trial on 1 February 1911.[144]

The case, in the King's Bench Division of the High Court of Justice, was heard before the Right Honourable the Lord Alverstone, Lord Chief Justice of England, and a Special Jury. The Attorney General, Sir Rufus Isaacs, led for the prosecution, assisted by Sir John Simon, the Solicitor General;[145] Mylius represented himself. He was informed, prior to the jury being sworn, that he was free to challenge any of the jurors. He refrained from doing so, but got into a dispute with Lord Alverstone about the absence of the King from the court and demanded his presence. He was overruled: 'This has already been the subject of an application before me. You are perfectly well aware that the King cannot be summoned here. The King is not present.'[146] Nor would he be. Mylius had made several attempts to secure the attendance of King George V at his trial, all of which had been rebuffed.[147]

The case was in essence quite simple. The prosecution had to show that Mylius' accusations were false. Mylius had to demonstrate they were true. Witnesses for the prosecution included Admiral Sir Michael Culme-Seymour, three of his sons and one of his daughters. All testified to the impossibility of the alleged marriage. The marriage registers for the period 1886 to July 1893, which had been fetched from Malta along with the Crown Advocate (Attorney General) of that territory, were shown to the jury and it was also demonstrated that Prince George had not been on the island at the time in any event.[148] Amongst those observing the proceedings was the Home Secretary. Churchill had stated beforehand that he would attend 'in order that it may be apparent that Ministers accept full responsibility for the course which has been taken'.[149]

Mylius sat through the evidence without attempting any cross-examination. Upon being asked to present his case, he resorted to demanding that the King be summoned as a witness: 'The King has made no sworn denial of the charges which have been made against him; the King has not contradicted of his own free will in the witness box any of those charges and I ask you to summon my accuser and let him deny the truth of my statement.' Upon being told again that this was not possible, Mylius refused to proceed any further. The Lord Chief Justice prompted him: 'You said you wished to call evidence?', to which came the reply 'That is my evidence, my Lord.' After being asked if he wished to say anything else, Mylius replied that he rested his case 'as I have been denied the Constitutional right of a fair trial'.[150]

Perhaps unsurprisingly, the jury did not even leave their box before, after only about a minute of deliberation, delivering a guilty verdict. Mylius was sentenced to twelve months' imprisonment in the Third Division; both he and, perhaps more importantly from the perspective of the King, his libel had undeniably been crushed. Indeed, as Smith argues, the whole purpose of the prosecution seems to have been less about punishing Mylius than vindicating the King's honour.[151] Sir John Simon noted in respect of the matter that:

> We were very lucky to bring the Mylius case to so satisfactory an end. If Mylius, instead of justifying, had pleaded guilty and explained that he was only repeating what thousands of reputable people have said for years without being prosecuted for it, we could never have established the falsity of the lie so effectually.[152]

The King was indeed pleased: 'both Sir Rufus and Sir John Simon were rewarded by appointment to be Knights Commander of the Royal Victorian Order as a mark of His Majesty's personal gratitude for their services.'[153] Churchill, who according to his official biographer had been in charge of the affair throughout and had taken the responsibility upon himself, received a letter of thanks from the monarch.[154] He also received one of reproach from his colleague Viscount Morley of Blackburn, the Lord President of the Council:

> I have written to the PM, that I should wish to raise at the Cabinet the proceedings about the libel on the King. It seems to me to be a profound mistake – and in any case, as it affects the Sovereign personally, the Cabinet ought to have been consulted.[155]

There do not appear to have been any repercussions in respect of the matter and, as noted, Churchill had taken care to keep Asquith up to date and had received his approval. He had, though, expended some considerable energy in pursuing the Mylius case; his correspondence with the various actors takes up over twenty-two pages of Randolph Churchill's official biography.[156]

It may be that this workload, especially when combined with the various other problems that he was dealing with at the time, plus the second general election of the year, contributed to Churchill's relative neglect of a scandal that arose publicly on 22 October 1910. On that date, the weekly magazine *John Bull* published an exposé pertaining to the ill treatment of boys at Heswall Nautical Training School, a reformatory school at Heswall, Cheshire, dubbed colloquially the Akbar, after a ship that was its former home.[157] The accusations were sensational: 'Reformatory School Horrors, How Boys at the Akbar School are Tortured – Several Deaths.'[158]

Neither the magazine, nor its editor and proprietor Horatio Bottomley, were what might be termed reputable. McEwan says of the latter: 'Bottomley was a thorough-going scoundrel and the use he made of *John Bull* is notorious; suffice to say that his weekly effusions pandered to the worst instincts of the mob.'[159] Scholarly opinion is virtually unanimous on that score, a recent opinion being he 'was the archetypal British demagogue, the godfather of today's anglocentric populists' and that 'When it came to fusing self-advertisement with the pursuit of profit, he has had few rivals.'[160]

He was also the Liberal MP for Hackney South, first elected there in 1906. He held the seat in the January 1910 election, though used the pages of *John Bull* to vilify his Tory opponent, Conway Wertheimer, as a Jew and a foreigner.[161]

The account given in *John Bull* was based on information disclosed by Ronald Adams, a former deputy superintendent of the school, and his wife, a former matron appointed in 1909. Mr Adams had tendered his resignation in March 1910 on health grounds, though both he and his wife were dismissed in May after she complained about the way the superintendent of the establishment, Captain Edward Beuttler, allowed the boys to be treated.[162] According to the article, this was brutal, with pupils being gagged and birched until blood was drawn; out of some eighty boys punished with birching or the cane twenty-seven were scarred for life.[163]

It was also stated that those who reported sick were often caned as malingerers, and that being drenched in freezing water was used as a chastisement.[164] Another punishment involved sleep deprivation: 'made to stand up, each boy by the side of the hammock in which he ought properly to have been sleeping, from ten o'clock at night until five o'clock the following morning, alternately for fifteen minutes at attention and for fifteen minutes at ease.'[165] These were all lads aged under 16, it may be remembered, and there is no doubt that in all essentials the abuses itemised had actually taken place. Further, and whether as a direct result of being punished or not was debatable, five had perished in 1909.[166]

The Home Office was not directly responsible for the Akbar. It formed part of, and was administered by, the Liverpool Reformatory Association. This was an organisation responsible for four institutions containing, in the words of Joan Rimmer, 'naughty children'.[167] These were, as the House of Commons was informed, 'private schools, privately owned and privately managed by groups of philanthropic persons' and the Home Office had 'no concern' in their administration apart from being the inspecting authority. In that regard, and as a former pupil of a reformatory school recollected, the inspector 'never did any good and never any harm and certainly never discovered or saw anything he was not wanted to discover or see'.[168]

Even if the inspector had seen or discovered something against the institution, the only sanction the Home Secretary could wield was to withhold the Home Office certificate of approval. Without this document magistrates would no longer be able to send youngsters to the establishments; 'the directors might in that case, of course, close the school altogether'. Six months' notice was required to withdraw the certificate.[169]

Bottomley lobbied Churchill following the revelations in *John Bull* and requested that the Assistant Editor of the journal should be present at the enquiry Churchill subsequently instigated. This was refused, with the Home Secretary pointing out that 'the enquiry is administrative' and so there would be no evidence given under oath. Public attendance would therefore not be 'advantageous'. The report of the enquiry would be presented to Parliament 'if necessary'.[170]

A later generation might well consider that the only kind of enquiry required was one by the police, and that it would reasonably conclude with Captain Beuttler and his underlings spending a lengthy period in an institution that, unlike the Akbar, came directly under the Home Office.[171] In fact, the person sent to conduct the investigation was Charles Masterman, Liberal MP for West Ham North and, as Under-Secretary for the Home Department, Churchill's deputy. Masterman was a substantial figure in his own right, with several well-regarded books[172] to his name, and has been described by one of Bottomley's biographers, Julian Symons, as 'an intellectual member of the Liberal party's left wing' who felt that 'the information about the Akbar came from a tainted source'.[173] There can be no doubt that he possessed the ability to get to the bottom of the matter, though. Carlebach, however, characterises the Home Office attitude to the matter as 'suspicious', inasmuch as it declined to take into account further evidence of abuse supplied by *John Bull* before Masterman reported.[174] His report, delivered in February 1911, raised a storm of protest and accusations of a whitewash when it exonerated Beuttler and his regime. One example, with respect to the freezing water episode, will suffice to illustrate the tone:

> The Superintendent himself recognised that this punishment was a mistake, and ought not to have occurred ... If punishments, either of standing boys all night or of throwing water over boys, had been in habitual usage, I should certainly have recommended the dismissal of the present superintendent.[175]

Churchill backed his Under-Secretary, stating in a debate on the matter in the House of Commons that 'I had an opportunity of reading the report ... before it was published, and I accept the fullest responsibility for everything in it.'[176] Masterman told Parliament that under Beuttler the incidences of corporal punishment inflicted upon the boys was actually on a downward trend:

> In the year 1907 – in the last six months of that year, which was before the school was under its present management, the number of corporal punishments administered was 119, whereas in the last six months of 1909 the number fell to fifty-six, and six months later it came down to thirty-five. That is a very considerable diminution, and it seems to redeem the superintendent from the charge of having some unnatural delight in the administration of corporal punishment for the boys.[177]

He went on to make a point that, in its implications, was extremely disturbing; seven of the thirty-five cases of corporal punishment mentioned were administered 'in consequence of a most disastrous revelation of organised immorality in which a large number of small boys were involved, and which was a corrupting influence to the whole school'. One dreads to consider what lay behind the euphemistic term 'organised immorality'. Indeed, it is difficult to controvert Henry William Massingham in *The Nation*: 'if the Home Office concludes that the case for the dismissal of the superintendent ... fails on the grounds that he had greatly ameliorated the boys' condition, what kind of hell on earth must this institution once have been?'[178] Sir William Watson Rutherford, the Conservative MP for Liverpool West Derby, argued that little appeared to have changed: 'The fact that out of some eighty boys punished with birching or the cane twenty-seven have been admittedly found to bear permanent marks ... shows that, as a rule, the corporal punishment administered in the school was excessive and inhuman.'[179]

The row over the 'Akbar Affair' rumbled on, largely through the actions of Bottomley, who began a vendetta against Masterman, though not Churchill, through the pages of *John Bull* and in Parliament. This damaged, and arguably eventually ruined, Masterman's political career.[180] As noted above, Churchill backed Masterman and his report in the House of Commons, and did so because he believed that his deputy was correct in his findings. Evidence for this can be found in the letter he wrote to the King concerning the attempt 'to censure the Home Secretary for not insisting upon the dismissal of the superintendent of the Akbar Nautical School for certain irregular floggings and other punishments which he had been responsible for'. He continued, writing in the third person as was the custom when communicating with the sovereign:

> This unpleasant case has attracted a great deal of public attention and knowing beforehand the strong views of the House of Commons on corporal punishment, Mr Churchill had taken the precaution to have a special enquiry made by Mr Masterman the Under Secretary of State. Mr Masterman is an extremely able minister and is greatly esteemed in the House for his high personal character, and remarkable for an unusual combination of being a strong churchman and an admired radical. He carried a great many guns for the purposes of this debate, and his striking report and earnest and effective speech broke the back of the attack. In any case Mr Churchill would not have been prepared to sacrifice the Superintendent who though guilty of irregularities is a thoroughly good man and has worked wonders with the school.[181]

Churchill had, though, already conceded to Parliament that 'there is a great deal more flogging going on in these reformatory schools than is necessary or desirable'. Accordingly he had decided to 'appoint a strong Departmental Committee which should be able to go into the whole question of the present methods of maintaining discipline in reformatory and industrial schools, and which will deal with the methods by which these schools should be brought into close and suitable contact with the Home Office'.[182] This, the Departmental Committee on Reformatory and Industrial Schools,[183] delivered an 'extremely critical' report in 1913, which was long after Churchill had left the Home Office.[184] The question of the administration of these establishments was, without question, long overdue. As Isaac Briggs, who had direct experience, was to put it: 'By maintaining certain institutions we might alter, we perpetuate certain evils we might cure.'[185]

Churchill had unquestionably demonstrated that he was indeed the 'Prisoners' Friend' in the case of adults, but declined to replicate this approach in respect of the Akbar children, and indeed the reformatory system more widely. It is clear that there were serious issues with the way that the Akbar was administered, to put it mildly, yet despite his instigating an investigation into the over-use of flogging in such establishments, he adopted a hands-off policy generally. Whether, as suggested, this was due to workload is unknown. What can be said with more certainty is that he was fortunate that he was not associated with the 'Akbar Affair' from then onwards. Indeed, a glance at the index of several Churchill biographies, spanning the spectrum from the voluminous official version by Randolph Churchill (and later Martin Gilbert) to the highly critical, revisionist, work of Clive Ponting,[186] reveals no mention of the matter. Perhaps the more spectacular events that he was, and remains, associated with such as Tonypandy and the Battle of Stepney left no space for the issue. He was in any event spared the vituperation that Bottomley, and then the Northcliffe Press (*Daily Mail, Daily Mirror, The Times*), poured upon Masterman with significant effect.[187]

Chapter Six

Mrs Pankhurst's Army of Amazons

'Frail little Mrs Pankhurst led an army of Amazons, autocratically organized, disciplined and commanded, [and] trained in the tactics of direct action ...'[1]

'... that copious fountain of mendacity, the Women's Social and Political Union.'[2]

*   *   *

As Home Secretary, Churchill was, initially at least, fortunate with respect to the ongoing suffragette campaign which had bedevilled his predecessor. This was so because shortly after his assumption of office, Emmeline Pankhurst, leader of the Women's Social and Political Union (WSPU), called for a truce in the struggle. Whilst addressing an audience at the Queen's Hall, Westminster, on 31 January she announced that militancy would end, at least for the time being.[3] 'Militancy' in the context of that period meant disruption or, as Emmeline Pankhurst had it, 'Peaceful Militancy'.[4] Christabel Pankhurst termed it 'mild militancy' and reckoned that by early 1910 it was 'more or less played out'. 'The Government', by her account, had 'closed every door to it, especially by excluding suffragette questioners from their meetings. Cabinet Ministers had shown their contempt for the mildness of our protests and had publicly taunted us on that score.' There was also strategy at play: 'a pause in militancy would be valuable, for it would give time for familiarity to fade, so that the same methods could be used again with freshness and effect'.[5]

Emmeline Pankhurst's announcement came as a surprise to the public at large, and led to speculation that some sort of deal had been agreed with the Government. Asquith, who was known to be opposed to the enfranchisement of women, now of course depended for a majority in the House of Commons on Irish Nationalist and Labour MPs, and the latter in particular were known to be generally supportive of female suffrage. Further, an initiative by the journalist Henry Brailsford, one of the founders of the 'Men's League for Women's Suffrage', led to the formation of what was known as the 'Conciliation Committee for Woman Suffrage in the House of Commons'. It was supported by thirty-six MPs from all parties and chaired by a member of the House of Lords, Victor Bulwer-Lytton, the 2nd Earl of Lytton.[6] Lytton was the brother of Lady Constance Bulwer-Lytton, of whom more later.

The question of the enfranchisement of the female population fell, as Constance Rover has described it, between two stools politically.[7] Very broadly speaking, many in the top rank of the Conservative Party were somewhat favourable but the rank and file were antagonistic, whilst the opposite applied vis-à-vis the Liberals. The leadership of the latter as represented by the Cabinet were divided on the question, though with a majority in favour but Asquith firmly against. There was also a fear that if women were enfranchised on the same basis as men then, given the 'property vote in the counties', this would simply increase the size of the Tory-voting electorate.[8] Lloyd George, who was in favour of enfranchising women, saw this potential danger clearly.[9] Compounding that issue from the Liberal perspective was the prospect of the 'faggot vote' coming into play. A faggot (sometimes rendered as 'fagot') voter could be created if a property-owner subdivided his holding, thus allowing others – the wives, daughters, and other female relatives of wealthy men – to qualify for the franchise.

These matters were just as obvious to Conservatives as to their opponents, and there were those in leadership positions who were favourably disposed to female suffrage. These did not include Lord Curzon. He authored 'Fifteen Good Reasons Against the Grant of Female Suffrage', and became a leading member and future president of the 'National League for Opposing Woman Suffrage'. The lesser lights, however, tended to view it as a radical measure, and so automatically repugnant, that would disadvantage them at some point. This was particularly so given the obvious solution to the problems the Liberals comprehended was universal adult suffrage, which few, if any, Conservatives would support.[10] That there was an obvious linkage was plain to many commentators. One such was Albert Venn Dicey, Professor of Law at Oxford University and the London School of Economics, who 'dominated the study of constitutional law in his own lifetime'.[11] Writing in January 1909, he warned that 'woman suffrage' was merely a portent of a vaster, more detrimental, development; that it 'must lead to adult suffrage, and will increase all the admitted defects of so-called universal or, in strictness, manhood suffrage'. This, he foresaw, would lead to catastrophe: 'Who can contemplate without dread a state of things under which democratic passion, intensified by feminine emotion, may deprive the country both of the calmness which foresees and the resolution which repels the onslaught of foreign enemies?'[12]

Despite the profound difficulties of arriving at measures around which these various divergent views might compromise, Lytton's Committee put forward the provisional text of a Bill that would provide a solution along non-party lines. The answer they arrived at was simple: women who were ratepayers had, so long as they were unmarried, been able to vote in local government elections since 1869.[13] This was extended in 1884, and further legislation in 1894 included some married women, but a husband and wife could not both qualify in respect of the same property. Thus, by allowing those women who were already able to vote in local government, or municipal, elections the same right at parliamentary elections, a 'working compromise' was arrived at 'which no party can consider objectionable or unfair'.[14] This measure, if adopted, would confer the vote on about a million new electors.[15] Formally entitled the 'Parliamentary Franchise (Women) Bill', and generally known as the 'Conciliation Bill', it would be introduced as a private bill,[16] and the Committee were of the opinion that there would be a majority in the House of Commons that would vote for it.[17]

Brailsford, as Secretary to the Committee, wrote to the Home Secretary on 13 April 1910 telling him of documents that he intended circulating to all MPs in respect of the proposed bill. He also asked if Churchill would 'allow us to quote you in the covering letter ... as one ... who welcome[s] the formation of the committee and would favour a solution on non-party lines'. Several prominent politicians – Sir Edward Grey (Foreign Secretary), Lloyd George (Chancellor of the Exchequer), Arthur Balfour (Leader of the Opposition), Alfred Lyttelton (a former Conservative Colonial Secretary), and Andrew Bonar Law (a senior Conservative politician) – were mentioned as being prospective supporters also.[18] Churchill replied on 19 April, apologising for the delay in doing so, which had been occasioned by 'great pressure of business'. He agreed in principle, but with conditions:

> I should be willing to allow myself to be quoted in the manner you suggest ... provided that the others whom you mention, or most of them, are willing to come forward too. [...] I do not wish to be committed at the present juncture to any special form or basis in or upon which the franchise is to be granted to women. I have not sufficiently studied the bearings of the municipal franchise which you now favour. I am, however, anxious to see women relieved in principle from a disability which is injurious to them whilst it is based on grounds of sex.[19]

Of the luminaries alluded to by Brailsford only Sir Edward Grey and Alfred Lyttelton were actually named on the end result. Churchill featured alongside them, as did three other MPs not originally mentioned,[20] but his inclusion was to be a source of friction in the near future.[21] There was, though, a more immediate cause of concern for the Home Office in respect of the female franchise. This revolved around the treatment of those suffragettes who had been sent to prison for militant action prior to Emmeline Pankhurst's cease-fire, and their tactic of refusing food once inside.

A linked factor that had the potential to cause controversy was class related. The official position of the authorities was that all the suffragette prisoners were treated the same irrespective of their background. This was a claim which was treated with grave suspicion and was put to the test by Lady Constance Bulwer-Lytton, the second daughter and third child of the Conservative politician and poet, Robert Bulwer-Lytton, Viceroy of India 1876–1880, created 1st Earl of Lytton in the latter year.[22] The 2nd Earl was, as already noted, her brother and chairman of the Conciliation Committee.

Born in 1869, Lady Constance was later to write that 'I had been more or less of a chronic invalid through the greater part of my youth. An overmastering laziness and a fatalistic submission to events as they befell were guiding factors in my existence.'[23] She found a mission in life, what she termed her 'conversion', when in August and September 1908 she came into contact with two prominent suffragettes, Emmeline Pethick-Lawrence and Annie Kenney.[24] Taking up their cause, she was arrested twice, the second time at Newcastle in October 1909, which was after the forced-feeding regime had been introduced. She refused both food and answers to medical questions put to her but, after examination by the prison doctor, was released due to a serious pre-existing heart condition which made her 'unfit to submit for forcible feeding'.[25] Or at least ostensibly so.

Lady Constance was convinced that her discharge had been occasioned because of her station in life. Given her aristocratic origins and connection, plus the fact that her sister, Lady Elizabeth or 'Betty', was married to Gerald Balfour, the elder brother of the leader of the Conservative Party, then this belief seemed plausible. That plausibility increased to near certainty when, after changing her appearance and reinventing herself as distinctly working class 'Jane Warton', she was once more arrested, and imprisoned at Liverpool on 15 January 1910. On 18 January, and after her refusing food since being incarcerated, the Senior Medical Officer decided she would be force-fed. According to her account: 'He did not examine my heart nor feel my pulse; he did not ask to do so, nor did I say anything which could possibly induce him to think I would refuse to be examined.'[26] After a graphic description of the process of force-feeding, following which the doctor slapped her on the cheek 'not violently, but, as it were, to express his contemptuous disapproval', she describes an out-of-body experience:

> suddenly I saw Jane Warton lying before me, and it seemed as if I were outside of her. She was the most despised, ignorant and helpless prisoner that I had seen. When she had served her time and was out of the prison, no one would believe anything she said, and the doctor when he had fed her by force and tortured her body, struck her on the cheek to show how he despised her! That was Jane Warton, and I had come to help her.[27]

Help her she did: 'She exposed the double standards of a government that released her from prison with little harm once she was identified as Lady Constance whilst meting out harsh, vicious and dangerous treatment when she disguised herself as Jane Warton, a poor unknown nobody.'[28] Indeed so, for Constance Lytton had powerful connections and was able to gravely embarrass the Home Office. Despite official obfuscation, her brother demanded an explanation from the Home Office, which became a matter that devolved onto Churchill after he took over. Gladstone had dubbed her behaviour 'a very contemptible trick',[29] for officialdom naturally regards such deception as deplorable. The standard response in such situations involves a closing of ranks, denial and deflection. This was far from satisfactory to the outraged Lord Lytton, who was a 'close personal friend' of the new Home Secretary.[30] He was thus able to write a private letter, beginning 'Dear Winston', on 18 March stating that he was 'rather unhappy at being so long delayed from publicly vindicating my sister against the charge of untruthfulness which was brought against her by the Home Office'. It continued:

> My complaint is that in a matter of this sort the kind of enquiry instituted by the Home Office has not really the object of arriving at the truth but rather

of making out a case against the alleged grievances. The fact that my sister concealed her identity and refused to answer medical questions does not relieve the prison officials at Liverpool of any responsibility. The fact that they knew nothing of her physical condition made it all the more incumbent upon them to find it out for themselves ...

Jane Wharton [*sic*] had not received that careful medical examination which your predecessor publicly declared was the indispensable preliminary to forcible feeding in the case of every prisoner, and nothing the Home Office officials may now say can get over that fact.[31]

Despite being confronted with evidence of how his departmental policy had impacted someone in his social milieu, albeit unwittingly, Churchill was, and remained, in favour of forcible-feeding. Wilfred Scawen Blunt records him being 'obstinate' on the matter despite being told that it closely resembled 'torture and the Spanish inquisition'.[32] He had, nevertheless, already taken steps that would likely prevent it happening even before receiving Lytton's letter.

The prison system in force in England and Wales at the time, established by the Prison Act 1898, placed convicted offenders into one of three divisions. Put basically, these represented a hierarchy of severity with the harshest regime reserved for those in the Third Division. At the opposite end of the scale was the First Division, into which very few prisoners were placed. These included those convicted of sedition and of offences under the Vaccination Acts. Sentencing to the Second Division was based on the 'character and antecedents of the offender and the circumstances in which the offence was committed'. Persons of bad character, of the criminal class, or generally of criminal or disreputable habits, were definitely excluded.[33] The court that sentenced the offender was left to decide in which division the sentence was to be served but, in practice, this was rarely done. The third division then became the default category, applying to over 90 per cent of those sentenced to prison without hard labour.[34]

Marion Dunlop had undertaken her pioneering hunger strike in furtherance of achieving political prisoner status, which effectively meant being moved to the First Division. On 15 March 1910, in reply to a question by John O'Connor, the MP for North Kildare, in the House of Commons about whether he had considered such a claim, Churchill replied that he had 'given my best consideration to this subject'. He went on to state that it was his 'duty' to ensure that 'the treatment of prisoners should not be inappropriate or harmful' and that he felt, as had his predecessor, that rules 'which are suitable to criminals guilty of dishonesty or cruelty, or other crimes implying moral turpitude, should not be applied inflexibly to those whose general character is good and whose offences, however reprehensible, do not involve personal dishonour'. Accordingly he was proposing to mitigate prison conditions 'which are generally regarded as of a degrading character' with a Rule which would 'acquire statutory force in the ordinary manner':

In the case of any offender of the second or third division whose previous character is good, and who has been convicted of, or committed to prison for, an offence not involving dishonesty, cruelty, indecency, or serious violence, the Prison Commissioners may allow such amelioration of the conditions prescribed in the foregoing rules as the Secretary of State may approve in respect of the wearing of prison clothing, bathing, hair-cutting, cleaning of cells, employment, exercise, books, and otherwise. Provided that no such amelioration shall be greater than that granted under the rules for offenders of the first division.[35]

This, codified as Rule 243A, was an implicit concession to suffragette prisoners. The substance of their demands was conceded in that they were subjected to substantially the same regime as prisoners of the First Division, though they remained officially categorised as being in the Second Division. Politically adroit though this move was, it caused the newly ennobled Lord Gladstone to complain that Churchill had merely taken credit for schemes that he, Gladstone, had put in motion prior to leaving the Home Office:

The form of your announcement in the House of Commons … to me is a matter of rather more than surprise. Apart from the merits of the proposal two deductions will inevitably be made – first that you initiated the changes and I did not; secondly that you have done the obviously right thing, and that I from foolishness and inhumanity did not.[36]

Churchill replied that he was sorry that Gladstone had reason to complain, and blamed newspaper coverage for failing to report that he had mentioned him, as his 'predecessor', in the speech. He did, though, reject the charge of political plagiarism, insisting that he had 'acted in entire independence of your views & gave instructions upon my own initiative wh[ich] I have felt v[er]y strongly should have been carried out three years ago, & might have been carried out at any time'.[37]

Given that his version is correct, then the origins of this stratagem may be found in a minute from Churchill to Troup of 28 February. Therein, the Home Secretary stated that he was 'anxious to prescribe a special code of regulations dealing with the treatment of political prisoners'. He also defined what he thought a political prisoner was: 'a person who has committed an offence, involving no moral turpitude, with a distinct political object'.[38] Troup's response warned of the dangers of 'prison treatment being made to depend on the political motive of the offender'. He also pointed out that the Prison Act had 'settled the classes of prisoner' and that a new class could not be introduced by rule of the Home Secretary. He went on, though, to state: 'But I think the same result can be obtained by other means.' He came up with a form of wording to achieve these 'other means', which then formed the basis of Churchill's speech to the House of Commons quoted above.[39] This proved popular, at least in certain quarters, as was evidenced by a letter from Charles Scott, the editor of the *Manchester Guardian*:

I want to send a line personally of thanks for your decision about the treatment of the suffragettes & similar persons. It strikes one as just common sense but it needed courage as well as sense. More & more one comes to think that courage is the first & the last of political virtues.[40]

It was then, during a period of relative peace in the 'war' over women's suffrage, when David Shackleton, the Labour MP for Clitheroe, moved that the Parliamentary Franchise (Women) Bill should be given its First Reading on 14 June 1910. This motion, and that it was 'to be read a second time upon Tuesday next', passed without a division (no vote being taken).[41] Asquith, according to his Cabinet colleague Jack Pease,[42] dubbed the whole matter a 'most repulsive subject', but agreed to receive deputations from both suffragists and antisuffragists on 21 June. The twenty-strong pro-suffrage group was led by Millicent Fawcett, the head of the National Union of Women's Suffrage Societies, otherwise known as suffragists. They were distinguishable from Emmeline Pankhurst's suffragettes[43] in that they eschewed militant action and believed in a peaceful, non-confrontational, approach to the question of female enfranchisement.[44] According to Mrs Fawcett's speech to a meeting of the NUWSS on 28 June, Asquith was a 'man of his word' and had 'left the door ajar':

It is for us to throw ourselves against the door … a heavy door … and its hinges are rusty with prejudice and cant. We must use all our strength and all our sense; we must press for an early day and further facilities.[45]

Asquith might have left the door ajar, but the resultant gap was exceedingly narrow; only two days, 11–12 July, were allowed for the Second Reading. Indeed, during a private meeting at the Home Office on 6 June, Churchill later claimed, in a 'Not for publication' memorandum, to have informed Lytton that 'there was no possible chance of any facilities being given for any women's suffrage measures this session [of Parliament]'.[46] Lytton had responded at the time, telling Churchill that the talk:

had made me very sad. I felt so incapable of conveying to you the depth of feeling which is behind the question. For me it has become so much more than a question of politics. It touches everything which I most value in my private life. It involves serious risk to my sister's life, it has broken the health & spirits of my mother, and it is a cause of much sorrow and bitterness in my relations with Pamela.[47]

Brailsford was not terribly optimistic either, writing to the Home Secretary a few days before the Bill was debated that whilst he hoped 'you will be able to speak as warmly as you honestly can for our Bill', he was 'afraid that we shall not fare well'. The letter continued:

I had hoped that Lloyd George would have consented to be neutral, but he is quite determined to do his best to smash us. On the other hand the Unionists cannot do away with their fear that the Bill means adult suffrage. It is a grotesque situation. [Lloyd] George will smash us because it is not adult suffrage, and the Unionists will desert us because it will lead to adult suffrage. Our best hope is that men like yourself & Mr [Augustine] Birrell who really want a moderate solution should say so.[48]

Whether this analysis of Lloyd George's position is entirely accurate is beside the point; he was against the Bill. Clearly Brailsford considered Churchill onside just then, as he probably was. However, at some point immediately before the Second Reading, the Home Secretary had a change of mind, or perhaps of heart. The second-hand account retrospectively related by Lucy Masterman has it thus:

Winston and Charlie had a very curious morning over the Conciliation Bill (Women's Suffrage). He is, in a rather tepid manner, a suffragist (his wife is very keen) and he came down to the Home Office intending to vote for the Bill. Charlie, whose sympathy with the suffragettes is rather on the wane, did not want him to, nor did Lloyd George. So Charlie began to put to him the points against Shackleton's Bill – its undemocratic nature, and especially particular points, such as that 'fallen women' would have the vote but not the mother of a family, and other rhetorical points. Winston began to see the opportunity for a speech on these lines, and as he paced up and down the room, began to roll off long phrases. By the end of the morning he was convinced that he had always been hostile to the Bill and that he had already thought of all these points himself ... Charlie thinks that his *mind* had up till then been in favour of the suffrage but that his *instinct* was always against it. He snatched at Charlie's arguments against this particular Bill as a wild animal snatches at its food. At the end the instinct had completely triumphed over the mind.[49]

Lucy Masterman is not necessarily a wholly reliable source, as will be discussed at more length in Chapter 8, so whether this account as to why Churchill's opinion changed is entirely accurate must remain arguable. That he became a vehement opponent of the Bill is, however, beyond dispute, though he did not speak at all on the first day of the debate, whilst Lloyd George only did so on a point of order. He intervened early the next day, though, being the fifth MP to speak, and began by stating that he believed 'there is a proportion of women capable of exercising the Parliamentary franchise, not merely for their own satisfaction, but to the public advantage' and that disqualification from voting on the grounds of sex 'is not in accordance with obvious facts'. This was followed, though, by a contrariwise point:

On the other hand, I think the grievance is greatly exaggerated. I think the great mass of women are not in any sensible degree losers by the disability under which they lie. It cannot be proved that they suffer any disadvantage in legislation. The Statute Book in fact leaves them a privileged class.[50]

Neither did he believe that 'the great mass of women want a vote'. He went on to add that 'they have made singularly little use of the immense opportunities of local and municipal government which have been thrown open to them.

Although there are numerous brilliant exceptions, these exceptions do not alter the actual fact.'

Continuing, he added that he was not 'in the least convinced that the male electorate of the country is in favour of making a change'. Furthermore, and this moved from the general to the particular in respect of the Bill in question, he foresaw 'a grave danger in creating without great consideration a vast body of privileged and dependent voters, who might be manipulated and manoeuvred in this direction or that'.

The potential for manipulation, as he explained it, related to plural voting: 'At present a man can exercise the franchise several times, but he has to do it in different constituencies. But under this Bill, as I read it, he would be able to exercise his vote once or twice or three times in the same constituency if he were a wealthy man.' The method by which this might be achieved was via faggot voting; if the Bill passed into law, then the wealthy man:

> if he owned a house and stable, or other separate building ... could give one vote to his wife in respect of the house, and take the other himself in respect of the stable. I am told it is quite open to question whether it would not be possible for a wealthy man with a large family or retinue of dependents to multiply faggot votes by letting to them any property of the value of £10 within his own residence. From every point of view it is clear that there would be a great multiplication of property votes, while no such expedients would be open to the working people and the poor.[51]

There was more in much the same vein, as well as the observation that 'There is no end to the grotesque absurdities that would follow the passing of this particular measure. It would be possible for women to have a vote while living in a state of prostitution; if she married and became an honest woman she would lose that vote, but she could regain it through divorce.'

Throughout he emphasised that the points he was making were his own personal opinions, as opposed to those of the Government or Liberal Party, but towards the end he indulged in a dig at both the Opposition and those on his own side who espoused a different perspective:

> I think it very creditable ... [that] ... the Unionist party opposite ... should resist a measure which I have not the slightest hesitation in saying would be a great party and electoral advantage to them. I can easily understand some of them voting for it ... but I am bound to say when I see a Liberal Member or a Labour Member voting for provisions like this I feel he must either be very innocent or must have been intimidated.

Having characterised the Bill as not merely undemocratic but actually anti-democratic – 'It is not merely an undemocratic Bill; it is worse. It is an anti-democratic Bill' – he would obviously not vote for it. His final sentence was: 'I shall, after long reflection, and without any doubt whatever, give my vote this evening for the rejection of this measure on the Second Reading.'

Lloyd George later observed that he didn't think it was necessary for him to take part in the debate, because his point of view had been 'presented with such power and force by my right hon. Friend the Home Secretary earlier in the evening'.[52] Nevertheless, as Sylvia Pankhurst observed, 'he refrained from depreciating the abstract principle of Women's Suffrage as the Home Secretary had done, and directed his attack wholly against the terms of the Bill'.[53] Arthur Balfour, who had spoken before the Chancellor, had, though, indulged in a modicum of mockery at Churchill's expense:

> There is no use in manipulating the word 'democracy' and turning it round and round when we all know exactly why it is used. It is used in order to enable hon. Gentlemen opposite, who willingly or unwillingly have allowed themselves to become inconveniently pledged to women suffrage, to get out of those pledges on some broad ground.[54]

This shaft might well have gone home. Certainly the general, opening, remarks of Churchill's speech did not utilise the language of someone totally committed to the principle of female suffrage. However, and despite some heavyweight opposition, the question 'That the Bill be referred to a Committee of the Whole House' was carried by 320 votes to 175. Given that the House of Commons adjourned on 3 August, and did not reconvene until 15 November 1910, the Bill was effectively killed.

Notwithstanding that, Churchill's attacks on measures he was thought to support outraged those behind the Conciliation Bill. Brailsford wrote to him following the debate in terms which, in only a slightly earlier age, would have resulted in pistols at dawn:

> I beg to inform you that in discussing your conduct in today's debate, I shall be obliged to describe it as treacherous. You knew when you 'welcomed the formation' of the Conciliation Committee the nature of the Bill it was drafting ... If you consider yourself insulted, I am at your service, and will study your convenience in making arrangements for a meeting.[55]

There was to be no trading of gunfire but this missive heralded a furious epistolary exchange, one which intensified when Lord Lytton joined in. Whereas previous communications between the two had been of the 'Dear Winston/ Lytton' and 'Yours ever' variety, they now began with 'Dear Sir/My Lord' and ended 'Yours faithfully'. Churchill defended himself vigorously and at length, though of course the debate was essentially sterile, and went so far as to compose a substantial memorandum marked 'Not for publication', the object of which was to 'place on record a full account of the circumstances'.[56] Written in the third person, it deals mostly with the minutiae of who said what and when, but it also offers some insight into the mind of its author. For example:

> Lord Lytton's attitude has always assumed that it was Mr Churchill's duty, without delay, to remedy the great injustice under which women suffer by

being excluded from the franchise, and to atone for his neglect to do so in the past. Mr Churchill's view has been that although in principle the absolute sex barrier is illogical, yet there has been no great practical grievance; and, further, that in any case the militant suffragists have less claim on him than any other public man. For the last five years, these people have attempted in the course of their agitation to break up every meeting he has addressed in any part of the country. They have opposed him with the whole strength of their organisations at four successive elections. If Mr Churchill has been returned three times out of four, it has been in spite of the utmost opposition which the Women Suffragists could offer. They have at all times treated him with the vilest discourtesy and unfairness. They have assaulted him physically. Shortly before the last election at Dundee he informed a deputation of his woman constituents that he would give them no pledge whatsoever of any assistance in the immediate future. In consequence of this he was again opposed by the suffragist organisations throughout the campaign, and his return by a majority of six thousand clearly left him with the fullest liberty of action. There could be no question of his being under any obligation or of any claim of any sort being urged against him.[57]

The Memorandum goes on to state that he did not finally decide what action he should take as regards the Bill and its second reading until two days before the debate. Two issues prompted him to speak as he did, the first being that it was only at that point that he actually studied the Bill properly, and thereby discovered 'a long succession of vices and faults of which he had no previous knowledge'. The Bill, he was now convinced, was 'not only absurd and indefensible in itself, but deeply injurious to the Liberal cause by reason of its partiality'. The second reason was in order to support Asquith and Lloyd George:

Mr Churchill felt that the Prime Minister's position after the debate and division would become one not unattended with danger. He thought it would be very cowardly if in face of such threats he allowed the Prime Minister and the Chancellor ... to take the whole burden of this upon their shoulders, while all the time he agreed with them, and was known to agree with them, that the Bill was a bad bill and ought not to pass ...[58]

The Bill did, however, pass, even if its prospects were decidedly inauspicious, and Churchill obviously knew this when he authored the memorandum. The wording he used in respect of the general principle of female suffrage echoed that of his speech in the House of Commons: that although denying women the vote was illogical, yet there 'has been no great practical grievance'. This, as already argued, was not the phraseology typical of someone committed to eradicating that illogicality.

His arguments about the vices and faults inherent in the Bill, albeit discovered rather late in the day, are founded on somewhat firmer ground; Churchill had, for example, publicly stated at the Manchester Free Trade Hall in February 1907 that he 'would not vote for a Bill to enfranchise women on the same terms as men'.[59] Yet the 'Conciliation Bill' did not seek to do that. It was, as the popular name given it suggested, a compromise; an attempt to find a formula that a majority in Parliament could agree on. It would not have doubled the electorate. Rather, by merely adding those women who already held the municipal franchise to the Parliamentary electoral roll, it would have increased the latter by around one million.[60] The stated concerns both in the Commons and the Memorandum about faggot voting, although they were shared by many others, could be said to display a distinct lack of faith in female capacity to act independently. No matter how wealthy the man, he could not monitor how his wife or daughters might use the vote he had gifted them; all electors, since the 1872 Ballot Act, whether voting in municipal or parliamentary elections, cast their votes in secret.

All in all, it is little wonder that Churchill's attitude to female emancipation was considered ambivalent and, as Lucy Masterman recalled, 'tepid'. This could not have contributed to domestic bliss in the Churchill household. Clementine was in favour of female suffrage[61] and, according to the recollection of Llewelyn Williams, the Liberal MP for Carmarthen Boroughs, whose wife and sister-in-law observed the proceedings from the Ladies' Gallery of the House of Commons, she was 'very angry and disappointed in her husband's attitude [as] she understood from him until 2 or 3 days previously that he was going to vote for the Bill'.[62]

However, and despite his hostility, the Bill passed, the dangers he perceived, and wanted to share with Asquith and Lloyd George, did not materialise, and the truce declared by Emmeline Pankhurst in January held. As she put it: 'Those who still had faith that the Government could be induced to do justice to women set their hopes on the autumn session of Parliament.'[63] Sylvia Pankhurst noted, however, that in October there were already signs that 'the truce of the militants, which had lasted for nine months, would soon be at an end'.[64] According to her account it was Asquith who finally broke it. A group of women from his East Fife constituency met him on 27 October 1910, and were told that facilities for progressing the Bill could not be granted before the end of the year.[65] As for the following year, he would only answer 'wait and see'. Therefore:

> at a great meeting in the Albert Hall on November 10th the truce broke – war was once more declared. Mrs [Emmeline] Pankhurst announced that another deputation would march to the House of Commons to carry a petition to the Prime Minister. She herself would lead the deputation ...[66]

The march was set for 18 November, coincidentally the same day that Asquith announced that, since the constitutional crisis had not been resolved, he intended to call a general election to obtain a mandate for the reform of the House of Lords. Though the truce was over, there is no suggestion that the marchers, generally regarded to have been some 300 strong, though Sylvia Pankhurst reckoned 450, were bent on trouble.[67] Nevertheless, trouble there certainly was.

It was claimed by Sylvia Pankhurst in an article published the following week that the contingent ordinarily responsible for the Houses of Parliament and environs, the men of A (Whitehall) Division of the Metropolitan Police, had been replaced in the front line. Instead, on 18 November, the officers of A Division were:

> only on duty close to the House of Commons and at the police station, and that those with whom the women chiefly came in contact had been especially brought in from the outlying districts. During our conflicts with the A Division they have gradually come to know us, and to understand our aims and objects, and for this reason, whilst obeying their orders, they came to treat the women, as far as possible, with courtesy and consideration. But these men with whom we had to deal on Friday were ignorant and ill-mannered and of an entirely different type.[68]

This report is probably the origin of the accounts which state that police from the East End, who were more accustomed to dealing with the great unwashed than (mainly) middle-class ladies, were responsible for the scenes that followed. Christopher Bearman has, however, shown that police from at least nine divisions (of the twenty-two operational divisions into which the Metropolitan Police were divided) were present, not all of whom were based in the East End.[69] It is also the case that available police manpower had been depleted by the despatch of 758 officers to south Wales.[70] In any event, and according to the Commissioner of Police's subsequent explanation of the tactics adopted on the day, the police were instructed to act with restraint and moderation, to use minimum force to disperse the demonstration, and to remain calm in the face of 'any provocation they might receive'. No other orders as to how to deal with the demonstrators were disseminated.[71]

The women's attempts to pass through the police cordon, which included contingents of mounted officers, swiftly degenerated into violence. This resulted, according to the accounts of many involved, in ferocious brutality towards the suffragettes. The next day's edition of the *Daily Mirror* published a photograph[72] of one of the women laid out on the street, which was captioned: 'Above is illustrated one of yesterday's incidents. A woman has fallen down while struggling, and she is in a fainting condition. The photograph shows how far women will go for the vote.'[73] In fact, rather than having fainted and fallen, or vice versa, the stricken woman had been felled by the police. Or at least according to Sylvia Pankhurst's account, which identified her as 50-year-old Miss Ada Cécile Granville Wright; a woman of 'culture and refinement and of sheltered upbringing',[74] she was also a veteran suffragette.[75] In an account published some eight days after the event, she claimed to have seen Ada Wright when:

> several police seized her, lifted her from the ground and flung her back into the crowd. A moment afterwards she appeared again, and I saw her running as fast as she could towards the House of Commons. A policeman struck her

with all his force and she fell to the ground. For a moment there was a group of struggling men round the place where she lay, then she rose up only to be flung down again immediately. Then a tall, grey headed man with a silk hat was seen fighting to protect her, but three or four police seized hold of him and bundled him away. Then again I saw Miss Ada Wright's tall, grey-clad, figure but over and over she was flung to the ground, how often I cannot say. It was a painful and degrading sight. At last she was lying against the wall of the House of Lords, close to the Strangers' Entrance, and a number of women, with pale and distressed faces, were kneeling down round her. She was in a state of collapse.[76]

The photograph of Ada Wright – 'lying prostrate at the feet of her tormentors', as Churchill was informed by an outraged correspondent the following month[77] – became iconic for the suffragette movement and an embarrassment to the Government. That day, 18 November 1910, was subsequently dubbed Black Friday by the suffragette movement, and Ada Wright was far from being the only suffragette to claim to have suffered outrage at the hands of the police that day.

As noted, Churchill's promotion to Home Secretary more or less coincided with the truce called by Emmeline Pankhurst. The events of 18 November were then the first significant raid, the contemporary term for a suffragette demonstration, to occur on his watch. According to him, as he later explained the matter to the House of Commons, the Home Office policy adopted by Gladstone during his tenure had been for the police 'to avoid so far as practicable arresting women for merely technical obstruction'. This had the effect, as he described it, of 'allowing the disorder to continue for a long time, during which the women work themselves into a high state of hysteria, expose themselves to rough horseplay at the hands of an unsympathetic crowd, and finally collapse from the exhaustion of their own exertions'.[78] In adhering to this policy the police, rather than arresting those attempting to approach Parliament, simply blocked their way and pushed them back. As a press report explained it:

the police in front of the gate at the corner of Parliament-street and Bridge-street were kept busy repelling the raiders, some of whom came up smiling every time to the attack, while a few scolded like viragoes and most were simply stolid. They were in every case seized and pushed, sometimes carried, to the other side of Bridge-street. The horse and motor traffic there was not stopped, but was somewhat hindered.[79]

It was during this seizing and pushing, the latter meaning they were thrust into the mainly male crowd gathered to watch, that a large number of violent attacks, including sexual assaults, were alleged to have taken place.[80] To quote David Mitchell: 'Clothes were ripped, hands thrust into upper and middle-class bosoms and up expensive skirts.'[81] These scenes continued for some five hours, and only towards the end were arrests made: thus it was that four men and 115 women were scheduled to appear before stipendiary magistrate Henry Curtis Bennett at

Bow Street Police Court the following morning. Or rather, as Emmeline Pankhurst related it:

> they were kept waiting outside the court room while Mr Muskett [police
> solicitor Herbert Muskett], who prosecuted on behalf of the Chief Com-
> missioner of Police, explained to the astounded magistrate that he had
> received orders from the Home Secretary that the prisoners should all be
> discharged. Mr Churchill, it was declared, had had the matter under careful
> consideration, and had decided that 'no public advantage would be gained by
> proceeding with the prosecution, and accordingly no evidence would be
> given against the prisoners'.[82]

Christabel Pankhurst concluded that 'Public policy apparently meant election
policy ...'.[83] Elements of the press were of much the same opinion even before
the event:

> a deputation of about 300 women will march in procession to Parliament-
> square with the object of fighting its way into St Stephens Hall. Should a
> large number of women be imprisoned on the eve of the election, the
> suffragists hope that that course would provoke a revolt among the Liberal
> women who work for the party at the election.[84]

Emmeline Pankhurst, in a widely syndicated interview given to the Press Association soon after the court proceedings, proclaimed the decision as 'an admission
... of the great injustice practised by the Government in the past in imprisoning
many women for long periods as common criminals for the same action as that
taken by the deputation on Friday'.[85] Conservative opinion, as expressed in
The Times, was outraged:

> What does the Home Secretary mean? That question will be asked by many
> who read our report of the proceedings ... and the extraordinary ending to
> those proceedings ... There was no question of an accidental breach of the
> peace. The raid on Friday was deliberate and persisted in ... It was not a
> sudden outburst of passion ... The persons charged belonged to the well-to-
> do classes, and doubtless after assaulting the police they went to comfortable
> homes or clubs. What extenuating element is there in these circumstances?[86]

What the Home Secretary meant can only be conjectured. Randolph Churchill
records that 'hostile critics' viewed it as 'a device for preventing their [suffragette]
grievances being publicly aired in court'.[87] Some scholars consider it a tacit quid
pro quo; if there were no prosecution of suffragettes, then the behaviour of the
police towards them would not require investigation either.[88] If this was indeed
the exchange Churchill had in mind, then he miscalculated, or at least inasmuch
as there arose a loud clamour for just such an enquiry.

Whatever the reason for his decision, and it was most likely to have been based
on 'election policy', the Home Secretary was displeased with how the police had
handled matters on the day. He wrote to the Metropolitan Police Commissioner,

Sir Edward Henry, on 22 November expressing his discontent and laying down how he wanted the suffragettes dealt with from then on:

> I am hearing from every quarter that my strongly expressed wishes conveyed to you on Wed[nesday] evening & repeated on Fri[day] morning that the suffragettes were not to be allowed to exhaust themselves but were to be arrested forthwith upon any defiance of the law, were not observed by the police on Friday last, with the result that v[er]y regrettable scenes occurred. It was my desire to avoid this even at some risk; to arrest large numbers & then subsequently to prosecute only where serious grounds were shown & I am sorry that, no doubt through a misunderstanding, another course has been adopted. In future I must ask for a strict adherence to the policy outlined herein.[89]

There appears to be no documentary record of Churchill's 'strongly expressed wishes', though it seems entirely possible that he conveyed them verbally, perhaps by telephone. In any case, Sir Edward did not have time to impress upon his subordinates this written restatement of Churchill's policy. As he informed the Home Secretary, his men were 'already out on the streets' dealing with their next large-scale encounter with the suffragettes.[90] This became known as the 'Battle of Downing Street', and took place on the date of Churchill's letter.

The 'battle' came about following an announcement by Asquith, in response to a question from Keir Hardie concerning female suffrage, that: 'The Government will, if they are still in power, give facilities in the next Parliament for effectively proceeding with a Bill which is so framed as to admit of free Amendment.' Awaiting this answer was a large contingent of suffragettes assembled at Caxton Hall, a mere half mile or so away from Downing Street, with Emmeline Pankhurst at their head. Also present was Christabel Pankhurst who, upon receiving news of what Asquith had said, announced that it was 'an absurd mockery of a pledge'. Her mother then informed the gathering that 'I am going to Downing Street. Come along, all of you.'[91] Thus 'Frail little Mrs Pankhurst' personally led her 'army of Amazons' into battle.[92]

According to one contemporary report, 'a column of militant suffragists over a hundred strong left Caxton Hall for the Prime Minister's residence'.[93] It seems likely that Emmeline Pankhurst's spontaneity wrong-footed the police, who were not deployed at Downing Street in any strength. Those who were there attempted to keep the women out but were unable to do so completely. In the vanguard was the distinguished mathematician and physicist Hertha Ayrton, the first woman to be proposed for fellowship of the British Royal Society.[94] She described a close-combat technique used by the police, and what it was like to be on the receiving end of it:

> I was marching immediately behind Mrs Pankhurst when she entered Downing Street, but was prevented from reaching No. 10 by an attempt at strangulation on the part of a policeman ... Twice, policemen seized me by

the throat and jerked my head back till it felt as if my neck would break, so that I quite lost my breath and half lost consciousness for a time; indeed I must have fallen down and been trampled on, as were other women ...[95]

Many of the suffragettes were undoubtedly of somewhat advanced years for fighting policemen and rolling around on the cobbles. Nevertheless, according to one press report: 'they hurled themselves on the thin line of police so fiercely that they won inch by inch ... It was not a pleasant sight. The police met force with force. Over a dozen women were lying on the ground and several policemen were also thrown down.'[96] Some of the women got through the police cordon and attempts were made to smash windows in Number 10, but police reinforcements arrived at the run and began the process of clearing the street and pushing the suffragettes back. The fight, as newspaper accounts had it, was 'short, sharp, and decisive' and lasted for some ten minutes.[97] The Home Secretary also arrived on the scene at about this time and was reported to be 'angry', particularly when he observed someone he knew: 57-year-old Anne Cobden-Sanderson. Her husband noted in his journal her version of what happened:

> Annie was in one of the raids on Tuesday on Downing Street, and was left by the surging police alone, after they had driven out all the main mass of them, for she had fallen to the ground. On getting up she saw Winston Churchill approaching with a bevy of policemen. She went towards him to speak to him. 'What is that woman doing here?' he exclaimed, addressing his police. And instantly they laid hands on her, he looking on, and hustled her down the stairs into the Park, she protesting the while and claiming her freedom, or, if she had done an illegal act, to be arrested and charged with it, and not to be thus violently assaulted.[98]

An essentially similar account appeared in the newspapers, though this had her sitting 'quietly on the sill of one of the Colonial Office windows' rather than lying on the ground. According to this version, upon her approaching Churchill to speak to him, he 'angrily' asked a police inspector 'Why do you allow these women to hang about in the streets in this way? Clear them out.'[99] Though he gives no source, Randolph Churchill has a slightly different form of words: 'Take that woman away; she is obviously one of the ringleaders.'[100] Whatever he might have said, this event was to figure in an event with personal consequences for the Home Secretary some four days later, but more immediately the mass of suffragettes ejected from Downing Street had been pressed down Whitehall in the direction of Parliament Square.

There the Prime Minister, who had left the House of Commons on foot, was spotted and 'the angry and baffled women made for him with angry cries and gestures'.[101] The attack made international news, with the *New York Times* featuring a syndicated report stating that: 'Shrill police whistles brought officers from all nearby quarters, and as the women struggled frantically among themselves for the privilege of getting at him, the premier was hustled into a taxicab.'[102]

Not so closely guarded, nor as fortunate, was Augustine Birrell. Also on foot, and heading for the Athenaeum Club in Pall Mall, he was spotted in the vicinity of St James Park and set upon: 'They knocked Mr Birrell's hat over his eyes, hustled him, and one of them kicked him on the shin. Police and others intervened, and a gentleman offered the Cabinet Minister the use of his car, but Mr Birrell limped on to the Athenaeum.'[103] Whilst he was there some windows of his London house were smashed, as were those of several other ministers including John Burns, Churchill, Sir Edward Grey and Lewis Harcourt.[104] Alice Hawkins, a middle-aged working-class suffragette from Leicester, explained the rationale behind this, or at least as she perceived it:

> The police were simply horrid, and they banged and fought like a lot of tigers at times. After a large number of arrests they eventually got us out of the street into Whitehall. After about an hour, I was simply done up and made up my mind to do something else ... When a number of women went out to break Cabinet Ministers' windows, I volunteered to lead twelve to Mr Harcourt's house ... It was easier to break windows than have my body broken.[105]

Some scholars have seen this calculation, that it was 'easier to break windows' than attempt to fight an almost inevitably losing battle with policemen, as applying more widely. In other words, that after their experiences on Black Friday and at the Battle of Downing Street many suffragettes decided on a change of tactics.[106] Given the superior physicality of their opponents – Shpayer-Makov describes the Metropolitan Police manpower of the period as being low-paid and indifferently educated, but physically strong and taller than average[107] – this made perfect sense. Christabel Pankhurst phrased it thus: 'More and more, our women were insisting that a broken window was a lesser evil than a broken body, besides being, seemingly, more impressive to political opponents.'[108]

Those arrested during the course of the day, some 150 in total, duly found themselves arraigned before Chief Magistrate Sir Albert de Rutzen at Bow Street the following morning. Once again Herbert Muskett was prosecuting and, once again, he found himself explaining that, following consultation with the Home Secretary on the previous evening, he would ask that all cases of simple obstruction and resistance to the police should be withdrawn. Only those charges that related to stone-throwing and other malicious damage would be proceeded with. Sir Albert enquired as to whether he was to understand that 'the police are responsible for the course of action which you now take?' The reply, that Muskett was acting on behalf of the police authority for the Metropolis, the Secretary of State for the Home Office, caused de Rutzen to protest:

> This course of action appears to me to impose a hardship on certain prisoners. I have had one or two letters from people who happened to be charged who said that they absolutely did nothing which justified their being taken into custody, and then, when they are brought here, no evidence is

offered and no opportunity is given them of proving that they gave no reason for being taken to the [police] station. That is the effect of it, and, in my opinion, it throws great hardship upon the individual.[109]

Muskett could only reply that 'Any observations made by the court will be reported to the proper quarters', which drew the response that, 'This practice has never been adopted in the 30 years I have sat here as magistrate.'[110] Churchill's novel approach on this second occasion can likely be again attributed to 'election policy' and there is no doubt that he cleared his decision with the Prime Minister. Asquith mentioned the subject in a short note concerning the attack on Augustine Birrell, which being still under investigation was not dealt with at that time: 'The assault on Birrell seems to have been a serious one, and I think that case should be proceeded with: also all cases of *serious* assault on the police.'[111]

Two days later, in the House of Commons, Henry Chancellor, the Liberal MP for Shoreditch Haggerston, questioned his colleague about what instruction had been issued to the police the previous Friday. He also asked whether the Home Secretary was aware that in many cases unnecessary violence, requiring medical treatment, was used before arrests were carried out. Finally: 'whether he will inquire into the conduct of the police on that occasion and issue instructions to prevent a repetition of such conduct'. Churchill's reply was to encompass several themes from which he was never to deviate:

I find on inquiry that the police for the most part acted under the instruction which has been in force for some time, that they should avoid, as far as prac-ticable, making arrests. The result was that some of the ladies who desired to be arrested, made repeated efforts, and no doubt a few of them exhausted themselves and may have required medical treatment. Several used a good deal of force, as six of the police were reported injured. I am sorry that the arrests of those who violated the law and endangered their own safety in the crowd were in some cases so long delayed. My intention was that arrests should be made as soon as there was a lawful reason. On subsequent occa-sions those who have resisted the police in the performance of their duty have, in their own interest, been promptly taken into custody.'[112]

As already noted, many of those taken into custody were released before trial, but one case that did proceed through the Bow Street Court, though not until 28 November, involved an attempted assault on the Home Secretary himself. This had occurred two days earlier and the assailant was male: one Hugh Frank-lin. Franklin was well connected, being private secretary to Lieutenant Colonel Sir Matthew Nathan, Secretary of the Post Office, a position he had undoubtedly obtained through the influence of his uncle, Herbert Samuel the Postmaster General.[113] He was also a member of the recently founded militant 'Men's Polit-ical Union for Women's Enfranchisement'. These 'Suffragettes in Trousers'[114] were able to access political meetings from which women were often auto-matically excluded in case they were suffragettes and Franklin had attended, and been ejected from, a meeting which Churchill had addressed at Bradford on 26 November. According to his later testimony, it was by chance that he later found himself on the same London-bound train as the Home Secretary.[115] Whilst en route Franklin attempted to attack Churchill. The evidence given by Sergeant Joseph Sandercock of New Scotland Yard, who was accompanying the Home Secretary, had it thus: 'the prisoner [Franklin] jumped up, drew a dog whip from his pocket and shouted "Winston Churchill, take that, you dirty cur".'[116] Sandercock intervened, thwarting the assault, and though Franklin disputed the words used, he admitted that he had intended to whip Churchill. He also stated that one motivating factor was a conversation he had with Anne Cobden-Sanderson on 22 November after she had been ejected from Downing Street.[117] Franklin was jailed for six weeks,[118] but accusations he made about the Home Secretary ordering the police to use brutal methods on the suffragettes echoed the case being propagated by the WSPU. He expanded on this, and indeed the entire episode, in an article he must have authored whilst inside:

> When a man is responsible for having women knocked about and physically injured by others – when, in addition, he insults them to their face and slanders them behind their back – he deserves a whipping ... It was because I held Mr Churchill guilty on every one of these counts that I determined to punish him in the only way which was open to me ... On Tuesday, November 22 ... I encountered Mrs Cobden-Sanderson faint from exhaustion from a struggle in which she had taken part. She is the daughter of the man whom Liberal statesmen profess to honour. But how does Mr Churchill deal with her? 'Turn that woman away! Don't let anyone within here.' These are the words he addresses to the police with regard to her. When will Cabinet Ministers know that their position does not give them the right to insult women?[119]

It is clear that the activities of the militant suffragists, both of the skirted and trousered variety, exasperated Churchill to a large degree. The appearance of Franklin's piece led him to propose raising an action for libel, and he went so far as to have the offending article clipped and sent to the Solicitor-General, Sir John Simon.[120] The advice he received was firmly against the notion:

> I would strongly urge you *not* to take proceedings ... the cases are very rare in which a Minister ought to defend himself by himself taking action in the Courts for injurious statements, and it seems to me that for the Home Secretary personally to pursue a creature who has already [been] sentenced for an assault on him would be most unwise ... I think it is probable that you will have arrived at the same conclusion as I. I feel quite clear about it.[121]

Advice along similar lines had been received from the Director of Public Prosecutions earlier, concerning whether or not it would be feasible to take action against suffragettes who advocated violence; the particular case involved a suffragette meeting at the Queen's Hall on 28 November.[122]

Churchill likely received that letter whilst at Dundee. He was in his constituency on 1 December and is recorded as receiving a delegation from the Dundee branch of the National Union of Women's Suffrage Societies in the Queens Hotel on that day. He assured his visitors that he had 'not wavered in his opinion that the sex disqualification should be removed. He had always been a supporter of this movement ...'. However, he went on to add that:

there was nothing he more bitterly regretted, for he had been assailed by accusations of hypocrisy and treachery, by outrageous insults of every kind ... He dwelt with warm indignation on the policy of the militant societies, and expressed a strong conviction of their disastrous effects upon the public mind.[123]

Great precautions were taken by Churchill to avoid the attentions of 'the militant societies' during his campaign. On 5 December he was back in his constituency to speak at the King's Theatre to a male-only audience. All women were excluded, and four men spent the previous night on the roof of the building in order to prevent attempts at female infiltration.[124]

He didn't manage to avoid trouble entirely, however. Ethel Moorhead, 'Dundee's Rowdiest Suffragette', managed to get into one of his meetings and at an opportune moment, attempted to hit him with an egg. It missed, falling at the feet of Sir Charles Barrie, a former Lord Provost of Dundee, whereupon she was 'ejected with great violence by three Liberal stewards, while attempting to hit Mr William Smith the Liberal Organiser with her umbrella. Many women stood on the seats to watch; Mr Churchill was a silent observer of the proceedings.'[125] He was, though, spared anything like the attention he remembered many years later receiving from 'la Belle Maloney', that 'peculiarly virulent Scotch virago armed with a large dinner-bell'.[126]

Following the General Election, and with the parliamentary arithmetic much the same as before, a new Women's Enfranchisement Bill, or second Conciliation Bill, had its First Reading in the House of Commons on 9 February 1911.[127] Whilst that was looking to the future, an account of the events of the previous November had been compiled and handed to the Home Office a week earlier (it was also published as a short booklet which sold for sixpence). The authors, Jessie Murray and Henry Brailsford, had collected 135 statements from those involved in the demonstrations, nearly all of them describing overly violent acts by policemen, with twenty-nine of that total being deemed 'consciously sensual' – what a later legal age would probably deem indecent and/or sexual assaults.[128]

Churchill was asked in Parliament on 1 March if he had received the document, had considered it, and 'what reply had been given to the request for an inquiry?' The answer, in terms of accusations both general and particular, was dismissive. The 'memorandum', he stated:

contains a large number of charges against the police of criminal misconduct, which, if there were any truth in them, should have been made at the time and not after a lapse of three months, and should, if they could be supported by evidence, have been preferred in a police court ... There is no truth in the statement that the police had instructions which led them to terrorise and maltreat the women.[129]

There would, of course, be no public enquiry into what he deemed 'vague and general charges' which had only been collected via advertisements in *Votes for Women* and 'brought forward by irresponsible persons long after the event'. The alleged sexual assaults were likely the work of men in the crowd which had gathered. This multitude, he argued, had only come together in response to invitations 'scattered broadcast' by the suffragettes and 'it contained a large number of undesirable and reckless persons quite capable of indulging in gross conduct. It is perfectly possible that some of these were guilty of the indecencies alleged, and for their presence in Parliament Square the women themselves are responsible.'[130] This was indeed 'warm indignation on the policy of the militant societies', though difficult to distinguish from what might, with a high degree of accuracy, be termed victim-blaming.

Churchill was questioned about his role in the November 1910 disturbances nine days later by Henry Cavendish-Bentinck, known as Lord Henry Bentinck, the Conservative MP for Nottingham South. Bentinck wanted to know 'the exact wording of the instruction to make as few arrests as practicable, under which the Metropolitan Police were acting in dealing with the women's deputations on 18th and 22nd November last'. Bentinck also asked whether the orders had been verbal or written, and whether they had actually reached the men involved.[131] The Home Secretary's written answer stated that: 'No fresh instructions, verbal or written, were issued to the police on or before 18th November.'[132]

This unqualified statement jars somewhat with his message to Sir Edward Henry of 22 November 1910 already quoted. The difference between his twice transmitted 'strongly expressed wishes' and 'instructions' or 'orders' is surely a matter of semantics. That communication was, though, not in the public domain, so any contradictions arising remained unknown. Churchill did, however, reiterate the final part of it and once more blamed the women for the nature of the disturbances which had occurred: 'I have given explicit instructions that in the future, with a view to the avoidance of disagreeable scenes, for which no one is responsible but the disorderly women themselves, police officers shall be told to make arrests as soon as there is lawful occasion.' His peroration too was a variation on that theme:

I have given the Noble Lord a full answer on the subject of his question, but I cannot conclude it without reaffirming my conviction, that the Metropolitan Police behaved on 18th November with the forbearance and humanity for which they have always been distinguished, and again repudiating the unsupported allegations which have issued from that copious fountain of mendacity, the Women's Social and Political Union.[133]

Christabel Pankhurst was having none of it. At a WPSU meeting held that evening in Steinway Hall she laid into the Home Secretary in no uncertain, though not necessarily entirely accurate, terms. According to a report of the speech she stated:

> It was quite notorious, a matter of everyday and universal knowledge ... that the women who went to Westminster in November, 1910, were brutally and in many cases indecently ill-treated by the police acting under the orders of the Home Secretary ... They knew perfectly well that had the police been left to their own devices, they would have behaved as men and gentlemen.[134]

This seems to have annoyed Churchill to the extent that legal advice as to the possibility of prosecuting Christabel Pankhurst or *The Times*, or presumably both, for libel was sought by Sir Edward Troup from the Director of Public Prosecutions.[135] It is possible, though there is no evidence, that Christabel Pankhurst said what she did in order to provoke just that reaction. Formidably intelligent, she had graduated with a First Class Degree in Law in 1906, being the only female on the course and sharing that level of attainment with only one other student.[136] Despite being debarred from pursuing law as a career, she had nevertheless defended herself in court in the 1908 'Rush the Commons' Case, calling Lloyd George and Herbert Gladstone as witnesses and skilfully questioning them both.[137] She may well have relished subjecting Churchill to cross-examination, and the publicity would have been colossal. No reply to Troup's letter seems to have survived, but given that no action was taken it seems likely that it would have contained advice, as per previous opinion in the same context, not to proceed.

Churchill's claim that charges against the police of criminal misconduct should have been made at the time, and not after a lapse of three months, provoked a public response from Mrs Saul Solomon (Georgiana Margaret Solomon). She wrote an indignant letter to *The Times* stating that she had complained of police brutality on Black Friday in a letter to the Home Secretary of 17 December 1910. This date, she explained, was the first occasion on which she had been capable of writing as a 'consequence of the shameful brutality which I experienced [at the hands of the police]'.[138] The Home Secretary also received a communication from one of his parliamentary colleagues, Ellis Griffith, the MP for Anglesey and a distinguished lawyer. This urged him to reconsider his refusal to hold an enquiry into police behaviour on 18 November, given subsequent statements made by women. The response was that there could be no departure from the 'position indicated in H[ouse] of C[ommons] answers'.[139]

This argument, basically that there was no case to answer, was of course fiercely contested, and the Home Secretary's supposed behaviour in respect of Black Friday became fixed in suffragette and indeed popular mythology alongside Tonypandy, the riots there having taken place only some ten days earlier. In fact, the evidence that Churchill issued orders to utilise policemen drafted in from the East End, with the specific intent of inflicting brutal treatment on the suffragettes, is non-existent. It is also the case, as Caroline Morrell has noted, that the events of Black Friday were largely unexceptional in terms of violence towards suffragette raids: 'It was one of a long series of deputations to Parliament and violence had occurred on nearly all of them.'[140] She cites Ray Strachey in support.[141]

There were many comparable accounts, an example being by the 'radical suffragette' Kitty Marion, who wrote, in her unpublished autobiography, that after an attempt to approach Parliament in 1908 she found her 'arms and shoulders black, blue and painful, as were every woman's who had taken part'.[142] Sylvia Pankhurst told similar tales, one such concerning marches on Parliament in 1907: 'a large section of both Press and public were unanimous in condemning the Government for the violent measures which it had employed to suppress the women's deputation. Many compared the sending out of mounted police against a procession of unarmed women to the employment of Cossacks in Russia ...'[143]

It follows that Christabel Pankhurst's claim that the police on Black Friday would have behaved differently, 'as men and gentlemen', without Churchill's instruction to do otherwise was probably baiting him; she knew that they had always acted in much the same way.[144] However, what seems to have marked out Black Friday as exceptional, apart from being the first raid after a hiatus occasioned by the truce, was that the degree of violence was extraordinary compared to earlier confrontations, and that there were multiple accusations of sexual/indecent assault. The complaints arising were, as has been shown, contemptuously dismissed by the Home Secretary, whilst scepticism concerning his involvement was only increased by the decision to discontinue prosecutions of those charged. This gave rise to the belief that he, and the Government more widely, had something to hide; suspicions were raised that, as Sophia A. van Wingerden put it, 'the Government had somehow played a part in authorizing the extensive violence'. She also notes, however, that the differing accounts of the events of that day make it difficult to determine the truth about what happened.[145]

Whilst that is undoubtedly the case, the fact that attempts to investigate the matter were summarily rejected raised reservations concerning the motives behind that dismissal. Lord Robert Cecil, a younger son of the Marquess of Salisbury and a lawyer of high standing, pointed out that Churchill's accusation of mendacity in respect of the WSPU and police violence 'requires more than the *ipse dixit*[146] of a Minister to support it'. He also argued that it was not 'in accordance with the principles of British justice to reject without investigation the evidence of scores of apparently respectable women'.[147]

There would be no investigation; the response, as with the Constance Lytton case, was a closing of official ranks, denial, deflection and victim-blaming. Indeed, Black Friday and the subsequent fallout are generally held to have been a turning point, marking 'a watershed in the relationship between the militant suffrage movement and the police'.[148]

There was, though, no immediate return to militancy on the part of the suffragettes. The 1911 'Women's Enfranchisement Bill' received its Second Reading in the House of Commons on 5 May 1911, passing by 255 to 88: 'The Party leaders,

Mr Asquith, Mr Balfour, and the rest, took no part in the Debate, apparently by agreement.'[149] Churchill, if he attended at all, neither spoke nor voted, though Lloyd George is recorded as being amongst the 'Ayes' but not intervening.[150] Christabel Pankhurst wrote that the 'magnificent majority justified every hope' that facilities, that is time, would be granted in the current session of Parliament for progressing the Bill.[151]

That hope was not to be fulfilled; Lloyd George announced on 29 May that a week's-worth of time to consider the Bill would not be granted until the following year.[152] This seemed to be backsliding in no uncertain terms. As Christabel Pankhurst retrospectively wrote: 'Militancy or no militancy at Coronation time[153] was still hanging in the balance – for the Government it seemed, and we were told, had perhaps not said their last word.'[154] Indeed not; a speech at the National Liberal Club by Sir Edward Grey on 1 June, and a subsequent letter from Asquith to Lord Lytton of 17 June, confirmed that sufficient time would be allowed. Asquith's words were clear: 'The Government, though divided in opinion on the merits of the Bill, are unanimous in their determination to give effect, not only in the letter, but in the spirit, to the promise in regard to facilities ...'[155]

So it was that Bertha Mason, parliamentary secretary to the National Union of Women's Suffrage Societies, wrote that: 'These declarations remove all possible misconceptions as to the intentions of the Government, and indicate that, barring unforeseen accidents, the Women's Suffrage ship is at last within reach of land.'[156] Emmeline Pankhurst remembered that the WSPU was now convinced that the Government was sincere and would allow time for the Bill to pass the following year. Accordingly she again declared that 'warfare against the Government was at an end'.[157] But then, as George Dangerfield recorded, the suspicion arose that this 'shining truce' had been engineered by the Government in order to prevent suffragette riots during the Coronation, which was held on 22 June. The WSPU, Dangerfield remembered, became very uneasy but 'it kept its part of the bargain; there were no demonstrations'.[158]

There were to be no more 'demonstrations' during the remainder of Churchill's tenure as Home Secretary; it was not until November 1911 that the 'shining truce' lost its lustre. Then, Emmeline Pankhurst, who reckoned that in June 'we had something yet to learn of the treachery of the Asquith Ministry and their capacity for cold-blooded lying', was in the United States and did not return to the UK until early January. By that time 'great deeds had been done. Our movement had entered upon a new and more vigorous stage of militancy.'[159] It was, though, Churchill's successor who had to deal with this, which eventually led to elements of the WSPU carrying out a 'nationwide campaign of terror that has never been truly acknowledged in our history'.[160]

There is no doubt that the female suffrage question generally, and the suffragette campaign particularly, baffled and frustrated Churchill. Whilst he was not an out-and-out anti-suffragist such as, for example, Asquith, his commitment to it was, as described by Lucy Masterman, tepid. As his quoted words show, he could not, or would not, accept that the great mass of women wanted the vote nor that they were disadvantaged by disenfranchisement.

That the suffragettes considered him an enemy of 'the cause' before his accession to cabinet rank has been shown in Chapter 1, and this viewpoint did not change. Whether he would have been less equivocal had there been less militancy is difficult to say. It seems unlikely, given that even their heckling discomfited him; Lloyd George's witticism about him being very bitter towards suffragettes 'because they ruin his perorations' has already been remarked upon.[161]

His words, as recorded, express ever greater bitterness at the calumny heaped upon him for his actions as Home Secretary and there is some justice in this; as the evidence demonstrates, he was not the malevolent force behind the police brutality of Black Friday and the Battle of Downing Street. However, his later defence or denial of it, plus his habit of victim-blaming, hardly endeared him to those with suffragette sympathies. Further, his decision not to prosecute those arrested raised suspicions that he had something to hide, and made him a hate figure in suffragette circles. Even the non-militant NUWSS had given up on him by mid-1911[162] a time when, we have it at several removes, he informed George V that he was 'sick of the Home Office'. The cause of this was largely down to the suffragettes: 'These women,' he is reported as saying, 'will be the death of me.'[163]

Chapter Seven

A Whiff of Cordite

'The Home Office was 'responsible for all matters of domestic administration not specifically assigned to any other department'.[1]

* * *

When King Edward VII opened Parliament following the Liberal victory in January 1910, his speech included the following statement:

> Recent experience has disclosed serious difficulties, due to recurring differences of strong opinion between the two branches of the Legislature. Proposals will be laid before you, with all convenient speed, to define the relations between the Houses of Parliament, so as to secure the undivided authority of the House of Commons over Finance, and its predominance in Legislation.[2]

Measures for abolishing, or at least limiting, the veto power of the House of Lords did not, however, proceed with any kind of discernible speed, and the matter was still in a state of flux when King Edward died on 6 May 1910. It was, said *The Times*, a 'public calamity':

> That the loss of a sovereign so experienced, so sagacious, so popular with the statesmen of both parties, as well as with the nation, so cautious, so courageous, and so tactful in the management of men and of affairs, the moment when we stand committed to the gravest domestic crisis of our time, is indeed a public calamity.[3]

The grave domestic crisis was ameliorated somewhat when, in respect of both the Liberal and Conservative parties, the accession of the relatively inexperienced George V resulted in 'a kind of political moratorium'.[4] A joint effort was made to solve the House of Lords problem by establishing a Constitutional Conference of eight members, four Liberals and four Conservatives, to seek an agreed solution. Churchill was not directly involved, the Government being represented by Asquith, Lloyd George and Augustine Birrell (the Chief Secretary for Ireland)[5] from the Commons, and the Earl of Crewe, Leader of the House of Lords, from the upper house. Balfour headed the Conservative and Unionist group, consisting of: Austen Chamberlain, a former (and future) Chancellor of the Exchequer; the Marquess of Lansdowne, a former Secretary of State for Foreign Affairs, Secretary of State for War, and Leader of the House of Lords; and the Earl of Cawdor, who had served as First Lord of the Admiralty in Balfour's administration.[6] As Lord

Lansdowne's biographer declared, this conference was 'approved of by the moderate men of both parties, but much disliked by the extremists'.[7]

There were twenty-two meetings between 17 June and 10 November but the initiative ultimately failed despite Lloyd George's novel idea of morphing the forum into a coalition Government: 'a direct extension of the conference, sitting as a kind of ad hoc super-Cabinet to guide the passage of an agreed plan of legislation'.[8] Though not directly involved in the negotiations, Churchill was kept closely informed, and onside, by Lloyd George. The latter, in one analysis, needed the Home Secretary's support for his coalition plan: 'it would have been fatal for him to move towards the centre while a man of Churchill's talents remained on the left, in a position to do to him what Disraeli had done to Peel'.[9]

That Churchill would indeed have turned on Lloyd George had the need, as adjudged by the former, arisen seems probable. He is recorded as becoming 'very offensive' towards the Chancellor and 'almost threatening' him on one occasion. Lloyd George had 'to deal very faithfully with him, and remind him that no man can rat twice'.[10] Nothing ultimately came of the coalition idea, nor was it likely to if Churchill were included; Conservatives still remembered him as the 'Blenheim Rat'. There was also a factor which applied to both Churchill and Lloyd George. Sir Robert Chalmers, a senior civil servant and Chairman of the Board of the Inland Revenue between 1907 and 1911, opined after being consulted by the Chancellor that becoming involved in any such scheme was definitely not for a young, ambitious, politician: 'anyone who joined the Coalition would probably be done for by the end of it, and it could not possibly last any great length of time'.[11]

Use of the referendum was also discussed but, perhaps predictably, the ultimate stumbling block was Ireland: 'The Liberals, dependent as they were on the Irish Nationalists, could not agree to any plan of reform that did not remove the Lords' veto on Home Rule, whereas the Conservatives would not accept any proposal that reduced the constitutional barriers to Home Rule becoming law. The Irish thus determined the outcome ... even though they had not been present at its deliberations.'[12] Lloyd George phrased it in his own way: 'when Mr Balfour proceeded later on to sound the opinion of the less capable and therefore more narrowly partisan members of his party, he encountered difficulties which proved insurmountable'.[13]

There was only one solution. Asquith announced in the House of Commons on 18 November that the King had been advised, and had agreed, to dissolve Parliament, which would occur on 28 November. Churchill wrote to the King between those dates, telling him that Asquith's statement had 'effectually extinguished the pallid flickering light of this House of Commons. No one cares about it any more.' He trusted that 'Your Majesty will excuse a brief report. He [Churchill] does not remember having been so hard-pressed before. The general situation, the South Wales Strike, and no fewer than eight capital cases which have descended from the summer assizes have been a great burden in the last few days.'[14]

Not quite so brief, but certainly direct and to the point, was his address 'To the Electors of Dundee' of 23 November. This laid out in no uncertain terms the question over which the election was to be fought, and also stated that the author would be ranging widely across the country during the campaign rather than concentrating his efforts in his constituency. Churchill's points are, I think, worth quoting at some length:

The case against the House of Lords has now reached the final Court of Appeal. Either this election is to settle it once and for ever, or all democratic processes of government have come to a full stop and must begin again [. . .] For five years I have seen every controversial measure which has been passed by the House of Commons rejected or mangled by the House of Lords. We can go no further on these terms . . .

No one can persuade the Tory Party to give up their Veto. They regard themselves as the ruling caste, exercising by right divine superior authority over the whole nation. They treat us as if we were a conquered race to be allowed by their goodwill and modern condescension to air our opinions, and to play at self-government only within such limits as they think fit and at such times as they shall appoint . . .

[. . .] the Veto of the House of Lords is no aid to our counsels. It poisons our politics; it perverts our social balance; it has handicapped our Constitution. To-day the chance to end that oppressive Veto is within your grasp. The opportunity is there, and the power. I am sure you will not fail. No one on such an issue could doubt Dundee [. . .] I am confident that Dundee will carry the banner of Scottish Radicalism in the forefront of the people's victory.[15]

Voting took place between 2 and 19 December[16] but an event that was to push politics aside and dominate the news burst forth on the evening of 16 December. Dubbed 'The Houndsditch Affair' or 'The Houndsditch Murders', it involved the slaying by gunfire of three Metropolitan policemen, Sergeant Charles Tucker, Sergeant Robert Bentley and Constable Walter Choate, with two others being wounded out of a total complement of six. The officers had disturbed a group attempting to burgle a jeweller's shop by driving a hole through a party wall from next door.

All the criminals escaped, though one was fatally wounded by, given that the policemen were unarmed, 'friendly fire'. Identifying the perpetrators proved difficult and a statement given to the newspapers on 19 December contained limited information. The police were looking for three men and one woman, all aged in their 20s or 30s. The men all had dark moustaches and at least one of them spoke with a foreign accent.[17] According to the press, a squad of forty officers was assembled and set to scour the East End, but despite 'six days of London's biggest hue-and-cry since the "Jack the Ripper" murders in 1888, the wanted men remained as elusive as ever'.[18]

One of the main difficulties facing the investigation was that the community in the area included a large East European element with whom the police, having little in the way of foreign linguistic skills, could only interact with difficulty. Nor was it a settled society; there were many 'vagabond people' who seemingly appeared and disappeared at will.[19]

The killing of the three policemen by, it was suspected, East Europeans was certain to raise xenophobic sentiment. This was particularly so given the belief, as famously expressed in one newspaper article, that immigrants from that part of the world were 'dirty, destitute, diseased, verminous and criminal'.[20] An example, taken as reinforcing the stereotype, had been the somewhat surreal 'Tottenham Outrage' of 23 January 1909. On that day two Latvian Jews carried out an armed robbery which led to a fantastic conclusion as the perpetrators were chased for more than two hours, and over 6 miles, through the streets of Tottenham and Walthamstow by a huge crowd. The escape attempt involved hijacking a tram, and several hundred rounds were discharged by the pursuees in their attempts to escape. Indeed, two of the chasers, a policeman and a young boy, were killed by gunfire, whilst more than twenty others received wounds. The affair ended when the fugitives turned their guns on themselves, committing suicide rather than be taken prisoner.[21]

Churchill, it may be recalled, had been particularly opposed to the legislation on immigration proposed by the Conservatives in 1904, and the Liberal Party in general was considered lukewarm on the matter. Outrage, as measured in press reports, was severe in respect of the Tottenham murders and, more pertinently, the alien perpetrators. For example, the *Globe* argued that such outrages occurred because 'alone among European countries the United Kingdom ... [offers] ... comparatively safe quarters in which these crimes against humanity are conceived and organised'.[22] These sentiments were echoed in the *Daily Mirror*, which contended on the same day that the culprits were foreign criminals who, having been expelled from their own country, could 'find no refuge in any place on earth but England'.[23]

Now it, and worse, seemed to have happened again, but this time the murderers appeared to have escaped. With no sign of them being apprehended, their victims were laid to rest on 22 December with all the trappings of a state funeral. Following a service at St Paul's Cathedral, the funeral corteges passed through the streets, watched by huge crowds. One observer wrote: 'It seemed as though all of London had turned out yesterday to get a glimpse of the imposing ceremonial with which the three City Policemen who lost their lives at the call of duty were to be laid to rest.'[24] An editorial in *The Times* solemnly intoned that the funeral demonstrated 'the depth of the impression made upon the public mind by this murderous outrage, which, coming after the similar affair at Tottenham, proves the existence in our midst of a social peril from which we have hitherto flattered ourselves upon being exempt'.[25]

It has to be said, however, that any rise in xenophobia that may have been occasioned by the Houndsditch killings was either too late, or too little, to affect the outcome of the General Election. Churchill and Wilkie were returned at Dundee, though with a reduced share of the vote in both cases, and the Liberal Party retained power; the composition of the House of Commons effectively remained unchanged.[26] Thus, when the dénouement of the 'Houndsditch Affair' unfolded, it was on Churchill's watch as Home Secretary.

The police got their first break when a local GP, John James Scanlon, reported that he had called to treat a man at a house in Grove Street, Stepney. The patient had been shot but refused hospital treatment and, as a second visit by Scanlon confirmed, subsequently perished. When the police went to the address they were, according to Frederick Wensley who led the squad, 'let in by the landlady, a fat old Jewess who couldn't or wouldn't understand our questions'. Having no time to waste, the detective rather ungallantly made her lead the way up the stairs: 'Her bulk amply protected me from any possible bullet, although, maybe, I might have been crushed to death if she had fallen backwards.'[27] The dead man was identified as George Gardstein, though he had several other aliases, and was adjudged to be a Latvian anarchist. Also found on the premises were several firearms and much ammunition. Three people who were known to be associated with the place, one unidentified woman and two men, one being Peter Piatkov better known to history as 'Peter the Painter', had fled the scene.

These, evidence suggested, were the culprits who had shot the three policemen. A massive manhunt was set in motion and they were eventually tracked, or so it was thought, to an address at 100 Sidney Street. This house was accordingly surrounded by police, who armed themselves with whatever firearms they could extemporise from various sources. A gunfight broke out with the inhabitants, who possessed superior firepower, and one policeman, Detective Sergeant Ben Leeson, was seriously wounded.[28] Assistance was urgently required. Churchill, some twenty years after the event, related an account of what happened from his perspective:

> At about ten o'clock on the morning of January 3 I was in my bath, when I was surprised by an urgent knocking at the door. 'There is a message from the Home Office on the telephone absolutely immediate.' Dripping wet and shrouded in a towel I hurried to the instrument, and received the following news: 'The Anarchists who murdered the police have been surrounded in a house in the East End – No. 100 Sidney Street – and are firing on the police with automatic pistols. They have shot one man and appear to have plenty of ammunition. Authority is requested to send for troops to arrest or kill them.'
>
> I replied at once, giving the necessary permission and directing the police to use whatever force was necessary ... No one knew how many Anarchists there were or what measures were going to be taken. In these circumstances I thought it my duty to see what was going on myself, and my advisers concurred in the propriety of such a step.[29]

Though written long after the event, and bearing in mind that great men, or those who thought they were, often indulged in a 'well attested habit of improving the historical record',[30] the above account is generally in accord with those produced contemporaneously.[31]

By the time the Home Secretary arrived, a contingent of Scots Guards, based at the Tower of London, had been deployed and gunfire was being exchanged. According to his later recollection, there was 'a considerable crowd of angry and alarmed people' surrounding the scene who were unfriendly towards him. He records several shouts of 'Oo let 'em in?', which he took to be an 'allusion to the refusal of the Liberal Government to introduce drastic laws restricting the immigration of aliens'.[32]

It was a spectacle unlike anything ever seen on the streets of London and, as well as a host of press photographers taking still photographs, moving pictures of the affair were captured for newsreel footage by a team from Pathé News.[33] Hugh Martin, a journalist with the *Daily News* recorded his impressions:

> As soon as I reached Fleet-street that morning I was ordered to Sidney-street, and found the whole region congested with police, stiffened with a sprinkling of soldiers. Now and again a pistol shot, fired, one would say, more in general defiance than with deliberate aim, would come from an attic window of No. 100, every pane of glass in which had by this time been smashed by the besiegers. The police were 750 strong. Seventeen men, with two non-commissioned officers, of the Scots Guards, and a Maxim gun had also been fetched from the Tower. Some of the soldiers were sniping from a brewery; others were lying in the street on newspaper bill-boards (to protect them from the bitter slush), looking very much as though they were trying to score bulls at Bisley.
>
> This was the position when, soon after midday, I saw Mr Churchill arrive in a car from Whitehall. He was wearing a silk hat and a fur-lined overcoat with astrakhan collar – altogether an imposing figure in the exceedingly drab surroundings ... Here was a priceless piece of characteristic personal drama ... to add tone to the otherwise rather garish colours of what looked likely to be the most sensational London crime story of the decade ... I watched him moving restlessly hither and thither among the rather nervous and dis-traught police, a professional soldier among civilians, talking, questioning, advising ... Peeping round corners, he exposed himself with the Scots Guards to the random fire of the besieged burglars, or consulted with his 'staff' in tones of the utmost gravity.[34]

Churchill was certainly no stranger to being shot at; he had first experienced being 'under fire' in Cuba in 1895, and though he has been mainly absolved of giving direct orders to the police or soldiers he was, as noted by Martin, rather more than just a passive observer:

> I made it my business ... after seeing what was going on in front to go round the back of the premises and satisfy myself that there was no chance of the criminals effecting their escape through the intricate area of walls and small

houses at the back of No. 100 Sidney Street. This took some time, and when I returned to the corner of Sidney Street I was told that the house had caught on fire, and I could see smoke coming out from the top-floor window.[35]

The fire inside the house was, it seems, set by the inhabitants. The besiegers believed that 'the men inside caused it, possibly with the idea that means of escape might be afforded by the smoke and confusion attendant on a fire'.[36] If that was the intention then it failed, and the conflagration was left to burn itself out. This was a matter in which Churchill did intervene, accepting 'full responsibility' for the decision not to deploy the Fire Brigade in an attempt to fight the fire, his rationale for this decision being that 'it would have meant loss of life and limb to any fire brigade officer who had gone within effective range of the building'.[37] He explained his part in the affair to the Prime Minister in a letter dated the same day. According to this account he had been composing a memorandum concerning the House of Lords when the 'Stepney affair' interrupted the process. Whether he had actually been dictating it from the confines of his bathtub, as per his later description already quoted, is unknown. In any event, he added a paragraph on the siege to this missive before despatching it:

> I was interrupted in copying out this letter by the Stepney affair from wh[ich] I have just returned. It was a striking scene in a London street – firing from every window, bullets chipping the brickwork, police and Scots Guards armed with loaded weapons, artillery brought up etc. I thought it better to let the House burn down rather than spend good British lives in rescuing those ferocious rascals.[38]

He had to repeat that information at the inquest, held on 18 January before Wynne E. Baxter, Coroner for the County of London, into the deaths of two men whose 'charred and unrecognisable bodies' were found in the burned-out house.[39] These were later identified as being Fritz Svaars and William Sokoloff *aka* 'Joseph', both of whom were known to be associates of George Gardstein, but of 'Peter the Painter' there was no sign. There never was to be, and several authors have wondered whether he actually existed.[40] Later scholarship has established that he probably did exist, and whether a real person or not, he became a renowned figure in the mythology of the East End and indeed internationally.[41]

Though he didn't actually interfere overmuch there, Churchill's presence at the Siege of Sidney Street also entered the realm of myth, and attracted a good deal of censure into the bargain. In particular it provided a focus for Conservative criticism, and was the subject of wild reports in the newspapers. In an attempt to clear this up he wrote a letter to *The Times*, dated 11 January, highlighting that his only action there had been with respect to holding back the Fire Brigade. It went on: 'For the rest, I can claim no more personal responsibility than I can for the sensational accounts which appeared in the newspapers or the spiteful comments based upon them.'[42]

These accounts were replicated in the foreign press. His Under-Secretary, Charles Masterman, had been in France at the time where, according to Lucy, his wife and biographer, he noted that: 'The story was told in heightened terms in the foreign press ... every English person we encountered demanded what was happening, with vocal complaints that they did not expect this sort of action by a British Government.'[43] Her account states that by the time Masterman reached home again his 'official loyalty was beginning to show signs of wear and tear':

> He burst into Mr Churchill's room at the Home Office with the query 'What the hell have you been doing now, Winston?' The reply, in Winston's characteristic lisp, was unanswerable. 'Now Charlie. Don't be croth. It was such fun.'[44]

Balfour's criticism of him, in the House of Commons on 6 February 1911, which Churchill deemed 'especially sarcastic', is often mentioned as an example of Conservative reproach:

> I understand that he did not call out the troops or assemble the police, and that he had nothing to do with the massing of artillery. He was there in – well, I do not know the position he was in. He was, I understand, in military phrase, in what is known as the zone of fire – he and a photographer were both risking valuable lives. I understand what the photographer was doing, but what was the right hon. Gentleman doing? That I neither understood at the time, nor do I understand now. I must frankly say that I should have thought that anything more embarrassing to those responsible for the operations than to have the head of the office who is over them all present with the photographer as irresponsible spectators, could not be imagined.[45]

Churchill, many years later, in writing of 'The Battle of Sidney Street', was to judge Balfour's contribution as a 'not altogether unjust reflection'.[46] He also admitted that 'convictions of duty were supported by a strong sense of curiosity which perhaps it would have been well to keep in check'.[47]

To his detractors, both at the time and later, the episode epitomised his defects. That there were both many detractors and defects is unarguable; his friends, and there were many of those as well, could not fail to notice the latter. Lucy Masterman wrote that 'His great weakness, which is growing on him more and more, is his love of the limelight ...'[48] Lloyd George saw something more portentous according to his confidant, Sir George Riddell. Riddell, the managing director of the *News of the World*,[49] was 'Lloyd George's Boswell' according to John Grigg,[50] and his diary entry for 8 February 1913 is illuminating in respect of how the Welshman viewed his colleague and friend:[51]

> Spent the evening alone with LG. Long chat. [...] We talked of Winston. I said, 'His career looms large with him.' 'Yes,' said LG, 'more than with any other statesman I know. We are all keen on success, but there is a difference.'

I said, 'The absence of the Napoleonic idea.' 'Yes,' replied LG, 'that is what I mean.'[52]

As noted, following the events at Tottenham, Houndsditch, and Sidney Street, the presence of foreigners in Britain became contentious. Churchill wrote to Asquith on 3 January reflecting this. The letter concluded: 'I think I shall have to stiffen the administration and the Aliens Act a little, and more effective measures must be taken by the police to supervise the dangerous classes of aliens in our midst.'[53] Such measures were also on the mind of, and appealed to, the King. One of his private secretaries (there were two) wrote to the Home Secretary on 5 January, telling him that His Majesty was sorry to hear about the 'injured fireman' at Sidney Street and that 'He hopes that these recent outrages by foreigners will lead you to consider whether the Aliens Act could not be amended so as to prevent London from being infested with men and women whose presence would not be tolerated in any other country.'[54]

A correspondent in *The Times* of the same date gives an example of the thoughts of those from humbler backgrounds: 'It is entirely due to the action of the late Home Secretary, Mr Herbert Gladstone (now a wicked peer), that the operations of the [Aliens] Act were rendered non-effective, and this country is still an asylum for Anarchists, criminals, and the mentally and physically afflicted of all nations.'[55] Needless to say there was much more of the same in newspapers of every political persuasion.

The subject of foreigners (aliens) and their treatment constituted something of a perennial problem for the Home Office. It was 'constantly nervous' regarding 'vigorous attacks' from liberal politicians anxious that the principles of asylum were being observed whilst, from the opposite direction as it were, it came under fire from 'an authoritarian, not to say zenophobic [sic], sector of the magistracy for taking too lenient a line'.[56]

Churchill was now drawn, or was driven by public concern as it manifested itself in the press, to the authoritarian end of that spectrum. This was evidenced by a draft of the 'Aliens (Prevention of Crime) Bill' that he circulated to the Cabinet on 19 January 1911. His accompanying Memorandum stated that 'two naughty principles are involved in it'. These were, he explained: 'a deliberate differentiation between the alien, and especially the unassimilated alien, and a British subject, and ... that an alien may, in certain circumstances, be deported before he has committed any offence'.[57] The Bill, complete with 'naughty principles', received its First Reading[58] in the House of Commons on 18 April 1911.[59] Churchill informed the King the following day about this, adding in what can only be described as a rather syrupy tone: 'Your Majesty was pleased earlier in the year to take some interest in this question, and Mr Churchill has endeavoured to profit by the expression of Your Majesty's wishes ...'[60]

Though it made further progress, it was not destined to advance as far as passing into law, being eventually, and formally, withdrawn in December 1911.[61] A similar fate befell a private Bill along the same lines, which had been introduced by Edward Goulding, Conservative MP for Worcester.[62] The reason for these failures was relatively straightforward: 'more urgent domestic crises and the increasingly tense international situation put anarchist and immigration issues low on the agenda'.[63] The whiff of cordite from Sidney Street was overlaid by the much more powerful, if metaphorical, gunpowder scent of domestic political revolution and the potential for war abroad.

When Asquith had announced to the House of Commons on 18 November 1910 that the King had been advised, and had agreed, to dissolve Parliament, he kept to himself another matter upon which the monarch had been 'advised' and had also agreed. This was outlined in a memorandum from the Cabinet to the King dated 15 November 1910:

> Ministers cannot, however, take the responsibility of advising a dissolution, unless they may understand that in the event of the policy of the Government being approved by an adequate majority in the new House of Commons, H[is] M[ajesty] will be ready to exercise his constitutional powers (which may involve the prerogative of creating Peers) if needed, to secure that effect shall be given to the decision of the country.
>
> H[is] M[ajesty's] Ministers are fully alive to the importance of keeping the name of the King out of the sphere of party and electorial controversy. They take upon themselves, as is their duty, the entire and exclusive responsibility for the policy which they will place before the electorate. H[is] M[ajesty] will doubtless agree that it would be inadvisable in the interest of the State that any communication of the intentions of the Crown should be made public unless and until the actual occasion should arise.[64]

George V had agreed, albeit 'most reluctantly', to give the Cabinet this 'secret undertaking'; indeed one of his recent biographers considers that he had been 'shafted' by Asquith over the matter.[65] The King wrote in his diary the following day that 'in the event of the government being returned with a majority ... I should use my prerogative to make peers if asked for', before adding that 'I disliked having to do this very much.'[66] Disliked or not, what it meant in effect was this; that having been returned as Prime Minister for the second time, and with the Liberals having won three consecutive General Elections, Asquith now possessed the power to comprehensively breach the hitherto impregnable Conservative obstacle represented by the House of Lords. This was something he, and his Cabinet colleagues, concealed for the moment.

The passage of the Parliament Bill 1911, which was exactly the same as a Bill that had failed to get past the Upper House the previous year, began on 21 February in the House of Commons.[67] It eschewed any attempt at altering the composition or function of the House of Lords at that time, though mentioned the possibility for the future. What it did do, though, was propose changing the law, and thus the constitution of the United Kingdom, in three main respects. Firstly it would largely strip the House of Lords of its power over money bills.[68]

The second proposal contained the substance. It would remove the absolute veto completely, and put in its place the power to delay legislation for up to two years spread over three parliamentary sessions. After that, it would automatically pass into law without the approval of the House of Lords. Finally, the maximum life of the House of Commons, and thus the period between General Elections, would be reduced from seven years to five years.[69]

The Bill's Second Reading, where it was debated, took place between 27 February and 2 March. This process 'followed a largely familiar pattern. The Unionists denounced the Government for forcing through a constitutional revolution at the behest of the Irish Party ... and Government speakers denounced the Opposition for refusing to accept the clearly expressed verdict of the electorate.'[70] Hansard records that the Home Secretary did not contribute anything significant during this period. However, after the Bill had passed through its Committee and Report stages, involving detailed examination, he delivered the final, 'winding up', speech for the Government during the Third Reading on 15 May. This occasion allowed him to indulge in some withering sarcasm at Balfour's expense:

there are only two arguments which have been brought forward in the course of to-day's discussion which require a very brief reference from the Government Bench to-night. Both arguments have been adduced by the Leader of the Opposition. The first argument was that we had no mandate for this Bill, and the second was that it sets up Single-Chamber Government. I am always interested in the right hon. Gentleman's theories, and, as far as I could gather, his theory about mandates is this. It used to be that a General Election won by the Liberals only entitled them to settle one thing, but he has now improved upon that, and his theory now is that a General Election won by the Liberals decides nothing, and never could in any circumstances decide anything ... The hon. Member for Anglesey (Mr. Ellis Griffith), in his excellent speech this afternoon, referred to the theory of the Leader of the Opposition as 'One Bill, one election'. That was the old theory, but the new theory is 'Two elections, no Bill'. I shall leave these conclusions in their original simplicity.[71]

There was, needless to say, much more in that vein but the crux of the whole matter came during his peroration:

I agree with the hon. and learned Gentleman the Member for Waterford (Mr J[ohn] Redmond) that once the absolute Veto was gone the House of Lords and the Conservative party would come to terms on many of the great questions which have long delayed the harmonious development of our nation. The passage of the Parliament Bill marks a new era in our politics – an era not of strife but of settlement. The time has surely come when this country should clear off its arrears. The time has surely come when the outworn controversies of the Victorian period should be honourably settled and cleared out of the way; and when the House of Commons, freed from the tyranny of congested business, freed also from the tyranny of a partisan Veto, may turn with all its strength to those problems of social, national, and Imperial organisation on which the welfare and future of our country depend.[72]

This was of course a polite way of saying that, in the event that the Parliament Bill succeeded, one of the problems the House of Lords and the Conservative Party would have to 'come to terms' with was Irish Home Rule.

The Bill now had to be passed by the House of Lords, but a hiatus in the procedure was occasioned by the Coronation of King George V and Queen Mary on 22 June 1911. When it was considered at length by the Upper House, the Committee Stage there beginning on 28 June, the Conservative and Unionist peers used their majority to amend it; they substituted their own proposals for those of the Government. According to Asquith the Bill had, by 5 July, been 'as completely transformed as if no General Election had been held'.[73] On 14 July, the Committee Stage having been completed, the Cabinet sent a minute to George V:

> The Amendments made in the House of Lords to the Parliament Bill are destructive of its principle and purpose, both in regard to finance and to general legislation. There is hardly one of them which, in its present form, the Government could advise the House of Commons, or the majority of the House of Commons could be persuaded, to accept. The Bill might just as well have been rejected on Second Reading. It follows that if, without any preliminary conference and arrangement, the Lords' Amendments are in due course submitted to the House of Commons they will be rejected en bloc by that House, and a complete deadlock between the two Houses will be created. Parliament having been twice dissolved during the last eighteen months, and the future relations between the two Houses having been at both Elections a dominant issue, a third Dissolution is wholly out of the question. Hence, in the contingency contemplated, it will be the duty of Ministers to advise the Crown to exercise its Prerogative so as to get rid of the deadlock and secure the passing of the Bill. In such circumstances Ministers cannot entertain any doubt that the Sovereign would feel it to be his Constitutional duty to accept their advice.[74]

The Conservatives, or their leaders at least, were aware that the King might well be asked to create peers in order to secure a Liberal majority in the House of Lords. Balfour had written to Lansdowne in December 1910, putting himself in the monarch's position – 'If I were the King' – and relating what he would do in relation to any such request:

> I should say to them – 'Am I to understand that, under the threat of leaving me without a Ministry, and the country without a Government, you propose to compel me to give a promise that, under circumstances which no man can

foresee, I am to raise to the peerage 500 gentlemen, whose names have not been submitted to me, in order to pass a Bill which has never yet been discussed in Parliament, and which, under the pressure of discussion, may be moulded into some quite unexpected shape? If this be your real policy, although I have no power to prevent it, I must enter my solemn protest against it.'[75]

The operative phrase in this premise was of course that the King, ultimately, would 'have no power to prevent' such a thing occurring. That Balfour considered the creation of peers at least likely is evidenced by his closing line: 'I have written the above on the assumption that, terrified by their followers, the Government will use their full power of coercion.'[76] Balfour had, in January, reiterated this belief to a select group consisting of Viscount Esher and Francis Knollys (Lord Knollys), one of the King's two private secretaries. He told his dining companions that 'if he were King and were asked by Mr Asquith ... to promise the creation of peers in sufficient numbers to pass the Parliament Bill ... he would make a strong remonstrance but he would not feel in a position to give a definite refusal'.[77]

Knollys not only knew that George V had already agreed to exercise his prerogative if asked, but had been instrumental in advising the King that he should do so. This advice had been wrongly tendered according to Ridley, who argues that 'he deceived the King by withholding a crucial piece of information' – that being, if George V refused to create peers and Asquith resigned, then Balfour would make an attempt to form a government.[78] Needless to say, Knollys kept the secret.

The King too maintained confidentiality during a talk he had with Lord Lansdowne in late January. According to Lansdowne's record of the event, they discussed the possibility of peers being created, and he opined that whilst he 'could conceive that the step might become inevitable ... it was one which had been universally condemned as violently straining the Constitution'. He added that he was sure the King would be reluctant to take such a step and that the Government would be 'not less reluctant to advise' that it should be taken. He did, though, warn the monarch that he:

> should be careful how he took it for granted that in no circumstances might the House of Lords take a line which would render it impossible for him to overcome them except by the creation of peers (I dwelt upon this because I gathered Knollys had told HM that he was under the impression that the Lords would in no circumstances push the king to extremities).[79]

Jenkins postulates, surely correctly, that Lansdowne's tactics were essentially Micawberish; he sought delay in the hope that something would turn up.[80] The impression that he simply could not accept that Asquith and his Cabinet would actually try to go through with what many Conservatives considered a revolutionary action is strong. A later generation would probably diagnose him as being in a state of denial about the question which, as Balfour's cool analysis had shown, postulated that the only sensible option was a policy of retreat under protest.[81] The Prime Minister was of an essentially similar mind, according to Margot Asquith. She recalled her husband had been confident following the King's acceptance of the Cabinet advice on his 'prerogative' in November 1910 that the matter was essentially academic: 'If we are beaten at the General Election the question will never arise, and if we get in by a working majority the Lords will give way, so the King won't be involved.'[82] Both had, it seems, underestimated the inability of some Conservatives to acknowledge that they faced certain defeat.

There were, though, partisans on both sides. In the absence of Lloyd George, who was unwell during the early part of 1911 and had been ordered to take a break from politics,[83] Churchill was the most vociferous amongst the Liberals. A lengthy letter he sent to Asquith on 3 January contained a section demonstrating his desire to confront the House of Lords head on: 'We ought to go straight ahead with the Parliament Bill and carry it to the Lords at the earliest date compatible with full discussion,' he argued. When it came to the creation of peers he was uncompromising and decidedly iconoclast:

> We ought as early as possible to make it clear that we are not a bit afraid of creating 500 peers if necessary: that we believe ourselves beyond doubt possessed of the power, and will not shrink from using it. Such a creation would be in fact for the interest of the Liberal party and a disaster for the Conservatives. It w[oul]d be possible to make a list of men whose local and civic reputations stood so high with both parties in cities and councils that the attempts to ridicule their character or to compare them unfavourably with the present nobility w[oul]d fall flat. We should at a stroke gain a great addition of influence in the country. The wealth and importance of British society could easily maintain 1,000 notables much more easily than 300 a century ago.[84]

That this missive had been sent from Blenheim Palace, the seat of Churchill's cousin the Duke of Marlborough, may have amused Asquith, but it is safe to say he ignored the contents. The Parliament Bill progressed slowly through the House of Lords though, as already noted, not without gross mutilation. That Balfour knew such resistance to it would be useless was evidenced by a 'long talk' he had with Lord Esher on 5 July, which the latter then related to George V:

> Mr Balfour told Viscount Esher that he and Lord Lansdowne had never quite agreed upon the probable creation of peers.
> Lord Lansdowne has refused to believe that this step could ever actually be taken.
> Mr Balfour has held the contrary opinion, and he perfectly realises now that when members of the Government assert that no general election can take place, and that the [Parliament] Bill must pass into law, they have solid ground for their statements.[85]

According to Balfour's niece and biographer, who had access to his private papers, he first learned 'privately' that the King had already agreed to create peers on 'a day in the first week of July'.[86] Given what he told Esher, then it would seem to have been prior to that conversation. Jenkins, however, gives the exact date as 7 July,[87] though provides no source, and was probably inferring the date from Dugdale's account of how Balfour, upon hearing the news, 'at once summoned his Conservative colleagues to review the situation in the light of this knowledge. The "Shadow Cabinet" met on July 7th at his house in Carlton Gardens.'[88] Jenkins also credits, if that is the correct term, Knollys with 'probably' being the bearer of the information.[89] The identity of the communicant, and the precise date of the communication, are somewhat academic. What can be said is that by the time of the Shadow Cabinet meeting Balfour knew, for certain, that the game was up; the Parliament Bill could not be stopped. Many of his colleagues disagreed and were all for having the House of Lords continue to resist: 'There for the first time surrender by the House of Lords was discussed as practical politics. There for the first time appeared the crack in the unity of the Party, which very soon developed into the "Die-hard" revolt.'[90] Thus began, in Jenkins' phraseology, the 'Disunion of the Unionists'.[91]

Lloyd George, acting as Asquith's 'agent',[92] met with Balfour and Lansdowne on 18 July. The two Conservative leaders were informed that 'a pledge to create peers had been obtained from the King as far back as November: that nothing would induce the Government to run the risk of losing the Parliament Bill in the House of Lords; and that the Government were reluctant to create peers.'[93] Lansdowne communicated with Knollys the following day and stated that he wanted the fact of the agreement to be put in writing before, as was the suggestion, Asquith revealed its existence in the House of Commons.[94] This was imminent; the Third Reading in the House of Lords was scheduled for the next day.

Then, as John Morley, 1st Viscount Morley of Blackburn, put it when opening the debate on 20 July, the Parliament Bill that was under consideration 'is not the Bill that was submitted to the judgment of the country. It is not the Bill that was passed by a great majority in the House of Commons ...'[95] Morley did not reveal the 'secret undertaking' which Asquith and the Cabinet had received from the King. He did, though, albeit in an understated way, warn those who had amended the Bill out of all recognition that they were acting undemocratically:

> I will only say this further – to pass this Bill tonight and to allow the real Bill to pass by-and-by is not surrender to the House of Commons, it is not surrender to the Government; it is a surrender to the verdict and the judgment of the country at the last General Election.[96]

Lansdowne in replying defended the amendments, but made no direct reference to the King's pledge. He did state that the Lords were sending the Bill 'down to the House of Commons asking for it – I do not know whether we shall ask successfully – that it may be treated in accordance with the ordinary decencies of

Parliamentary warfare'. He then finished with a passage which went unnoticed at the time, but appears significant in retrospect:

> My Lords, we believe that you have ready to your hand all the materials for an honourable settlement, and, therefore, it seems to us almost inconceivable that His Majesty's Government should prefer to resort to other methods, methods which have been condemned by statesmen of both great political Parties, and which seem detestable in the eyes of all right thinking men.[97]

The Parliament Bill, as amended, was then passed by the House of Lords and returned to the Commons. That same evening Asquith, who had previously agreed with Knollys that he should do so,[98] wrote to Balfour and Lansdowne:

> I think it is courteous and right, before any public decisions are announced, to let you know how we regard the political situation.
>
> When the Parliament Bill in the form which it has now assumed returns to the House of Commons we shall be compelled to ask that House to disagree with the Lords' amendments.
>
> In the circumstances, should the necessity arise, the Government will advise the King to exercise his prerogative to secure the passing into law of the Bill in substantially the same form in which it left the House of Commons; and His Majesty has been pleased to signify that he will consider it his duty to accept, and act on, that advice.[99]

The letter was then published in the following morning's newspapers. Randolph Churchill noted that 'the proposed swamping of the Upper House was to appear even to many objective people as an act of constitutional indecency'.[100] To the non-objective it was worse. In Bates' apposite phraseology: 'Their fox shot on the assurance of the unhappy King, the Tories in Parliament went berserk.'[101]

This frenzy expressed itself on 24 July when the House of Commons met for consideration of the House of Lords' amendments. In the sober words of Hansard: 'The PRIME MINISTER rose in his place to move "That the Lords Amendments be now considered," and was immediately assailed with Opposition cries of "Traitor".'[102] Churchill's letter to the King gives his perspective:

> The Prime Minister was this afternoon subjected to prolonged organised insult & interruption from a section of the Conservative party, among whom Lord Hugh Cecil[103] & Mr Goulding were the most prominent. For more than 25 minutes he attempted to deliver his speech, but in spite of the Speaker's appeals the Conservatives continued their rowdy and unreasonable disorder. He therefore confined himself to stating the course wh[ich] the Government would adopt without further argument or explanation.
>
> It was therefore a great triumph of restraint on the part of the majority of the House, including as it does the Labour & Irish parties, that they listened patiently and politely to a long & controversial speech from Mr Balfour, who

acknowledged their courtesy & expressed regret for the behaviour of his friends.[104]

Balfour, amongst many other things (it was a very long speech), accused the Prime Minister, and by extension the Government and Liberal Party, of 'misusing the prerogative of the Crown and destroying the independence of the Second Chamber', the purpose behind it all being 'one object, and one object only, to prevent the people of this country expressing any verdict – any new verdict I ought to say – on a question on which they have twice expressed a verdict before – I mean the institution of Home Rule in the Sister Island.'[105] Though Balfour was indeed heard, attempts by Tory backbenchers, particularly 'Mr F E Smith who had been himself v[er]y disorderly',[106] to continue the debate resulted in chaos and the Speaker adjourned the House.[107]

Churchill was to note some further unruly behaviour two days later which reflected the 'Disunion of the Unionists' over the best way to proceed when the Parliament Bill, with its amendments removed, returned to the House of Lords. Of those involved, he wrote that: 'The ringleaders are ... making themselves a distinct force against Mr Balfour & there is no doubt that a great many Unionists in the country who are dissatisfied with his leadership will take the opportunity of supporting the rebels.'[108]

Dissatisfaction with Balfour's leadership revolved around his realism. In his estimation, allowing the Bill to pass was the lesser of two evils, albeit the loss of the Lords' veto power would ensue. On the other hand, 'fighting to the last' would lead to exactly the same result, with the addition of a permanent Liberal majority in the Upper House. This was too cerebral for many Tories to comprehend. Motions of censure were laid in both Houses of Parliament, that in the Commons taking place on 7 August with Churchill winding up for the Government. He was in defiant and provocative mode:

> You censure us because you say we are going to pass Home Rule in this Parliament. So we are. .... Censure us then if you will, by all means, for that. Censure us for that if you have the power. You have not the power. We repel your censures to-night, and we are sure that this censure will be even more decisively repudiated before these matters have passed from action into history.[109]

He was as safe in doing so as he was correct in saying to the Opposition 'you have not the power'; the motion was defeated. The Lords debated the same measure the following day with, as expected, a different result[110] but to no effect whatsoever; 'nobody paid any attention to the peers'.[111]

When it came to considering the Lords' amendments in the House of Commons the following day, Asquith absented himself with laryngitis and responsibility for making the Government's case was delegated to the Home Secretary.[112] As expected, certain Opposition MPs laced the occasion with bitterness, Lord Hugh Cecil stating that 'I conceive that the Government and the Prime Minister have been guilty of high treason ... Undoubtedly it is high treason to overthrow the liberties of either House of Parliament, and that is the whole argument I am addressing to the House, for that is precisely what they have done.'[113] Churchill's response, when it came, was sharp: 'His definition of high treason is when the majority of the nation claim for themselves the same political rights as the other portion of the nation have long enjoyed.'[114]

Sir Edward Carson, the Irish Unionist Alliance MP for the University of Dublin, brought up Home Rule: 'the Irish question, which was put forward in such a bombastic way by the Home Secretary last night largely dominates, if it does not entirely dominate, the present situation'.[115] He later opined that:

> If anything ever justified resistance to Home Rule it is the conduct of the Government in relation to this Parliament Bill. You are going to attempt to pass it, according to the Home Secretary, without putting it before the electors, and by a pure act of force. I do not want in the least to boast, but I may at least express my own hope, made most solemnly, that your act of force will be resisted by force. I believe myself it will, and I believe that those who resist will have constitutional right on their side.[116]

This might well have been a dig at Churchill, who had written four years earlier of how, in 1886, 'The jingling phrase, "Ulster will fight, and Ulster will be right," was everywhere caught up. It became one of the war-cries of the time and spread with spirit-speed all over the country.'[117] If it was an attempt to get the Home Secretary to denounce his father's words, it failed. Churchill did not rise to the bait, merely retorting that:

> The right hon. and learned Gentleman and the Noble Lord are very wrong in using language of this kind at the present time when there is very grave labour unrest all over the country. There are 70,000 dockers on strike in London. Those men have just the same strong feelings as the Noble Lord. Some of them are hungry, some of them are suffering, and I should like to know if they were to break out into rioting who would be the first to come here and urge that the soldiers should be sent. We deprecate the use of this language. It is not suitable for the House of Commons, it is injurious and injudicious in the times in which we live, and least of all is it suitable for the party which prides itself as being the party of law and order, and the party which undoubtedly has the most to lose by any scenes of turbulence and riot.[118]

No matter how vituperative, earnest or long-winded their contributions, the Opposition were ultimately at the mercy of the majority the Government could command. Accordingly, when Lloyd George, who argued that the discussion had gone on 'at very unusual length', moved that the House proceed to actually consider the Lords' Amendments, this was carried.[119] The result was a foregone conclusion and on 10 August the House of Lords assembled to consider the returned Parliament Bill in its more or less original form.

Here the result was very much in doubt, though Lord Morley, 'on my full responsibility as the spokesman of the Government', warned the House that every vote given against the Bill 'is a vote given in favour of a large and prompt creation of Peers'.[120] Though it is likely that most of those present had already made up their minds as to whether they were going to 'die in the last ditch' or not,[121] one member claimed the debate had changed his mind. Randall Davidson, Archbishop of Canterbury, had, he said, intended to abstain. However:

The course of the debate, I will honestly admit, has induced me to change my mind. Especially I have been influenced by the callousness – I had almost said levity – with which some noble Lords seem to contemplate the creation of some five hundred new Peers, a course of action which would make this House, and indeed our country, the laughing-stock of the British Dominions beyond the seas and of those foreign countries whose Constitutional life and progress have been largely modelled upon our own. We are now told that the issue whether or not these Peers are to be created for the swamping of the House may depend to-night upon a few votes, perhaps upon a single vote. That being so, I cannot hold the position of one of those who might have averted that calamity and did not.[122]

When the vote was taken, the Archbishop of York and eleven Bishops of the Church of England followed Davidson. So did thirty-seven Conservative peers; the majority in favour of the Parliament Bill was seventeen.

Heaven did not fall, but to say there was disappointment in some quarters would be an understatement. George Wyndham, Conservative MP for Dover and one of the hardest of 'die-hards', wrote: 'It was a shrewd blow to be beaten in the Lords by 13 Prelates and 31 traitors and 6 mountebanks. My "book" on the morning of the 10th allowed for 10 Prelates and 21 traitors. And, behold, there were more. But so things befall in these days. And we must begin all over again like Robert Bruce's tiresome spider.'[123] Perhaps predictably, the *Daily Mail* saw it in apocalyptic terms:

To-day the floodgates of revolution are opened, and the two-chamber Government is swept away ... The ministers have made the King the un-willing agent in a coup d'état, but the battle for English liberty has only just begun. Under the lead of Mr Balfour the Unionists will close their ranks for the supreme effort to restore the balance to our constitution, punish the outrage on the King and repeal the Parliament bill.[124]

Balfour, though, had had quite enough, and had left the country on 9 August for a holiday at Bad Gastein in Austria-Hungary. Whilst en route, and on the day of the vote in the Lords, he wrote to his close friend Lady Elcho, formerly Mary Wyndham, a sister to the George Wyndham mentioned above: 'Politics have been to me quite unusually odious. I am not going into the subject but I have, as a matter of fact, felt the situation more acutely than any in my public life – I mean from the personal point of view [...] You must not ask me to tell you anything about the last ten days. I am trying to forget it all.'[125] He had in fact become seriously disenchanted at the lack of intellectual rigour and discipline he perceived at senior levels in the Conservative and Unionist Party of late. Just before he left for Bad Gastein, he had discussed the matter with Jack Sandars, his private secretary, who recorded Balfour's views in his diary:

> after a full discussion, a minority decline to accept my advice, which commanded the majority of votes at the Shadow Cabinet, and the dissentient members have gone out into the world and have embarked upon a policy of active resistance. I confess to feeling that I have been badly treated. I have no wish to lead a Party under these humiliating conditions. It is no gratification to me to be their leader. If they think that someone else is better able to discharge the duties of leadership, I am quite willing to adopt that view.[126]

This was, of course, before the conclusion of the affair in the House of Lords, but there seems little doubt that he would have shared the views of the Archbishop of Canterbury as expressed during that debate concerning 'levity' over the creation of hundreds of new Peers. Balfour was, of course, a patrician intellectual who had been mentored by his uncle, Lord Salisbury, early in his career. The latter's views on how the country should be governed, and by whom,[127] were well known and, one suspects, he too would have been appalled at politics directed by 'the music-hall attitude of mind', as his nephew had termed it in his suppressed memorandum. The Home Secretary shared, at least to some degree, that viewpoint. His letter to the King of 11 August referenced 'the memorable and dramatic events in the Lords'. It went on:

> Mr Churchill ventures to offer to Your Majesty his respectful congratulations upon the conclusion of this long drawn & anxious constitutional crisis ... it was a shocking thing that the tremendous issues of last night's division should have depended on the votes of a few score persons quite unversed in public affairs, quite irresponsible & undistinguished who refused to accept guidance from all the most notable leaders of every political party in the State.[128]

Other matters, though, had absorbed Churchill's attention on the day of the House of Lords vote, which he had alluded to in his speech to the Commons of 8 August: '70,000 dockers on strike in London'. Efforts at conciliation were in progress, but if these failed, he now informed the King that 'extraordinary measures will have to be taken to secure the food supply of London wh[ich] must at all cost be maintained. Twenty-five thousand soldiers are being held in readiness & can be in the capital in six hours from the order being given.'[129] What the Home Secretary and the Government were having to deal with has been dubbed by historians as t'The Great Labour Unrest'. It was, according to one, the most prolonged and largest incidence of industrial unrest since the mid nineteenth century Chartist movement.[130]

Chapter Eight

'a dim spectre of revolution'

'In August 1911 a national, in other words a general, strike developed on the railways. During those days a dim spectre of revolution hung over Britain.'[1]

'Labour is robbed of the wealth and means of life created by the genius of toil; the exploiters are on trial for their malefactions; the charge is that capitalist ownership of the land and material wealth is the cause of poverty.'[2]

* * *

If Churchill and Balfour were puzzled or annoyed, or both, at those who refused to accept advice and guidance from them and their ilk, much the same could be said for those at the other end of the social scale. According to Philip Snowden, the Labour MP for the Blackburn and a future Chancellor of the Exchequer:

The year 1910 has been an exceedingly trying time for all who have had any responsibility for the management of trade unions and the direction of the Labour movement. The men connected with a number of important trade unions have shown a good deal of dissatisfaction with the actions of their responsible officials, and this dissatisfaction has expressed itself in some cases in rebellion against the agreements entered into by the Union Executive and in unauthorised strikes.[3]

The year 1911 was worse: 'In 1911, 9 per cent of the total industrial population was involved in strikes of various length, as compared with 2.6 per cent for 1902, 1.4 per cent for 1907, and an average of 2.9 per cent for the period 1902–1911.'[4] One of the reasons, and undoubtedly a major one, behind this general upsurge was the disparity between incomes and expenditure which badly affected many working people. A negligible increase in nominal wages had in no way compensated for a greater rise in prices, thus causing a decline in real wages and purchasing power.[5] To quote Snowden again:

The years 1911–13 were a time of great unrest in the labour world. From the point of view of the condition of the working classes there was ample justification for it. It was a period of trade prosperity. Since the beginning of the century our foreign trade increased by nearly 50 per cent. The Income Tax returns showed a great expansion of trade profits. Prices were rising and wages remained stationary.[6]

That this was a socially dangerous condition for the country to be in had been foreseen, perhaps most particularly in the current context by Churchill's deputy

Charles Masterman. In his 1909 book, *The Condition of England*, he had pointed out that: 'Sixty years ago, Disraeli described the rich and poor of England as two nations. Today, even national distinctions seem less estranging than the fissure between the summit and basis of society.'[7] His conclusion was that this 'horizontal division between rich and poor' was one factor which made 'the future of progress ... doubtful and precarious'.[8]

Progress, and what it entailed, was of course a matter of perspective and, as has been well attested, the period in question was one when large sections of the working class organised themselves in an effort to ensure it was their version which prevailed. Indeed, there is evidence that substantial numbers of workers were losing faith in the political method of making gains.[9] That the Liberal Party had been in power for some four or five years, supported by the Labour Party, seemed not to have made much difference to their overall lot, despite the various reforms made. Indeed, the 1910 Cambrian dispute was 'still dragging its slow length along' in mid-1911.[10]

It is then, as Coates and Topham phrased it, 'not surprising that in 1911 industrial unionists and syndicalists alike were fully convinced of the hostile malevolence of the state'.[11] Syndicalism aimed 'to overthrow capitalism through revolutionary industrial class struggle and to build a new social order free from economic or political oppression'.[12] It disregarded the possibility of achieving this through parliamentary methods, though it has to be said that there was no unanimity concerning what it actually was at the time. To again quote Snowden, this time writing in 1913:

> The difficulty one experiences in attempting to understand the nature and the aim of Syndicalism is that there is no authoritative and definite statement of its philosophy or its policy or its aims. Syndicalism is one thing according to one of its exponents and something very different according to another.[13]

Industrial Unionism, which was 'by no means equivalent to syndicalism', was theoretically less extreme.[14] It sought to organise all workers within an industry into one union, though propounded vigorous sympathetic and national strikes.[15] There was, though, a substantial intersection of interest between syndicalists and industrial unionists, as is evidenced in the words and actions of one trade union leader who stood outside the mainstream: Ben Tillett, founder and General Secretary of 'The Dock, Wharf, Riverside and General Labourers Union of Great Britain and Ireland' (a forerunner of the Transport and General Workers' Union created in 1922).[16] Whilst 'never an out and out syndicalist',[17] Tillett was committed to industrial unionism and was censorious in respect of the Parliamentary representation that the working class had thus far achieved via the Labour Party:

> The House of Commons and the country, which respected and feared the Labour Party, are now fast approaching a condition of contempt towards its Parliamentary representatives.
> The lion has no teeth or claws, and is losing his growl too [...]

This is lamentable, although it requires a deal of character to sustain the part; the foolishness of which can only be estimated by the loss of opportunity to force the supreme issue of poverty in general.

To procrastinate is the motive of all governments, the aim of their being, so long as they are capitalistic and protecting their privileges.

The safety of a Parliamentary seat is too big a price to pay for the neglect of the millions of homes affected detrimentally by poverty; even at the risk of losing the empty vanity of Parliamentary honours the Labour Party should be rebels in everlasting and open warfare with the powers that be.[18]

Tillett moved swiftly to exploit what George Askwith, Comptroller-General of the Commercial, Labour and Statistical Departments of the Board of Trade and expert conciliator, termed 'the great outburst of 1911', which began with a strike of seafarers at Southampton in early June. Rather than staying a local dispute, however, it rapidly spread, beginning in earnest on 14 June 'when the National Sailor's and Fireman's Union (NSFU) declared a seamen's strike throughout Britain and Ireland'.[19] Plans for mass action had been laid and the call was heeded both in terms of breadth (most of the principal ports of the United Kingdom were soon affected) and depth (the dock and transport workers stopped work at these ports in support of the seamen).[20] Askwith records a discussion he had with an unnamed shipowner, evidently from Yorkshire, who was baffled by the situation:

he spoke of it as a revolution, and so it was. The dockers at Goole and Hull, he said, had new leaders, men unknown before; the employers did not know how to deal with them; the military were close by, but they were Territorials from Hull, what would be their attitude? The shipowners could not recognise the Seamen's Union: the [Shipping] Federation forbade [it]. Metropolitan police had been asked for and were on their way. Fires, looting, riots had started at once. They were thoroughly surprised; and could not understand the cause.[21]

Askwith, in testimony that no doubt unwittingly supported Tillett's point about Labour MPs, grass-roots trade unionists and their mutual estrangement, recalled an unnamed 'leading' Labour politician observing that 'I don't know what has come over the country. Everyone seems to have lost their heads.'[22] A piece from the *Manchester Guardian*, pertaining to Salford, agreed:

The nerves of the dockers were in a jumpy state ... They were in the mood for anything, either to leave their work or to go on with it, and the bare shouting of the word 'strike' seems to have turned the balance of their minds on the side of leaving it ... The movement spread unchecked. Men ran along the docks shouting 'Strike! Strike!' and with scarcely an inquiry as to why they were striking men stopped work.[23]

If the strikes were incomprehensible to the likes of the Yorkshire shipowner quoted, to the *Manchester Guardian* and to the anonymous Labour politician, amongst many others, that wasn't the case with those taking the action. There was, though, at least according to the prominent Socialist Henry W. Lee, no 'deep-laid plot on the part of certain agitators to hold up the country's food, and put a pistol to the head of the general public'.[24] It was rather a grassroots-driven affair, motivated by, as Lloyd George phrased it, 'a tidal wave of impatience'. He was referring to the exasperation felt by working-class people with respect to the unequal relationship between them and the rest of society, and the snail's-pace of change.[25] Those involved then knew what they wanted and, more to the point, their efforts were attended with success.

At Glasgow, where action began on 11 June, the majority of shipping movements and thus seaborne trade was brought to a standstill within little more than a week. Whilst the Shipping Federation was attempting to organise blackleg labour, three large ocean liner companies, the Allan Line Steamship Company, Anchor Line (Henderson Brothers) and Donaldson Line, came to terms with the strikers and conceded wage increases and union recognition.[26] Many smaller companies then followed suit, and by the end of June the 'main phase' of the seamen's action was concluded, even though some employers still held out.[27]

A similar pattern was observed at Liverpool, where the first withdrawal of labour had taken place on 14 June. Success there for the strikers, who were led by the veteran organiser and syndicalist Tom Mann,[28] was rapid; on the first day four shipping lines, the Cunard Steamship Company, Elder Dempster Lines, Alfred Booth & Company and Alfred Holt & Company (Blue Funnel), agreed to meet deputations from the Sailors' and Firemen's Union, whilst the White Star Line agreed to hear the men's complaints, though not to meet their union. Sympathetic action was also taken by the men ashore, the end result, as explained by historian Harold Hikins, being:

> The display of solidarity among the seamen, the support they received from the dockers on every ship involved in strike action, and the evident sympathy of the carters, must have convinced the firms that negotiation would be less disadvantageous than tying up ships in a protracted struggle. The Cunard, Booth and Canadian Pacific all conceded the seamen's terms in full by the following Wednesday and recognised the unions' right to negotiate.[29]

Tom Mann recorded the extent of the seamen's victory:

> Shipowners who had absolutely refused to have anything to do with the workmen, now earnestly endeavoured to arrange for a conference. The Shipping Federation proved utterly incapable of helping its clients, and, after having dictated conditions for over twenty years, it had in a single day lost all its power.[30]

Despite these successes, which were more or less replicated nationally, industrial peace was not forthcoming. For example, all work on the Liverpool docks ceased on 28 June. This was, in Hikins' view, the day that the nature of the 1911 strike movement changed fundamentally: 'the dockers had decided for themselves that

The 'terrible twins', *circa* 1907. (*Author's Collection*)

The Glamorgan Colliery,
Llwynypia. (*Author's Collection*)

Leonard Wilkinson Llewellyn.
(*Newport Past Picture Library*)

(*Above left*) Captain Lionel Lindsay.
(*Author's Collection*)

(*Above right*) Wyndham Childs.
(*Author's Collection*)

(*Left*) Nevil Macready. (*Author's Collection*)

David Davies, the Dartmoor Shepherd.
(*Author's Collection*)

Edith Carew. (*Author's Collection*)

Heswall Nautical Training School. (*Author's Collection*)

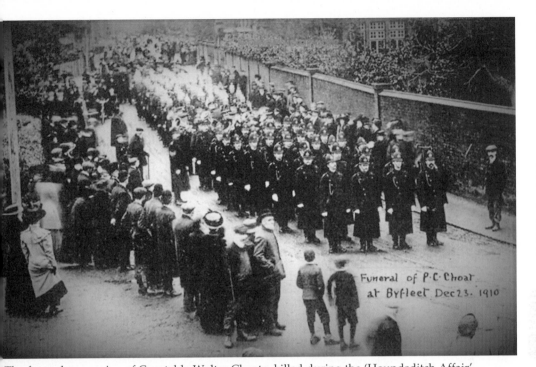

The funeral procession of Constable Walter Choate, killed during the 'Houndsditch Affair'. (*Author's Collection*)

Stinie Morrison in court. (*Author's Collection*)

Edward Mylius. (*Author's Collection*)

The Battle of Stepney:
Churchill surrounded
by armed police.
(*Author's Collection*)

The Battle of Stepney:
Churchill at the inquest.
(*Author's Collection*)

Charles Masterman. (*Author's Collection*)

Lucy Masterman. (*Author's Collection*)

John Galsworthy, *c*.1910. (*Author's Collection*)

Wilfred Scawen Blunt, *c*.1910. (*Author's Collection*)

Churchill and La Belle Maloney. (*Author's Collection*)

Lord Curzon's 'Fifteen Good Reasons Against the Grant of Female Suffrage.' (*Author's Collection*)

LORD CURZON'S
FIFTEEN GOOD REASONS AGAINST THE GRANT OF FEMALE SUFFRAGE.

LORD CURZON OF KEDLESTON has said that there are fifteen sound, valid, and incontrovertible arguments against the Grant of Female Suffrage. He summarises them as follows :—

(1) Political activity will tend to take away woman from her proper sphere and highest duty, which is maternity.

(2) It will tend by the divisions which it will introduce to break up the harmony of the home.

(3) The grant of votes to women cannot possibly stop short at a restricted franchise on the basis of a property or other qualification. Married women being the women, if any, best qualified to exercise the vote, the suffrage could not be denied to them. Its extension to them would pave the way to Adult Suffrage. There is no permanent or practicable halting-stage before.

(4) Women have not, as a sex, or a class, the calmness of temperament or the balance of mind, nor have they the training, necessary to qualify them to exercise a weighty judgment in political affairs.

(5) The vote is not desired, so far as can be ascertained, by the large majority of women.

(6) Neither is the proposed change approved, so far as can be ascertained, by the large majority of men.

(7) If the vote were granted, it is probable that a very large number of women would not use it at all. But in emergencies or on occasions of emotional excitement, a large, and in the last resort, owing to the numerical majority of women, a preponderant force might suddenly be mobilised, the political effect of which would be wholly uncertain.

(8) The presence of a large female factor in the Constituencies returning a British Government to power would tend to weaken Great Britain in the estimation of foreign Powers.

(9) It would be gravely misunderstood and would become a source of weakness in India.

(10) The vote once given, it would be impossible to stop at this. Women would then demand the right of becoming M.P.'s, Cabinet Ministers, Judges, &c. Nor could the demand be logically refused.

(11) Woman, if placed by the vote on an absolute equality with man, would forfeit much of that respect which the chivalry of man has voluntarily conceded to her, and which has hitherto been her chief protection.

(12) The vote is not required for the removal of hardships or disabilities from which woman is now known to suffer. Where any such exist, they can equally well be removed or alleviated by a legislature elected by men.

(13) Those persons ought not to make laws who cannot join in enforcing them. Women cannot become soldiers, sailors, or policemen, or take an active part in the maintenance of law and order. They are incapacitated from discharging the ultimate obligations of citizenship.

(14) The intellectual emancipation of women is proceeding, and will continue to do so, without the enjoyment of the political franchise. There is no necessary connection between the two.

(15) No precedent exists for giving women as a class an active share in the Government of a great Country or Empire, and it is not for Great Britain, whose stake is the greatest, and in whose case the results of failure would be the most tremendous, to make the experiment. It would not, indeed, be an experiment, since if the suffrage were once granted, it could never be cancelled or withdrawn.

Printed by the National Press Agency Limited, Whitefriars House Carmelite Street ; and Published by the NATIONAL LEAGUE FOR OPPOSING WOMAN SUFFRAGE, Caxton House, Tothill Street, Westminster, S.W.   Price 4s 6d. per 1,000.

Constance Lytton. (*Author's Collection*)

Jane Warton. (*Author's Collection*)

Emmeline, Christabel and Sylvia Pankhurst. (*Author's Collection*)

VOTES FOR WOMEN.

The Women's Social and Political Union.

Head Office: 4, CLEMENT'S INN, STRAND, W.C.

Telegraphic Address: "WOSPOLU, LONDON."

Telephone No. 2724 HOLBORN.
(Three lines.)

Founder and Hon. Secretary—Mrs. PANKHURST.
Joint Hon. Secretary—Mrs. TUKE.
Publishing Office—The Woman's Press, 156, Charing Cross Road, W.C.
Bankers—Messrs. Barclay & Co., Fleet Street, E.C.

Hon. Treasurer-Mrs. PETHICK LAWRENCE.
Organising Secretary—Miss CHRISTABEL PANKHURST, LL.B.
Newspaper—"VOTES FOR WOMEN."
Colours—Purple, White and Green.

BLACK FRIDAY.

A LETTER SENT BY Mrs. SAUL SOLOMON, Widow of the late Saul Solomon, of Cape Town ("The Gladstone of South Africa") to Mr. WINSTON CHURCHILL, Secretary of State for the Home Office, on Dec. 17, 1910.

Reprinted from "VOTES FOR WOMEN," Jan. 6, 1911.

SIR,—Will you of your courtesy allow me to refer to you with regard to certain facts relating to the women's deputations to the Prime Minister on November 18, 1910? These deputations consisted of over 300 honourable women, who walked—in groups of 12 only, according to the legal requirement—towards the House of Commons. We know of no existing law to prevent us from going there, whether the Government of the day choose to receive us or not. And, not only was our cause a *just,* but also a *reasonable* one, we being desirous of drawing the attention of the Government to our righteous dissatisfaction with the shelving of the "Conciliation Bill" by Mr. Asquith, and his utter ignoring of Woman Franchise when he announced the dissolution of Parliament.

It would appear to be generally admitted that unrepresented citizens have hitherto been unable to find a more constitutional or effective method than the above for bringing their grievances immediately to the notice of the Cabinet, the Parliament and the country. You are doubtless well aware that this is a time-honoured mode of procedure, and one fully proven to be practically convincing by the perusal of British history. Well, sir, we continued our progress in the most orderly and ladylike manner as far as *we* were concerned, hoping, as the

precedents alluded to gave us every reason to expect, that a few of our representatives—headed by our leader, Mrs. Pankhurst—would be graciously received, more especially seeing that the "Conciliation Bill" had passed its Second Reading in the House by a majority of 110 larger than that accorded to the Budget, or against the Lords' Veto! Naturally, we held, in these circumstances, that we women of the National Women's Social and Political Union would meet with some consideration worthy of our Liberal Cause, and more particularly at that moment in deference to the increasing volume of public opinion openly expressed during Suffrage Week in favour of the speedy granting of the Woman's Vote. In our hands we carried a small roll of paper upon which was written the resolution passed at the Caxton Hall. The women possessed no other weapon.

But, how were we met? By the relentless engine of physical force—the Metropolitan Police—an instrument under the control of the Government, presumably in your Department. Therefore, whatever I may have to say about the police in this letter or statement, refers to them merely as the *irresponsible, obedient tools* of the Government; and I do not mention their actions in any respect or instance whatsoever as actions for which I deem them

The first page of Mrs Saul Solomon's letter to Churchill. (*Author's Collection*)

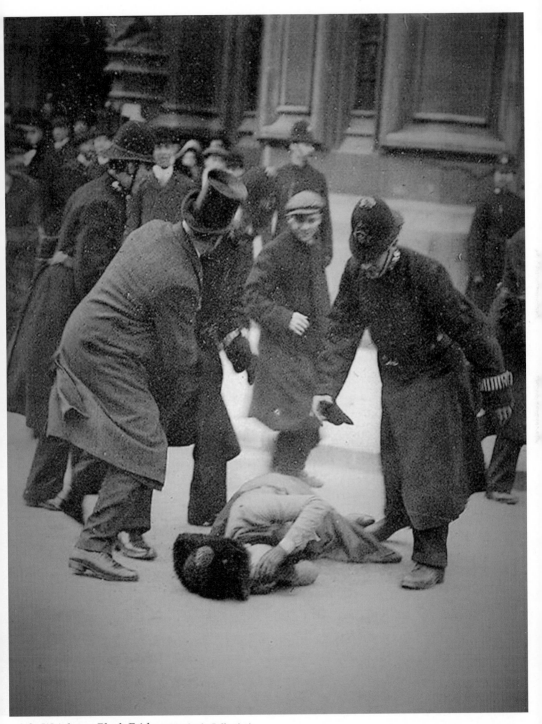

Ada Wright on Black Friday. (*Author's Collection*)

CITY OF LIVERPOOL.

PUBLIC WARNING.

I, the Lord Mayor and Chief Magistrate of the said City, hereby warn and urge all persons not having any business to transact in the centre of the City, to keep away from those parts of the City, especially the neighbourhoods of St. George's Hall, Lime Street, Christian Street, Scotland Road, and any other parts where trouble has taken place or is likely to take place. Especially do I request all women and children to remain at home as much as possible during the disturbed condition of the City.

Large numbers of persons have assembled in the disturbed streets for the purpose of seeing what is going on, and I warn all such persons that if the Authorities are called upon to act, innocent citizens are as likely to be injured as those against whom any drastic measures on the part of the Police or the Military are directed.

S. M. HUTCHINSON,

Lord Mayor.

14th August, 1911.

A 'Public Warning' by the Lord Mayor of Liverpool. (*Author's Collection*)

HMS *Antrim* in the Mersey. (*Author's Collection*)

The gathering outside St George's Hall, Liverpool, on Bloody Sunday. (*Author's collection*)

THE CHANCE OF A LIFETIME.

Our Mr. Asquith. "Five hundred coronets, dirt-cheap! This line of goods ought to make business a bit brisker, what?"

Our Mr. Lloyd George. "Not half; bound to go like hot cakes."

[December 28, 1910.]

'Swamping the House of Lords!' (*Author's Collection*)

REVELATIONS OF THE SECRET SERVICE

BEING THE AUTOBIOGRAPHY OF HUGH MORRICE, CHIEF TRAVELLING AGENT OF THE CONFIDENTIAL DEPARTMENT OF HIS BRITANNIC MAJESTY'S GOVERNMENT

CHRONICLED BY

WILLIAM LE QUEUX

LONDON

F. V. WHITE & CO. LTD.

17 BUCKINGHAM STREET, STRAND, W.C.

1911

William Le Queux and some of his titles. (*Author's Collection*)

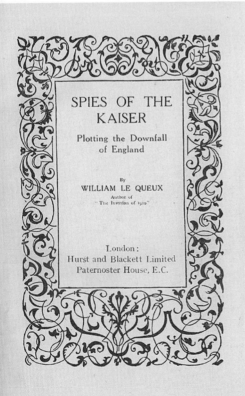

SPIES OF THE KAISER

Plotting the Downfall of England

By

WILLIAM LE QUEUX

Author of
"The Invasion of 1910"

London:
Hurst and Blackett Limited
Paternoster House, E.C.

THE INVASION OF 1910

WITH A FULL ACCOUNT OF THE SIEGE OF LONDON

BY

WILLIAM LE QUEUX

NAVAL CHAPTERS BY H. W. WILSON

INTRODUCTORY LETTER BY
FIELD-MARSHAL EARL ROBERTS, K.G., K.P., ETC.

Toronto

THE MACMILLAN COMPANY OF CANADA, LIMITED

1906

All rights reserved

Richard Haldane. (*Author's Collection*)

Reginald McKenna. (*Author's Collection*)

Sir Arthur Wilson. (*Author's Collection*)

Henry Wilson. (*Author's Collection*)

what won the seamen's demands could win theirs too'.[31] Salford saw a similar, and if anything even more widespread, change. Over the period 29 June–3 July the strike escalated until all road transport throughout Manchester and Salford was stopped, and on 5 July some 1,500 miners also walked out to join the action.[32]

Neither was social peace maintained. There had been a significant clash between strikers and police at Glasgow on 19 June, when the latter baton-charged a crowd estimated at between five and six thousand strong after being pelted with bottles. They also, according to those involved, obstructed peaceful picketing and interfered with pickets and protestors. Further violent scenes occurred on 3 July when strikers and blacklegs clashed, the police again baton-charging the strikers.[33]

Widespread violence also occurred at Cardiff, where the seamen were led by their local organiser, the 'bizarre and quixotic' Captain Edward Tupper.[34] There the Shipping Federation attempted to introduce Chinese blackleg labour, the result being that 'we had the spectacle of a force under the Home Office being used to escort and protect Chinese blacklegs by the Government that was returned to power in 1906 largely on the question of the abolition of Chinese labour in the South African gold mines!'[35] This tactic, and the reaction to it, led to crowds attacking Chinese laundries and businesses, and much fighting with those thought to be strike breakers.[36] The Home Office force mentioned was a 220-strong Metropolitan Police contingent requested by the Chief Constable of Cardiff City Police, William McKenzie. These were augmented by reinforcements from other South Wales forces but at this time there was no call for military assistance.[37]

The introduction of 400 police from Birmingham and Sheffield into the dispute at Hull was, it has been argued, a factor in the strikes there turning violent. Previously the union leaders, pickets and local police had kept a lid on things until, and 'largely as a result of representations made to the government by provision merchants, ship-owners, and consulates in a bid to safeguard business interests', these reinforcements arrived.[38] The police attempted to protect blacklegs engaged to unload ships, famously including the cargo of *Titania*, which on 27 June was being handled by female workers under police protection. These women were rolling barrels of butter from the ship into railway wagons under the jeers of a large crowd of strikers when a single picket asked permission of George Morley, the Chief Constable of Hull City Police, to go aboard and speak to them. This was refused, whereupon 'the crowd got angrier [and the] police requested the unloading be suspended'.[39] Unpacified, the crowd attempted to storm the ship, leading to a pitched battle with the police. According to the *Daily Mail*:

> There was an ugly rush ... towards the stern of the *Titania*. The police emerged from the struggle without any injury although a number of the men fell to the ground. Some stones were thrown at the police and as they came

away their clothes were covered with dust and dirt. The remarkable scene continued for some little time. [...] The following day as the strikers tried to escalate the unrest by enlisting support from other workers trouble broke out at Reckitts.[40] Initially the workers here refused to stop work and fighting broke out. Thirty Birmingham policemen who were guarding the factory were forced into baton charges to restore order and many bystanders were swept unwillingly into the conflict ...[41]

Even uglier scenes were to follow, with syndicated reports published worldwide claiming that 'There is a threatening situation at Hull, the whole of the working population being involved.' The piece continued: 'The police charged and truncheoned a section of a mob of 10,000 who were perambulating the streets of the city calling upon the mill hands to cease work and help to paralyse the trade of the port. The workers at a number of creosote works and timber mills were forced to stop work by the mob.'[42] Even allowing for the usual journalistic hyperbole, there was clearly large-scale disruption occurring. However, and according to the same account, the rioting stopped when news was released that G.R. Askwith of the Board of Trade was journeying to the city 'to confer with the employers and strike leaders'.

If Askwith, and his colleagues elsewhere, formed one arm of the Government's response to the widespread unrest, then the other involved Home Office intervention. This, of course, had two functions: to suppress disorder and maintain the movement of materials, the chief one being food. Once again, Major General Sir Nevil Macready found himself summoned to assist:

> At 7-15 p.m. on 5th July I was suddenly sent for to the Home Office, and at 10-30 p.m. the same night found myself with 200 Metropolitan Police en route for Salford, where the transport strikers were causing anxiety. Two squadrons of the Scots Greys and a battalion of infantry arrived the next morning. There were no exhibitions of violence on the part of the strikers, and having distributed the troops at various centres in case of accidents, there was little fear that any outbreak would occur.[43]

Peace had come to Hull in the meantime. Despite some serious difficulties, Askwith, accompanied by Isaac Mitchell, had managed to broker an agreement which was accepted by the dockers on 3 July, and a return to work began.[44] Their next port of call was Salford and Manchester, where after the normal difficulties a settlement was achieved. Askwith related the sight that greeted him on the morning of 10 July:

> in the large square opposite the Manchester Town Hall, on one side were riding out the Scots Greys, who had been garrisoning Salford, on the other side were the Metropolitan and Birmingham police going to the railway-station to leave the city; and in the main street were mile upon mile of lorries laden with goods coming from the docks to be distributed in the city and to the cotton-mills.[45]

Macready reflected that his assignment 'had been quite pleasant, entailing no hardships on troops or police, and no collisions with the strikers'.[46] There remained, however, other areas of the country where collisions with strikers continued, one such being South Wales where around 700 Lancashire Fusiliers and 250 Metropolitan Police were eventually deployed to protect blackleg labour and maintain order.[47] Nevertheless, with Askwith's settlements in mind, 'some of the newspapers expressed a hope that "the strike fever" had closed and that the holiday season would be passed in peace'.[48]

The broker of the settlements knew better. He sent a long memorandum to Churchill on 23 July dealing with his proposals for establishing new machinery for industrial conciliation (the shortly to be set up 'Industrial Council').[49] Two days later, however, he forwarded him a draft memorandum entitled 'The Present Unrest in the Labour World' which offered his, and Isaac Mitchell's, analysis of the subject.[50] The cause of the 'present unrest' had, the memorandum argued, economic underpinnings: 'There has been during the last fifteen years a marked and almost unbroken increase in the cost of living.'[51] Wages had not kept pace, whilst returns on investment had markedly improved. Thus increasing disparities between classes had become marked, and were observable as such:

All classes are seeking to secure some of the amenities of existence, and are becoming more impatient of the bare struggle for a livelihood. The wealthier classes, in those types of luxurious expenditure now favoured, possibly display that luxury more than was the custom in the preceding generation. The use of motor-cars, for example, cannot fail to attract the attention of those who might be unobservant of other even more lavish types of expenditure. Further, the more extravagant of the doings of the wealthy classes secure a publicity of ever wider extent through the agency of the cheap newspaper. In affording a basis for discontent with his lot in life to the wage-earner, this publicity of private luxury may not be without importance.[52]

Having established the motivation of the strikers as he saw it, and buttressing his argument with copious statistical evidence, Askwith moved on to describe the tactics they had most recently deployed. These had come as a surprise, forcing the employers into a change of approach, and since they had proved largely successful, they were likely to be replicated:

The outstanding features of the present unrest amongst certain sections of workers are the rapidity and success of the movement amongst the transport workers, and the readiness with which the better organised trades such as miners and railwaymen show a disposition to give support. A strike of seamen, which had been threatened for some time but was not generally expected to be serious, commenced on the 16th June[53] and has affected all the principal ports. The Shipping Federation knew that if the strike did break out it might give some trouble owing to a shortage in the supply of seamen, but no one foresaw the extent of the support which has been given to the seamen by the other transport workers, such as dockers, carmen, and railwaymen, or the manner in which these different sections have acted together. The Seamen's Union was not a strong body, and the Transport Workers' Federation was only in process of formation, yet, so far as it has gone, the movement has been successful, as concessions have been given to each class of workers where a settlement has been effected, and the men feel that by acting together they can stop the trade of any port. No doubt the fact that owners are averse to laying up their ships while trade is good has helped the men, and initial successes have increased their confidence, but this does not account for the spontaneous manner in which the outbreak has taken place, and it looks as if we were in the presence of one of those periodic upheavals in the labour world such as occurred in 1833–34, and from time to time since that date, each succeeding occurrence showing a marked advance in organisation on the part of the workers and the necessity for a corresponding change in tactics on the part of employers. In this last instance the change of tactics on the part of employers has been practically to concede the men's demands – a development which must have the effect of encouraging the leaders to renewed efforts.[54]

The coda of this document, the 'Joint opinion of Mr Askwith and Mr Mitchell', offered a bleak prognosis: 'Successful as the Board of Trade may generally have been in finding a solution of difficulties which appeared almost insurmountable, it must be remembered that these difficulties are becoming daily greater, and one failure may mean the letting loose of forces which would irreparably damage our trade and commerce.'[55]

Churchill annotated the memorandum's covering letter on 30 July, stating that he found it 'most interesting and disquieting'. He also wrote that he would see Asquith about it on 'Tues morning', that day being 1 August.[56] As Randolph Churchill noted,[57] the Home Secretary accepted Askwith's warnings and, likely in preparation for his meeting with the Prime Minister, composed a memorandum of his own on the subject:

There is grave unrest in the country. Port after port is called out. The police and the military are asked for at place after place. Fresh outbreaks continuously occur and will go on. The railways are not sound. Transport workers everywhere are getting to know their strengths, whilst the 'hooligan' element are causing riots: and those conversant of labour matters *in practice* anticipate grave upheaval. Serious crises have been in recent years, and very often lately, surmounted only by a narrow margin of safety, and now specially a new force has arisen in trades unionism, whereby the power of the old leaders has proved quite ineffective, and the sympathetic strike on a wide scale is prominent. Shipping, coal, railways, dockers etc etc are all uniting and breaking out at once. The 'general strike' policy is a factor which must be dealt with.

While control can probably be maintained, even in a dozen or more simultaneous Tonypandys or Manchesters, control would be more difficult if the railways went, and inadequate control must mean great uncertainty, destruction of property, and probably loss of life. Such protection or repression must be coupled with civil action on the lines of prevention and peace.[58]

The document went on to outline, in pursuit of 'prevention and peace', Askwith's proposed machinery for industrial conciliation. The Prime Minister was, of course, used to being on the receiving end of Churchill's multitudinous memoranda, and did not always receive them appreciatively; he had been apt to perceive at least some of them as being 'born of froth out of foam'.[59] It was also the case that he, and the Government generally, were also deeply immersed in matters of great moment at that time in any event. As his biographers put it: 'Never in the memory of men living had a Ministry been beset with so many and great dangers as Asquith's Government in these weeks.'[60] Nevertheless, there is no doubt that Churchill's concerns as he laid them out were very real and, as it happened, were soon realised.

On 5 August 1911 about 1,000 Liverpool railwaymen, employed by the Lancashire & Yorkshire Railway (LYR), struck without union authorisation and other transport workers followed suit.[61] On 8 August the entire docks rail traffic was at a standstill with some 4,000 men on strike, and the action was spreading to railwaymen in Manchester, Preston, Crewe and other north-western centres.[62] At Liverpool, the strike was becoming general and Leonard Dunning, Head Constable of Liverpool City Police, feared what might happen next. Accordingly, he contacted the Home Office asking for assistance, a move justified by the Lord Mayor of Liverpool Samuel Mason Hutchinson, also Chief Magistrate of the city, who claimed that 'acts of violence and other unlawful acts have been committed by persons in connection with the present labour dispute'.[63] The Home Office approved the reinforcements sought, as Masterman telegraphed on 9 August:

War Office are sending a battalion of troops tonight to Seaforth Barracks ... In the event of their being required they will have to be requisitioned by Magistrates in the usual way. You should see the Officer in Command as soon as possible. Another battalion has been ordered to stand by at Rhayader [Radnorshire, Mid Wales].[64]

The following day Dunning was informed that a regiment of cavalry were being held in readiness at York. If these were actually required, he was told, 'send [a] requisition to General Officer Commanding, Western Command, Chester; at the same time inform General Officer Commanding, Northern Command, York'.[65] With some three-quarters of the goods that were usually handled in the city and port immobilised in warehouses and the like,[66] the local authorities requested and received 200 police reinforcements from Birmingham and Leeds on 10 August.[67] Churchill informed the House of Commons that day that the authorities in Liverpool had 'been supplied with the military forces that they require'.[68] More police followed, and military assistance was requisitioned on 11 August; this included the infantry battalion already in the city, at Seaforth Barracks, and the second battalion at Rhayader. Also called upon were the cavalry from York.[69] All in all, it was estimated that there were 5,000 troops and 2,400 police at the disposal of the Head Constable.[70]

On the afternoon of Sunday, 13 August, the hottest day Liverpool had seen since 1873, according to local press reports,[71] a crowd estimated at more than 80,000 attended a mass meeting around St George's Hall in the city centre. This had been announced previously and permission to gather on 'the Plateau in front of the ... building' had been granted by the corporation.[72] Fred Bower, a stonemason from the USA who had made his home in Liverpool, was an eyewitness to the occasion: 'It was glorious weather when, from a dozen wagons on the Plateau in Lime Street, speeches being made in support of the railway workers ...'[73] By all accounts the gathering was entirely peaceful until, as Bower recalled: 'From my wagon, facing the great St George's Hall, I heard a rumpus behind me. It seemed a small skirmish.'[74] According to the official report, violence broke out in a side street behind the Empire Theatre, initiated by 'roughs from the adjoining Irish district'.[75] For reasons that are still largely unexplained, the police overreacted to this 'small skirmish' and decided to clear the crowd, and to do so violently, in fact extremely violently: 'An hour later, after the mounted police had cleared the streets, and all the hospitals in the city were filled with people with cracked skulls, "peace" was restored for a time ...'[76]

It was a very short time. Rioting and general disorder spread to surrounding areas and intensified during the evening. It soon became apparent that whatever the intention had been in attacking the crowd, all that had been achieved was to exacerbate an already tense situation. Indeed 'Red' or 'Bloody' Sunday, as the day was named, formed the catalyst for massive unrest and a widening of the strike.

The next day the offices of the Shipping Federation were torched and it was estimated that 100,000 men were on strike.[77] Hutchinson issued a 'Public Warning' urging all persons, unless they had business to transact, to keep away from 'those parts of the city where trouble has taken place or is likely to take place'. Women and children were especially warned to stay at home. His proclamation concluded by cautioning those who had assembled in 'large numbers' in the 'disturbed streets' in order to see what was 'going on' that 'if the Authorities are called upon to act, innocent citizens are as likely to be injured as those against whom any drastic measures on the part of the Police or Military are directed'.[78] Churchill was obliged to inform the King that the situation in Liverpool had worsened:

> The dockers have not gone back to work and the shipowners have declared a general lockout from this afternoon to apply to all dock workers. There is a good deal of riotous disturbance particularly in the Irish quarter ... The riot last night started with the hooligans not strikers but was quickly taken up by the latter.[79]

He also informed the monarch that military reinforcements were being sent to the city and, in a reminder that whilst the situation in Liverpool was probably the most serious, there were also problems elsewhere: 'Two more battalions [of infantry] will be moved to Lichfield to be available for Manchester if necessary ... Aldershot has been told to have ten thousand men ready to move at short notice into London.'[80] Much the same information was given to the House of Commons, where the Home Secretary revealed that in order to:

secure the restoration of public order and the observance of the law [...] Orders have been ... given for the movement of further troops, which will raise the force in Liverpool to a complete brigade of Infantry and two regiments of Cavalry. It is believed that this force will be sufficient for all emergencies.[81]

Also sent to Liverpool was the General Officer Commanding Western Command, Lieutenant General Sir Henry MacKinnon.[82] His command consisted of regular troops, with the local Territorials ordered to hand in the bolts of their rifles,[83] and was by any standards a serious military force. However, whilst it was capable of controlling the streets, the same did not necessarily apply to the water. On 15 August the Home Secretary received a joint message from Hutchinson in Liverpool and his counterpart on the opposite side of the Mersey, Arthur Washington Willmer, the Mayor of Birkenhead:[84]

Strike so serious that ferry traffic may be suspended at any moment. We think that you should consider [the] desirability of sending a War Ship to [the] Mersey with instructions that if need be Blue Jackets should work the ferries.[85]

Sir Edward Troup replied the following day affirming that 'arrangements have been made with [the] Admiralty to send [a] vessel for purposes of protection'.[86] Churchill also sent a message stating that any further applications for aid would be 'promptly supported by the Government'.[87] The Admiralty did indeed send a ship, which arrived on 17 August, in the shape of the largely obsolete, and reserve, armoured cruiser HMS *Antrim*.[88] Some have seen the arrival of the cruiser as an attempt to 'overawe' the population, and there may be something in that.[89] It was certainly a powerful symbol remembered long afterwards even amongst the various other traumas during what some considered to be a virtual civil war. The journalist and writer Philip Gibbs,[90] at that time reporting for the *Daily Chronicle*, reckoned:

It was the nearest thing to civil war I have seen in any English city ... the whole of the transport service was at a standstill, and the very scavengers [street sweepers] left their work. The Mersey was crowded for weeks with shipping from all the ports of the world, laden with merchandise, some of it perishable, which no hands would touch. No porters worked in the railway goods yards, so that trains could not be unloaded. There was no fresh meat, and no milk for babes. Not a wheel turned in Liverpool. It was like a besieged city, and presently, in hot weather, began to stink in a pestilential way, because of the refuse and muck left rotting in the streets and squares.[91]

Margaret Isabel Postgate,[92] the 18-year-old daughter of Professor John Percival Postgate of Liverpool University, who had recently moved to the city after leaving school, recalled that time in her autobiography. She reckoned that the strikes:

> loosed what was almost a small civil war in my new home of Liverpool ... I remember the stench of the unscavenged streets – the Corporation employees came out in sympathy – and of the truck-loads of vegetables rotting at Edge Hill station. I remember bits of broken bottle, relics of battles down by the Docks, the rain-patter of feet walking the pavements when the trams ceased to run and clank, the grey *Antrim* lying on guard in the Mersey, the soldiers marching through the streets, special editions of the evening papers coming out every half-hour, and American tourists, decanted from the *Baltic*, sitting at Pier Head on their Saratoga trunks with no porters to carry them away. I gathered from my father's thunderous noises that it was the beginning of the end of the world.[93]

There had also been deaths. On 15 August two men, John Sutcliffe and Michael Prendergast, were killed when cavalrymen opened fire during a disturbance involving attempts to stop prison vans taking those arrested on Bloody Sunday towards Walton Prison. As Hikins put it: 'In the general deterioration, such an event was all but inevitable.'[94] That day the Home Secretary received a confidential communication from Lord Derby, the hugely influential Tory grandee dubbed (by some) the 'King of Lancashire'.[95] Derby had been contacted by Samuel Hutchinson, who was concerned that 'the serious position' pertaining in Liverpool had not been realised by the Home Office and Government more widely. The Lord Mayor, Churchill was told, reckoned that the riots were not of the ordinary kind:

> but that a revolution is in progress. He fears that tonight there may be no light in the town and that looting will be wholesale [...] The city is in a state of siege, the hospitals have but two days' supply, and in 48 hours all the poor people will be face to face with starvation, and God knows what will happen when that moment arrives.[96]

The House of Commons was sitting on 15 August, and Churchill reported that the military in Liverpool had opened fire prior to the fatal shootings mentioned and, in fact, before they were known about:

> In Liverpool the situation yesterday was unsatisfactory. There was rioting in certain districts. The troops had to be called out, and the Riot Act was read. The statement that volleys were fired, to which currency has been given in the Press, is incorrect, but some individual shots were fired at the windows

or roofs of houses from which missiles were being thrown at the troops [...]
The total number of shots fired were seven revolver shots by officers, five
rifle shots. No casualties are reported to have resulted, and the disturbance was at once quieted down. The troops returned to barracks at 3 a.m.
Three men were injured among the troops, but nothing serious. Bayonets
were fixed, and the troops advanced down the street with their weapons at
the "charge", but no bayonet charge occurred, nor did they use their
bayonets, as the crowd immediately dispersed down a side street.[97]

When reports concerning the shooting of Sutcliffe and Prendergast came in
later, Churchill had departed. The reports were then dealt with by the Under-
Secretary of State for War, John Edward Bernard Seely, known as Colonel Seely
from his rank in the Hampshire Yeomanry.[98] He told the House that he had
received information direct from General MacKinnon stating that 'a party of
the 18th Hussars were attacked to-night in Liverpool and one man was killed
and three wounded'.[99] Subsequent information corrected the number killed.
This represented a serious escalation and indeed, on Churchill's own estimation,
a calamity. As he had phrased it less than six months earlier: 'For soldiers to fire
on the people would be a catastrophe in our national life. Alone among the
nations, or almost alone, we have avoided for a great many years that melancholy
and unnatural experience.'[100]

No less a person than George V expected, and indeed urged, more of these
'melancholy and unnatural' experiences, at least if his message to the Home
Secretary of 16 August is anything to go by. It echoed Lord Derby in noting that
the situation in Liverpool was 'more like revolution than strike' and urged a
settlement be 'forced on both parties'. Unfortunately the monarch didn't specify
how this might be achieved, but went on to 'strongly deprecate the half hearted
employment of troops'. His advice was that 'they should not be called upon
except as a last resource but if called upon, they should be given a free hand and
the mob should be made to fear them'.[101]

Churchill telegraphed the King the following day and updated him on the
situation in both London and Liverpool, the latter in particular, and also related
that a battalion of Gordon Highlanders had been despatched to Sheffield, where
'disturbances of a serious character' had broken out. The perhaps nervous
monarch was also offered some reassurance that he wasn't actually facing the
same type or scale of revolutionary challenge which his cousin, Nicholas II of
Russia, had met some six years earlier:[102]

Although a spirit of unusual unrest and discontent is stirring the whole
Labour world due mainly to the fact that wages have not in late years kept
pace with the increased cost of living there is no ground for apprehension.
The forces at the disposal of the Government are ample to secure the
ascendancy of the Law. The difficulty is not to maintain order but to maintain order without loss of life.[103]

If the general tenor of Churchill's telegram was reassuring, a mention in it of a meeting of the railway unions at the Board of Trade was perhaps less so. He told George V that 'the signal for a general strike on the railways has not yet been given' and that in the event of such 'it is believed that the necessary services can in all circumstances be maintained'. Any hopes that the four unions representing railway workers – the Amalgamated Society of Railway Servants (ASRS), the United Pointsmen and Signalmen's Society (UPSS), the General Railway Workers' Union (GRWU)[104] and the Associated Society of Locomotive Engineers and Firemen (ASLEF) – would be exempt from the 'spirit of unusual unrest and discontent' were to be dashed later that very day. As the historian of one of them put it: 'by 1911 the railway service was full of outstanding grievances. The Transport Workers' Strike at Liverpool proved a match to the combustible material, and ... the revolt spread to every station.'[105]

The 'outstanding grievances' largely revolved around the workings, or perceived lack thereof, of the Conciliation Boards which had been set up in November 1907 in order to avoid a general railway strike. The Board of Trade, then headed by Lloyd George, had brokered the arrangement whereby these Boards would arbitrate on matters revolving around railwaymen's hours of work and rates of pay.[106] According to Lord Claud Hamilton, a former (and future) Conservative MP and Chairman of both the Great Eastern Railway and of the Railway Companies' Association, the employers accepted the settlement because 'it did not involve recognition of the Union'. He went on to add:

> The Union, of course, is not recognised in any way. Not a loophole, so far as I can see, has been left open for them ... No official of the Union who is not an employee can have anything to do with the boards. The agreement secures what the companies have been contending for, namely – the separate entity of each company, and the non-recognition of trade unionism.[107]

The Boards proved unpopular with the workers and, perhaps unsurprisingly, with their unions, who dubbed them 'Confiscation Boards'. The system was sluggish and, according to one author, 'The whole scheme proved clogged and inadequate ...'[108] It was in an attempt to resolve these issues that the employers and unions were holding talks at the Board of Trade. However, according to the diary of civil servant Sir Almeric Fitzroy, the Clerk of the Privy Council,[109] the talks failed partly because of an intervention by the Prime Minister, who proposed a royal commission be convened to investigate the questions at issue:

> I saw a Minister at luncheon, who told me the breakdown of the negotiations was directly due to the Prime Minister's roughness in dealing with the men's representatives as he flung his Commission at their heads in the form of an ultimatum, without taking the trouble to explain its constitution and the arrangements for its immediate sitting and report at the earliest possible moment. His brusquerie at such a juncture may not be irretrievable, but it

has undoubtedly aggravated discontent and made the chances of an accommodation more remote.[110]

Asquith had also publicly warned the unions that 'he would employ all the forces of the Crown to keep the railways open',[111] which, as one of his biographers phrased it, 'had the counter-productive outcome of precipitating the strike, not preventing it'.[112] Though observance of this national stoppage was stronger in some areas, mainly the midlands and north of England, than in others, it nevertheless threatened to paralyse the national network. As one of Lloyd George's biographers stated it: 'This railway strike of August, 1911, was much the most serious industrial dispute that England had ever known.'[113] This is unarguable, and if it endured for any length of time then a general stoppage of industry, with consequential economic damage and severe food shortages, would result. There was, of course, one further corollary, in that without the railway, troops and police could not be moved quickly to where they might be required.

Deployment of police and military forces formed one arm of the Government's response. The Home Office despatched a letter to Chief Constables on the day the strike was called, informing them that:

> it will be the duty of each Police Force to give effective protection to life and property and also to all railwaymen within their jurisdiction who wish to work. If the force at your command is not adequate for this purpose, it will be necessary for you to have special constables sworn in, and the Home Secretary strongly recommends that you should take immediate steps to have suitable men ready to be sworn ...[114]

The Home Secretary, having taken advice from the Attorney General Sir Rufus Isaacs and the Solicitor General Sir John Simon on 18 August that he was acting legally in doing so and in conjunction with the War Office, changed the rule whereby military aid had to be requested by the local authorities: 'The Army Regulation which requires a requisition for troops from a civil authority is suspended.' The military were now charged with:

> the duty of protecting the railroads and all railwaymen who continue at work and the general officers commanding the various military areas are instructed to use their own discretion as to whether troops are or are not to be sent to any particular point.[115]

The officers chosen by Haldane, the Minister of War, to 'control the distribution and movements of all troops employed in protecting the railways throughout the country'[116] were Major General Sir Nevil Macready and, as his staff officer, Captain Wyndham Childs. Asquith's statement that he would utilise 'all the forces of the Crown' had been no exaggeration; according to Childs, the regular army in its entirety was involved:

> We had got every soldier we could secure out on duty with the police. We had even reached the stage of making up composite companies of men on

foot from field and garrison gunners, and ended by actually taking the depot staffs of instructors. Literally there was not a man left in barracks.[117]

Macready explained how: 'Practically the whole of the troops in Great Britain were on duty scattered along the railway systems, many unimportant lines being closed down, and on the main lines arrangements made for trains to run long distances by locking the signals at intervening points.'[118] This had, according to one account, an unfortunate effect: the Birmingham Police contingent sent to Liverpool were compelled to march 40 miles to a station on the main line in order to board a train when they were urgently needed in their home city.[119] Further, Arthur Willmer, Mayor of Birkenhead, telegraphed Churchill on 19 August informing him that fifty infantrymen had been withdrawn from the town by the army and thus, despite enrolling 374 special constables, he did not 'consider that I have sufficient force at my disposal. If you cannot send me more military or naval support I cannot answer for the safety of life and property.'[120] Receiving no reply, he followed up with a telegram to Sir Edward Troup some five-and-a-half hours later: 'Please send more troops at once. It is urgent. I cannot see my way to preserve life and property unless I get more assistance. Food supply running short.'[121]

Churchill had reported to the King the same day on the situation. Reports from Chief Constables nationwide indicated that in South Wales about 75 per cent of railwaymen were on strike, whereas in 'the triangle Bristol Gloucester Reading' the proportion was about fifty-fifty. In the 'great manufacturing provinces', which Harold Butler recalled him naming 'the great quadrilateral of industrialism',[122] meaning an area encompassing 'Carlisle Newcastle Grimsby Leicester Coventry Wolverhampton Crewe Chester Liverpool Bradford', probably 70 per cent were strikers. What was worse, however, was that 'Over large parts of these areas 90 per cent of the drivers have come out.' As for the rest of England: 'there is inconvenience and dislocation but no serious stoppage except in cases of through trains cancelled through strike areas. London is quiet. Stoppage of goods trains in main strike areas perfectly complete.' The 'paralysed areas', as he termed them, contained a population of around twenty million and almost all the UK's principal manufacturers. Both groups were dependent upon the railways for food and raw materials. He concluded that: 'Any prolonged interruption of traffic in these areas must involve comparative arrest of industry of all kinds coupled with severest famine.'[123]

Despite the report being telegraphed, a method which generally limits expression, that the sender was pessimistic is fairly obvious. In fact, and even though the army tried to maintain a skeleton service of trains carrying foodstuffs and essential freight, the effort met with meagre success: 'Trains were stoned, signal-wires cut, rails torn up, stations attacked.'[124] The effort made to keep the railways going was, though, intense. Macready related that he and Childs stayed constantly in their room at the War Office, where an extra telephone, along with a large railway map, was installed, from 17 to 23 August. Apart from taking it in turns to go home for a 'wash up' each morning, they 'put in one hundred and forty-four hours practically on end' of continual telephoning. As he put it: 'I never before realized the physical exhaustion of long-distance telephoning.'[125]

There was a broadly similar set-up at the Home Office. Butler recounted the Home Secretary 'marching up and down his room ... before a large map of the country',[126] whilst Lewis Harcourt, Asquith's Secretary of State for the Colonies, wrote that 'Winston is much too fond of acting as Commander in Chief and moving thousands of troops about ...'[127] That was an exaggeration; the Home Secretary had devolved responsibility for troop deployments, as already mentioned. There was, though, liaison between Churchill's office and Macready's, as was evidenced when a telegram was received at the former at 13.00 hours on 18 August. It had been sent by magistrates at Llanelli, Carmarthenshire, and was brief and to the point, if somewhat cryptic: 'Troops unable to cope with mob. Desire augmentation of force by nightfall.'[128]

Llanelli (also spelled Llanelly at the time) was an industrial town with significant steel and tinplate works. Given that 'the kind of contacts with dockers and other workers which, elsewhere in Britain, had generated unofficial strike action did not exist in Llanelli', then it appeared for a time 'as though the turbulent events of 1911 might by-pass Llanelli altogether'.[129] It was not to be, and when the railway strike was called on 17 August the station was picketed and traffic brought to a halt. This was, as Hopkin noted, particularly easy to achieve given the location of Llanelli station between level crossings to east (Station/New Dock Road) and west (Glanmor Road). By the evening of 17 August three trains were held up and unable to pass through the blocked crossings, one of which was the Cork Express from London to Fishguard. Attempts to clear the pickets using the small number of local police failed, and even the arrival of a 120-strong military force from Cardiff on the morning of 18 August proved insufficient, the number of pickets present being estimated at anywhere between 1,000 and 5,000 strong at various times – a number which greatly exceeded the total of railway employees in the area. It was this event that led to the sending of the telegram to the Home Office.

Macready reacted immediately, though he blamed the magistrates for letting the situation get out of hand, and despatched a further 250 men from Cardiff. In overall command was Major Burleigh Francis Brownlow Stuart, who led 150 officers and men of the Worcestershire Regiment, reinforced with a further 100 of the Devonshire Regiment. With these at hand, the police, also reinforced, were able to get the level crossing gates open and traffic began moving again. The trouble, however, was not over.

At around 14:30 on 19 August a train left Llanelli station, heading westwards, and passed successfully over the level crossing. A little further along the line traversed a cutting with embankments on both sides, that on the northern side being topped by the back gardens of High Street. Here the train slowed so that the gates at a further level crossing, at Victoria Road, could be opened. It was now that a number of men ran up to the locomotive. They physically removed the driver, during which operation he was injured, according to some accounts, then extinguished the fire and blew-down the steam before sabotaging the brake. The train was now completely immobilised. Major Stuart, at the head of some eighty men of his regiment, was quickly on the scene, along with a trio of local magistrates. A large crowd had by now gathered, mainly on the northern embankment, and began throwing stones down onto the soldiers below, who were obviously at a tactical disadvantage.

Stuart got one of the magistrates, Henry Wilkins, to read the Riot Act before ostentatiously consulting his watch and stating that the crowd had one minute to disperse before the troops would open fire. Whether any of those on the embankment heard any of this is uncertain, but before the minute was up a rifle was discharged accidentally whilst being loaded. This led to five further rounds being fired, these presumably being aimed at individuals. In any event two men, John 'Jack' John and Leonard Worsell, fell dead in the garden of 6 High Street, whilst a further two were wounded.[130]

As had been the case in Liverpool, these further examples of a 'melancholy and unnatural experience' had the opposite effect of that intended: Llanelli exploded into a massive, uncontrollable, riot that went on through the night. The railway was again interdicted and at 22:00 an explosion in a siding where goods wagons were being looted killed four people and seriously injured eleven more. Within twenty-four hours rioting had also broken out in several other South Wales towns including Tredegar, Ebbw Vale, Rhymney, Bryn Mawr and Bargoed, with those at Tredegar being particularly severe. The connection between the events at Llanelli and these later disturbances, which were undoubtedly racially motivated initially, are, though, tenuous.[131] Whatever the impetus behind them, the police and military had to be deployed in response and these forces had been, as has been seen, stretched thin.

Ironically, the shootings at Llanelli occurred on the same day as the other arm of the Government's response, the effort to bring both sides to an agreement, bore fruit. Lloyd George, who 'swoops down on opportunity like a hawk on its prey',[132] had interposed himself into the dispute seemingly on his own initiative; there is no evidence that he sought the Prime Minister's permission, nor that of the President of the Board of Trade, Noel Buxton, before intervening.[133] We have, albeit at several removes, Lord Haldane's account of the result being conveyed to him:

> I was left alone in London one day in charge not only of the War Office but of the Foreign Office also, the Prime Minister having gone to Wiltshire and particularly requested that he might not be summoned back unless his presence was imperatively necessary. There I sat in the War Office ... with a General in each room with his ear glued to the telephone receiving reports as to military arrangements. At last I felt that the situation was too grave for me to take the whole responsibility on my own shoulders and I telegraphed for the Prime Minister. Suddenly Lloyd George burst into our room

exclaiming, 'A bottle of champagne! I've done it! Don't ask me how, but I've done it! The strike is settled!' And ... from that day to this I have never known and none of his colleagues have ever known how it was done.[134]

The settlement had been signed by representatives of the Board of Trade, the railway companies and the unions at 23:00 on the evening of 19 August. Under its terms the strike was terminated, and the strikers were to return to work at once. The Conciliation Boards were to be convened to settle outstanding disputes and a royal commission would be urgently convened to investigate the running of the railway industry. A telegram was despatched to all branches of the railway unions: 'Joint Committee have settled strike. Victory for trade unionism. All men must return to work immediately.'[135]

Shortly afterwards, at 01:00 on 20 August, the Mayor of Birkenhead received a reply from Churchill to his already quoted, and somewhat frantic, telegrams of the day before. He was reassured: 'Railway Strike settled by unanimous agreement. Publish the fact and that peace is made and be specially careful to avoid collisions with those who do not know this yet.'[136] It actually took a little longer to settle matters in that part of the world, particularly given that part of the settlement involved the reinstatement of all who had been dismissed. This was resisted in respect of Liverpool tram workers, who were employed by the local corporation, which 'held itself immune from the conditions facing other employers'.[137] When 250 tram workers were told that they would remain sacked, the Strike Committee rescinded the decision to return to work, and for two days it remained uncertain whether there would be any return at Liverpool. Only after the Strike Committee threatened to reactivate a national strike in sympathy did the Corporation come to terms; the Strike Committee ordered a general resumption of work, and wound itself up on 24 August.[138]

Hattersley reckons that Lloyd George had 'browbeaten' the employers in order to overcome their reluctance to meet with the unions, which is likely the case.[139] According to Jenkins, Lloyd George achieved the settlement by employing 'all the cajolery, all the psychological insight, all the appeals to patriotism which Asquith had disdained to use'.[140] This judgement reflected contemporary opinion, as recorded by Sir Almeric Fitzroy: 'The end of the Railway Strike is another triumph of Lloyd George's genius for conciliation. According to Nash [the Prime Minister's private secretary, Vaughan Nash], he plays upon men round a table like the chords of a musical instrument ...'[141] Asquith too paid fulsome tribute,[142] as did the King, who congratulated the Chancellor on 'averting a most disastrous calamity'.[143]

If Lloyd George was perceived to have had a 'good strike', then the same cannot be said for his 'terrible twin' in the Home Office. As the 'recognized guardian of the public safety',[144] Churchill had become extremely frustrated at the failure to maintain a functioning railway system. Lucy Masterman's biography of her husband, from whom she must have received the information, has the Home Secretary 'prostrate' on the evening of 19 August and exclaiming that 'The men have beaten us. We cannot keep the trains running. There is nothing we can do. We are done!'[145] However, and according to the same author, upon learning of the settlement Churchill 'immediately telephoned Lloyd George' but, rather than congratulating him, admonished his colleague: 'I'm very sorry to hear it. It would have been better to have gone on and given these men a good thrashing.'[146]

This is often cited as an example of Churchill's belligerence towards those whom he considered socialists and indeed organised labour in general.[147] It may be, however, that it is a poor example, inasmuch as it is probably false. There are a few reasons to suspect this.

It is, for instance, barely compatible with his earlier despondency concerning the inability to keep the trains running, which whilst from the same source does accord with the known situation. Nor does it chime with the tone of his telegram to Willmer at Birkenhead despatched about two hours after news of the settlement. Moreover, at much the same time as the latter message was sent, a telegram was also sent to the King. This too was moderate and emollient in tone, if inaccurate in content regarding Llanelli:

> reports from South Wales this morning show that everything is perfectly quiet. Order has been restored at Llanelly and the railwaymen are returning to work. The military officers report that the railwaymen were not themselves responsible for the rioting at Llanelly. The Commissioner of [Metropolitan] Police reports that everything is peaceful and quiet in London and that all arrangements are being made to facilitate the meeting of railwaymen in Hyde Park this afternoon. The troops are being withdrawn from the railway stations and other points and are being concentrated preparatory to returning home. The news from Liverpool and Birkenhead is that everything is quiet and orderly. It is expected that the settlement of the railway strike will promote a solution of the special difficulties which exist in those two places.[148]

Further evidence that Churchill was relieved rather than exasperated at the strike ending comes from his colleague John Burns, the President of the Local Government Board. He recorded in his diary visiting the Home Office 'after tea' on 20 August to find 'WC in velvet lounge suit unduly elated at end of dispute ...'[149] Burns undoubtedly considered the elation out of place due to his belief that the 'settlement' had not really settled anything at all, but merely postponed further confrontation.[150] He was, of course, proved right in the fullness of time but peace, as brokered by Lloyd George, reigned for the moment. Indeed the Chancellor would likely have taken a dim view of any carping about his 'champagne' moment.[151] It was indeed something to celebrate, inasmuch as the railway strike directly involved 145,000 men from forty-one companies, and amounted to roughly 485,000 working days lost.[152] This was, by any standards, a vast economic cost.

Moreover, none of Lloyd George's biographers seem to have recorded this telephone conversation, which suggests that he wasn't the source of the story even though he and Lucy Masterman were close, though platonic, friends.[153] Almost by default then, she must have got it from her husband whose biography, published twelve years after his death and nearly thirty years after 1911, was based on her diary. She notes, however, that the entries were often made according to her recollection of conversations that occurred days earlier. Accordingly, some scholars, such as Roy Jenkins and Bentley Gilbert, consider it a secondary source.[154] John Grigg described the book as 'an altogether outstanding source for the period, though it is not always clear when the author is quoting a contemporary record or narrating (less reliably) from memory',[155] whilst Roy Hattersley opined that 'the basic facts are usually right, though the details are often woefully wrong'.[156]

Even with these caveats it remains an important work, and Lucy Masterman was indisputably an acute, if not always entirely accurate, observer and recorder of things she saw, heard and remembered. To quote Peter de Mendelssohn: 'Gifted with a sparkling intelligence, great charm, and a high sense of humour, her memoirs and diaries, together with her husband's letters, furnish us with a wealth of felicitous "snapshots" of Churchill and his circle of friends during these exciting and harassing years.'[157]

Even if Churchill had not then wanted the railway strike to continue in order to 'thrash' the men into submission, he still had to explain and justify his and the Government's conduct during it to Parliament. A debate on 'Labour Disputes' and the employment of the military in them took place in the House of Commons on 22 August 1911 when he was called upon to account for the matter. As might have been expected, criticism was levelled at him from both right and left of the political spectrum. Labour members were particularly exercised about the deployment of military forces to areas where there had been no request for them from the civil authorities. Philip Snowden, for example, asked the Home Secretary why troops had been sent into his constituency and under whose authority this had been done. The answer was:

> the troops were sent to Blackburn by the officer commanding the troops in the district as part of his general scheme for the protection of the railways. The military authorities have complete discretion in this respect ... and are under no legal obligation to await a request from the civil authorities.[158]

Hansard records an unnamed MP shouting 'Martial law' during this answer, and whilst he did not respond to the interjection the Home Secretary was pressed on the matter. George Lansbury, the Labour member for Tower Hamlets, Bow and Bromley, put it thus: 'When a district is perfectly peaceful, is it at the whim or discretion of an officer commanding in the Army to draft in soldiers against the will of the local authorities?'[159] Churchill explained that the rule which 'we have usually followed has been that soldiers should be sent in aid of the civil power

when they have been advised by the local authority' but, after being pressed
further by Lansbury, explained that 'in the present situation'

> the military authorities have been charged with ... protecting the property
> of the railways and for securing law and order in the maintenance of traffic.
> For the purpose of discharging that duty it has been necessary to employ a
> large number of troops ... under the orders of different generals who are
> responsible for certain areas in the country. Those ... have been given and
> will continue to enjoy full discretionary power to move troops along the
> lines of [the] railway to such points as may enable them to safeguard as far as
> possible the ordinary working of all necessary traffic.[160]

Snowden then asked whether his reply meant 'that the Home Office have given
authority to the military authorities to send troops where they like and when they
like, without there being any indication of disturbance?'[161] He was told that:

> The military authorities always enjoy power to move troops in their own
> country – to move British troops about the country wherever it is found to
> be convenient or necessary, and the regulation which has hitherto restricted
> their employment in places where there was disorder until there had been
> a requisition from the local authority was only a regulation for the con-
> venience of the War Office and generally of the Government, and has in
> these circumstances necessarily been abrogated in order to enable the
> military authorities to discharge the duties with which at this juncture they
> were officially charged.[162]

Leo Chiozza Money, the Liberal MP for East Northamptonshire and a close ally
of Lloyd George, asked if there was 'any precedent for these relations between
the War Office and the Home Office?',[163] to which Churchill replied that no
precedent was needed. The matter was entirely in accord with existing law and
did not violate constitutional practices. He added that 'the conditions which have
undoubtedly occurred in the last week have been without any previous experience
in this country'.[164]

Though Churchill was obviously defending Government, rather than specifically Home Office, policy, it was his department that came under fire, particularly
from the Labour MP for Leicester, Ramsay MacDonald, and Keir Hardie.
MacDonald had been involved alongside Lloyd George in settling the railway
strike, and he went on the attack following Asquith's motion 'That this House
do now Adjourn until Tuesday, the 24th October.'[165] After praising all sides in
the dispute and commending their willingness to come together, he moved on to
commenting that: 'I should like, if we were able, to stop here, but that is absolutely impossible. The Department which has played the most diabolical part in
all this unrest is the Home Office. The Home Office has taken two departures,
both of which ought to be censured by this House.'[166]

The first 'departure' he deprecated was essentially minor: the Home Office had
issued 'strike bulletins' which, he claimed, were 'prejudiced, ill-informed and

inaccurate' and had an inflammatory effect. Churchill dismissed this charge as 'small and trumpery'. The second was of far greater consequence and related to 'the new doctrine' preached by the Home Secretary concerning the deployment of troops:

> I always understood that the military have no right to quarter itself in districts where there was civil peace unless the authorities were first of all consulted, or unless it was in the ordinary operation of the drafting about from place to place of the military contingents ...[167]

He went on to state that if the 'the constitutional law and practice' as outlined was 'going to be the rule of the Home Office in future', then trouble lay ahead: 'Organised labour in the country will not allow it, and, what is more, I think every person who has got the least idea of what civil liberty is will support us.'[168] The methods employed, he said, were a 'recurrence to medieval ideas of how law and order are going to be maintained'. Britain, however, was 'not a medieval State, and it is not Russia. It is not even Germany ...' Churchill was then criticised directly and personally:

> If the Home Secretary had just a little bit more knowledge of how to handle masses of men in those critical times, if he had a somewhat better instinct of what civil liberty does mean, and if he had a somewhat better capacity to use the powers which he has got as the Home Secretary, we should have had much less difficulty during the last four or five days in facing and finally settling the very difficult problem we have had before us. I have spoken warmly, and I hope it may induce the Home Secretary just to think a little bit more before he starts drafting his troops into places where they are very unwelcome and unbidden guests; and before he tells his generals to do what they like in Leicester or Manchester I think he might consult people who know something more about the condition of those places and how to keep law and order in them.[169]

The Home Secretary also drew criticism from the Opposition, albeit in a more oblique fashion. Gershom Stewart, the Conservative MP for Wirral (which adjoined Birkenhead), complained of intimidation by strikers of men who wanted to work and of 'the violent scenes which we have lately witnessed'. He implied that the Government had not acted forcibly enough: 'Surely,' he argued in reference to the strike leaders, 'the time has come to put the law into operation and not allow the continuance of such action by people who are preaching public sedition in the way they do.'[170] This drew a reaction from Labour members, particularly from the MP for Glasgow Blackfriars and Hutchesontown, George Barnes, and an argument that fills several columns of Hansard ensued.[171]

When Churchill eventually rose to speak, however, he addressed himself mainly to the attack made by MacDonald. He denied absolutely that any 'illegal or extra constitutional action of any kind' had been taken, but acknowledged that the Government had made 'exceptional use of obvious and well-known legal powers, and that exceptional use we submit the emergency fully justified'.[172]

The next portion of his speech, during which he related the nature of the emergency referred to, was described by Randolph Churchill as seeming to be 'high flown and even absurdly exaggerated' when read 'in the cold light of historical analysis more than fifty years later'. However, he added that at the time it was made, there can be little doubt that 'it reflected the considered views and attitudes of the overwhelming majority of responsible opinion'.[173]

> I have a right to ask the House, to look at the emergency with which we were faced, and which alone would justify the strong and unusual measures which we thought it necessary to take. Let the House realise it. In that great quadrilateral of industrialism, from Liverpool and Manchester on the West to Hull and Grimsby on the East, from Newcastle down to Birmingham and Coventry in the south – in that great quadrilateral which, I suppose, must contain anything between 15 to 20 millions of persons, intelligent, hard-working people, who have raised our industry to the forefront of the world's affairs – it is practically certain that a continuance of the railway strike would have produced a swift and certain degeneration of all the means, of all the structure, social and economic, on which the life of the people depends. If it had not been interrupted it would have hurled the whole of that great community into an abyss of horror which no man can dare to contemplate.[174]

He argued that no Minister, 'even the hon. Member for Leicester himself, if he sat on this Bench', would have acted differently in using 'the whole power of the State' to direct 'the vital service of the food supply and the scarcely less vital service of transport of the goods indispensable to the industrial production'.[175] Also re-enunciated was the philosophy which had inspired the Government in regard to deployment of the military:

> The task which was entrusted to the military forces was to keep the railways running, to safeguard the railways, to protect the railway men who were at work, to keep the railways running for the transport of food supplies and raw material. And it was necessary, if they were to discharge that task, that the general commanding each area into which the country is divided, the general responsible for each of the different strike areas, should have full liberty to send troops to any point on the line so that communication should not be interrupted. That is how it arose, of course, that ... soldiers arrived at places to protect railway stations, signal-boxes, goods yards, and other points on the line without their having been requisitioned by the local authorities. There is nothing against the law in that. Let no man imagine that there is.[176]

Though there was, as had been established by the opinions of Simon and Isaacs already mentioned, nothing 'against the law' in utilising the military as a centrally directed gendarmerie, it was certainly a departure from traditional methodology. As has been discussed, by long-established custom and practice it was not central

Government that was responsible for the preservation of order. Rather it had been the responsibility of magistrates and other local authorities who were autho-rised, in the last resort, to call upon the army for assistance as and when required. Now these powers had been usurped and superseded, the 'existing procedure' for dealing with industrial strife and disorder, though it had been previously strained, had now been completely overturned. As had been foreshadowed earlier in Churchill's tenure as Home Secretary, industrial strife and concomitant disorder on a large scale was seen for the first time as a national, rather than local, emergency which required a co-ordinated response, both civil and military, from the state.[177]

The journalist and editor William T. Stead adopted a somewhat idiosyncratic, and arguably hagiographic, view of Churchill's role over the period in question. According to an article of his which appeared in November 1911, the Home Secretary had 'been through it all before', albeit only in his imagination:

> Mr Winston Spencer Churchill last month had the unusual opportunity of verifying by the experience of a Minister of State the accuracy of his imagi-nation as a novelist. When the Home Secretary, finding himself face to face with the General Strike, gave orders for the occupation of the railways by an army of 50,000 men, and despatched armed cruisers to the Mersey to protect the docks at Liverpool, he must have realised, at least momentarily, in the stress of his arduous labours, that he had been through it all before. In his early youth, when he had only turned his first quarter of a century, Winston Churchill had thought it all out, had pictured the stirring scenes when a furious populace surges through the streets, to be checked by the sharp, stern voice of the rifle, and had realised in advance how he would feel if he were Minister of State confronting a revolution, and also if he were a popular hero leading it.[178]

The piece went on to review, over three double-column pages, the novel in question: 'I ignore the books of last month, and revive the almost forgotten "Savrola" as the book of this month, containing, as it does, the sketch in outline of the picture which the author, as Home Secretary, had to complete in the mosaic of actual fact.' This wasn't a tongue-in-cheek exercise:

> 'Savrola', although an interesting romance, is chiefly important for the light which it throws up in the working of the Home Secretary's mind. It is part of the irony of circumstance that Mr Winston Churchill personified himself as the leader of the forces of discontent and not as the President who repre-sented the executive Government of the day.

Determining whether this analysis has any validity is perhaps best left to others, but that the author was impressed by the Churchill's performance is clear:

> The Home Secretary is undoubtedly the most commanding outstanding figure of the group of Ministers who had to handle the strike last month.

Mr Lloyd George was the most winning, Mr Buxton the most laborious, and Mr Asquith the least successful of the Ministerial junta upon whom was thrown the *rôle* of saviours of a society threatened with dissolution. But Mr Winston Churchill, as the Home Secretary, held the post of danger. On him devolved the responsibility for maintaining order. It was he, and he alone, who had to give the command to use troops, who in case of need would not, and who, as a matter of fact, did not, hesitate to shoot. He was the hero of his own romance.

Politics as performance art? Perhaps. Jonathan Rose thought so, and contended that whilst *Savrola* 'arguably ranks among the worst novels of the nineteenth century', it nevertheless 'offers remarkable insights into the author's core political convictions and methods'.[179] This was as Churchill had intended. He had informed his mother prior to publication that 'All my philosophy is put into the mouth of the hero.'[180] Journalist and author Alfred George Gardiner was less impressed than Stead, though also described Churchill as an actor, and one who possessed an 'abnormal thirst for sensation'. This, he argued, was combined with 'an unusual melodramatic instinct':

He is always unconsciously playing a part – an heroic part. And he is himself his most astonished spectator. He sees himself moving through the smoke of battle – triumphant, terrible, his brow clothed with thunder, his legions looking to him for victory, and not looking in vain. He thinks of Napoleon; he thinks of his great ancestor.[181]

Others found his 'performance' rather more prosaic, along with that of the Government as a whole. According to Keir Hardie's interpretation:

It was left to a Liberal Government to ride roughshod through the Civil law, trample down the entire framework of the constitution and introduce Russian methods into England ... Generals were given instructions to act without any request from the civil authorities ...[182]

Some scholars have viewed Churchill as having his 'old martial instincts ... re-awakened', whereby he 'threw himself into the fight with all his energy'.[183] There is some contemporary evidence of this. Gardiner relates a story that John Burns found him studying a map upon which had been marked the positions of military contingents. 'What do you think of my military arrangements?' he asked. 'I think you are mistaking a coffee-stall row for the social revolution' was the reply.[184]

As has been argued, the Home Secretary judged that the 'great unrest' was more about discontent with economic and working conditions than it was about revolution as such. This was despite many opinions, including that of the King as already noted, having it the other way around. Even Leon Trotsky, writing in 1925, by which time he knew a thing or two about revolutions, opined that 'During those days a dim spectre of revolution hung over Britain.'[185]

It was also the case that many Conservative-leaning newspapers, undoubtedly reflecting the opinions of their readers, were appalled by what Stead termed the 'elemental forces' which had been wakened and let loose.[186] The *Sunday Referee*, for example, reckoned that what it called the 'popular disturbances' had approached 'more nearly to red revolution on an extensive scale than anything that our oldest inhabitants can remember' and had 'undoubtedly increased political animosity ... both within and without Parliament'. The blame was firmly attached to the current Government, via its pandering and giving way to 'selfish and insatiable factions' such as 'extreme Radicals, Labour-Socialists, and [Irish] Nationalists'. These factions, the paper contended, were attacking 'all the established and venerated institutions of the country, endangering the existence of the Crown, and the unity of the nucleus of the Empire – Great Britain itself ...'[187] This was *The City of Brass*, as envisioned by Kipling, made real.

The *Morning Post* had gone further and, believing that 'this country was nearer to open revolution than at any time within the memory of living man!', thundered that 'The time has come for the "whiff of grape shot" which is the only final answer of authority to the clamour of an undisciplined mob.'[188] A 'whiff of grape shot attitude' was exactly what Churchill was reputed to possess[189] and Gardiner had noted some three years previously that 'the whole spirit of his politics is military ... The smell of powder is about his path, and wherever he appears one seems to hear the crack of musketry and to feel the hot breath of battle.'[190] Yet despite this reputation the 'grape shot' remained largely unused. Indeed, and particularly given the national scale of the strikes and the numbers involved, there is something in William T. Stead's November 1911 observation that: 'The chief marvel ... is that an enterprise which dealt so fatal a blow at the vitals of the nation should have been baffled with such little loss of life.'[191]

It is the case, though, and despite him having far less direct involvement than he had with the South Wales strikes the previous year, that the Home Secretary found the 1911 unrest vexing. This may have been due to him being forced to curb 'the spirit of his politics'. According to George Riddell, who 'usually played golf with Winston twice a week' at that time:

> During the period of strikes, Winston had a very difficult job. He started out being perhaps too lenient, and was gradually forced into a very awkward and difficult position in relation to the working classes. I could see that the situation was weighing upon him very seriously and that his position at the Home Office was gradually becoming intolerable to him. It was obvious that he was gradually setting his teeth, and being a soldier he would be likely to act in a thorough and drastic manner in the event of further labour troubles.[192]

Whatever he did, or was perceived to be doing, would inevitably attract opprobrium from both ends of the political spectrum. That the deployment of military forces had not succeeded in keeping the railways working at anything like sufficient capacity, and that Lloyd George's success was based around conceding much to the unions, may also have rankled. As Addison notes: 'he saw it as the duty of his class, and hence of the state, to protect the weak and the poor. The strong and rebellious were an altogether different matter.'[193] Robert Rhodes James quotes Charles Masterman in a similar vein: 'He desired in England a state of things where a benign upper class dispensed benefits to an industrious, *bien pensant*, and grateful working class.'[194] That was a description which singularly failed to encompass the working class recently encountered, a version moreover which was likely to be clashed with more and more in the future. It seemed quite clear from the general unrest which accompanied the strikes, and the sympathy and active support other workers afforded those taking action, that industrial and social relations in Britain had entered upon a novel and, to some, alarming phase. This new era, as it might be termed, had then at least the potential for repeats of Liverpool and Llanelli. If so then Churchill, according to the retrospective opinion of his close, lifelong, friend Violet Bonham Carter, would not shrink from it:

> he was never quite a Liberal. He never shared the reluctance which inhibits Liberals from invoking force to solve a problem. And though he revelled in discussion he was by temperament an intellectual autocrat. He never liked having other people's way. He infinitely preferred his own.[195]

Gardiner provided a similar and rather more contemporary opinion: 'Remember, he is a soldier first, last and always. He will write his name big in our future. Let us take care he does not write it in blood.'[196]

That was for a future which was, of course, dependent upon, to steal the apocryphal phraseology of a future Prime Minister, 'events, dear boy, events'.[197] That these 'events' might well be in the international sphere was known in late August 1911. For, in addition to the political crisis occasioned by the House of Lords reforms, and the social and industrial conflict experienced during the strikes, both of which had calmed somewhat towards the end of the month, the potential for a conflict of arms with Kaiser Wilhelm's Germany remained very much a live issue. Indeed, according to Sir Almeric Fitzroy's diary, the Home Secretary perceived a connection between the last two, inasmuch as he was 'said to be convinced that the whole trouble [the Railway Strike] is fomented by German gold, and claims to have proof of it, which others regard as midsummer madness'.[198] Midsummer madness or not, the international crisis was to have profound effects on Churchill's life and career.

Chapter Nine

As Dead as Queen Anne

'There is a well-defined class of people prone to "Spy-mania" and whose minds are peculiarly affected by anything in the nature of espionage or counterespionage.'[1]

'What sells a newspaper? A former associate of Lord Northcliffe answers:

The first answer is "war". War not only creates a supply of news but a demand for it. So deep-rooted is the fascination in war and all things appertaining to it that ... a paper has only to be able to put up on its placard "A Great Battle" for its sales to mount up.

This is the key to the proclivity of the Press to aggravate public anxiety in moments of crises.'[2]

* * *

In 1903 Erskine Childers published his bestselling novel, *The Riddle of the Sands*, the plot of which dealt with the uncovering of a dastardly Prussian plot to invade Britain.[3] It was by no means the first, and was most definitely not the last, example of 'invasion' or 'invasion/spy' literature, though it remains the best known and is still in print.[4] It was Childers' sole novel, whilst the most prolific writer of such works during the late Victorian–Edwardian period was undoubtedly William Le Queux. An author who 'masqueraded as an expert in espionage and claimed to be a spy with his life under threat from the Germans'.[5]

As with several of his contemporaries, Le Queux began his career by depicting the invaders as being French and/or Russian.[6] Following perceived German support for the Boers during the South African War, the advent of Anglo-German naval rivalry, the signing of the Entente Cordiale in 1904 and the visit of Kaiser Wilhelm II to Tangier in 1905 (which sparked the so-called Moroccan Crisis), the identity of the prospective enemy changed. Such tales proved lucrative, and were taken up in the expanding market epitomised by the 'new journalism' of organs such as the *Daily Mail*. Founded in 1896 by Alfred Harmsworth with 'the explicit object of entertaining as well as informing its readers',[7] this became 'a newspaper where sensationalism and spy/invasion stories met'.[8]

Credited with believing that his readership, both actual and potential, relished a 'good hate'[9] and that wars whether fictitious or real sell newspapers, Harmsworth commissioned Le Queux in 1905 to compile an account of a fictitious invasion of Britain set in the near future.[10] This would be serialised in the *Daily Mail* between March and July the following year before appearing in book form. Field

Marshal Lord Roberts, the British Commander in Chief during the Boer War, lent his name to the venture and advised on the most likely path that the invaders would take. Harmsworth had them rerouted: he wanted larger towns and cities, with their greater populations and thus potential readers of his paper, 'imperilled'. To generate publicity Lord Northcliffe, as Harmsworth had become,[11] sent men dressed as Prussian soldiers, complete with spiked helmets and wearing sandwich-boards, to parade around the streets of the places in question as the 'invasion' progressed.[12] When it, and they, reached London, their presence caused proverbial 'questions in the House' from, amongst others, Hugh Arnold-Forster, a former Secretary of State for War from 1903 to 1905 and Liberal Unionist MP for Croydon.[13] They were assured by the then Home Secretary, Herbert Gladstone, that 'the Commissioner of Police is taking steps to deal with the matter under the Metropolitan Streets Act'.[14] Northcliffe was likely delighted with the extra publicity; it is said that the serial publication and associated advertising boosted circulation by 80,000 per day.[15] The book when it appeared was translated into twenty-seven languages and supposedly sold over a million copies.[16]

The tale was written as a narrative military history complete with maps and plans and the object of the exercise, apart from making money, was to reveal 'the truth that the Government are strenuously seeking to conceal from our people the appalling military weakness and the consequent danger to which the country is constantly open'.[17] Needless to say, a great part of this 'danger' related to the stated 'fact' that the majority of German immigrants in Britain were part of a spy network – a recurring theme in Le Queux's works and those of others who wrote similar stories. As one scholar has noted: 'Scaremongering had been a regular feature of the yellow press for many years, but Le Queux became its high priest. Even serious journals began to succumb to panic.'[18]

One 'serious journal', the *Quarterly Review*, then under the editorship of the distinguished academic Sir George Prothero, did indeed succumb. In *The Invasion of 1910* Le Queux wrote of the 'marvellous system of spies and advance agents – Germans who had lived for years in England',[19] and this theme was taken up and explained as fact:

> Nothing can be much more certain than that, if we are locked in a life-and-death struggle with Germany, she will attempt invasion. Her naval officers have sounded and sketched our harbours and studied every detail of our coasts. Her military officers have carried out staff-rides in this country. [...] There are, in this country some 50,000 German waiters;[20] and a large number of these are employed in connexion with the hotels at railway stations. Many keepers of public houses near our forts are German. The nakedness of our land is spied out; and, as we are habitually very vocal and the German General Staff is very silent, the blow will fall when and where we least expect it.[21]

The next year Le Queux wrote another work, *The Spies of the Kaiser*, which was, prior to publication, serialised in the *Weekly News*.[22] The book became another bestseller, and given the 'uncomfortable feelings' it engendered it is then small wonder that 'spy mania' flourished. This manifested itself, at least in part, via multitudinous missives to Le Queux from concerned readers. The quantity of these was no doubt related to the fact that the publishers of the *Weekly News*, D.C. Thomson of Dundee, offered their readers a reward of £10 for information on 'spies' and appointed a 'spy-editor' to collate the results. This information was passed to Le Queux, who incorporated elements into his stories, thus responding 'directly to the imagination of his audience'.[23] The same information was forwarded by the author to Major James Edward Edmonds, who headed, from 1907, the Military Operations Directorate 5 (MO5) at the War Office.[24]

Le Queux, and indeed Childers before him, as well as contemporary writers in the genre, claimed the existence of a British 'secret service' which sought to thwart the Kaiser's dastardly designs. The truth was, as might be expected, rather more mundane. Up until 1907 the only approximation to a British 'secret service', which might engage in espionage, consisted of 'small and underfunded military and naval intelligence departments, both with little capacity to collect secret intelligence'.[25] These 'spies in uniform' were severely constrained in their abilities to access intelligence: 'If they were sent to the Reich in an official capacity ... the German authorities would, by definition, be aware of their presence and could take steps to ensure that their "guests" only saw what they wanted them to see.'[26]

This was a known problem. Colonel Edward Gleichen,[27] head of the European Section of the Directorate of Military Operations at the War Office and a former military attaché at Berlin, wrote in 1907 asking for funds to set up a 'Secret Service for Europe' which would relieve military and naval attachés of the difficulty of conducting espionage. If there was a conflict, any failure in discerning enemy intentions would, he argued, mean that the 'whole blame would fall on this Directorate'. Since the works of Le Queux and similar were translated into German, and several other languages, he concluded that: 'The only consolation in the present state of affairs is that every foreign government implicitly believes that we already have a thoroughly organised and efficient European Secret Service!'[28] He was probably being ironic,[29] inasmuch as critiques of the British Army's performance during the Boer War, and the failure of intelligence particularly, were widely and openly discussed.

That was all in the public domain. What was not so widely advertised was that the year 1903 also saw two 'diminutive departments' established within the Directorate of Military Operations at the War Office. One, MO2, was responsible for gathering foreign intelligence, whilst the second, MO3, had a counterespionage role. Since the only official organisation with any expertise in these areas, albeit minimal in the required context, was the Special Branch of the Metropolitan Police,[30] then the recruitment of the head of that organisation, Superintendent William Melville,[31] to carry out investigative work for both departments was a logical step.[32]

MO3 was renamed MO5 in 1907, during a period when concentration on suspected German espionage intensified, which was, as noted earlier, the same year that Edmonds took over.[33] His resources were miniscule: other than himself, there were just two other personnel involved, one being Melville and the other an unnamed major who had little interest in the position.[34] Melville had given credence to reports of German spies, but could get neither the police nor the Home Office to take him seriously when he attempted to highlight such matters with them.[35] Edmonds held similar opinions and had the opportunity of presenting them when, pressured by 'popular opinion', as represented by much of the press, the Prime Minister Sir Henry Campbell-Bannerman authorised the convening of a sub-committee of the Committee of Imperial Defence to consider the invasion threat.[36] It heard several witnesses, including Edmonds and Lord Roberts, and their confidential report was completed on 22 October 1908. Asquith, now Prime Minister, summed it up for the House of Commons on 29 July 1909:

> the conclusion to which we unanimously arrived ... may be summed up under two heads. In the first place that, so long as the naval supremacy of this country is adequately assured, invasion on a large scale ... is an absolutely impracticable operation ... it is the business of the Admiralty to maintain our naval supremacy ... The second proposition is, we ought to have a home Army ... sufficient in numbers and organisation for two purposes – in the first place, to repel what are called raids ... [and] ... to compel an enemy which contemplates invasion to come with such substantial force as to make it impossible for them to evade our Fleet.[37]

Balfour, as Leader of the Opposition, largely concurred with the conclusions outlined. Indeed, given that the sub-committee's decisions as laid out by Asquith were accepted, the threat of large-scale invasion was vanishingly small and any so-called raids, though strategically imbecilic, would be of little more than nuisance value. Nevertheless the obsession with spies continued and indeed intensified, which caused Haldane, a level-headed logician if ever there was one, concern. Initially at least he doubted such tales, describing the 'circumstantial stories' which reached the War Office as being 'almost always ridiculous'. What troubled him more was what they represented: 'the index of a dangerous state of nervousness which if it is allowed to grow might lead to a public outcry against our sending the Expeditionary Force, which we have created with such pains, overseas when it was needed to go'.[38] He also remained anxious to build bridges to Berlin,[39] so even more troubling was 'the effect on the public mind that Germany is the enemy, which renders any attempt to improve relations increasingly difficult'.[40]

Haldane had a change of heart, however, becoming concerned about foreign espionage, and Asquith seemingly shared his anxiety.[41] The result, at the suggestion of the Army's General Staff, was the setting up under Haldane's chairmanship of yet another sub-committee on 25 March 1909.[42]

Edmonds appeared and presented such evidence as he had of German espionage in Britain, a proportion of which had been sourced from Le Queux and all of it from members of the public. It was, to say the least, thin. One example will suffice:

> [The] Informant, while motoring last summer in an unfrequented lane between Portsmouth and Chichester, nearly ran over a cyclist who was looking at a map and making notes. The man swore in German, and our informant getting out of his car to apologize, explained in fair English, in the course of the conversation, that he was studying at Oxford for the Church, and swore in German to ease his conscience. He was obviously a foreigner.[43]

The Naval Assistant Secretary to the Committee of Imperial Defence, Maurice Hankey, was to relate that Edmonds' 'revelations' were initially received with 'incredulity and regarded almost as the aberration of minds suffering under hallucination'.[44] Esher's journal entry for that day recorded: 'A defence committee on "espionage" this afternoon. A silly witness from the W[ar] O[ffice]. Spy catchers get espionage on the brain. Rats are everywhere – behind every arras.'[45] Notwithstanding this, and according to Hankey 'almost against its will', the sub-committee became convinced that the danger was a real one.[46]

When the sub-committee reconvened on 20 April 1909, Haldane informed them that though he did not think there was an invasion plan as such, he did consider that 'the German General Staff is collecting information systematically in Great Britain'. Therefore methods of preventing them making use of this data, which could be used 'in time of war or of strained relations ... [for] injuring our defences, stores, or internal communications', must be evolved. Coming from an ardent Germanophile, who had been educated at the renowned University of Göttingen in Saxony and was known to be a devoted admirer of Germanic culture,[47] his views 'conveyed unusual conviction'. In fact he proposed that five members of the sub-committee, Hardinge, Murray, Henry, Ewart and Bethell, should form what might be termed a sub-sub-committee in order to consider 'how a secret service bureau could be established'.[48] The quintet recommended, and the sub-committee agreed, that a Secret Service Bureau was essential for dealing both with counter-espionage at home and intelligence gathering abroad.[49]

Two officers were appointed to the Secret Service Bureau that was formed in October 1909: Captain Vernon Kell and Commander Mansfield Cumming were selected by the War Office and Admiralty respectively.[50] They came under MO5, with Edmonds being responsible for directing their activities, and shortly afterwards 'it was found necessary, in order to avoid over-lapping' to divide their responsibilities; Cumming was entrusted with gathering foreign intelligence, whilst Kell was made responsible for counter-espionage within the British Isles.[51] This division of labour provided the acorns from which were to grow the mighty oaks of MI6 (*aka* SIS, the Secret Intelligence Service) and MI5.

Churchill, as President of the Board of Trade in 1909, was not directly involved in the process whereby the Secret Service Bureau came into being. In fact, and perhaps ironically, he was at Würzburg in northern Bavaria during mid-September 1909 observing, as a guest of Kaiser Wilhelm II, the annual German Army manoeuvres.[52] This was the second such occasion he had witnessed, having also been at those held around the city of Breslau, Silesia, three years earlier. That experience had caused him to remark to his Aunt Leonie afterwards that 'I am very thankful there is a sea between that army and England.'[53] He was no less impressed with the later version, writing that he had:

been out all day watching these great manoeuvres. There are no less than five Army corps and three cavalry divisions engaged [...] This army is a terrible engine. It marches sometimes 35 miles in a day. It is in number as the sands of the sea – & with all the modern conveniences.[54]

He did, however, note that politically there was 'a complete divorce between the two sides of German life – the Imperialists & Socialists. Nothing unites them. They are two different nations. With us there are so many shades. Here it is all black & white (the Prussian colours).'[55] He wrote a few days later how 'The manoeuvres finished with a tremendous cannonade in a fog' and that he had:

only two minutes speech with the Emperor – just to say goodbye and thank him for letting me come. He was v[er]y friendly ... but I saw nothing of him. Perhaps it was just as well. I rather dreaded the responsibility of a talk on politics. It is so easy to say something misunderstandable – and foreign affairs are not – after all – my show.[56]

This passage is noteworthy for recording what was, probably, the only time in his adult life that Winston Churchill dreaded talking politics or, indeed, felt the need to respect departmental boundaries.

Upon his return from Germany he had his officials prepare 'a most careful report' on the structure of German finance for the Cabinet. This described the difficult position in which the Empire found itself in that context, and expanded upon his earlier observation about the 'divorce' in German society. 'These circumstances' he said:

force the conclusion that a period of severe internal strain approaches in Germany. Will the tension be relieved by moderation or snapped by calcu-lated violence? Will the policy of the German Government be to soothe the internal situation, or to find an escape from it in external adventure? There can be no doubt that both courses are open. Low as the credit of Germany has fallen, her borrowing powers are practically unlimited. But one of the two courses must be taken soon, and from that point of view it is of the greatest importance to gauge the spirit of the new administration from the outset.[57] If it be pacific, it must soon become markedly pacific, and conversely.[58]

That one of the functions of the Secret Service Bureau was indeed to 'gauge the spirit' of the German government, and to discover and measure how this spirit manifested itself in relation to 'external adventure' particularly, was obvious. What isn't clear is when Churchill learned of its existence: 'the Bureau remained so secret that its existence was known only to a small group of senior Whitehall officials and ministers, who never mentioned it to the uninitiated'.[59] This, at least, was something that Le Queux got right; he had written a decade earlier that 'The British Secret Service ... works in silence and secrecy ...'[60]

In any event, it was with Major General Ewart that Churchill met, at Haldane's instigation, in order to discuss the Board of Trade report on 15 November.[61] Ewart disliked Asquith's government generally, seeing it as Kipling had in *The City of Brass* as ruinous to tradition and a socialist advance guard, and Churchill and Lloyd George particularly.[62] Despite this antipathy, the meeting was productive, with the military man explaining how useful the Board of Trade could be in helping to assess German intentions and strength. The abnormal purchase of materiel such as preserved foods, boots, clothing, medical supplies and horses might indicate a military campaign was in the offing. Churchill agreed that if the War Office sent a comprehensive list of questions, then he would see that they were addressed. The resultant document ran to some sixty pages, but it contained no guarantee that advance notice of war could be had from scrutiny of economic data.[63]

If the ice between Churchill and Ewart had been broken somewhat by these exchanges, it seemed not to have improved the military man's opinion of the politician. He was to write on 17 December 1909, following the calling of the General Election of January 1910, that 'There is an ugly rumour that if the Radicals return to power Winston will come to the War Office. God forbid.'[64] If God did indeed forbid, then he worked through the agency of Asquith, and Ewart was spared the ordeal of having a man he regarded as a 'fussy interfering gasbag' as his political head.[65] He was, though, even had he wanted to, unable to avoid interaction with Churchill completely. Kell's first six-monthly progress report of 25 March 1910 detailed one reason why:

> For the effective working of the Counter-espionage movement, it is essential to ensure the co-operation of the Chief Constables. Those who have already been approached by me in this matter are willing to help us in every way. It has been suggested by one of them that the subject be laid before the whole body of Chief Constables, at their annual meeting in London, in May next [May 1910] when a definite understanding as to the working of a system could be arrived at. The matter is now under the consideration of the DMO [Director of Military Operations].[66]

There were, though, two types of Chief Constable: those in the counties who were able to act discreetly, and those leading borough forces in the larger towns and cities who faced greater scrutiny by their Watch Committees.[67] It followed that briefing all Chief Constables, as Kell had suggested, could compromise his clandestine activities. This was something Ewart was seemingly aware of and had indeed considered. In fact, when he introduced Kell to the recently appointed Home Secretary, on 27 April 1910, it was via a letter requesting assistance in approaching the Chief Constables of *county* forces only:

> This officer, who is attached to my Intelligence Department, is employed by me in making enquiries regarding the many alleged instances of Foreign Espionage and other suspicious incidents which are frequently brought to our notice. The nature of his work makes it desirable that, with your permission, he should be brought into private communication with the Chief Constables of counties, and, if you could see your way to give him some general letter of introduction, which he could produce when necessary, it would help us very materially.[68]

Churchill ordered compliance, and over the signature of his Private Secretary, Edward Marsh, an introductory letter requesting Chief Constables to give him 'the necessary facilities for his work' was despatched to Captain Kell.[69] He was able to use it profitably. At a meeting of 'about twenty' county Chief Constables held on 2 June 1910, 'they unanimously agreed to help all they could' after the 'President' of the gathering, Major Otway Mayne, read out Churchill's letter. One of them, Major Atcherley of the West Riding force, suggested, however, that 'it would be a good thing to get in touch with the Chief Constables of Boroughs'. Kell recorded that he then asked Atcherley and Captain Sant to lunch in order to 'discuss the advisability of meeting these Borough Chief Constables'. Following a 'long discussion', the trio arrived at the conclusion that 'it would be more prudent not to meet them en bloc, as there were perhaps some among them who would not be of much use to me [Kell] – and who might prove to be obstructionists'.[70]

Kell's diary is silent on the matter thereafter, but it does record him asking Edward Marsh for a letter of introduction to the Scottish Office so that he might have 'some authority to show the Scottish Chief Constables'.[71] His intention was to travel to Aberdeen, and then work his way southwards into England. Marsh provided a missive addressed to P.J. Rose, private secretary to Lord Pentland, the Secretary of State for Scotland, and Rose in turn furnished him with a suitable document.[72]

Kell's first visit was to Major Duncan Forbes Gordon, the Chief Constable of Aberdeenshire, on 15 June 1910 but it was not a success: 'He was not enthusiastic, and said there were no cases of suspicious Germans anywhere about. He asked me to send him a copy of the Scottish Secretary's Letter of Introduction. I told him I would do so on my return home.'[73] Kell left for Perth after his talk with Gordon. There he received a warmer welcome, one which formed the pattern for the rest of his tour. His second General Report, covering the period April–October 1910, detailed how: '40 Chief Constables (33 in England and 7 in Scotland) have been got in touch with. They have all expressed themselves most willing to assist me in every way.' Presumably Major Gordon was not included in this tally. The report went on to add that

> Early in the coming year I hope to have returns in from the Chief Constables, giving details of every alien residing in the Coast Counties of N[orth] Riding, E[ast] Riding, Lincoln, Norfolk, E[ast] Suffolk, Essex, Kent, ... W[est] Sussex, Cornwall, Isle of Wight; also Surrey, Wilts[hire] and Bucks [Buckinghamshire].[74]

Stafford has argued that Churchill 'readily believed in the existence of a foreign spy menace ... [and] uncritically embraced Kell's nightmares of such an army preparing the way for a German invasion'.[75] It is certainly the case that the Home Office was extremely accommodating to the Counter Espionage Section, and helped to draw up a form, dubbed 'Alien Returns', which was to be completed by Chief Constables. Following Kell's submission of a draft version, Troup suggested that 'a note should be put on the form saying that all information was to be collected confidentially and no questions of an inquisitorial nature asked. He asked me to get a proof printed and he would submit it for approval to the Home Secretary.' The proof met with Churchill's approval.[76]

This confidential registering of suspicious foreigners by Chief Constables, though the actual work was delegated to superintendents, causing concern that it would 'do away with a good deal of secrecy of the matter',[77] proved useful. There remained, however, a problem. As Kell explained in January 1911:

> I took a bundle of Alien Returns to Sir Edward Troup to show him what excellent work the Chief Constables had done in that way. He was very pleased ... I told Sir Edward that although these returns were of the greatest assistance to us, our real difficulty still remained unsolved, viz: that it was impossible to get at the names of Aliens in the large cities and boroughs; and that only some sort of compulsory legislation would enable us to deal effectively with that side of the question. He said that so far Mr Churchill was not in favour of any compulsory registration.[78]

Churchill's disfavour was likely related to the fact that it would be politically impossible to introduce any such scheme, as already existed in other European states, to peacetime Britain. What he was prepared to sanction was the clandestine expansion of existing procedures. He had been appointed chairman of a 'Standing Sub-Committee of the Committee of Imperial Defence', with the brief of considering the 'nature and degree' of both postal and press censorship during time of war, on 1 March 1910. The question of censorship of the press was held over,[79] so postal censorship was the subject at the first meeting on 11 July 1910. Three of the sub-committee members, Esher, Bethell and Brigadier Murray, had featured on the Foreign Espionage sub-committee which examined Edmonds. In addition, Lieutenant Colonel George Macdonogh of the General Staff, Alfred Hull Dennis, Assistant Solicitor to the Treasury, Lieutenant Colonel Sir

Matthew Nathan, Secretary of the Post Office,[80] Walter Langley, Assistant Under-Secretary at the Foreign Office, and of course Churchill were present.[81]

Macdonogh explained that the Army General Staff advocated the 'desirability of preventing as far as possible the transmission to foreign powers of information regarding our naval and military preparations, especially in time of war and of strained relations'.[82] He suggested that it was important to have a list of aliens residing in certain naval and military centres, as this would form the 'ground-work' for intercepting and censoring their letters following the signing of a warrant by the Home Secretary.[83] A copy of the proposed warrant was provided, though the entire business was very much a murky area in legal terms.[84] This was pointed out by Dennis, who argued that it was 'doubtful whether the Home Secretary could issue such a comprehensive warrant, but this was a legal matter which would require further consideration'. This was brushed aside:

> MR CHURCHILL said that there did not appear to be any need for further legislation with a view to increasing our powers of censoring correspon-dence. The powers at present possessed by the Home Secretary, which can be set in motion at the request of the War Office, appear to be ample ... he considered that the Police, working with the War Office, should have lists of individuals who might be suspected of sending information to foreign Governments in a time of strained relations, and a warrant might be issued in time of emergency authorising the correspondence of these individuals being censored. This authority should be used sparingly, in order that public confidence in the Post Office should not be shaken ...[85]

The Sub-Committee agreed with him, concluding that: 'The power at present possessed, and secretly exercised on rare occasions, of opening, examining, and impounding correspondence believed to be contrary to the public interest, should be used whenever the necessity arises.' The hope that a 'register of aliens resident in the United Kingdom' would be compiled was also expressed, as was the belief that their correspondence 'might be subjected to censorship in [a] time of strained relations without resort being had to any further legislation'.[86]

Thus, as Christopher Andrew puts it, 'Churchill added a major weapon to Kell's armoury ... what soon became his main counter-espionage tool.'[87] This was intensified by extending the system, which had previously required an indi-vidual warrant for each letter opened, to encompass 'general warrants'. As Churchill later explained:

> Hitherto the Home Secretary had to sign a warrant when it was necessary to examine any particular letter passing through the Royal Mails. I now signed general warrants authorizing the examination of all the correspondence of particular people upon a list, to which additions were continually made. This soon disclosed a regular and extensive system of German-paid British agents.[88]

Quite what constituted a 'time of strained relations' was never defined exactly, though that the Sub-Committee met during just such a period seems undeniable: it was held in the midst of the Second Moroccan, or Agadir, Crisis.[89]

Once again, as with the First Moroccan Crisis of 1905 in particular, German action had the effect of pushing Britain into opposition, rather than, as was Bethmann's general policy, of forging a closer relationship in order to break the 'encirclement' of Germany. Indeed, instead of shattering the *entente cordiale*, German bullying had the exactly opposite effect. As Charmley so eloquently put it in relation to the First Moroccan Crisis, 'Where Bismarck had played chess, Bülow and the Kaiser played poker – and badly.'[90] Replacing Bülow with Bethmann had not, it seemed, changed that. What did change, though, were British attitudes; henceforth, as Strachan argues, Europe rather than the Empire became the focus of British foreign policy, a course from which the Government was not to be deflected.[91]

Though Churchill as Home Secretary had not, as he phrased it, 'had any special part to play in this [the Agadir] affair', he had followed it with the 'utmost interest'.[92] A special Cabinet meeting concerning it had been summoned for 4 July 1911,[93] and the British position debated. Though no minutes were taken,[94] Churchill related to his wife that 'We decided to use pretty plain language to Germany and to tell her that if she thinks Morocco can be divided up without John Bull, she is jolly well mistaken ...'[95] This may have been something of an overstatement, of which more below.

At about this time Churchill composed a memorandum on Home Office paper, which his official biographer says was never circulated to the Cabinet but the content of which formed the basis of his conversations with Asquith, Grey and Lloyd George concerning the matter. It certainly utilised 'pretty plain language':[96]

> It is true G[ermany] has some (minor) claims about Morocco wh[ich] if amicably stated we should be glad to see adjusted either there or elsewhere – subject to Britain being safeguarded – wh[ich] ought not to be difficult.
>
> Her action at Agadir has put her in the wrong & forced us to consider her claims in the light of her policy & methods.
>
> We are bound to give diplomatic support to F[rance] in any discussion about Morocco: but are entitled to tell France if necessary & to make public fact that this is only diplomatic if we think she is unreasonable [...]
>
> If Germany makes war on France in the course of the discussion or deadlock (unless F[rance] has meanwhile after full warning from us taken unjustifiable ground) we sh[oul]d join with France.
>
> Germany should be told this now.[97]

If this had reached the Cabinet it would likely have caused an almighty row. As Randolph Churchill pointed out: 'It is doubtful if at this time any other member of the Cabinet, except Grey, would have gone so far as Churchill was prepared to go in the hypothetical circumstances which he had predicted.'[98]

That was probably optimistic, inasmuch as it is unlikely that Grey would have gone that far, and Churchill was at the extreme end of a spectrum of ministerial opinion. A Cabinet meeting held on 19 July decided, after a long and animated discussion, only to inform the French Government that, if all else failed, Britain would 'suggest a Conference in which it will be our aim to work in concert with French diplomacy'.[99] Asquith's Government was far from being united on such matters. Indeed, if Lloyd George's famous Mansion House Speech of 21 July 1911, which had been cleared by Asquith and Grey,[100] irritated German ministers, then it had a similar effect on some of their British counterparts; Earl Loreburn and John Morley, Lord High Chancellor and Lord President of the Council respectively, were 'extremely alarmed'.[101]

The Home Secretary also felt alarm, though from a different quarter. Kell had reported in February 1911 that he had information via an informant that 'the Germans were very anxious just now to find out the positions of all our ammunition stores and secret magazines'.[102] It seems that Churchill didn't learn of this piece of intelligence, whether accurate or not, at that time. Some six months later, on the afternoon of 27 July 1911 and whilst at a garden party at 10 Downing Street, he received what he called a 'rude shock':

> I met the Chief Commissioner of [Metropolitan] Police, Sir Edward Henry. We talked about the European situation, and I told him that it was serious. He then remarked that by an odd arrangement the Home Office was responsible, through the Metropolitan Police, for guarding the magazines at Chattenden and Lodge Hill, in which all the reserves of naval cordite were stored. For many years these magazines had been protected without misadventure by a few constables. I asked what would happen if twenty determined Germans in two or three motor cars arrived well armed upon the scene one night. He said they would be able to do what they liked. I quitted the garden party.[103]

After some difficulty with a recalcitrant admiral who refused to assist, he managed to get the War Office to deploy infantry to the locations in question. And so, he declared, 'By the next day the cordite reserves of the Navy were safe.'[104] Churchill's account first appeared in 1923. He told a slightly different tale at the time if Lord Riddell's diary is to be believed:

> Winston told me that in the night it had occurred to him that our ammunition stores were practically unprotected and that he had telephoned to the War Office giving instructions that they should be guarded by the military. Curious that no one should have thought of this.[105]

Whatever the origins of his fears of German sabotage, which he admitted may have been unfounded, this incident marked a change in Churchill's thinking. He claimed that 'once one had begun to view the situation in this light, it became impossible to think of anything else'.[106] Given what else was going on in the domestic sphere at that time, this is an extraordinary statement and cannot possibly be true. Or not completely. Even his critics, and there were, and still are, many, were struck by his enormous capacity for work.[107] There is then no reason to disbelieve his statement that 'I now began to make an intensive study of the military position in Europe. I read everything with which I was supplied. I spent many hours in argument and discussion. The Secretary of State for War told his officers to tell me everything I wanted to know.'[108] He also came into contact with, and claimed to have learned most from, Brigadier Henry Wilson, who had succeeded Ewart as Director of Military Operations in August 1910.[109] Sir Edward Grey noted this in his memoirs, commenting that Churchill 'followed the anxieties of the Foreign Office with intense interest and, I imagine, saw much of Sir Henry Wilson ... he insisted on taking me once to see Wilson, and their talk was keen and apparently not the first that they had had.'[110]

Wilson was and is a controversial figure. Strachan characterises him as 'a noted Francophile, convinced that war in Europe was inevitable and possessed of political instincts few British soldiers could match'.[111] That he had indeed exercised a large influence on the Home Secretary is evidenced by a memorandum that Churchill prepared for the Committee of Imperial Defence. Dated 13 August, and running to some 1,500 words, it began by stating that 'The following has been written on the assumption ... that a decision has been arrived at to employ a British military force on the continent of Europe. It does not prejudge that decision in any way.' It also presupposed that 'an alliance exists between Great Britain, France and Russia, and that these Powers are attacked by Germany and Austria'.[112]

This memorandum, 'one of the most prescient strategic documents that Churchill ever wrote', according to Randolph Churchill,[113] forecast a German invasion of France through Belgium and proposed the deployment of a British 'expeditionary army' to operate 'in rear of the French left',[114] The qualities of this document, whether prophetic or otherwise, do not, however, appear to have been widely appreciated at the time. To quote Randolph Churchill again: 'This memorandum did not make much impact upon the Committee of Imperial Defence.'[115] Nor, despite it being entirely based on Wilson's predictions of how a German campaign against France would unfold, did it impress the Director of Military Operations: 'Winston had put in a ridiculous and fantastic paper on a war on the French and German frontier, which I was able to demolish. I believe he is in close touch with Kitchener and French, neither of whom knows anything at all about the subject.'[116]

Britain and France were not formal allies. Therefore British strategy, and particularly the despatch of an expeditionary force to fight alongside the French Army in the event of war with Germany, was far from being a settled matter. Churchill was well aware of this, hence the qualifications in the preamble of his memorandum. In fact Britain had no single established strategy. What had evolved over the period since 1905 were two separate schemes for fighting Germany, one developed by the War Office and the other by the Admiralty.

These had been formulated in isolation from each other and, indeed, from the Government.

That the continental strategy favoured by the War Office, as outlined by Churchill, existed in detailed form, and had been discussed with the French high command, was largely due to the influence and actions of Sir Edward Grey. Grey served twice as Foreign Secretary, firstly from 1892 to 1895 in Gladstone's final administration, and then from 1905 to 1916 in the Campbell-Bannerman and Asquith administrations. From 1906 he authorised secret 'discussions' between the General Staffs of France and Britain but kept these hidden from most of his cabinet colleagues, though of course Haldane knew, and the full import of them even from Campbell-Bannerman.[117] He probably briefed Asquith on the matter in July 1908, some three months after the latter became Prime Minister, and five other members of the Government were also let into the secret around that time.[118] Churchill and Lloyd George were only brought into the picture in 1911, and the former 'discussed the staff plans in considerable detail with Wilson'.[119] Churchill was later to write that 'our Entente with France and the military and naval conversations that had taken place since 1906, had led us into a position where we had the obligations of an alliance without its advantages' but also opined that the policy was, in all essentials, the right one.[120] Lloyd George was, retrospectively, less positive; he told Charles Prestwich Scott, editor of the *Manchester Guardian*, in 1918 that 'Grey is one of the two men primarily responsible for the war'.[121] He was only slightly less censorious in his memoirs:

> the Cabinet as a whole were never called into genuine consultation upon the fundamental aspects of the foreign situation. There was a reticence and a secrecy which practically ruled out three-fourths of the Cabinet from the chance of making any genuine contribution to the momentous questions then fermenting on the continent of Europe ... I can recall no such review of the European situation being given to us ... nothing was said about our military commitments. There was in the Cabinet an air of 'hush hush' about every allusion to our relations with France, Russia and Germany ... We were made to feel that, in these matters, we were reaching our hands towards the mysteries, and that we were too young in the priesthood to presume to enter into the sanctuary reserved for the elect.[122]

A.J.P. Taylor considered that Grey 'followed a resolute line ... but he consulted the cabinet very little, and he informed the public hardly at all'. He also argued that whilst Grey repudiated the phrase the 'Balance of Power', he was 'concerned about the European Balance in a way that no British foreign secretary had been since Palmerston'.[123] The maintenance of this 'balance' was an enduring concern as the readers of *The Times* were informed, or reminded, in 1908:

> The policy of England [*sic*] has always been consistent. This policy, whether the executive agent is Cecil,[124] William III,[125] Marlborough,[126] Chatham,[127] the younger Pitt,[128] or another, is to prevent the overlordship of Europe by

any single Power, and, if any Power either aspires to or begins to acquire a dangerous position of predominance, to use the utmost diligence of state-craft and of arms to redress the scales.[129]

Later scholarship largely agrees that Grey sought, via his willingness to allow hypothetical war planning, to dissuade the French government from seeking an accommodation with Germany: 'Had the French preferred to discuss joint operations in Antarctica, Grey would have been equally content.'[130] At bottom, though, it was politically impossible for Grey to publicise his diplomacy. It risked dividing the cabinet, the Liberal Party and probably the country as well.

Whatever restraints domestic politics might place on the question, there was a practical side to it which, with the Agadir Crisis in full swing, Haldane sought to address. According to his biographer, he was 'persuaded' that the situation was so threatening that he asked the Prime Minister to call together the Committee of Imperial Defence to consider what British actions should, or indeed could, be taken if Germany were to attack France.[131] Asquith agreed, and a secret meeting was arranged for 23 August, which he would chair.

That this might prove a difficult time for the Navy, or at least what might be termed its strategic philosophy, was recognised by Hankey. He sent a letter of warning to Reginald McKenna, the First Lord of the Admiralty, on 15 August:

> you will have received a notice of a CID meeting to be held on Wednesday the 23rd, at which the question of military intervention on the Continent of Europe in certain eventualities is to be discussed ... It is of course notorious that ... General Wilson, who has brought this question to the front, has a perfect obsession for military operations on the continent.[132]

Five days later Wilson conferred with General Augustin Dubail, Chief of Staff of the French Army. The resultant 'agreement' that both put their signatures to called for 'the dispatch of six divisions of British troops to France on certain specified days after mobilization, and enumerated the French ports where they were to disembark and the zone of concentration in France to which they were to proceed'.[133] It was, however, prefixed with the following statement:

> The negotiations which had been initiated were devoid of any official char-acter, and could in no way bind the English and French Governments. The purpose of the conference was only to elucidate certain essential questions and to provide for the necessary preparatory measures so as to ensure, in the best possible conditions, the effective co-operation of their armed forces.[134]

Thus all was set for 'the battle of the Wilsons',[135] the First Sea Lord at that time being Sir Arthur Wilson, who would put the case for a naval strategy. Churchill's later account of the meeting of 23 August is often quoted: 'We[136] sat all day. In the morning the Army told its tale; in the afternoon, the Navy.'[137] He rather glossed over an initial disagreement, or misunderstanding, which arose even before the Army began its tale. Asquith opened the meeting by stating that he 'had called the Committee together as the European situation was not altogether clear, and it was possible that it might become necessary for the question of giving armed support to the French to be considered'. He referred to a previous meeting of a CID Sub-Committee which had considered similar matters in 1909.[138] This had concluded that any such decision was a matter of policy that could only be determined by the Government of the day on the day. However, given that there was the possibility of such a decision being made, the Sub-Committee had examined the General Staff's plan for such an event, and determined that it was valuable. It also concluded therefore that 'the General Staff should accordingly work out the necessary details'.

He added that, 'given recent developments', the General Staff had prepared a fresh Memorandum on the subject, the crucial point of which was that, in the event the Cabinet did decide to support France militarily, 'we should mobilise and dispatch the whole of our available regular army of six divisions and a cavalry division immediately upon the outbreak of war, mobilising on the same day as the French and Germans'. Consequently, the General Staff asked the Admiralty for an assurance that 'the Expeditionary Force could be safely transported across the Channel ... and that the Navy will protect the United Kingdom from organised invasion from the sea'.[139]

Sir Arthur Wilson said it could, but did so in an exceedingly indirect way:

> The Navy could spare no men, no officers, and no ships to assist the Army. The whole force at the disposal of the Admiralty would be absorbed in keeping the enemy within the North Sea. Ordinarily the Navy would furnish transport officers and protecting ships. These could not be furnished in these circumstances. The Channel would, however, be covered by the main operations, and provided the French protected the transports within their own harbours, the Admiralty could give the required guarantee as to the safety of the expedition.[140]

Sir William Nicholson expressed himself satisfied on that point, and added that he presumed the 'ungrudging assistance' of the Admiralty's Transport Department would be forthcoming. McKenna responded that no such support could be given during the first week of a war; the Transport Department would be fully occupied otherwise.[141] In other words, whilst it could transport the Expeditionary Force across the Channel in safety, it couldn't do so in the timeframe required by the War Office. Therefore, even if the Army mobilised on the same day as the French and Germans as planned, it wouldn't be able to reach the battlefront for at least a week.

Thus, during the very first stage of the proceedings, the problem of the Army and Navy developing strategies in isolation was brought into sharp focus. Haldane cut to the heart of the matter as regards the provision of transports: 'could the Admiralty carry out the scheme as worked out or not?' McKenna replied that the matter would be looked into, and that he regretted any misunderstanding. Asquith responded that it was necessary that it should be understood that the question of time was all important; simultaneous French and British mobilisation and concentration were essential features of the scheme. He then moved on, asking the Committee to 'consider the desirability of carrying out the operations proposed by the General Staff or the alternative scheme suggested by the Admiralty on their merits'.[142] Now the Army 'told its tale'.

> General Wilson ... stated the views of the General Staff. Standing by his enormous map, specially transported for the purpose, he unfolded, with what proved afterwards to be extreme accuracy, the German plan for attacking France ... It was asserted that if the six British divisions were sent to take position on the extreme French left, immediately war was declared, the chances of repulsing the Germans in the first great shock of battle were favourable [...] There was of course a considerable discussion and much questioning before we adjourned at 2 o'clock.[143]

Henry Wilson was master of his brief, and was able to answer questions convincingly. He was also noted for being a skilled lecturer[144] and, according to one of Lloyd George's biographers, possessed 'an engaging *bonhomie*, a trenchant vocabulary, and a power of surmounting friction with badinage of a tonic quality which commended him to Lloyd George'.[145] Sir Arthur Wilson possessed few of these attributes, though was far from the reactionary dunderhead he is sometimes portrayed as being.[146]

Upon the Committee reconvening after an hour's lunch, and before Sir Arthur could present the Admiralty case, he was asked directly by Haldane if the War Office 'might assume that the Admiralty could arrange for the sea transport of the Expeditionary Force across the Channel within the time contemplated in the General Staff scheme'. He replied that whilst he had not enquired into the matter, he 'thought that the Admiralty could carry out this service without serious difficulty'.[147]

Admiral Wilson began his presentation by criticizing the General Staff proposals on three main grounds. Firstly, if the entire regular Army left the country, there was a 'grave possibility' of panic amongst the public, which might result in 'the movements of the Fleet being circumscribed with serious effect on our naval operations'. Secondly, there would be no regular troops left to assist the Navy in defence matters. Small enemy raids might cause serious damage unless 'very promptly met' and there were many undefended points on the North Sea littoral that might become important to the Navy, and which the Army would need to protect. Lastly, there would be no regular troops available for direct co-operation in naval operations.[148]

He then outlined the 'policy of the Admiralty on the outbreak of war with Germany', which was 'to blockade the whole of the German North Sea coast'. The important portions of this were the estuaries of the Elbe, Weser and Jade rivers. He explained that this blockade would largely be achieved by the deployment of destroyers, which would be backed up by 'scouts and cruisers' upon which they could retire if driven off by the enemy's larger ships, 'whose own retirement would then, if possible, be intercepted'. The rationale for this close blockade, though he did not make it entirely clear at the meeting, was that it was imperative to stop German submarines – a type of vessel he (apocryphally) considered 'underhand, unfair, and damned un-English'[149] – from getting out.[150]

There were several places, the occupation of which would facilitate the matter: Wangerooge, easternmost of the East Frisian islands; Schillighorn on the west coast of the Jade estuary; an unnamed point at the mouth of the Weser; and Büsum, a coastal town in Schleswig-Holstein from which the southern end of the Kiel Canal could be threatened. As well as assisting the Navy directly, the capture of these places would keep the German North Sea coast in a state of constant alarm. The British force would be highly mobile and could be landed and embarked again before superior enemy forces could be concentrated. In this way, Sir Arthur explained, ten German divisions could be retained in the area and thus the operations would make a material contribution to the Allied cause. At least one regular British army division would be required to carry them out, and subsequent operations could include an attempt to 'destroy or drive out the German Fleet at Wilhelmshaven'. When Churchill pointed out that this would involve 'regular siege operations', the minutes merely record that Sir Arthur 'assented'.[151]

Unlike the plans laid out by his military namesake, Wilson's schemes lacked any sort of detail; he was unable to state how many men would be landed at each place mentioned, but could only say that 'troops for such enterprises must be good and have the best officers'. Upon being informed by French that without horses neither guns nor troops could move, and that horses could not be kept long aboard ships without 'very rapid loss of condition', the admiral responded that infantry would be the chief requirement.[152] Artillery support for the onshore force would be supplied by ships close inshore; Wilson did not respond to an enquiry from Nicholson as to how guns were to be landed.[153] There was one landing operation which would not require Army support: the island of Heligoland would be taken by Marines 'as soon as possible after the outbreak of war'.[154]

This policy, in general, was more or less the same as the one Sir Arthur had advocated in 1907 when he had argued that 'The only way in which we could give serious assistance to France would be by a floating army, making raids on different parts of the German coast and so diverting troops from the main theatre of war.'[155] Or, as Admiral Sir John Fisher is reputed to have put it: 'The British Army should be a projectile to be fired by the British Navy.'

There was much criticism of the notion, particularly from those who cleaved to the continental policy as described earlier. Nicholson stated that: 'The truth was that this class of operation possibly had some value a century ago, when communications were indifferent, but now, when they were excellent, they were doomed to failure. Wherever we threatened to land the Germans could concentrate superior force.'[156] This was echoing, whether consciously or not, the expressed view of Lieutenant Colonel Repington, the highly influential military correspondent of *The Times*:[157]

> Every one knows, or ought to know, that the next continental war will be decided on shore, and many believe that it will be decided within a very brief period of time. A hundred thousand British troops at this decisive point will be of greater moral and material service to a friend than three times their number dabbling in amphibious warfare off the enemy's coast, supported though they might be by the whole strength of the British Navy. If we contemplate the reproduction of Rocheforts, St Malos, and Cherbourgs[158] on the German coast we are not fit to be at large without attendants. This strategy is as dead as Queen Anne.[159]

Nicholson went further, asking Sir Arthur if the Admiralty would continue to press its view 'even if the General Staff expressed their considered opinion that the military operations in which it was proposed to employ this division were madness'.[160]

Retrospectively it has generally been adjudged that this meeting saw the final defeat of the Navy's strategy; that it was found to be something like 'madness' and, therefore, was indeed as 'dead as Queen Anne'. Churchill's version told how the Navy's view, 'which was violently combated by the Generals, did not commend itself to the bulk of those present' and that 'the military and naval authorities were found in complete discord'.[161] Hankey's account, published some fifty years after the event, related that 'the grim old First Sea Lord was no match for the witty and debonair Director of Military Operations'. Consequently, he pointed out, 'From that time forward there was never any doubt what would be the Grand Strategy in the event of our being drawn into a continental war in support of France.'[162] His view at the time was, however, completely different, as evidenced by his letter to Sir John Fisher of the following day:

> A tremendous battle was fought in yesterday's packed meeting. ... After a battle which raged from 11.30 am to 5.30 pm no decision was arrived at. No further meeting will be held in the CID, and, if discussed again it will be in the Cabinet, where the forces will be more evenly balanced. AK W[ilson] put up a rare fight – considering that the thing had been sprung on him almost at a moment's notice, with his DNI [Director of Naval Intelligence] on leave – but, as you know, he is no dialectician and I don't think he made a good impression ... The great thing is that we are safe. The PM began by being pro-military, but possibly this was a bluff ... for afterwards he veered considerably ... The great point is that no decision was arrived at – this means, in my opinion, defeat of our opponents.[163]

Given how mistaken this judgement proved to be, it is perhaps unsurprising that Hankey did not include the document in his later book.[164] Having said that, Keith Wilson produces evidence that it was originally to have featured in the appendices, but these were cut for reasons of space.[165] McKenna too, who had been primed by Hankey as already noted and of course backed the Admiralty position, felt he had achieved some success. According to the diary of Hilda Runciman, the wife of his closest parliamentary friend and colleague Walter Runciman, the President of the Board of Education, he claimed to have been 'calm, dignified and pitiless'.[166] That may have been so, but that this availed him naught, and that Hankey was seriously mistaken, is evidenced by Churchill's letter to Grey of 30 August, in which he said 'I am not at all convinced about the wisdom of a close blockade, and I did not like the Admiralty statement.' He also asked that this message be forwarded to the Prime Minister.[167] Much more portentous, though, was Asquith's letter of 31 August to Haldane:

> Sir A[rthur] Wilson's 'plan' can only be described as puerile, and I have dismissed it at once as wholly impracticable. The impression left on me, after consideration of the whole discussion is:
>
> 1. That, in principle, the General Staff scheme is the only alternative but
> 2. That it should be limited in the first instance to the despatch of four divisions. Grey agrees with me, and so (I think) does Winston.[168]

Haldane says in his autobiography that after the meeting on 23 August had broken up, and before they both departed for Scotland, he took the Prime Minister aside and informed him that he 'could not continue to be responsible for military affairs unless he [Asquith] made a sweeping reform at the Admiralty'.[169] Sir Frederick Maurice, Haldane's biographer, includes a letter from Haldane to Asquith which is undated, but from the wording would appear to have been written in early September 1911, likely in response to Asquith's letter of 31 August, and which expands upon that theme:

> You have recognised that the position disclosed ... on August 23rd is highly dangerous. By good fortune we have discovered the danger in time, but had war come upon us last month, as it very nearly did, the grave divergence of policy between the admirals and the generals might well have involved us in disaster. The fact is that the Admirals live in a world of their own. The Fisher method, which Wilson appears to follow, that war plans should be locked in the brain of the First Sea Lord, is out of date and impracticable. Our problems of defence are far too numerous and complex to be treated in that way. They can only be solved correctly by a properly organised and scientifically trained War Staff, working in the closest co-operation with the Military General Staff under the general direction of the War Office. [Admiral] Wilson's so-called plan disclosed an ignorance of elementary military principles which is startling.
>
> I have after mature consideration come to the conclusion that this is, in the existing state of Europe, the gravest problem which confronts the Government to-day and that unless it is tackled resolutely I cannot remain in office. Five years' experience of the W[ar] O[ffice] have taught me how to handle the generals and get the best out of them and I believe that the

experience makes me the person best qualified to go to the Admiralty and carry through as thorough a re-organization there as I have carried out at the W.O. In any event I am determined that things at the Admiralty shall not remain any longer as they are.[170]

These were not just serious criticisms of the Admiralty in general, but of its political head, McKenna, in particular; and now, quite explicitly, Haldane wanted him removed in favour of himself. Churchill too was undermining McKenna, though less overtly if his letter to Lloyd George of 14 September is any guide:

I cannot help feeling uncomfortable about the Admiralty. They are so cock-sure, insouciant and apathetic, so far as one can judge from all that one sees and hears. I cannot feel much confidence in Wilson's sagacity after his per-formance the other day.[171]

According to Haldane, during his discussion with Asquith on 23 August the Prime Minister had asked him to 'motor over from Cloan[172] to Archerfield[173] in East Lothian, where he would be in residence, to discuss what should be done'.[174]

At some point between the CID meeting of 23 August and Haldane's arrival at Archerfield, Asquith decided what 'should be done'; he would reshuffle his cabinet and, rather than Haldane, move Churchill to the Admiralty. It is possible that he had this in mind earlier, hence the Home Secretary's presence at the meeting. As Churchill later put it: 'I was invited to attend, though the Home Office was not directly concerned.'[175] Lloyd George claimed, according to Lord Riddell, to have had a hand in it, and a large one at that: 'I think I am entitled to the credit. I went to Archerfield ... in August, and told the Prime Minister that we must make the change.'[176] He may have been misremembering. Asquith had written to his daughter Violet on 24 August stating that 'We go to Archerfield a week this Saturday,' that day being 2 September.[177] Plans can, of course, change. Lloyd George was, though, to make much the same claim some four years later: 'The Prime Minister was proposing to make Haldane First Lord of the Admiralty when I happened to appear on the scene ... I knew Winston was unhappy at the Home Office and I pressed the PM to give him the Admiralty.'[178]

Whatever impelled Asquith, and his own account is spectacularly uninfor-mative,[179] there are two versions, both retrospective, of what happened at Archerfield: Haldane's and Churchill's. The former states that he 'drove over to Archerfield as soon as I got to Cloan. As I entered the approach I saw Winston Churchill standing at the door. I divined that he had heard of possible changes and had come down at once to see the Prime Minister.'[180]

This suggests that the drive from Cloan, a distance of some 80 miles, took place in late August. Churchill, however, dates his visit rather later: 'Early in October Mr Asquith invited me to stay with him in Scotland.'[181] There is no doubt that Churchill's dating is the more accurate, and his account continues: 'The day after I had arrived there ... he asked me quite abruptly whether I would like to go to the Admiralty ... I accepted with alacrity ... He said that Mr Haldane was coming to see him the next day and we would talk it over together. But I saw that his mind was made up.'[182]

Haldane told a different tale: 'It was as I thought. Churchill was importunate about going himself to the Admiralty ... He had told Asquith that the First Lord must be in the Commons. As I was now in the Lords[183] this looked like a difficulty.' But not, he thought, an insuperable one.[184] Haldane further relates that he returned home to Cloan, but revisited Archerfield the following day to find Churchill still there. On this second occasion 'the Prime Minister shut me up in a room with him', whereupon he [Haldane] explained to the Home Secretary that, amongst other things, he did not 'think, to be frank, that Churchill's own type of mind was best for planning out the solution that was necessary'. He added that 'Churchill would not be moved, and Asquith yielded to him.'[185]

That Asquith would choose his ministers via a process somewhat approximating dialectical single combat sounds inherently unlikely; more likely is that they thrashed out the outlines of their future relationship as heads of fighting departments. There is also the contemporaneous account of Asquith's daughter Violet, who was at Archerfield during Churchill's visit. Her diary entry for Sunday, 1 October is unambiguous:

> I went for a walk with Winston after tea – and he told me Father had offered him the Admiralty – & to put McKenna at the Home Office. He is over the moon about it (as it has long been his Mecca in the Cabinet) – & tremendously fired by the scope & possibilities of the office. 'Look at the people I've had to deal with so far – Judges & convicts – this is a big thing' etc. etc. He is determined to make a success of it & will put every inch of himself into it ...[186]

The editors of her diary and letters state that the actual offer was made by Asquith on 27 September, but they give no source.[187] Despite this, there is some evidence that it may be largely accurate. Churchill's mother was also in Scotland, and she sent him a letter dated 1 October which refers, albeit indirectly, to the matter: 'Dearest Winston, You thrill me with curiosity. Is it a change of office? – I hope a good one.'[188] The inference is obvious; he had previously hinted to her that he was leaving the Home Office, but not stated where he was going. His letter, if that is what it was, seems not to have survived but she had also written to him on 28 September and it seems likely that it was his response to that which had contained the news.[189]

Churchill had been at Balmoral on 26 September, from where he had written to the Permanent Under-Secretary for Foreign Affairs, Sir Arthur Nicolson, concerning the imminent outbreak of the Italo-Ottoman War,[190] but had left earlier than expected: 'They thought you were leaving early in order to visit your "Mommer"! [mother].'[191] Churchill's letter to Nicolson asked that he 'send me a line to Archerfield to let me know whether I rightly apprehend the bearings of this affair'.[192] He wrote again three days later, this time from Archerfield: "Many thanks for your long and interesting letter which I showed to the Prime

Minister.'[193] All in all then, it would seem that Churchill was invited to Archerfield by Asquith, which curtailed his stay at Balmoral, and was then informed of the Prime Minister's decision during the period 27–29 October 1911.

If Haldane was disappointed at Asquith's verdict, Reginald McKenna was gravely affronted. The news broke for him, at least officially, on 10 October, when he received a letter informing him of the decision:

> As we are on the eve of completing our sixth year of office I am contemplating a certain amount of reconstruction both inside and outside the Cabinet ... and I am going to ask you to undertake what is undoubtedly one of the most difficult and responsible places in the Government – the Home Office ... You know well how highly I appreciate the invaluable service which you have rendered at the Admiralty during the best part of four years, and I hope that a change of scene will not be unwelcome to you.[194]

Though technically he had been offered a promotion, McKenna's immediate inclination was to refuse the post and to resign from the Cabinet.[195] The choice of his replacement at the Admiralty was a particularly galling prospect. Churchill was the man with whom, just a few years earlier, he had fought bitter political battles over the size of the Royal Navy.[196] As Admiral Sir John Fisher, the then First Sea Lord, had phrased it to King Edward VII in 1909:

> McKenna, who when he came here was an extreme 'Little Navy' man, is now an ultra 'Big Navy' man and Your Majesty would be astonished by his memorandum to Grey and to the Prime Minister as to building more Dreadnoughts next year than intended, and we shall certainly get them![197]

Fisher was proved correct. In Churchill's famous phraseology: 'The Admiralty had demanded six ships; the economists offered four: and we finally compromised on eight.'[198] Churchill had been, alongside Lloyd George, the most high-profile of the 'economists' and thus a 'Little Navy' man. Now he was to inherit the fruits of McKenna's labours, a 'Big Navy', and would undoubtedly discard the policies and strategies that McKenna 'had spent three-and-a-half-years promoting'.[199] Further, his earlier campaigning for a reduction of the naval estimates would ensure that the Navy's senior ranks would hardly view his appointment with equanimity.[200] It was, as Asquith's biographers remarked, 'an odd turn of the wheel which brought to the Admiralty the man who only two years earlier had been one of the leaders in the fight against the eight Dreadnoughts, and displaced the man who had fought that fight so gamely and successfully'.[201]

McKenna sought to turn back, or at least halt, that wheel. One of those he confided in was Grey, who wrote: 'I think it would be an awful pity if you chucked office altogether. I have learnt nothing from Asquith. I am as much in the dark as to what is really in his mind and that is why I should like you to talk it all over with him before coming to a decision ...'[202] Other confidants offered similar advice, the outcome being that he asked the Prime Minister to delay the move for two months on the grounds of his, McKenna's, ill health.[203] Asquith agreed initially but when the news leaked and was reported in the press, he rapidly changed his mind; the move was to be immediate.[204] McKenna demurred: 'It is repugnant to me not to acquiesce in any proposal made by you', he informed the Prime Minister, who replied that he was 'much disappointed' and appealed to him to 'reconsider your position'.[205]

McKenna did reconsider his position, but only after arriving at Archerfield on 20 October in order to, as Grey had suggested, talk the matter over and tell the Prime Minister 'all that was on my mind'.[206] According to Martin Farr, McKenna's biographer, he 'pressed his case several times, and Asquith resisted, with increasing indignation'. One of the main planks of his argument was that the military conversations with France were exceedingly dangerous: they 'encouraged the French in the belief that we should fight on their side and led them to provoke Germany. If we failed to join them we should be charged with bad faith. If we joined in fact we should be plunged into war on their quarrel.'[207]

Asquith was able to mollify him to the degree that he did agree to move to the Home Office rather than resign completely, but Farr considers that this 'almost desperate trip to Archerfield and the variety of pleas made to support his case was, and remained, the greatest trauma of McKenna's career'.[208] Asquith's opinion of the matter comes to us second hand. According to his wife's account of what he told her, the Prime Minister 'had the greatest difficulty in explaining [to McKenna that] it was not from rumour gossip or want of efficiency that this change was made ... but he minded terribly & was rather pathetic over it'.[209] If Lord Riddell's recollection is accurate, Lloyd George was scathing: 'I can remember L[loyd] G[eorge]'s sneering account of how McKenna ... had wept at the proposal to eject him from the Admiralty and how he had ignominiously gone to the Home Office like a chastened dog.'[210]

It is certainly the case that McKenna had appeared 'very bitter against Lloyd George and Winston Churchill'[211] over the dispute about the naval estimates in 1909, and had become estranged from the former even before then.[212] However, his enmity in respect of Churchill now turned into something more: an enduring hatred. According to Lucy Masterman, writing soon afterwards: 'McKenna's removal ... left him rather sore. I was rash enough once to mention Winston in his house. I was never received with a more chilling silence.'[213] Lord Riddell noted much the same sentiment, only more so, some three years later: 'Called to see McKenna, who I am beginning to think is a wrong-headed, ineffective person ... His hatred of Winston amounts to an obsession ... McKenna was treated badly when he was ejected from the Admiralty, but his state of mind is not conducive to the public weal.'[214]

That he believed Churchill had indulged in skulduggery in order to replace him seems the only explanation for this level of animosity, though he blamed Haldane even more.[215] There is, though, no real evidence that Churchill engaged in intrigue, certainly before the CID meeting of 23 August, and it was of course only after that meeting that Haldane threatened to resign if McKenna were not removed. Whether Asquith's decision to make a change, not quite as Haldane wished but rather in favour of Churchill, was indeed prompted by Lloyd George remains unverifiable. In any event the Prime Minister justified his decision to Lord Crewe on 7 October, before McKenna had been informed, thus: 'the First Lord ought to be in the H[ouse] of Commons, and the Navy would not take kindly in the first instance to new organisation imported direct from the War Office. On the whole I am satisfied that Churchill is the right man, and he would like to go ...'[216] Haldane, as has been seen, reckoned Churchill to be 'importunate' about going to the Admiralty, which meant, if true, that he had approached, indeed pestered, Asquith about it. Again, there is no documentary evidence to support that claim, though McKenna alleged shortly afterwards that the matter had been 'settled at Archerfield on September 18th, certainly before September 25th ... I know this absolutely ...'[217] Churchill, as has already been shown, wasn't at Archerfield on 25 September,[218] so if it was indeed settled at that time then it is unlikely that he would have had any direct, face-to-face, input, though of course he and Asquith could have spoken by telephone.

The Cabinet reshuffle was announced on 23 October, the day before Parliament reconvened, and the changes were made on 25 October:

Mr McKenna and I changed guard with strict punctilio. In the morning he came over to the Home Office and I introduced him to the officials there. In the afternoon I went over to the Admiralty; he presented his Board and principal officers and departmental heads to me, and then took his leave. I knew he felt greatly his change of office, but no one would have divined it from his manner. As soon as he had gone, I convened a formal meeting of the Board, at which the Secretary read the new Letters Patent constituting me its head, and I thereupon in the words of the Order-in-Council became 'responsible to Crown and Parliament for all the business of the Admiralty'. I was to endeavour to discharge this responsibility for the four most memorable years of my life.[219]

Chapter Ten

'Home Secretaries never do have an easy time'

'If you want to ruin a man send him to the Home Office.'[1]

'The quandary of Winston Churchill may be simply expressed: There were so many Winston Churchills. This baffled his contemporaries and often inspired their mistrust; it has caused historians and his biographers comparable problems.'[2]

* * *

Churchill's tenure at the Home Office served to demonstrate that, even though aged only 35 when appointed, he was competent to perform at a senior level administratively and politically. On the other hand he cannot be said to have been a great Home Secretary; he could boast of no major achievements other than attempts at penal reform, nor did he enunciate any grand or lasting principles. This, however, was hardly out of the ordinary and was, indeed, the norm.

He was the youngest to hold the position since Sir Robert Peel in 1822, and between the end of Peel's first period as Home Secretary and Churchill's appointment the office had changed hands on thirty-two occasions. Thirteen of these stints had, for various reasons, lasted less than the twenty months and five days he was in post. The names of very few of the men who held the position, and they were of course all men, were, or are now, remembered at all apart perhaps from Peel himself.

If the brevity of his tenure was not particularly remarkable relative to that of many of his predecessors, the same cannot be said to apply to his contemporaries: those who served in Asquith's Cabinets from 1908 until the formation of a coalition ministry in May 1915. The Prime Minister was not a great one for reshuffling, and there was little 'churn' involving his Cabinet and none at all with respect to the other great offices of state, for Asquith kept Lloyd George and Sir Edward Grey in their posts over the whole period. Thus the brevity of Churchill's tenure stands out in that context.

He was no doubt relieved that it was so for he neither liked, nor enjoyed performing, the role. Not many holders have, perhaps because, as a then far-in-the-future Prime Minister was to put it, 'Home Secretaries never do have an easy time; it is sometimes said that they possess a unique combination of responsibility without power ...'[3] Indeed whilst Churchill cannot be accused of shirking responsibility, he was to find his powers as Home Secretary strictly limited on occasion. This was undoubtedly amplified by the fact that, as the apocryphal curse has it, he lived in interesting times; his first senior role in politics encompassed a period of extraordinary turmoil in several areas. Politically and constitutionally there was the struggle over the House of Lords which, whilst he was obviously involved and had to fight two General Election campaigns within a year, did not greatly engage him departmentally. The social and industrial strife that took place on his watch most certainly did, and as has been seen he was forever after associated with 'Tonypandy'. That and the events at Stepney. Indeed, it is hard to disagree with Charmley, who argued that: 'It says something for Churchill's reputation that the most famous incident during his period at the Home Office was not his attempt at penal reform but rather his attendance at the "battle of Sidney Street".'[4]

If one accepts that analysis, then that single event overshadows what Sir Martin Gilbert considered to be one of Churchill's 'most productive periods'. He argued that: 'The penal reforms he [Churchill] envisaged, and in many cases carried out, were a high point of his imagination and achievement.'[5] They were also contentious, or potentially so, for although he was building upon processes which had been instigated by his predecessor, particularly in relation to the categorisation of suffragette prisoners, and which had been urged and were supported by Home Office permanent officials, penal reform is almost inevitably unpopular. This is particularly so if the reforms in question can be perceived as being 'soft' on prisoners. Having said that, a Home Secretary in Edwardian times did not face the same degree of obloquy from 'public opinion', as defined by elements of the press, that later proponents of prison reform would have.[6] Indeed, one wonders how a modern audience, perhaps viewing it through a tabloid lens, would receive his oft-quoted words regarding punishment and society: 'The mood and temper of the public in regard to the treatment of crime and criminals is one of the most unfailing tests of the civilisation of any country.'[7]

Randolph Churchill observed that as a backbencher Churchill had spoken as if he were an Under-Secretary and then, after elevation to the latter position, acted as if he were a Cabinet member. He went on to state that, after becoming a Cabinet minister, he became 'apt to speak as if he were Prime Minister'.[8] Whether that be the case or not, Churchill as Home Secretary certainly tried to push the boundaries of his authority, as with his attempts to thwart the system of preventive detention introduced by his predecessor, for example. That he maintained his hostility to that system, even after being severely, and thrice, embarrassed by the affair of the Dartmoor Shepherd, is testimony to the authenticity of his belief and his willingness to act on it.

Conversely, whilst he railed against, and succeeded in abating, preventive incarceration for non-violent and petty criminals, he was keen to have those identified as 'feeble minded' detained on a large scale and indefinitely. The point needs to be made, though, that eugenics was not at that time the sole preserve of oddballs and fanatics, so Churchill's adoption of the eugenicist agenda was not totally outside the mainstream:

it is often forgotten how pervasive eugenic assumptions about human inheritance were in learned and socially elevated circles in the early twentieth century. Belief in the inheritability of myriad physical, psychological and behavioural characteristics, identifiable, even quantifiable, in particular ethnic groups and social classes, was reinforced by expert scientific testimony, and, perhaps equally important, middle and upper class prejudices.[9]

As Home Secretary he was most definitely moving in a circle that was both socially and politically elevated, and so was in a position to at least try to put eugenicist solutions into practice. He did so on at least one occasion: the attempt to have that 'typical example of the village fool', Alfred Oxtoby, vasectomised. As was pointed out to him, though, the documentary evidence from the United States upon which he was basing his effort was 'a monument of ignorance and hopeless mental confusion', and nor could the question of consent be easily answered.[10] He was then obliged to drop the case, but there is no doubt that his espousal of the eugenic cause was sincere rather than, as Macnicol has noted in respect of many public figures, merely an opportunist tactic.[11] However, if the evidence leads to the conclusion that, as Home Secretary and immediately afterwards, he was a true believer, it also points to him ceasing to be so, or at least losing interest, at some point after 1912. Why this might have been so is impossible to say, but it was undoubtedly fortunate in terms of his later reputation.

Though his efforts concerning eugenics basically led nowhere, this was not so in other areas and contexts. For example, his instigation of general warrants authorising the interception of mails was a novel departure that was to endure. It may indeed be considered as exemplifying his 'temerity' in challenging 'principles and practices which had remained sacrosanct for many years'.[12] Whilst these initiatives remained hidden from the public gaze, his expansionist and interventionist 'hands-on' approach was plainly evident in other less clandestine areas where they could, and did, result in legal and constitutional stress and public controversy. One of the most obvious and well known examples was the usurpation of local responsibility for maintaining order, and particularly the appointment of Major General Macready as, in effect, Home Office commissioner to the Welsh coalfields in 1910. Having said that, this could not have been accomplished solely on Churchill's initiative as it required, at least, Haldane's approval. Asquith must have consented too, though the wider Cabinet were unlikely to have been consulted.

Despite the fact that the Home Secretary did not give orders directly to the troops, it was from this time that the fable of Tonypandy, that he instructed the shooting of striking miners, arose. The evidence, however, demonstrates that this was indeed a myth which, in the opinion of Randolph Churchill, likely arose through confusion ('muddle') with Llanelli, where deadly force was used by the military the following year. Also, and as he put it: 'Tonypandy comes easier to the English tongue than Llanelly [Llanelli].'[13]

The 'Great Unrest', of which those events at Llanelli formed a part, was of course industrial and social strife of much greater scope and consequence than the South Wales coal strike. Government attempts to maintain some sort of control, and in particular to keep vital railway communications open, eventually involved the deployment of almost the entire, unmobilised, regular army.[14] Though the Home Office remained ultimately responsible, the command arrangements were devolved to a large extent, with army officers taking regional control and deploying military contingents without further reference to civilian authority. As he phrased it: 'The military authorities have complete discretion in this respect ... and are under no legal obligation to await a request from the civil authorities.'[15] If the shootings at Llanelli on 19 August 1911 became confused with the previous year's events at Tonypandy, it was still erroneous to blame Churchill directly. Though the Home and War Offices ran parallel operations rooms, if Macready's and Childs' extemporised effort can be so called, the Home Secretary had marginal input into military operations generally, and none in that particular instance.

Nevertheless, that the situation vis-à-vis policing industrial disputes had developed into something at least approximating to the imposition of martial law was an accusation that the Home Secretary had to defend against. There seems little doubt that the Government was acting 'on the margins of the constitution',[16] but Churchill had sought the opinion of the Government's legal officers and been assured that the steps taken were legal. Thus when challenged on the matter and accused of introducing 'Russian methods into England [*sic*]', he brushed these complaints aside, basically arguing that the seriousness of the situation vindicated the methods used. That of course smacks somewhat of the argument that the end justifies the means, a rather dubious doctrine to say the least and not that easy to defend.

The future Prime Minister quoted earlier also opined, vis-à-vis Home Secretaries, that they must also take the blame for matters such as 'the occasional riot, when their power to prevent them is indirect or non-existent'.[17] Exemplifying this, Churchill saw much blame come his way concerning the handling of two public disturbances on his watch: the police struggles with the suffragettes on 'Black Friday' and the subsequent 'Battle of Downing Street'. Already something of a target for proponents of female suffrage even before his 'treacherous' behaviour in respect of the 1910 Conciliation Bill, Churchill was now held directly responsible by the suffragettes and their supporters for the behaviour of the Metropolitan Police. Although, once again, the evidence demonstrates that he was not guilty of ordering or otherwise instigating police brutality, the fact that he arranged for the unconditional release of many arrested suffragettes before they could be tried raised suspicions that he had something to hide.[18] This was particularly so given the widely reported words of the magistrate that such a practice had 'never been adopted in the 30 years I have sat here'.[19]

Further, and as has been evidenced, Churchill consistently demonstrated through his actions that he was personally and politically ambivalent regarding female suffrage, despite being on record that he was in favour. This, unsurprisingly, singularly failed to impress a group whose motto was 'Deeds, not Words'.[20] Even though he was never an out-and-out opponent of enfranchising women, as for example was Asquith, his verbal support, for what it was worth, was not based on the principle that women had any fundamental right to the vote. A letter he penned to the Government Chief Whip following his departure from the Home Office sets out his views on the political danger, as he saw it, inherent in the question of female suffrage. It concludes: 'The only safe & honest course is to have a referendum [*sic*] – first to the women to know if they want it: & then to the men to know if they will give it.'[21] That the permission of the all-male electorate was required before women were granted the franchise was not a proposition that the suffragettes, who considered they had a constitutional right to the vote, would have accepted in any event. Be that as it may, there is no doubt that Churchill was profoundly irked by suffragette activities and Addison's point about him and the working class – that whilst he 'saw it as the duty of his class, and hence of the state, to protect the weak and the poor. The strong and rebellious were an altogether different matter'[22] – is surely applicable to them too.

That Churchill was unhappy at the Home Office is undisputed, and to argue that he was not temperamentally suited to the role would hardly be contentious. Mention has been made of the investigations into, and retrospective diagnoses of, Churchill's mental health during his time as Home Secretary which is an area of study that, if it does not cross into, certainly veers perilously close to, 'the much-debunked field of psychohistory'.[23] The source of the belief that Churchill suffered from debilitating 'Black Dog' depression is the book published soon after his death by Charles Wilson, Lord Moran, who had been his personal doctor from 1940 onwards. Therein, Moran stated that 'Black Dog' was 'Winston's name for the prolonged fits of depression from which he suffered.'[24] This work drew a withering response from a number of those who had worked closely with Churchill. One of these, John Colville,[25] argued that Moran was:

> always pursuing his favourite analytical researches from a basis which was false as far as Churchill was concerned. The subject had to be made to fit into the accepted framework, and he therefore satisfied himself that Churchill suffered from long fits of depression, was a prey to bad dreams and was deeply apprehensive.[26]

Forcing the subject into 'the accepted framework' is surely a close cousin of 'psychiatric imperialism', a phenomenon which 'desires that all human conduct become a psychiatric symptom'.[27] Indeed so, and one example of recent neo-psychohistory is perhaps worth quoting:

> Blaming someone's sadness on external events is common sense, but that approach can be as often wrong as right. In Churchill's case, it would certainly

be wrong; there is no question his sadness came from within. In 1910 he was at the peak of success ... In 1910 he was happily married, wealthy, famous, politically powerful, and widely respected. He had no reason to be depressed ... Churchill suffered from more than depression, though. Many historians now acknowledge his depression, but they generally don't appreciate that when he was not depressed Churchill's moods shifted frequently. He was never 'himself,' because his 'self' kept changing. When his depressive episodes subsided, he became another person – disagreeable and aggressive.[28]

Though happily married and undoubtedly famous and widely respected, he was also widely, and bitterly, criticised and disrespected. For though he was, as the holder of a great office of state, undeniably 'politically powerful', this power was greatly constrained in practice. His, and the wider Government's, inability to keep the trains running during the Great Unrest is one example of where he was 'freely criticised by the Press and certain of his colleagues'. The same contemporaneous source noted that 'The situation weighed upon him, and obviously he was very unhappy at the Home Office.'[29] The problems associated with the suffragettes and their campaigns form another example of the limitations of his operational clout. Further, whilst he held the ultimate power, that of life and death in terms of condemned prisoners, he found this, as he put it, a 'nightmare' rather than something to be happy about.

Nor was he wealthy. Indeed, what might, and arguably should, have caused him a degree of worry was his financial position. He had confessed to his wife in October 1909 that he was '*décassé* [out of funds] for the moment'[30] and even the salary of a Secretary of State, which he began receiving in 1910, proved insufficient to meet his outgoings. This was, of course, a far from unusual situation for someone of his background; he had been 'born a member of the aristocracy and enjoyed the trappings of expensive clothes, fine food, personal servants and the delayed payment of bills'.[31] These bills could not be delayed indefinitely, even for the grandson of a duke, and 1911 saw him having to borrow money to reduce, not completely pay off, the amounts owed to 'his wine, cigar, shirt, and saddle suppliers, in each case more than £200'.[32] Using Lough's formula for converting 1911 money values into those of a century or so later,[33] these debts would each have equated to approximately £18,000 at the later date. The Bank of England inflation calculator has the figure even higher at a little over £24,000.[34]

There clearly were several reasons why any Churchillian sadness and depression might have extrinsic origins, if he had been sad or depressed. As previously evidenced, the idea that circa 1910–1911 he was suffering from depression in any inordinate or clinical sense has been comprehensively discredited.[35]

It is also interesting to note that the idea that 'his "self" kept changing' is echoed somewhat, though in a vastly different context, by Robert Rhodes James who was famously to write that there were 'many Winston Churchills':

The quandary of Winston Churchill may be simply expressed: There were so many Winston Churchills. This baffled his contemporaries and often inspired their mistrust; it has caused historians and his biographers comparable problems.'[36]

He went on to list some of these multiple, and overlapping, identities: 'politician, sportsman, artist, orator, historian, parliamentarian, journalist, essayist, gambler, soldier, war correspondent, adventurer, patriot, internationalist, dreamer, pragmatist, strategist, Zionist, Imperialist, monarchist, democrat, egocentric, hedonist, romantic ... the list seems endless'.[37] Indeed so, but even within the category of Churchill as politician there were graduations. John Colville, who was able to observe him closely from 1940 onwards, wrote that 'in politics and indeed all his life, he was as strange a mixture of radical and traditionalist as could anywhere be found'. He considered that despite being the leader of the Conservative Party, and the Prime Minister heading a Conservative Government from October 1951 to April 1955, 'He was certainly not conservative by temperament, nor indeed by conviction a supporter of the Conservative Party.'[38] This dovetails rather neatly with the opinion that the earlier Edwardian-era Churchill, with whom this work has concerned itself, wasn't 'any easily definable species of Liberal' either.[39] That observation also applied to his fellow 'terrible twin', with whom Churchill's fortunes were to become so closely intertwined, Shannon identifying them as 'statesmen of genius in search of great roles to play in politics'.[40]

Lloyd George did, of course, get to play a 'great role' during the First World War which, for Churchill, proved advantageous. This was so because, as Prime Minister, Lloyd George appointed him Minister of Munitions in 1917, thus resurrecting his political career. Churchill had, as is well known, been brought down two years earlier by the failure of the Dardanelles operation, a reverse which was amplified by Conservative hostility to him personally. This was mutual and enduring, with a veto being applied in respect of him serving in Lloyd George's 1916 coalition War Cabinet.[41] To many Tories he remained the 'Blenheim Rat'. As the parliamentary correspondent, Alexander Mackintosh, noted in 1921: 'The personal animosity which Mr Churchill aroused in the Unionist party when he turned against it and left it was maintained by his conduct in office.'[42] Lloyd George interpreted it thus in his memoirs:

> Had he remained a faithful son of the political household in which he was born and brought up, his share in the Dardanelles fiasco would have been passed over and another sacrifice would have been offered up to appease the popular anger. There was an abundant choice from which the altar could have been supplied. His mistakes gave resentful Tories an irresistible opportunity for punishing rank treason to their party, and the lash which drove Churchill out of office, although knotted with the insults he had hurled at them, was wielded with an appearance of being applied not by vindictive partisans but by dutiful patriots.[43]

Lloyd George's *War Memoirs* appeared during Churchill's 'wilderness years', a period when, after having 're-ratted'[44] and become a Conservative again, he was 'deprived, partly but not entirely through his own intransigence, of the sustenance of power'.[45] It was also a time when some, perhaps many, thought he was completely finished politically. As Duff Cooper, Conservative MP for Westminster St George's and a former (and future) acolyte, remarked in March 1934: 'Odd that he should not realise that the game is up. I suppose that he goes on intriguing and making speeches in the same spirit that my mother-in-law goes on painting her face and wearing a wig.'[46]

Indeed, he and his former 'Terrible Twin' were now only brethren in powerlessness, for though he was involved in 'cooking up bold schemes for economic construction' and leading 'The Council of Action for Peace and Reconstruction', these were wilderness years for Lloyd George too.[47] The Conservative-dominated National Government coalition, elected in 1931, enjoyed a massive and unprecedented majority in the House of Commons and its dominance, together with the shattering of the Liberal Party, meant that 'Lloyd George's last chance of office had gone.'[48] He turned to writing his *War Memoirs*.[49]

These proved controversial, both at the time and later, and were unsparing in respect of criticism of generals, admirals and their political masters. They have also been described as 'confusing ... when not actually mendacious'.[50] Other historians have agreed with that conclusion and indeed gone further.[51] This view was not, and is not, unanimous.[52] Churchill, in a *Daily Mail* review dated 21 September 1934, considered that the volumes which had appeared formed the 'dominating contribution to our knowledge, and to our descendants' knowledge, of Armageddon'.[53] Whilst it is axiomatic that memoirs, in general, must be approached with caution, and extreme caution in Lloyd George's case,[54] the *War Memoirs* nevertheless contain much that is useful. One early reviewer considered that the character portraits were 'the outstanding feature of the memoirs',[55] and the third volume dealt up just such a portrait in respect of Churchill.

It described him as 'one of the most remarkable and puzzling enigmas of his time' and went on to state, in relation to his proposed appointment to the War Cabinet in 1916, that: 'His fertile mind, his undoubted courage, his untiring industry, and his thorough study of the art of war,[56] would have made him a useful member ...' Membership would also have mitigated his weaknesses: 'his more erratic impulses could have been kept under control and his judgment supervised and checked, before plunging into action'. Lloyd George concluded by opining that: 'Men of his ardent temperament and powerful mentality need exceptionally strong brakes.'[57]

Conservative hostility ensured that he did not become a member, and this animosity was renewed the following year upon his elevation to Minister of Munitions. Then, 'the Tory antipathy to him was so great that for a short while the very existence of the Government was in jeopardy'.[58] The former Prime Minister lays out his thoughts on the controversy and on the man at the centre of it:

> For days I discussed with one or other of my colleagues Churchill, his gifts,
> his shortcomings, his mistakes, especially the latter. Some of them were

more excited about his appointment than about the War. It was a serious crisis. It was interesting to observe in a concentrated form every phase of the distrust and trepidation with which mediocrity views genius at close quarters. Unfortunately, genius always provides its critics with material for censure – it always has and always will. Churchill is certainly no exception to this rule.[59]

These characterisations were obviously complimentary in general, if backhanded at times, and largely echo similar assessments of Churchill's disposition and personality both earlier and later.[60] Judging the degree to which they affected his performance as Home Secretary, one way or the other, is problematical. It is also difficult, if not impossible, to directly compare and contrast his performance relative to other holders of the post; as Heraclitus of Ephesus is credited with aphorising, 'no man ever steps in the same river twice, for it's not the same river and he's not the same man'.[61] It is definitely the case that the 'river' into which Home Secretaries are required to step flows exceedingly fast, making it difficult to argue that Churchill was more, or indeed less, effective than his direct successor, even though they faced much the same problems at roughly the same time.

Certainly McKenna, a far less dynamic and very dissimilar personality, handled the ongoing social and industrial troubles somewhat differently than Churchill had. He was, for instance, much less inclined to use troops for policing industrial disputes.[62] However, and despite being considered less imaginative, he nevertheless found something of a solution to the furore over the force-feeding of suffragettes by introducing the infamous 'Cat and Mouse Act'.[63] Thus, as his biographer has it: 'by removing "torture" from public discourse he went some way to neutralising the force as an issue and starvation as a weapon'.[64] Other, extremely illiberal, measures he took in respect of the increasing violence of the suffragette movement involved banning their meetings, having members of the editorial board of The Suffragette newspaper arrested, and censoring the paper itself. Barbara Winslow records George Bernard Shaw's riposte: 'The Suffragettes have succeeded in driving the Cabinet half mad. Mr McKenna should be examined at once by two doctors. He apparently believes himself to be the Tsar of Russia, a very common form of delusion.'[65]

Accusations of autocratic tendencies, of introducing 'Russian methods into England', had also been levelled at McKenna's predecessor, and at the government more widely. That Churchill was possessed of the Napoleonic idea, and indeed thought of himself as Napoleon, were similar indictments. Nobody, however, accused McKenna of having an abnormal thirst for sensation or an unusual melodramatic instinct. The accuracy of charges of that type may, with justice, be questioned, but there is no doubt they captured how the Edwardian-era Churchill was often perceived both popularly and by those who knew him.

McKenna is recorded as remarking in 1913 that 'If you want to ruin a man send him to the Home Office.'[66] Indeed, the argument has been made that the Home

Office was, and perhaps still is, 'viewed by politicians as a political graveyard from which resurrection is impossible'.[67] If there is merit in this then Churchill was a political Lazarus who, despite demonstrating that he had a somewhat mercurial approach to politics, certainly disproved the notion that becoming Home Secretary was a career-ending move.

Notes

Introduction

1. Anthony Howard, *RAB: The Life of R.A. Butler* (London: Jonathan Cape, 1986), p. xiv.
2. John Charmley, *Churchill: The End of Glory – A Political Biography* (London: Hodder & Stoughton, 1993), p. x.
3. The great offices of state are: Prime Minister, Chancellor of the Exchequer, Home Secretary and Foreign Secretary. The latter was the only one Churchill didn't attain. Keith Dowding, 'Government at the Centre', in Patrick Dunleavy, Andrew Gamble, Ian Holliday and Gillian Peele, *Developments in British Politics 4* (Houndsmills: Macmillan, 1993), p. 186.
4. Geoffrey Annis and John Radcliffe, 'Notes on The City of Brass', available at: http://www. kiplingsociety.co.uk/rg_cityofbrass1.htm.
5. Randolph S. Churchill, *Lord Derby, King of Lancashire: The Official Life of Edward, Seventeenth Earl of Derby, 1865–1948* (London: Heinemann, 1959), p. 118.
6. Sir Edward Troup, 'The Functions and Organization of the Home Office', *Public Administration: The Journal of the Institute of Public Administration*, 1926, IV:127.
7. Winston S. Churchill, *The World Crisis 1915: vol. II* (London: Thornton Butterworth, 1923), p. 277; Winston S. Churchill, *The World Crisis 1911–1918: vol. II* (London: Odhams Press, 1938), p. 719. *The World Crisis* was originally published as five books over six volumes (or five volumes in six parts, with vol. III divided into two separate books) between 1923 and 1931. In 1938 a 2-volume edition, containing the first four books (or volumes) mentioned above, appeared. The latter is the best known and most widely available version, so references have been made to it as well as to the original volume: Hereafter 'WSC WC (1923)' and 'WSC WC (1938)'. For an explanation of the rather complex publishing history of *The World Crisis* see Richard M. Langworth, *A Connoisseur's Guide to the Books of Sir Winston Churchill* (London: Brassey's, 1998), pp. 101–8, 121–2.
8. Violet Bonham Carter, *Winston Churchill as I Knew Him* (London: Eyre & Spottiswoode and Collins, 1965), Preface (unpaginated).
9. Ibid., pp. 16–17.
10. Violet Asquith to Hugh Godley, 22 April 1907. Quoted in: Mark Bonham Carter and Mark Pottle (eds), *Lantern Slides: The Diaries and Letters of Violet Bonham Carter 1904–1914* (London: Weidenfeld & Nicolson, 1996), p. 127.
11. Roy Jenkins, 'Foreword' to Bonham Carter and Pottle, *Lantern Slides*, p. xxvi.
12. Howard, *RAB: The Life of R.A. Butler*, p. xiv.
13. Lord Moran, *Winston Churchill: The Struggle for Survival 1940–1965* (London: Constable & Co., 1966).
14. Martin Gilbert, *In Search of Churchill: A Historian's Journey* (London: HarperCollins, 1995), p. 233.
15. Douglas Jeffrey, 'Riddles, Mysteries, Enigmas', *Finest Hour: Magazine of The International Churchill Society*, May 2013, 142. Online edition at: https://winstonchurchill.org/publications/finest-hour/finest-hour-142/riddles-mysteries-enigmas-10/.

Chapter 1: The City of Brass

1. *The Story of the Malakand Field Force: An Episode of Frontier War* (London: Longmans Green, 1898); *The River War* in two vols (London: Longmans Green, 1899); *Savrola* (New York: Longmans Green, 1899).

2. Winston S. Churchill, *My Early Life: A Roving Commission* (London: Mandarin, 1991), p. 370. The book was originally published in 1930 by Thornton Butterworth.

3. J.L. Garvin, *The Life of Joseph Chamberlain vol. III: 1895–1900, Empire and World Policy* (London: Macmillan & Co., 1934), pp. 599–600.

4. Richard Price, *An Imperial War and the British Working Class: Working-Class Attitudes and Reactions to the Boer War 1899–1902* (London: Routledge & Kegan Paul, 1972), p. 105.

5. A coalition between Liberal Unionists and Conservatives. Liberal Unionists were former Liberals who had allied themselves with the Conservatives in 1886 in order to oppose Irish Home Rule. From 1895 the two parties were in coalition.

6. Unless otherwise stated, all information concerning elections, etc., is taken from: F.W.S. Craig (comp. and ed.), *British Electoral Facts, 1832–1987* (Dartmouth: Parliamentary Research Services, 1989).

7. Churchill to Lord Salisbury, 2 October 1900. Randolph S. Churchill, *Winston S. Churchill 1874–1965: vol. I Companion part 2 1896–1900* (London: Heinemann, 1967), p. 1,204. Hereafter RSC CV1, P2. Two books about the conflict and his adventures therein also appeared that year: *London to Ladysmith via Pretoria* and *Ian Hamilton's March*.

8. The phrase was coined by the then Liberal Party leader, Sir Henry Campbell-Bannerman, on 14 June 1901.

9. 'A war of annexation, however, against a proud people must be a war of extermination, and that is unfortunately what it seems we are now committing ourselves to …'. David Lloyd George, Hansard, vol. 86, col. 1,211, 25 July 1900.

10. Thomas Pakenham, *The Boer War* (London: Futura, 1988), p. i.

11. *The Times*, 29 July 1901.

12. In the House of Commons, 5 February 1900. Alexander Mackintosh, *Joseph Chamberlain: An Honest Biography* (London: Hodder & Stoughton, 1906), p. 236.

13. *The Examiner* (Tasmania), 2 October 1903.

14. Daily Mail, *The Ghastly Blunders of The War: A Guide to the Report of the Royal Commission on the South African War, 1899–1900* (London: Daily Mail, no date [circa 1903]), p. 12.

15. Ibid, p. 43.

16. M.W. Kirby, *The Decline of British Economic Power since 1870* (Abingdon: Routledge, 2014), p. 1.

17. Paul Warwick, 'Did Britain Change? An Inquiry into the Causes of National Decline', *Journal of Contemporary History*, January 1985, 20(1):100–1.

18. Andrew S. Thompson, 'Tariff Reform: An Imperial Strategy, 1903–1913', *Historical Journal*, December 1997, 40(4):1,035.

19. C. Knick Harley, 'Trade: Discovery, Mercantilism and Technology', in Roderick Floud and Paul Johnson (eds), *The Cambridge Economic History of Modern Britain vol. I: Industrialisation, 1700–1860* (Cambridge: Cambridge University Press, 2004), p. 176.

20. Peter Cain, 'Political Economy in Edwardian England: The Tariff-Reform Controversy', in Alan O'Day (ed.), *The Edwardian Age: Conflict and stability, 1900–1914* (London: Macmillan, 1979), pp. 35–59.

21. Eugene L. Rasor, *Arthur James Balfour, 1848–1930: Historiography and Annotated Bibliography* (Westport, CT: Greenwood Press, 1998), p. 30.

22. Winston Spencer Churchill MP, *Mr Brodrick's Army* (London: Arthur L. Humphreys, 1903).

23. Randolph S. Churchill, *Winston S. Churchill vol. II: Young Statesman 1901–1914* (London: Heinemann, 1967), p. 50. Hereafter RSC VII.

24. Ibid, p. 79.

25. Winston S. Churchill, *For Free Trade* (London: Arthur L. Humphreys, 1906).

26. RSC VII, p. 80.

27. See 'Party Changes Between Elections', in David Butler and Gareth Butler, *Twentieth-Century British Political Facts 1900–2000* (Houndmills: Palgrave Macmillan, 2000), pp. 242–3.

28. Henry Pelling, *Winston Churchill* (London: Book Club Associates, 1974), p. 83.

29. David Lloyd George to William George (his younger brother), 31 December 1903. W.R.P. George, *Lloyd George: Backbencher* (Llandysul: Gomer Press, 1983), p. 413. The author was William's son and Lloyd George's nephew.

30. Norman Rose, *Churchill: An Unruly Life* (London: Touchstone, 1998), p. 54.

31. Roy Jenkins, *Churchill* (London: Macmillan, 2001), p. 90.

32. RSC VII, p. 82.

33. Winston Churchill, *Mr Winston Churchill on the Aliens Bill: A Letter Addressed to a Manchester Correspondent: Leaflet 2006* (London: Liberal Publication Department, 1904). The leaflet was priced at 3 shillings per 1,000.

34. Jill Pellew, 'The Home Office and the Aliens Act, 1905', *Historical Journal*, June 1989, 32(2):370.

35. Randolph S. Churchill, *Winston S. Churchill 1874–1965: vol. II Companion Part I 1901–1907* (London: Heinemann, 1969), p. 397. Hereafter RSC CVII, P1.

36. Richard A. Rempel, *Unionists Divided: Arthur Balfour, Joseph Chamberlain and the Unionist Free Traders* (Newton Abbot: David & Charles, 1972), p. 133.

37. Jenkins, *Churchill*, p. 103.

38. R.J.Q. Adams, *Balfour: The Last Grandee* (London: Thistle, 2013), Kindle edition, Loc. 4,914.

39. J.A. Spender, *The Life of The Right Hon. Sir Henry Campbell-Bannerman, GCB: vol. II* (London: Hodder & Stoughton, 1923), p. 190.

40. Ibid.

41. Ibid.

42. Campbell-Bannerman to Churchill, 9 December 1905. RSC CVII, P1, p. 411.

43. Rose, *Unruly Life*, p. 56.

44. Spender, *The Life*, p. 201.

45. Lord Elgin to Lord Crewe, May 1908. RSC VII, p. 207.

46. Edward Marsh, *A Number of People: A Book of Reminiscences* (London: William Heinemann, 1939), p. 150.

47. RSC VII, p. 112.

48. J.B. Priestley, *The Edwardians* (London: Sphere, 1972), p. 50.

49. Both seats in Churchill's former constituency were won by Liberals.

50. Adams, *Balfour: The Last Grandee*, Locs 5,022–30.

51. Hansard, vol. 152, col. 555, 22 February 1906.

52. Winston Spencer Churchill, *Lord Randolph Churchill* (London: Macmillan, 1906).

53. *Edinburgh Review*, July 1906, 417.

54. R.F. Foster, *Lord Randolph Churchill: A Political Life* (Oxford: Clarendon, 1981), p. 1.

55. Winston Spencer Churchill, *Lord Randolph Churchill: vol. I* (London: Macmillan, 1906), p. x.

56. The Earl of Oxford and Asquith, *Fifty Years of Parliament: vol. II* (London: Cassell, 1926), p. 38.

57. That for the Orange River Colony, which closely followed the Transvaal Constitution, was promulgated by Letters Patent in June 1907. Spender, *The Life*, pp. 242–3.

58. Memorandum from Lord Rosebery to Queen Victoria, 7 April 1894. The Marquess of Crewe, *Lord Rosebery* (London: John Murray, 1931), vol. II, p. 453.

59. Oxford and Asquith, *Fifty Years*, p. 39.

60. Though only in formal session for three days each week.

61. RSC VII, p. 321.

62. 'the House of Commons was the sole preserve of the wealthy, those of independent means and placemen of the rich': Mark Baimbridge and Darren Darcy, 'MPs' Pay 1911–1996: Myths and Realities', *Politics*, 1999, 19(2):72.

63. *Daily Canadian*, Friday, 15 March 1907, p. 2.

64. Alfred F. Havighurst, *Radical Journalist: H.W. Massingham (1860–1924)* (Cambridge: Cambridge University Press, 1974), p. 137.

65. Ronald Hyam, *Elgin and Churchill at the Colonial Office 1905–1908: The Watershed of the Empire-Commonwealth* (London: MacMillan, 1968), p. 317.

66. *Minutes of Proceedings of the Colonial Conference, 1907* (London: HMSO, 1907), p. 3.

67. Celia Sandys, *Churchill Wanted Dead or Alive* (London: Harper Collins, 1999), p. 62.
68. W.S. Churchill, *My Early Life*, p. 269.
69. Hyam, *Elgin and Churchill*, p. 318.
70. *Minutes of Proceedings of the Colonial Conference*, p. 422.
71. RSC VII, p. 320.
72. Hansard, vol. 176, col. 1,243, 25 June 1907.
73. Ibid, col. 1,254, 25 June 1907.
74. Ibid. It was during this debate that David Lloyd George coined his immortal phrase about the House of Lords. Rather than a 'loyal and trusty mastiff which is to watch over our interests', he categorised it as 'the right hon. Gentleman's [Arthur Balfour's] poodle. It fetches and carries for him. It barks for him. It bites anybody that he sets it on to. And we are told that this is a great revising Chamber, the safeguard of liberty in the country. Talk about mockeries and shams. Was there ever such a sham as that?' Hansard, vol. 176, col. 1,429, 26 June 1907.
75. John Winston Spencer-Churchill, 7th Duke of Marlborough.
76. William Manchester, 'Introduction' to W.S. Churchill, *My Early Life*, p. x.
77. Sebastian Haffner (trans. John Brown), *Churchill* (London: Haus, 2003), p. 35.
78. Lord Elgin to WSC, 5 June 1907. RSC CVII, P1, p. 661.
79. Sir H. Campbell-Bannerman to WSC, 9 September 1907. RSC CVII, P1, pp. 667–8.
80. Hyam, *Elgin and Churchill*, p. 349.
81. Douglas Austin, *Churchill and Malta: A Special Relationship* (Stroud: Spellmount, 2014), p. 5.
82. WSC to Lord Elgin, 4 October 1907. Randolph S. Churchill, *Winston S. Churchill 1874–1965: vol. II Companion Part 2 1907–1911* (London: Heinemann, 1969), pp. 685–6. Hereafter: RSC CVII, P2. See also: Austin, *Churchill and Malta*, pp. 6–7.
83. WSC to Lord Elgin, Telegram, 13 October 1907. RSC VII P2, p. 688.
84. Memorandum by Mr Churchill. 'Condition of Cyprus', dated 19 October 1907. Printed for the use of the Colonial Office, November 1907. UK National Archives, CAB 24/89/85, pp. 1–4.
85. Sir Francis Hopwood to Lord Elgin, 27 December 1907. RSC VII, p. 228.
86. RSC VII, p. 229.
87. Lord Elgin to Lord Crewe, May 1908. RSC VII P2, p. 797.
88. Sir Francis Hopwood to Lord Elgin, 27 December 1907. RSC VII, p. 228.
89. The Holmes tale being 'A Reminiscence of Sherlock Holmes: I – The Singular Experience of Mr. John Scott Eccles.' This reappeared later as Part 1 of 'Wisteria Lodge', in Arthur Conan Doyle, *His Last Bow: Some Reminiscences of Sherlock Holmes* (London: John Murray, 1917).
90. RSC VII, p. 229.
91. The Right Hon. Winston Spencer Churchill, MP, *My African Journey* (London: Hodder & Stoughton, 1908), p. vi.
92. Marsh, *A Number of People*, pp. 161–2.
93. https://www.dailymail.co.uk/news/article-3811344/Winston-Churchill-escaped-bout-food-poisoning-killed-servant-trip-East-Africa.html.
94. Margot Asquith, *The Autobiography of Margot Asquith: vol. II* (London: Thornton Butterworth, 1922), p. 89.
95. RSC VII, pp. 244–5.
96. George R. Boyer, *The Winding Road to the Welfare State: Economic Insecurity and Social Welfare Policy in Britain* (Princeton, NJ: Princeton University Press, 2019), p. 207. G.R. Searle, *A New England? Peace and War 1886–1918* (Oxford: Oxford University Press, 2004), p. 366.
97. Martin Pugh, '"Queen Anne is Dead": The Abolition of Ministerial By-Elections, 1867–1926', *Parliamentary History*, 2002, 21(3):352–3.
98. T.G. Otte and Paul Readman, 'Introduction' to T.G. Otte and Paul Readman (eds), *By-Elections in British Politics, 1832–1914* (Woodbridge: Boydell Press, 2013), p. 5.
99. RSC VII, p. 253.
100. David Cesarani, 'The Anti-Jewish Career of Sir William Joynson-Hicks, Cabinet Minister', *Journal of Contemporary History*, July 1989, 24(3):462–3.

101. Martin Pugh, *The Pankhursts* (London: Allen Lane, 2001), p. 175.

102. June Purvis, *Christabel Pankhurst: A Biography* (Abingdon: Routledge, 2018), p. 155.

103. *Manchester Guardian*, 16 April 1908.

104. Diary entry, 6 February 1912. Lord Riddell [George Riddell], *More Pages From My Diary 1908–1914* (London: Country Life, 1934), p. 36.

105. RSC VII, p. 257.

106. *Daily Telegraph*, 25 April 1908. Ted Morgan, *Churchill: Young Man in a Hurry, 1874–1915* (New York: Simon & Schuster, 1982), p. 223.

107. WSC to Miss Clementine Hozier, 27 April 1908. RSC VII P2, p. 787.

108. Jenkins, *Churchill*, p. 130.

109. Pelling, *Winston Churchill*, p. 112. Anne Newman, 'Dundee's Grand Old Man', *Journal of Liberal History*, Spring 2005, 46:22.

110. WSC to Miss Clementine Hozier, 27 April 1908. RSC VII P2, p. 787.

111. WSC to Lady Randolph [his mother], 29 April 1908. RSC VII P2, p. 789. His address, 'To the Electors of Dundee', publicly stating that he had accepted the invitation, is dated 30 April 1908. *Evening Express and Evening Mail*, 1 May 1908.

112. Later printed in a 32-page booklet and sold for one penny. Winston S. Churchill, *For Liberalism and Free Trade, Principal Speeches of the Rt. Hon. Winston S. Churchill, MP during the campaign in Dundee, May 1908* (Dundee: John Leng, 1908 and London, 186 Fleet Street, 1908).

113. E. Sylvia Pankhurst, *The Suffragette: The History of The Women's Militant Suffrage Movement 1905–1910* (New York: Sturgis & Walton, 1911), p. 227.

114. RSC VII, p. 393. Pankhurst, *The Suffragette*, p. 228.

115. *London Evening News*, 6 May 1908.

116. He was noted as being 'in a very agitated condition' during the count. Tony Paterson, *Churchill: A Seat for Life* (Dundee: David Winter, 1980), p. 74.

117. 'The Irish vote, which was numerous here, was safe for the Liberals at this election …'. Pelling, *Winston Churchill*, p. 113.

118. RSC VII, p. 264.

119. Ibid, p. 263.

120. W. Hamish Fraser, 'The Labour Party in Scotland', in K.D. Brown (ed.), *The First Labour Party 1906–1914* (Abingdon: Routledge, 2019), pp. 50–1.

121. This was printed as 'The Dundee Election: Kinnaird Hall, Dundee, May 14, 1908', in Winston S. Churchill, *Liberalism and The Social Problem* (London: Hodder & Stoughton, 1909), pp. 147–70. Hereafter W.S. Churchill, *Liberalism*. The date as given in the book is a typographical error. For the capacity of the Kinnaird Hall see Brian King, *Rediscovered Dundee* (Kibworth Beauchamp: Matador, 2020), p. 75.

122. W.S. Churchill, *Liberalism*, p. 154.

123. Ibid, p. 153.

124. Ibid, p. 79.

125. Ibid, pp. 154–5.

126. The population in 1901 and 1911 respectively as determined by the National Census. See https://www.nrscotland.gov.uk/.

127. RSC VII, p. 261.

128. According to 1905 estimates, 73 per cent of labour in the jute industry was female, and therefore automatically disenfranchised. Dundee Social Union, *Report upon Housing and Industrial Conditions and Medical Inspection of School Children* (Dundee: John Leng, 1905), p. 48.

129. Jim Tomlinson, *Dundee and the Empire: 'Juteopolis' 1850–1939* (Edinburgh: Edinburgh University Press, 2014), p. 183.

130. George Dangerfield, *The Strange Death of Liberal England* (London: Constable, 1936), p. 29.

131. David Powell, 'The New Liberalism and the Rise of Labour, 1886–1906', *Historical Journal*, June 1986, 29(2):383.

132. RSC VII, p. 276.

133. R.E. Quinault, 'Lord Randolph Churchill and Tory Democracy, 1880–1885', *Historical Journal*, March 1979, 22(1):151, 165.

134. Max Egremont, *Balfour: A Life of Arthur James Balfour* (London: Collins, 1980), p. 63.

135. Paul Addison, 'The Political Beliefs of Winston Churchill', *Transactions of the Royal Historical Society*, 1980, 30:33.

136. John Grigg, 'Churchill and Lloyd George', in Robert Blake and Wm Roger Louis (eds), *Churchill* (Oxford: Clarendon, 1993), p. 101.

137. Bonham Carter, *Winston Churchill as I Knew Him*, p. 129.

138. Lord Boothby, *Boothby: Recollections of a Rebel* (London: Hutchinson, 1978), p. 52.

139. Richard Toye, *Lloyd George and Churchill: Rivals for Greatness* (London: Pan Books, 2008), p. 71.

140. Charmley observes that 'Churchill was the junior partner. Lloyd George shared Churchill's obsessive interest in politics, but in their private lives they shared only a taste for the best.' Charmley, *The End of Glory*.

141. Earl Lloyd George, *My Father, Lloyd George* (New York: Crown, 1960), p. 178.

142. John Grigg, 'Churchill and Lloyd George', p. 98.

143. Leo Maxse, *National Review*, January 1907, 287. Addison, 'Political Beliefs', pp. 25–6. The *National Review* supported Conservativism and Maxse was the editor from 1893 to 1932.

144. Richard Shannon, *The Crisis of Imperialism 1865–1915* (London: Paladin, 1986), p. 403.

145. Roger Davidson, 'Social Conflict and Social Administration: The Conciliation Act in British Industrial Relations', in T.C. Smout (ed.), *The Search for Wealth and Stability: Essays in Economic and Social History presented to M.W. Flinn* (London: Macmillan, 1979), p. 175.

146. For a succinct summary see James C. Docherty and Sjaak van der Velden, *Historical Dictionary of Organized Labor* (Plymouth: Scarecrow, 2012), p. 257.

147. Spender, *The Life*, p. 279.

148. James E. Cronin, 'Strikes and Power in Britain, 1870–1920', *International Review of Social History*, 1987, 32(2):158.

149. RSC VII, p. 285.

150. See 'Table 1. Strikes and strikers in Britain, 1870–1914', in Cronin, 'Strikes and Power', p. 148.

151. 'Under the term "sweating" the following features have been included: underpayment, excessive hours of labour, work performed in insanitary conditions, or tasking the worker's power to an unreasonable extent.' Henry Parkinson, *A Primer of Social Science* (London: P.S. King, 1920), p. 184.

152. Paul Addison, *Churchill: The Unexpected Hero* (Oxford: Oxford University Press, 2005), p. 43.

153. Henry Pelling, 'Churchill and the Labour Movement', in Blake and Louis, *Churchill*, p. 115.

154. Addison, *Unexpected Hero*, p. 43.

155. H.W. Massingham, Introduction to W.S. Churchill, *Liberalism*, p. xvi. On that 'Introduction' see Alfred F. Havighurst, *Radical Journalist: H.W. Massingham (1860–1924)* (Cambridge: Cambridge University Press, 1974), p. 186.

156. Kenneth O. Morgan, 'Lloyd George and Germany', *Historical Journal*, September 1996, 39(3):756.

157. RSC VII, pp. 268, 274. The best man was Lord Hugh Cecil, Hugh Richard Heathcote Gascoyne-Cecil, the youngest son of the late Lord Salisbury (the 3rd Marquess and former Prime Minister).

158. WSC WC (1938), p. 24.

159. Between 1906 and 1909 the Liberals lost twelve seats to the Opposition. P.F. Clarke, 'The Electoral Position of the Liberal and Labour parties, 1910–1914', *English Historical Review*, October 1975, XC(CCCLVII):829.

160. Roy Jenkins, *Mr Balfour's Poodle: People v Peers* (London: Papermac, 1999), p. 64.

161. John Grigg, *Lloyd George: The People's Champion 1902–1911* (London: Methuen, 1991), p. 192.

162. For details see Jenkins, *Mr Balfour's Poodle*, pp. 74–5.

163. Charmley, *The End of Glory*, p. 60.

164. Robert Rhodes James, *Rosebery: A Biography of Archibald Philip, Fifth Earl of Rosebery* (London: Macmillan, 1964), p. 465.

165. Act II of Caesar and Cleopatra in [George] Bernard Shaw, *Three Plays for Puritans: The Devil's Disciple, Caesar and Cleopatra, & Captain Brassbound's Conversion* (London: Grant Richards, 1901), p. 121.

166. Geoffrey Annis and John Radcliffe, notes on 'The City of Brass' at: http://www.kiplingsociety. co.uk/rg_cityofbrass1.htm.

167. Rudyard Kipling, *The Collected Poems of . . .* (Ware: Wordsworth Editions, 1994), p. 327.

168. Robert Lloyd George, 'Foreword' to Geoffrey Lee, *The People's Budget: An Edwardian Tragedy* (London: Shepheard-Walwyn, 2008), p. vii.

169. The Right Honourable Viscount Long of Wraxall, FRS (Walter Long), *Memories* (London: Hutchinson, 1923), p. 187.

170. RSC VII, p. 324.

171. 'The Spirit of the Budget, Leicester, September 5, 1909', in W.S. Churchill, *Liberalism*, pp. 382–3.

172. Blunt had been a friend of, and influence on, Lord Randolph. For the relationship between Blunt, Lord Randolph and then Winston Churchill, see Warren Dockter, 'The Influence of a Poet: Wilfrid S. Blunt and the Churchills', *Journal of Historical Biography*, Autumn 2011, 10:70–102.

173. Diary entry for Saturday, 2 October 1909. Wilfrid Scawen Blunt, *My Diaries: Being a Personal Narrative of Events, 1888–1914: Part Two 1900 to 1914* (London: Martin Secker, 1920), p. 286.

174. Jenkins, *Mr Balfour's Poodle*, p. 103.

175. Oxford and Asquith, *Fifty Years*, p. 77.

176. See journal entries for 12, 13 and 14 September 1908. Thomas James Cobden-Sanderson, *The Journals of Thomas James Cobden-Sanderson 1879–1922: vol. II* (London: Richard Cobden-Sanderson, 1926), pp. 120–2.

177. Journal entry for 11–13 December 1909. Cobden-Sanderson, *Journals*, pp. 159–60. Alderley Park was a country estate at Nether Alderley, Cheshire, the main residence of the Stanley family headed by Edward Lyulph Stanley, 4th Baron Stanley of Alderley. The later epistolary relationship between Venetia Stanley, Lord Stanley's daughter, and Asquith is well known. See Stefan Buczacki, *My Darling Mr Asquith: The Extraordinary Life and Times of Venetia Stanley* (London: Cato & Clarke, 2016). See also: https://www.lrb.co.uk/the-paper/v38/n22/bee-wilson/a-little-talk-in-downing-st.

178. *Daily Mail*, 8 December 1909.

179. S. Rosenbaum, 'The General Election of January, 1910, and the Bearing of the Results on Some Problems of Representation', *Journal of the Royal Statistical Society*, May 1910, 73(5):484.

180. Charles Seymour, *Electoral Reform in England and Wales: The Development and Operation of the Parliamentary Franchise, 1832–1885* (London: Humphrey Milford Oxford University Press, MDCCCCXV [1915]), p. 465.

181. Chris Cook, *The Routledge Companion to Britain in the Nineteenth Century, 1815–1914* (Abingdon: Routledge, 2005), p. 63.

182. National Unionist Association of Conservative and Liberal Unionist Organisations, *The Constitutional Year Book for 1899* (London: Conservative Central Office, 1899), p. 209.

183. Duncan Tanner, 'The Parliamentary Electoral System, the "Fourth" Reform Act and the Rise of Labour in England and Wales', *Bulletin of the Institute of Historical Research*, November 1983, 56(134):206.

184. Ibid, p. 208.

185. In Scotland the function was discharged by a Sheriff. James Badenach Nicolson, *Analysis of Recent Statutes Affecting Parliamentary Elections in Scotland, With Appendix Containing the Statutes, and a Digest of Recent Decisions of the Registration Appeal Court* (Edinburgh: Bell & Bradfute, 1885), p. 35.

186. Sir Hugh Fraser, *The Representation of the People Act, 1918 with Explanatory Notes* (London: Sweet & Maxwell, 1918), p. 107.

187. Tanner, 'The Parliamentary Electoral System', p. 210.

188. M. Ostrogorski and Frederick Clarke (trans.), *Democracy and the Organization of Political Parties: vol. I* (London: Macmillan & Co., 1902), p. 378.

189. Tanner, 'The Parliamentary Electoral System', p. 207, n. 13.
190. Ibid, p. 208, n. 17.
191. England and Wales: 36,070,000: Scotland: 4,761,000: Ireland: 4,390,000. https://www.1911 census.org.uk/ and http://www.census.nationalarchives.ie/.
192. Rosenbaum, 'The General Election of January, 1910', p. 507.
193. Homer Lawrence Morris, *Parliamentary Franchise Reform in England from 1885 to 1918* (London: P.S. King & Son, 1921), pp. 10–11, 20. Edward Porritt, 'Barriers Against Democracy in the British Electoral System', *Political Science Quarterly*, March 1911, 26(1):8. In one instance, an individual in 1867 was possessed of eighteen votes. Seymour, *Electoral Reform*, p. 473.
194. For an authoritative account see Neal Blewett, *The Peers, The Parties and The People: The British General Elections of 1910* (London: Palgrave Macmillan, 1972).
195. William D. Rubinstein, 'The Liberal Government, 1910–14: A "General Crisis"?', in William D. Rubinstein, *Twentieth-Century Britain: A Political History* (Houndmills: Palgrave Macmillan, 2003), p. 38.
196. Winston S. Churchill, *The People's Rights* (London: Hodder & Stoughton, 1910).
197. H.H. Asquith to WSC, 1 February 1910. RSC VII, p. 363.
198. The title of a 1904 play by George Bernard Shaw.
199. WSC to H.H. Asquith, 5 February 1910. RSC VII, p. 365.
200. Charmley, *The End of Glory*, p. 63.
201. Addison, *Unexpected Hero*, p. 32.

Chapter 2: South Wales Strife (1): Newport

1. Sir Edward Troup to Sir Edward Ward (Permanent Under-Secretary of State for War), 21 May 1910. RSC CVII, P2, p. 1,169. Emphasis in original.
2. Sir Edward Troup's report of his interview with Mr Houlder on the evening of 21 May 1910. RSC CVII, P2, pp. 1,172–3.
3. Dai Smith, *Wales: A Question for History* (Bridgend: Seren, 1999), p. 98.
4. Valentine Low, 'Tonypandy: The Miners' Strike that Blighted Churchill's Career', *The Times*, 14 February 2019.
5. 'Churchill Was a Caricature', *The Journal (Newcastle, England)*, 23 February 2019.
6. Philip J. Leng, *The Welsh Dockers* (Ormskirk: Hesketh, 1981), p. 48.
7. Clive Emsley, *The English Police: A Political and Social History* (Abingdon: Routledge, 2014), p. 117.
8. Leng, *Welsh Dockers*, p. 49.
9. *Kelly's Directory of Monmouthshire and South Wales: 1914* (London: Kelly's Directories, 1914), p. 125.
10. Leng, *Welsh Dockers*, p. 49.
11. John Stokoe, 'The Shipping Federation', *The Bulletin: Journal of The Liverpool Nautical Research Society*, June 2013, 57(1):11.
12. John Saville, 'Trade Unions and Free Labour: The Background to the Taff Vale Decision', in Asa Briggs and John Saville (eds), *Essays in Labour History in Memory of G.D.H. Cole, 25 September 1889–14 January 1959* (London: Palgrave Macmillan, 1967), p. 331.
13. Shipping Federation to Home Office, 19 May 1910. RSC CVII, P2, p. 1,164.
14. RSC VII, p. 368.
15. Sir Charles Edward Troup, Assistant Under-Secretary of State from 1903 to 1908 and Permanent Secretary since 1908.
16. Isaac Haig Mitchell. Former General Secretary of the General Federation of Trade Unions and, since 1907, an adviser at the Board of Trade.
17. Sir Edward Troup to WSC, 19 May 1910. RSC CVII, P2, p. 1,164.
18. WSC to Sir Edward Troup, 19 May 1910. RSC CVII, P2, p. 1,165.
19. Councillor William Miles Blackburn, Mayor of Newport 1909–1910.
20. Sir Edward Troup to Mayor of Newport, 19 May 1910. Quoted in: WSC to Sir Edward Troup, 19 May 1910. RSC CVII, P2, p. 1,165.

21. A title synonymous with that of Chief Constable.
22. Mayor of Newport to the Home Office, 19 May 1910. RSC CVII, P2, p. 1,165.
23. *Evening Express and Evening Mail*, 25 May 1910. See also: Islwyn Bale, *Through Seven Reigns: A History of the Newport Police Force 1836–1959* (Pontypool: Hughes, 1960).
24. Head Constable of Newport to Home Office, 20 May 1910. RSC CVII, P2, p. 1,166.
25. Sir Edward Troup to WSC and WSC to Sir Edward Troup, 21 May 1910. RSC CVII, P2, p. 1,166.
26. W.F.A. Archibald, J.H. Greenhalgh and James Roberts, *The Metropolitan Police Guide, Being a Compendium of the Law Affecting the Metropolitan Police* (London: HMSO, 1922), p. 3.
27. Tom Standage, *The Victorian Internet: The Remarkable Story of the Telegraph and the Nineteenth Century's On-Line Pioneers* (London: Phoenix, 1999).
28. Sir Edward Troup to Mayor of Newport, 21 May 1910. RSC CVII, P2, p. 1,167.
29. Chief Constable Newport to Home Office, 21 May 1910. RSC CVII, P2, p. 1,167.
30. Shipping Federation to Home Office, 21 May 1910. RSC CVII, P2, p. 1,169. Emphasis added.
31. Mayor of Newport to Home Office, 21 May 1910. RSC CVII, P2, p. 1,169.
32. Sir Edward Troup to Sir Edward Ward (Permanent Under-Secretary of State for War), 21 May 1910. RSC CVII, P2, p. 1,169. Emphasis in original.
33. Sir Edward Troup to WSC, 21 May 1910. RSC CVII, P2, p. 1,170.
34. Lieutenant General Sir Charles Burnett at Watergate House, Chester, General Officer Commanding Western Command.
35. Sir Edward Ward to Mayor of Newport, 21 May 1910. RSC CVII, P2, p. 1,170.
36. General the Rt Hon. Sir Nevil Macready, *Annals of An Active Life: vol. I* (London: Hutchinson, 1924), p. 178. See also: Anthony Mor O'Brien, 'Churchill and the Tonypandy Riots', *Welsh History Review – Cylchgrawn Hanes Cymru*, June 1994, 17(1):74 n.12.
37. Mayor of Newport to Sir Edward Troup, 21 May 1910. Quoted in: RSC VII, p. 371.
38. The allusion to him having 'dined', a euphemism for having taken drink, would not have passed Churchill by.
39. Sir Edward Troup's report of his interview with Mr Houlder on the evening of 21 May 1910. RSC CVII, P2, pp. 1,172–3.
40. Mayor of Newport to Home Office, 22 May 1910. RSC CVII, P2, p. 1,171.
41. I.H. Mitchell to Home Office, 10.36am, 22 May 1910. RSC CVII, P2, p. 1,171.
42. Sir Edward Troup to WSC, 22 May 1910. RSC CVII, P2, p. 1,171.
43. WSC to Sir Edward Troup, 22 May 1910. RSC CVII, P2, pp. 1,173–4. Churchill also informed Troup that he could be reached at the Grand Hotel Goeschenen [Göschenen], Switzerland, until 5pm the following day, 23 May 1910, and that he would thereafter be en route via Lugano to Venice, where he expected to arrive on Wednesday, 25 May 1910.
44. Leng, *Welsh Dockers*, p. 49.
45. Copy of a letter from Sir Edward Troup, Permanent Under-Secretary of State, Home Office, on behalf of WSC to John Macauley, General Manager of the Alexandra Works and Railway Company, 23 May 1910. The Churchill Archive, CHAR 12/6/18A.
46. Saville, 'Trade Unions and Free Labour', p. 340.
47. Shipping Federation to Home Office, 2.52pm, 23 May 1910. RSC CVII, P2, pp. 1,174–5.
48. Stokoe, 'Shipping Federation', pp. 13–14.
49. Sir Edward Troup to Shipping Federation, 23 May 1910. RSC CVII, P2, p. 1,175.
50. Shipping Federation to Sir Edward Troup, 23 May 1910. Received 7.45pm. RSC CVII, P2, p. 1,175.
51. Sir Edward Troup to Shipping Federation, 23 May 1910. RSC CVII, P2, p. 1,176.
52. For Sinclair's approach see Barbara Weinberger, *Keeping the Peace?: Policing Strikes in Britain 1906–1926* (Oxford: Berg, 1991), pp. 33–4.
53. Shipping Federation to Sir Edward Troup, 23 May 1910. Received 9.07pm. RSC CVII, P2, p. 1,176.

54. L.H. Powell, *The Shipping Federation: A History of the First Sixty Years 1890–1950* (London: Shipping Federation 1950), p. 124.

55. Anonymous, 'The Man at the Wheel', *The Seaman: The Official Organ of The National Sailors' & Firemen's Union*, 29 May 1914, 1(42 New Series):121. Available at Warwick University Library. https://wdc.contentdm.oclc.org/digital/collection/tav/id/5194.

56. Second Report by I.H. Mitchell, Dock Workers, Newport. RSC CVII, P2, pp. 1,176–7.

57. Note by Sir Edward Troup (appended to Mitchell's Second Report), 24 May 1910. RSC CVII, P2, pp. 1,177–8.

58. Chairman, Watch Committee, Newport, to Houlder Bros and the Shipping Federation, 9.30pm, 23 May 1910. *Evening Express and Evening Mail*, 25 May 1910.

59. Resolution passed by Newport Watch Committee on Tuesday afternoon. *Evening Express and Evening Mail*, 25 May 1910.

60. Mayor of Newport to the Secretary of State for War, 26 May 1910. Hansard, vol. 18, cols 374–5, 22 June 1910. Robert Rhodes James (ed.), *Winston S. Churchill: His Complete Speeches 1897–1963. vol. II: 1908–1913* (New York: Chelsea House/R.R. Bowker, 1974), pp. 1,575–6.

61. The Churchill Archive, CHAR 12/6/25. Letter from Sir Edward Troup to WSC at Venice, concerning the opinions of Sir Rufus Isaacs and Sidney Rowlatt on the actions of the Home Office during the dockers' strike at Newport, 30 May 1910.

62. UK National Archives, HO 45/10608/192905/22. Strikes: Strike at Newport Docks – Law Officer's Opinion (1910–1912), 25 May 1910.

63. Hansard, vol. 18, col. 378, 22 June 1910.

64. Ibid, col. 371, 22 June 1910.

65. Ibid, col. 402, 22 June 1910.

66. O'Brien, 'Churchill and the Tonypandy Riots', pp. 70, 76.

67. D.J.V. Jones, 'The New Police, Crime and People in England and Wales, 1829–1888', *Transactions of the Royal Historical Society*, 1983, 33:159.

68. Robert G. Neville, 'The Yorkshire Miners and the 1893 Lockout: The Featherstone "Massacre"', *International Review of Social History*, 1976, 21(3):342.

69. Jane Morgan, *Conflict and Order: The Police and Labour Disputes in England and Wales, 1900–1939* (Oxford: Clarendon Press, 1987), p. 44.

70. Hansard, vol. 17, col. 1,723, 20 September 1893. Roger Geary, *Policing Industrial Disputes: 1893 to 1985* (Cambridge: Cambridge University Press, 1985), p. 35.

71. See *Report of the Select Committee on Employment of Military in Cases of Disturbances*, 16 July 1908. Parliamentary Paper 236.

72. Morgan, *Conflict and Order*, p. 46.

Chapter 3: South Wales Strife (2): Tonypandy

1. Macready, *Annals*, p. 150.

2. Steve Bruce, *Politics and Religion in the United Kingdom* (Abingdon: Routledge, 2012), p. 89.

3. Ness Edwards, *The History of the South Wales Miners' Federation: vol. I* (London: Lawrence & Wishart, 1938).

4. Kenneth O. Morgan, *Wales in British Politics, 1868–1922* (Cardiff: University of Wales Press, 1991), p. 203.

5. E.W. Evans, *Mabon: A Study in Trade Union Leadership* (Cardiff: University of Wales Press, 1959), p. 143.

6. Roy Douglas, *The History of the Liberal Party 1895–1970* (London: Sidgwick & Jackson, 1971), p. 83.

7. *Rhondda Leader*, 8 August 1903.

8. A. Beacham, 'Preface' to Evans, *Mabon*, p. ix.

9. Kenneth O. Morgan, 'Review of *Mabon: A Study in Trade Union Leadership*', *Cymdeithas Hanes Lleol Morgannwg – Transactions of the Glamorgan Local History Society*, 1960, IV:75.

10. See E.D. Lewis, 'Population Change and Social Life, 1860–1914', in K.S. Hopkins (ed.), *Rhondda: Past and Future* (Ferndale: Rhondda Borough Council, 1975), pp. 110–28.

11. T. Alban Davies, 'Impressions of Life in the Rhondda Valley', in Hopkins, *Rhondda: Past and Future*, pp. 11–21.

12. J. Vyrnwy Morgan, *The Welsh Religious Revival 1904–5: A Retrospect and a Criticism* (London: Chapman & Hall, 1909), p. 171

13. James Keir Hardie, the Scottish trade unionist and politician, founder of the Labour Party, and its first parliamentary leader from 1906 to 1908.

14. Dubbed the 'philosopher of the proletariat' and now a forgotten figure, Joseph Dietzgen coined the term 'dialectical materialism'.

15. R.J. Barker, *Christ in the Valley of Unemployment* (London: Hodder & Stoughton, 1936), p. 15.

16. Evans, *Mabon*, p. 216.

17. Ibid, p. 66.

18. David Evans, 'The Captain of Industry', in Margaret Haig Mackworth (née Thomas, 2nd Viscountess Rhondda), *D.A. Thomas Viscount Rhondda: By his Daughter and Others* (London: Longmans, Green, 1921), p. 126.

19. Rhys Davies, *Print of a Hare's Foot: An Autobiographical Beginning* (London: Heinemann, 1969), p. 89. For information on Davies see http://www.rhysdaviestrust.org/.

20. J. Vyrnwy Morgan, *Life of Viscount Rhondda* (London: H.R. Allenson, 1918), p. 146.

21. O'Brien, 'Churchill and the Tonypandy Riots', p. 71.

22. Macready, *Annals*, p. 140.

23. David Evans, *Labour Strife in the South Wales Coalfield: A Historical and Critical Record of the Mid-Rhondda, Aberdare Valley and other Strikes* (Cardiff: Educational Publishing, 1911), p. 5. See also: R. Page Arnot, *South Wales Miners Glowyr De Cymru: A History of the South Wales Miners Federation (1898–1914)* (London: George Allen & Unwin, 1967), p. 176.

24. Evans, 'The Captain of Industry', p. 124.

25. Evans, *Labour Strife*, p. 9.

26. Ibid. Arnot, *South Wales Miners Glowyr De Cymru*, p. 176.

27. Richard Wilkinson, *Lloyd George: Statesman or Scoundrel* (London: I.B. Tauris, 2018), p. 180. The remark, or something essentially similar, has also been attributed to several others.

28. Quoted in: Arnot, *South Wales Miners Glowyr De Cymru*, pp. 176–7.

29. Evans, *Labour Strife*, p. 4.

30. Arnot, *South Wales Miners Glowyr De Cymru*, p. 177.

31. O'Brien, 'Churchill and the Tonypandy Riots', p. 72.

32. 76,978 to 44,868. Arnot, *South Wales Miners Glowyr De Cymru*, pp. 177–8.

33. Evans, *Labour Strife*, p. 13.

34. Arnot, *South Wales Miners Glowyr De Cymru*, p. 178.

35. *Evening Express and Evening Mail*, 28 September 1910.

36. For a history of the company see The Powell Dyffryn Steam Coal Company, *The Powell Dyffryn Steam Coal Co. Ltd, 1864–1914* (Cardiff: Business Statistics, 1914).

37. One perk of the job, of some forty years' standing, was that the mineworkers got to take home waste wood from the pit. Without notice, this practice was unilaterally prohibited by the management and enforced by the police. *South Wales Daily News*, 17 October 1910. Martin Barclay, '"The Slaves of the Lamp": The Aberdare Miners' Strike 1910', *Llafur: The Journal of the Society for the Study of Welsh Labour History*, Summer 1978, 2(3):27.

38. Arnot, *South Wales Miners Glowyr De Cymru*, p. 180.

39. Ibid, p. 182.

40. 'Aberaman Riots: Officials' Houses Assailed: Workmen's Train Attacked', *Aberdare Leader*, 5 November 1910.

41. Among the journals which Thomas controlled were the *South Wales Journal of Commerce, Y Baner, Y Tyst, Cambrian News, Tarian* and the *Merthyr Express*. He also had financial control of Cardiff's *Western Mail*. Evans, 'The Captain of Industry', p. 137.

42. Home Office to Chief Constable and Chief Constable to Home Office, 2 November 1910. *Colliery Strike Disturbances in South Wales: Correspondence and Report, November 1910* (London: HMSO, 1911), Documents 1 and 2.

43. Harold Tollefson, *Policing Islam: The British Occupation of Egypt and the Anglo-Egyptian Struggle Over Control of the Police, 1882–1914* (Westport, CT: Greenwood Press, 1999), p. xiii.

44. Hansard, vol. 334, col. 102, 18 March 1889. https://api.parliament.uk/historic-hansard/commons/1889/mar/18/the-superintendent-of-police-at-merthyr.

45. Richard Griffiths, *The Entrepreneurial Society of the Rhondda Valleys, 1840–1920: Power and Influence in the Porth-Pontypridd Region* (Cardiff: University of Wales Press, 2010), p. 227. Morgan, *Conflict and Order*, p. 32.

46. Jane Morgan, 'Police and Labour in the age of Lindsay, 1910–1936', *Llafur: Cymdeithas Hanes Pobl Cymreig – The Welsh People's History Society*, 1988, 5(1):19.

47. Arnot, *South Wales Miners Glowyr De Cymru*, p. 182.

48. Ibid, p. 183. Evans, *Labour Strife*, p. 40.

49. Arnot, *South Wales Miners Glowyr De Cymru*, p. 185.

50. Evans, *Labour Strife*, p. 41.

51. Ibid.

52. Ibid, p. 60.

53. Weinberger, *Keeping the Peace?*, p. 47.

54. The term 'Fort Chabrol', denoting a siege situation, had become common in France following an incident in 1899 pertaining to the Dreyfus case.

55. Arnot, who wrote from the opposite viewpoint politically, deemed him a 'class war correspondent' who took 'the standpoint of the side whose cause he espouses not only against their employees whom he calls "the mob" but also against the Home Office and the military authorities'. Arnot, *South Wales Miners Glowyr De Cymru*, p. 191.

56. Churchill had written that the garrison at Stormberg Junction, during the early stages of the Boer War in late 1899, dubbed their fortified position 'Fort Chabrol.' Winston Spencer Churchill, *From London to Ladysmith via Pretoria* (London: Longmans, Green & Co., 1900), p. 35.

57. Macready, *Annals*, p. 145.

58. O'Brien, 'Churchill and the Tonypandy Riots', p. 74. John D. Blake, *Civil Disorder in Britain, 1910–39: The Roles of Civil Government and Military Authority* (University of Sussex: D. Phil. Thesis, 1979), p. 85.

59. Arnot, *South Wales Miners Glowyr De Cymru*, p. 186.

60. Chief Constable to Home Office, 8 November 1910. *Colliery Strike Disturbances* …, p. 4.

61. Hansard, vol. 21, col. 229, 7 February 1911.

62. Arnot, *South Wales Miners Glowyr De Cymru*, p. 187. O'Brien, 'Churchill and the Tonypandy Riots', p. 77.

63. Evans, *Labour Strife*, p. 43. See also: RSC VII, p. 374. O'Brien, 'Churchill and the Tonypandy Riots', p. 77.

64. Macready, *Annals*, p. 137.

65. Hansard, vol. 21, col. 229, 7 February 1911.

66. Macready, *Annals*, p. 137.

67. O'Brien, 'Churchill and the Tonypandy Riots', p. 79.

68. Ibid.

69. Brigadier General Charles Burnett, *The Memoirs of the 18th (Queen Mary's Own) Royal Hussars, 1906–1922: Including Operations in the Great War* (Winchester: Warren & Son, 1926), p. 7.

70. Hansard, vol. 21, col. 229, 7 February 1911. Perhaps he was thinking of the visually impressive deterrent effect of men on horseback: cavalry horses were not trained in anything approaching what would now be called 'crowd control' methods.

71. Ibid, col. 230, 7 February 1911. In the original telegram he quoted, the number of mounted police was set at seventy and subsequently increased.

72. Ibid.

73. Ibid.
74. Arnot, *South Wales Miners Glowyr De Cymru*, p. 189. Evans, *Labour Strife*, p. 54.
75. Paul Young, *The Mid and the Mush: Mid Rhondda Ground and its Football Team* (Treorchy: Paul Young, 2003), p. 8. The Mid Rhondda Football Club are nicknamed *The Mushrooms*, which is contracted to *The Mush* locally.
76. Copies appeared in all the local newspapers. For example: *The Cambrian*, 11 November 1910.
77. Mrs Stuart Menzies (Amy Charlotte Menzies *née* Bewicke), *Modern Men of Mark: The Romantic Stories of Lord Armstrong, Sir Richard Burbidge, Lord Leverhulme, Lord Northcliffe, Sir Joseph Lyons, Sir Joseph Pease, Lord Rhondda and Others* (London: Herbert Jenkins, 1921), p. 284.
78. Sam G. Riley (ed.), *Consumer Magazines of the British Isles* (Westport, CT: Greenwood Press, 1993), p. 201.
79. 'The Welsh Riots', *The Spectator*, 12 November 1910, p. 5.
80. Evans, *Labour Strife*, p. 45.
81. David Smith, 'From Riots to Revolt: Tonypandy and The Miners' Next Step', in Trevor Herbert and Gareth Elwyn Jones (eds), *Wales 1880–1914* (Cardiff: University of Wales Press, 1988), p. 111.
82. Arnot, *South Wales Miners Glowyr De Cymru*, p. 190.
83. Evans, *Labour Strife*, p. 45. Arnot, *South Wales Miners Glowyr De Cymru*, pp. 190–1.
84. For his account of the matter see Evans, *Labour Strife*, pp. 46–8.
85. *Evening Express and Evening Mail*, 15 December 1910.
86. Evans, *Labour Strife*, p. 49.
87. From a post-event report put together by Captain Francis Farquhar, Coldstream Guards, who had been appointed to organise an intelligence unit by Macready. Quoted in: Evans, *Labour Strife*, p. 50. See also: *Colliery Strike Disturbances . .* , p. 20.
88. 'The Strike: Serious Riots at Aberaman: Sixty Persons Injured: Window Smashing at Aberaman', *Aberdare Leader*, 12 November 1910. See also: Barclay, 'The Slaves of the Lamp', p. 31.
89. Charles Townshend, '"One Man Whom You Can Hang If Necessary": The Discreet Charm of Nevil Macready', in John B. Hattendorf and Malcolm H. Murfett (eds), *Limitations of Military Power: Essays Presented to Professor Norman Gibbs on his Eightieth Birthday* (Houndmills: Palgrave Macmillan, 1990), p. 143.
90. Macready, *Annals*, p. 138.
91. A stipendiary magistrate was a salaried full-time judge who sat in a magistrates' court. In 2000 stipendiary magistrates became District Judges (Magistrates' Courts). See Courts and Tribunals Judiciary. https:// www.judiciary.uk/ about-the-judiciary / who-are-the-judiciary / judicial-roles / judges/chief-magistrate/. From 1909 to 1933 Daniel Lleufer Thomas was stipendiary magistrate for Pontypridd and Rhondda. See 'Thomas, Sir Daniel (Lleufer) (1863–1940), stipendiary magistrate', in *Y Bywgraffiadur Cymreig Dictionary of Welsh Biography*. https://biography.wales/article/s-THOM-LLE-1863.
92. Telegram from Lleufer Thomas, Stipendiary Magistrate, to the Home Office, sent at 7.45pm and received at 9pm on 8 November. *Colliery Strike Disturbances . .* , p. 6.
93. The Riot Act was passed in 1714 and took effect the following year. James Morton, 'Reading the Riot Act 100 years on', *Law Society Gazette*, 9 September 2019. Available online at: https://www.lawgazette.co.uk/obiter/reading-the-riot-act-100-years-on/5101379.article.
94. Evans, *Labour Strife*, p. 48.
95. O'Brien, 'Churchill and the Tonypandy Riots', p. 81, n. 57. For the Aberdare magistrates he cites the autobiography of Edmund Stonelake: Anthony Mor O'Brien (ed.), *The Autobiography of Edmund Stonelake* (Bridgend: Mid Glamorgan County Council, 1981), p. 141.
96. Evans, *Labour Strife*, p. 48. 'The Sack of Tonypandy. Looters in Court', *Rhondda Leader*, 17 June 1911.
97. 'Terror-Stricken Shopkeepers Abandon Premises. Thousands of Pounds Worth of Damage', *South Wales Daily Post (Extra Special Edition)*, 9 November 1910.
98. Arnot, *South Wales Miners Glowyr De Cymru*, p. 193.

99. *Evening Express and Evening Mail (Special Edition)*, 9 November 1910.
100. *South Wales Daily Post (Extra Special Edition)*, 9 November 1910.
101. 'Tonypandy, Wednesday', *Manchester Guardian*, 10 November 1910.
102. Richard C. Thurlow, *The Secret State: British Internal Security in the Twentieth Century* (Oxford: Blackwell, 1994), p. 31.
103. Major General Sir Wyndham Childs, *Episodes and Reflections: Being Some Records from the Life of Major-General Sir Wyndham Childs, KCMG, KBE, CB, One Time Second Lieut., 2nd Volunteer Battalion, the Duke of Cornwall's Light Infantry* (London: Cassell & Company, 1930), p. 82.
104. See, for example: David Smith, 'Tonypandy 1910: Definitions of Community', *Past & Present*, May 1980, 87:168. Gareth Elwyn Jones, *People, Protest and Politics: Case Studies in Twentieth Century Wales* (Llandysul: Gwasg Gomer, 1987), p. 48. John Williams, *Was Wales Industrialised?: Essays in Modern Welsh History* (Llandysul: Gwasg Gomer, 1995), p. 215.
105. Philippa Davies, 'Introduction', in Rhys Davies, *Ram with Red Horns* (Bridgend: Seren, 1996), p. 6.
106. Barclay, 'The Slaves of the Lamp', p. 36.
107. Smith, 'Tonypandy 1910', p. 162.
108. Hywel Francis and David Smith, *The Fed: A History of the South Wales Miners in the Twentieth Century* (London: Lawrence & Wishart, 1980), p. 45, n. 23.
109. Smith, 'Tonypandy 1910', p. 162.
110. David Smith, 'From Riots to Revolt: Tonypandy and The Miners' Next Step', in Trevor Herbert and Gareth Elwyn Jones (eds), *Wales 1880–1914* (Cardiff: University of Wales Press, 1988), p. 113.
111. *Evening Express and Evening Mail*, 9 November 1910.
112. He includes, in addition to labour problems, questions around Irish Home Rule ('Ulster'), votes for women, and the House of Lords. Bernard Porter, *The Origins of the Vigilant State: The London Metropolitan Police Special Branch before the First World War* (Woodbridge: Boydell Press, 1991), p. 161.
113. Weinberger, *Keeping the Peace?*, p. 51.
114. 'Order to Proceed', *Cardiff Times and South Wales Weekly News*, 12 November 1910.
115. *South Wales Daily Post (Extra Special Edition)*, 9 November 1910.
116. *The Times*, 9 November 1910.
117. W. Gascoyne Dalziel, Secretary, Monmouthshire and South Wales Coal-owners' Association, to Home Secretary, 10 November 1910. Quoted in: Evans, *Labour Strife*, p. 58.
118. Edward Troup, Home Office, to Monmouthshire and South Wales Coal-owners' Association, 12 November 1910. Quoted in: Evans, *Labour Strife*, pp. 58–9.
119. For a fuller account see Arnot, *South Wales Miners Glowyr De Cymru*, pp. 197–9.
120. WSC to the King, 25 November 1910. RSC CVII, P2, p. 1,214.
121. Quoted in: O'Brien, 'Churchill and the Tonypandy Riots', p. 93. Presaging Parker's aphorism: 'The business of the armed forces in wartime is to kill people and break things.' Geoffrey Parker, 'The Etiquette of Atrocity: The Laws of War in Early Modern Europe', in Geoffrey Parker (ed.), *Empire, War and Faith in Early Modern Europe* (London: Allen Lane, 2002), p. 143.
122. Macready, *Annals*, p. 144.
123. Churchill to Macready, 14 November 1910. Secret and Personal. DISTURBANCES: South Wales miners' strike (Tonypandy riots). UK National Archives, HO 144/1551/199768, 1910–1920.
124. Morgan, *Conflict and Order*, p. 45.
125. Macready, *Annals*, p. 148.
126. Ibid, p. 149.
127. Childs reckoned that Moylan's 'primary duty was to warn Winston if he saw any signs of the soldier-man being likely to do anything particularly drastic'. Childs, *Episodes and Reflections*, p. 79.
128. Quoted in: Weinberger, *Keeping the Peace?*, p. 51.
129. Alison Heath, *The Life of George Ranken Askwith, 1861–1942* (Abingdon: Routledge, 2016), p. 104.

130. Macready to Churchill, 6 December 1910. DISTURBANCES: South Wales miners' strike (Tonypandy riots). UK National Archives, HO 144/1552/199768, 1910–1920.

131. In 1993 the former Prime Minister Margaret Thatcher dubbed the year-long national miners' strike of 1984–85 an 'insurrection'. Margaret Thatcher, *The Downing Street Years* (London: Harper Collins, 1995), p. 339.

132. Macready, *Annals*, p. 150.

133. Macready to Churchill, 16 November 1910. *Colliery Strike Disturbances . . .*, p. 30. Reports of the theft of 'a considerable quantity of explosives and detonators' from the Glamorgan Colliery had appeared in the *Evening Express and Evening Mail*, 14 November 1910.

134. Superintendent T. Cole, Deputy Chief Constable, reports to the Chief Constable. Quoted in: Evans, *Labour Strife*, p. 78.

135. See reports in: *Merthyr Express*, 19 November 1910; *Cardiff Times and South Wales Weekly News*, 19 November 1910; *Welshman*, 25 November 1910.

136. 'Chicago Socialist', 'They Refused to Murder: Disarm Militia in South Wales – Territorials Refuse Orders to Act as Coal Bosses' Tools: London, Dec. 15', *Industrial Worker*, 22 December 1910.

137. Macready to Churchill, 25 November 1910. DISTURBANCES: South Wales miners' strike (Tonypandy riots). UK National Archives, HO 144/1552/199768, 1910–1920.

138. Burnett, *Memoirs*, p. 7.

139. For a discussion of this see Roger Geary, *Policing Industrial Disputes: 1893 to 1985* (Cambridge: Cambridge University Press, 1985), pp. 41–2.

140. Hansard, vol. 21, col. 1,242, 16 February 1911.

141. Macready, *Annals*, p. 157.

142. RSC VII, pp. 320–1.

143. Stephen Bates, *H.H. Asquith* (London: Haus, 2006), p. 76. Bates gives no source for this claim.

144. Weinberger, *Keeping the Peace?*, p. 52.

145. *Colliery Strike Disturbances . . .*

146. O'Brien, 'Churchill and the Tonypandy Riots', p. 87. He discusses the matter over pp. 86–91, identifying the editors as 'in the main' being Sir Edward Troup and John Moylan.

147. Evans, *Mabon*, p. 91.

148. From a subsequently deleted draft passage in his autobiography. Barbara Prys-Williams, 'Rhys Davies as Autobiographer: Hare or Houdini?', in Meic Stephens (ed.), *Rhys Davies: Decoding the Hare: Critical Essays to Mark the Centenary of the Writer's Birth* (Cardiff: University of Wales, 2001), p. 126.

149. RSC VII, p. 367.

150. P.G. Wodehouse, *Mr Mulliner Speaking* (London: Herbert Jenkins, 1921), pp. 167–8.

151. David Maddox and Gwyn Evan, *The Tonypandy Riots 1910–1911* (Bridgend: Mid Glamorgan County Council Education Department, 1992).

152. Picketing was, of course, the strikers' only weapon.

153. Neil Prior, 'Rhondda marks 100th anniversary of Tonypandy Riots', BBC News, Wales, 7 November 2010. https://www.bbc.co.uk/news/uk-wales-11655470.

154. Valentine Low, 'Tonypandy: The Miners' Strike that Blighted Churchill's Career', *The Times*, 14 February 2019.

155. John M. McEwen, 'Tonypandy: Churchill's Albatross', *Queen's Quarterly: A Canadian Review*, Spring 1971, 78:83–94.

Chapter 4: Cutting off 'this stream of madness'

1. Michael Crichton, 'Appendix I: Why Politicized Science is Dangerous', in Michael Crichton, *State of Fear* (London: Harper Collins, 2004), p. 577.

2. Diary entry for 20 October 1912 in: Wilfrid Scawen Blunt, *My Diaries: Being a Personal Narrative of Events 1888–1914: Part 2 1900 to 1914* (London: Martin Secker, 1920), p. 399.

3. The best biographical work on Galton is undoubtedly: Nicholas Wright Gillham, *A Life of Sir Francis Galton: From African Exploration to the Birth of Eugenics* (New York: Oxford University Press, 2001).

4. Francis Galton, *Memories of My Life* (London: Methuen & Co, 1908), p. 287.

5. Ibid, p. 288.

6. Available online at: https://galton.org/essays/1860-1869/galton-1865-hereditary-talent.pdf.

7. Francis Galton, *Hereditary Genius: An Inquiry into its Laws and Consequences* (London: Macmillan & Co., 1869).

8. B.S. Bramwell, 'Galton's "Hereditary Genius" and the Three Following Generations since 1869', *Eugenics Review*, January 1948, 39(4):146.

9. Francis Galton, *English Men of Science: Their Nature and Nurture* (New York: D. Appleton & Co., 1875), p. 11.

10. Charles Darwin, *The Descent of Man, and Selection in Relation to Sex: In Two volumes – Vol. I* (New York: D. Appleton & Co., 1872), pp. 162–3.

11. Ibid, p. 167.

12. Daniel J. Kevles, *In the Name of Eugenics: Genetics and the Uses of Human Heredity* (Cambridge, MA: Harvard University Press, 1999), p. 85.

13. G.R. Searle, 'Eugenics and Class', in Charles Webster (ed.), *Biology, Medicine and Society 1840–1940* (Cambridge: Cambridge University Press, 1981), p. 231.

14. William Cecil Dampier Whetham and Catherine Durning Whetham, *The Family and the Nation: A Study in Natural Inheritance and Social Responsibility* (London: Longmans, Green & Co., 1909), p. 148.

15. Pauline Mazumdar, *Eugenics, Human Genetics and Human Failings: The Eugenics Society, its Sources and its Critics in Britain* (London: Routledge, 1992), p. 1.

16. Kevles, *In the Name of Eugenics*, pp. 59–60.

17. Francis Galton, 'Eugenics: Its Definition, Scope and Aims', in Sir Francis Galton, *Essays in Eugenics* (London: Eugenics Education Society, 1909), p. 38.

18. Francis Galton, 'The Possible Improvement of the Human Breed Under the Existing Conditions of Law and Sentiment', in Galton, *Essays in Eugenics*, p. 8.

19. James Moore, *Good Breeding: Science and Society in a Darwinian Age* (Milton Keynes: Open University, 2001), p. 71.

20. Dorothy Porter, '"Enemies of the Race": Biologism, Environmentalism, and Public Health in Edwardian England', *Victorian Studies*, Winter 1991, 34(2):164. G.R. Searle, *Eugenics and Politics in Britain 1900–1914* (Leyden: Noordhoff International Publishing, 1976), p. 2.

21. Mazumdar, *Eugenics, Human Genetics and Human Failings*, p. 7.

22. Greta Jones, *Social Hygiene in Twentieth Century Britain* (London: Croom Helm, 1986), p. 21.

23. C.P. Blacker, *Eugenics: Galton and After* (London: Gerald Duckworth & Co., 1952), pp. 12–13. Carlos Paton Blacker was General Secretary of the Eugenics Society from 1931 to 1952.

24. Theodore M. Porter, *Karl Pearson: The Scientific Life in a Statistical Age* (Princeton, NJ: Princeton University Press, 2004), p. 10.

25. See, for example: Richard A. Soloway, *Demography and Degeneration: Eugenics and the Declining Birthrate in Twentieth-century Britain* (Chapel Hill, NC: University of North Carolina Press, 1995), p. 35. Mazumdar, *Eugenics, Human Genetics and Human Failings*, p. 2. Searle, 'Eugenics and Class', p. 219. Blacker, *Eugenics: Galton and After*, p. 139.

26. Donald MacKenzie, 'Review of Eugenics and Politics in Britain, 1900–1914 by G.R. Searle', *British Journal for the History of Science*, March 1978, 11(1):89–90.

27. Jakob Tanner, 'Eugenics before 1945', *Journal of Modern European History/Zeitschrift für moderne europäische Geschichte/Revue d'histoire européenne contemporaine*, 2012, 10(4):464.

28. Donald Mackenzie, 'Karl Pearson and the Professional Middle Class', *Annals of Science*, 1979, 36(2):137.

29. An account of Arthur Balfour's opening address at the banquet held at the Hotel Cecil on Wednesday, 24 July 1912 to celebrate the opening of the First International Eugenics Congress,

British Medical Journal, 3 August 1912, p. 253. The First International Eugenics Congress was held at the University of London, 24–30 July 1912.

30. Elaine Harrison (ed.), *Office-Holders in Modern Britain: vol. 10: Officials of Royal Commissions of Inquiry 1870–1939* (London: University of London, 1995), p. 47. https://www.british-history. ac.uk/office-holders/vol10/pp42-57#h3-0018.

31. After Jacob Pleydell-Bouverie, the 6th Earl of Radnor, who chaired the Commission.

32. *Report of the Royal Commission on the Care and Control of the Feeble-Minded: vol. VIII* (London: HMSO, 1908), pp. 180–1.

33. Ibid, p. 181.

34. Ibid. There were 'many others who have merely touched on the subject'.

35. Ibid, p. 182.

36. Ibid, p. 6.

37. Ibid, p. 8.

38. Francis Galton, 'Segregation', in Mrs Walter Slater, *The Problem of the Feeble Minded: an Abstract of the Report of the Royal Commission on the Care and Control of the Feeble Minded* (London: P.S. King & Son, 1909), p. 81.

39. 'Care of the Feeble-Minded. Deputation to the Home Secretary', *British Medical Journal*, supp., 4 September 1909, 2(2,540):210.

40. The Revd W.R. Inge, MA, DD, 'The Religious Aspect of the Problem', in Slater, *The Problem of the Feeble Minded*, p. 92.

41. 'Care of the Feeble-Minded. Deputation . . , p. 210.

42. Ibid.

43. Bodleian Archives & Manuscripts. Miscellaneous letters to Asquith or his private secretaries, 1909–1910. MS Asquith 12. Letter from Churchill to Asquith, 1910.

44. UK National Archives, HO 144/1085/193548. PRISONS AND PRISONERS – OTHER: Treatment of weakminded prisoners. Proposals by the Secretary of State (Mr Winston Churchill), 1910.

45. Bodleian Archives & Manuscripts. Miscellaneous letters to Asquith or his private secretaries, 1909–1910. MS Asquith 12. Letter from Churchill to Asquith, December 1910. Also quoted in: Desmond King, *In The Name of Liberalism: Illiberal Social Policy in the United States and Britain* (Oxford: Oxford University Press, 1999), p. 99, n. 258.

46. UK National Archives, CAB 37/108/189. 'The Feeble Minded – A Social Danger.' Circulated by WSC, 1911.

47. Ibid, Cover Note.

48. Ibid, p. 1, n. 2.

49. Ibid, p. 1.

50. Ibid, p. 2.

51. Ibid, pp. 2, 3, 4.

52. RSC VII, p. 426.

53. WSC to the King, 10 February 1911. Quoted in: RSC CVII, P2, p. 1,037.

54. Grigg, *Lloyd George: The People's Champion*, p. 225.

55. Lord Knollys to Vaughan Nash, 11 February 1911. RSC CVII, P2, p. 1,037.

56. WSC to the King, 13 February 1911. RSC CVII, P2, pp. 1,038–9. The published document is a copy containing several abbreviations. These have been expanded for the sake of easier reading.

57. Lord Knollys to WSC, 14 February 1911. RSC CVII, P2, p. 1,040.

58. Lord Knollys to Vaughan Nash, 17 February 1911. RSC VII, p. 438.

59. Lord Knollys to WSC, 17 February 1911. RSC VII, p. 438.

60. Kevles, *In the Name of Eugenics*, p. 93.

61. Angela Gugliotta, '"Dr Sharp with His Little Knife": Therapeutic and Punitive Origins of Eugenic Vasectomy – Indiana, 1892–1921', *Journal of the History of Medicine and Allied Sciences*, October 1998, 53(4):372.

62. Sharp's list of those he considered unfit encompassed: 'the diseased . . . the insane, the idiot, the epileptic, the imbecile, the backward, the criminal . . . the habitual vagrant: the syphilitic, the

consumptive, the inebriate, the drug habitue, the rake, the roue, the neurotic, the erotic, the sexual pervert … the reformed prostitute'. Gugliotta, 'Dr Sharp with His Little Knife', p. 389.

63. Unless all the patients gave their informed consent, Dr Sharp must have been acting illegally for some eight years if he had been performing his operations since 1899. According to Kevles, the Indiana law was passed in 1907. Kevles, *In the Name of Eugenics*, p. 100.

64. UK National Archives, HO 144/1098/197900. 'CRIMINAL: Sterilization of the mentally degenerate', 1910.

65. Obituary of Sir Horatio Bryan Donkin, MA, MD OXON, FRCP in *Journal of Mental Science*, January 1928, LXXIV(304):2–3, 5.

66. 'The time may not be very distant when a sounder knowledge may go far towards dispelling the ignorant and almost superstitious credulity which still exists, and rendering impossible much of the quackery and mystery which as yet disfigure the profession of medicine.' H. Donkin, 'Thoughts on Ignorance and Quackery', *British Medical Journal*, 9 October 1880, 2(1,032):580.

67. Houdini, *A Magician Among The Spirits* (London: Harper & Brothers, 1924), pp. 80–2.

68. UK National Archives, HO 144/1098/197900. 'CRIMINAL: Sterilization of the mentally degenerate', 1910. Donkin to Troup, 27 May 1910.

69. UK National Archives, HO 144/1088/194663. 'CRIMINAL: Expert opinions on the question of sterilisation; CRIMINAL: Oxtoby, Alfred: Court: Beverley (E. Riding): Offence: Attempted bestiality with mare; Sentence: Insane on arraignment', 1910–1911.

70. 'Programme of the First International Eugenics Congress, London 1912.' Published by the Eugenics Education Society, p. 2.

71. Diary entry for 20 October 1912 in: Blunt, *My Diaries*, p. 416.

72. Martin Farr, *Reginald McKenna: Financier among Statesmen, 1863–1916* (Abingdon: Routledge, 2008), pp. 237–8.

73. Hansard, vol. 53, col. 221, 28 May 1913.

74. Ibid.

75. Phil Fennell, *Treatment Without Consent: Law, Psychiatry and the Treatment of Mentally Disordered People Since 1845* (London: Routledge, 1996), p. 77.

76. Alexandra Hamlin and Peter Oakes, 'Reflections on Deinstitutionalization in the United Kingdom', *Journal of Policy and Practice in Intellectual Disabilities*, March 2008, 5(1):47.

77. Blacker, *Eugenics: Galton and After*, pp. 140–1.

78. John Macnicol, 'Eugenics and the Campaign for Voluntary Sterilization in Britain Between the Wars', *Social History of Medicine*, August 1989, 2(2):154.

79. Letitia Fairfield, *The Case Against Sterilisation* (London: Catholic Truth Society, 1934), p. 4.

80. Lord Riddell to Neville Chamberlain, 27 April 1929. Quoted in: Macnicol, 'Eugenics and the Campaign for Voluntary Sterilization', p. 151.

81. Martin Gilbert, *Prophet of Truth: Winston S. Churchill 1922–1939* (London: Minerva, 1990), p. 410.

82. Hansard, vol. 255, cols 1,253–6, 21 July 1931.

83. Ann Farmer, *By Their Fruits: Eugenics, Population Control, and the Abortion Campaign* (Washington, DC: Catholic University of America Press, 2008), p. 69, n. 320.

84. Soloway, *Demography and Degeneration*, p. 301.

85. Jack R. Fischel, *Historical Dictionary of the Holocaust* (Lanham, MD: Rowman & Littlefield, 2020), p. 102.

86. Quoted in: Macnicol, 'Eugenics and the Campaign for Voluntary Sterilization', p. 148.

87. Winston S. Churchill, *Great Contemporaries* (London: Reprint Society, 1941), p. 229. The chapter in the work quoted, entitled 'Hitler and his Choice', had as stated been written in 1935. It was, though, retitled for this edition from simply 'Hitler', which is how it had appeared in the first, 1937, edition of the book. Richard M. Langworth, *A Connoisseur's Guide to the Books of Sir Winston Churchill* (London: Brassey's, 1998), p. 184.

88. Winston S. Churchill, *The Second World War: vol. Two: Their Finest Hour* (London: Reprint Society, 1951), p. 192.

Notes 229

89. Richard Breitman, *Official Secrets: What the Nazis Planned, What the British and Americans Knew* (London: Allen Lane, 1999), p. 15.
90. For an examination of this see Larry V. Thompson, '*Lebensborn* and the Eugenics Policy of the Reichsführer-SS', *Central European History*, March 1971, 4(1).
91. Crichton, 'Appendix I: Why Politicized Science is Dangerous', in Crichton, *State of Fear*, p. 577.

Chapter 5: Crime, Punishment, and the 'Prisoners' Friend'

1. Undergoing a lengthy prison sentence.
2. Violet Bonham Carter, *Winston Churchill: An Intimate Portrait* (New York: Konecky & Konecky, 1965), p. 151.
3. Isaac G. Briggs, *Reformatory Reform* (London: Longmans, Green & Co., 1924), p. vii.
4. UK National Archives, PCOM 7/38. 'Departmental Committee on Prisons, 1895: The "Gladstone Committee" – report and minutes of evidence', 1894–1895, para 5.
5. Rupert Cross, *Punishment, Prison and The Public: An Assessment of Penal Reform in Twentieth Century England by an Armchair Penologist* (London: Stevens & Sons, 1971), p. 8.
6. Ibid, p. 7.
7. Philip Harling, 'The Trouble with Convicts: From Transportation to Penal Servitude, 1840–67', *Journal of British Studies*, January 2014, 53(1):88, 98, 99–100. Cross, *Punishment*, p. 9.
8. Colonel Sir Edmund F. Du Cane, *The Punishment and Prevention of Crime* (London: Macmillan & Co., 1885), p. 159.
9. Cross, *Punishment*, p. 11.
10. Alan S. Baxendale, *Winston Leonard Spencer-Churchill: Penal Reformer* (Bern: Peter Lang, 2009), pp. 16–17.
11. Walter C. Reckless, *The Crime Problem* (New York: Appleton-Century-Crofts, 1961), p. 552.
12. Baxendale, *Penal Reformer*, p. 20.
13. Calculated from 'The Annual Report of the Commissioners and Directors of Convict Prisons 1909–1910.' Baxendale, *Penal Reformer*, p. 180, n. 29.
14. RSC VII, p. 387.
15. Churchill, *My Early Life*, p. 273.
16. Ibid, pp. 275, 283.
17. Undergoing a lengthy prison sentence.
18. Bonham Carter, *Intimate Portrait*, p. 151. Interestingly, Churchill entitled the relevant chapter of *My Early Life* 'In Durance Vile'. Churchill, *My Early Life*, p. 273.
19. Mike Nellis, 'John Galsworthy's Justice', *British Journal of Criminology*, Winter 1996, 36(1):61
20. H.V. Marrot, *The Life and Letters of John Galsworthy* (London: William Heinemann, 1935), p. 261.
21. John Galsworthy, *Justice: A Tragedy in Four Acts* (London: Duckworth, 1911), pp. 82–5.
22. UK National Archives, PCOM 7/279. 'Standing Order (New Series), no. 10', 30 July 1897, p. 3.
23. Sir Evelyn Ruggles-Brise, *The English Prison System* (London: Macmillan, 1921), p. 37.
24. Great Britain Prison Commission, *Report of the Commissioners of Prisons and Directors of Convict Prisons 1903–4* (London: HMSO, 1904), p. 16.
25. Ruggles-Brise, *English Prison System*, p. 41.
26. Ibid, pp. 7–8.
27. Ibid, pp. 45–6.
28. Marrot, *Life and Letters*, p. 677. RSC CVII, P2, p. 1,149.
29. Marrot, *Life and Letters*, p. 678. RSC CVII, P2, p. 1,150.
30. Baxendale, *Penal Reformer*, p. 50.
31. Though admitting that Galsworthy with 'pen and play was deeply moving public sentiment', in respect of the matter. Shane Leslie (Comp.), *Sir Evelyn Ruggles-Brise: A Memoir of the Founder of Borstal* (London: John Murray, 1938), p. 150. For the Galsworthy-Churchill relationship see also: James Gindin, *John Galsworthy's Life and Art: An Alien's Fortress* (London: Palgrave Macmillan, 1987), pp. 202, 206–7, 209–10.
32. Baxendale, *Penal Reformer*, pp. 51–2.

33. Ibid, p. 53.
34. Ibid.
35. Harold Butler, *Confident Morning* (London: Faber & Faber, 1950), p. 78.
36. Hansard, vol. 19, col. 1,349, 20 July 1910.
37. See, for example: Monika Fludernik, *Metaphors of Confinement: The Prison in Fact, Fiction, and Fantasy* (Oxford: Oxford University Press, 2019), p. 397.
38. Hansard, vol. 19, col. 1,354, 20 July 1910.
39. Galsworthy's diary entry for Friday, 29 July 1910. Marrot, *Life and Letters*, p. 284.
40. WSC to John Galsworthy, 30 July 1910. Marrot, *Life and Letters*, p. 684. RSC CVII, P2, p. 1,190.
41. Chapter 4 of his book is titled: 'Humanizing Convict and Local Prison Regimes: Churchill's Initiatives.' Baxendale, *Penal Reformer*, pp. 65–99.
42. Alyson Brown, *English Society and the Prison: Time, Culture and Politics in the Development of the Modern Prison, 1850–1920* (Woodbridge: Boydell Press, 2003), p. 16. This remains the case.
43. Diary entry for 20 October 1912 in: Blunt, *My Diaries*, p. 399.
44. Sir Edward Troup, *The Home Office* (London: G.P. Putnam's Sons, 1925), p. 62.
45. Jenkins, *Churchill*, p. 183. By the time Jenkins became Home Secretary, on 23 December 1965, capital punishment in England, Wales and Scotland had been effectively, if not completely in the legal sense, abolished. He famously replaced the 'billiard marker' with a refrigerator 'presumably well stocked'. John Campbell, *Roy Jenkins: A Well-Rounded Life* (London: Jonathan Cape, 2014), p. 261.
46. Baxendale, *Penal Reformer*, p. 157. Randolph Churchill says that 'when it fell to him to take the decision in a particular case he found it most painful'. RSC VII, p. 418.
47. Diary entry for 19 October 1912 in: Blunt, *My Diaries*, p. 398.
48. Diary entry for 20 October 1912 in: Blunt, *My Diaries*, p. 399.
49. Hansard, vol. 453, col. 1,439, 15 July 1948.
50. Nassir Ghaemi, *A First-Rate Madness: Uncovering the Links Between Leadership and Mental Illness* (New York: Penguin Press, 2011), p. 34.
51. Allister Vale and John Scadding, *Winston Churchill's Illnesses, 1886–1965* (Barnsley: Frontline Books, 2020) Kindle edition, Loc. 9580.
52. Butler, *Confident Morning*, p. 77.
53. Troup, *The Home Office*, p. 64.
54. Ibid, p. 63.
55. John Ellis, *Diary of a Hangman* (London: True Crime Library, 1996), pp. 65–6.
56. S.O. Rowan-Hamilton (ed.), *Trial of John Alexander Dickman* (London: Butterworth & Co., 1914), p. 188.
57. Established by the 1907 Criminal Appeal Act.
58. Ellis, *Diary*, p. 8.
59. John J. Eddleston, *The Encyclopaedia of Executions* (London: John Blake, 2002), p. 195.
60. RSC VII, pp. 411–18; RSC CVII, P2, pp. 1,191–6. Dickman's name, 'following an unbroken tradition', was withheld in these works.
61. See the 'Introduction' to: Rowan-Hamilton, *Trial*, pp. 1–23. For a thorough investigation of the whole affair see John J. Eddleston, *The Murder of John Alexander Dickman: The Newcastle Train Murder 1910* (Sussex: Bibliofile Publishers, 2012).
62. Dickens and Doyle remain popular, whilst Morrison (no relation to the accused) is largely forgotten. See Eliza Cubitt, *Arthur Morrison and the East End: The Legacy of Slum Fictions* (Abingdon: Routledge, 2019).
63. According to Kirby this sobriquet was bestowed by the *Sunday Express*. Dick Kirby, *Whitechapel's Sherlock Holmes: The Casebook of Fred Wensley OBE KPM Victorian Crime Buster* (Barnsley: Pen & Sword, 2015), Kindle Edition, Loc. 93. See also: Paul Stickler, *The Murder That Defeated Whitechapel's Sherlock Holmes: At Mrs Ridgley's Corner* (Barnsley: Pen & Sword, 2018).
64. Edward Abinger, *Forty Years at The Bar: Being the Memoirs of Edward Abinger, Barrister of The Inner Temple* (London: Hutchinson & Co., 1930), p. 26.

65. Kirby, *Whitechapel's Sherlock Holmes*, Locs 2932–4.

66. Butler, *Confident Morning*, p. 77.

67. Frederick Porter Wensley, *Forty Years of Scotland Yard: The Record of a Lifetime's Service in the Criminal Investigation Department* (Garden City, NY: Doubleday, Doran & Co., 1931), p. 119.

68. An Italian phrase meaning 'do nothing' or 'idleness'. See James Main Dixon, *Dictionary of Idiomatic English Phrases* (London: T. Nelson & Sons, 1891), p. 110.

69. H. Fletcher Moulton (ed.), *Trial of Steinie Morrison* (London: William Hodge & Co., 1922), p. xx.

70. 'The witnesses who crowded the court nearly all belonged to the East End and revealed such exotic ways of life and ways of thinking that the honest British jury must have been bewildered.' From a review of Fletcher Moulton, *Trial of Steinie Morrison*, in *The Spectator*, 1 April 1922.

71. The Honourable Sir Patrick Devlin, *Trial by Jury* (London: Stevens & Sons, 1956), p. 20.

72. Abinger, *Forty Years at The Bar*, pp. 57–8.

73. Wensley, *Forty Years of Scotland Yard*, p. 114.

74. Ibid, p. 131.

75. Abinger, *Forty Years at The Bar*, p. 66.

76. Ibid, p. 63.

77. S. Theodore Felstead, *In Search of Sensation: Being Thirty Years of a London Journalist's Life* (London: Robert Hale, 1945), p. 149.

78. Abinger, *Forty Years at The Bar*, p. 66.

79. Felstead, *In Search of Sensation*, p. 11.

80. Moulton, *Trial of Steinie Morrison*, pp. xxv–xxvi. The case continued, and indeed continues, to be written about.

81. RSC VII, p. 418.

82. Ibid, p. 411.

83. Four women were sentenced to death in 1910, but all were reprieved: the same figure applied in 1909. Hansard, vol. 23, col. 197, 20 March 1911.

84. Christopher Roberts, *The British Courts and Extra-territoriality in Japan, 1859–1899* (Leiden: Global Oriental, Boston).

85. Butler, *Confident Morning*, p. 80.

86. Sir Ernest Satow to F.V. Dickins, 23 February 1897. Quoted in: Ian Ruxton (transcriber, annotator and indexer), *Sir Ernest Satow's Private Letters to W.G. Aston and F.V. Dickins: The Correspondence of a Pioneer Japanologist from 1870 to 1918* (Morrisville, NC: Lulu Press, 2008), pp. 219–20.

87. Butler, *Confident Morning*, pp. 80–1. For an account of the Carew case see Molly Whittington-Egan, *Murder on the Bluff: The Carew Poisoning Case* (Glasgow: Neil Wilson Publishing, 2012).

88. *Wanganui Herald*, 3 November 1910. *Los Angeles Herald*, 21 November 1910.

89. Katherine D. Watson, *Poisoned Lives: English Poisoners and Their Victims* (London: Hambledon Continuum, 2004), p. 208.

90. Thomas Babington Macaulay, 'Review of: Letters and Journals of Lord Byron: With Notices of his Life by Thomas Moore', in Thomas Babington Macaulay, *Reviews, Essays, and Poems Including Essays from 'The Edinburgh Review', Lays of Ancient Rome, and Miscellaneous Writings in Prose and Verse* (London: Ward, Lock, 1890), p. 179.

91. L. Radzinowicz, 'The Persistent Offender', *Cambridge Law Journal*, March 1939, 7(1):68 n.1.

92. R.F. Quinton, *The Modern Prison Curriculum: A General Review of Our Penal System* (London: Macmillan & Co., 1912), p. 259.

93. https://www.legislation.gov.uk/ukpga/1908/59/section/10/enacted.

94. Stephen Hobhouse and A. Fenner Brockway (eds), *English Prisons Today: Being the Report of the Prison System Enquiry Committee* (London: Longmans, Green & Co., 1922), p. 444.

95. Baxendale, *Penal Reformer*, pp. 114–15. RSC VII, p. 391.

96. Approximating to £12 in 2022 terms.

97. John Hainsworth, *The Llanfyllin Union Workhouse: A Short History* (Llanfyllin: Llanfyllin Dolydd Building Preservation Trust, 2004), p. 27.

98. A Welsh custom, this refers to an address associated with him or his family.

99. 'For sacrilege at Leaton and Myddle, between 1st and 3rd inst.', *Police Gazette*, 27 January 1899, XVI(1574).
100. Baxendale, *Penal Reformer*, p. 114
101. Sir Basil Thomson, *The Scene Changes: An Autobiography* (London: Collins, 1939), p. 220.
102. Hansard, vol. 24, col. 877, 19 April 1911.
103. 'Mr and Mrs Lloyd George. Visit to Crediton Liberal Club To-day', *Western Times*, 22 October 1910. 'Lloyd George opens Bazaar in aid of the Crediton Liberal Club', *Crediton Chronicle & North Devon Gazette*, 29 October 1910.
104. 'Mr Winston Churchill: Arrival at Exeter Last Evening', *Western Times*, Monday, 24 October 1910.
105. Jenkins, *Churchill*, p. 182.
106. Thomson, *The Scene Changes*, p. 220.
107. *The Times*, 22 November 1910. *Spectator*, 26 November 1910. *Y Llan a'r Dywysogaeth*, 2 Rhagfyr 1910 (*The Church and the Principality*, 2 December 1910).
108. Diary entry for 22 November 1910. In: John Vincent (ed.), *The Crawford Papers: The Journals of David Lindsay, Twenty-Seventh Earl of Crawford and Tenth Earl of Balcarres, 1871–1940, During the Years 1892 to 1940* (Manchester: Manchester University Press, 1984), p. 169.
109. Frank Owen, *Tempestuous Journey: Lloyd George His Life and Times* (London: Hutchinson, 1954), p. 18.
110. 'Chancellor and the Gaol-Bird: Sentiment Over an Aged Convict Exposed: Another "Lloyd-Georgism" Shown Up' *South Wales Daily Post*, 26 November 1910.
111. Andrew Ashworth and Lucia Zedner, *Preventive Justice* (Oxford: Oxford University Press, 2014), p. 45.
112. Sir Leon Radzinowicz and Roger Hood, 'Incapacitating the Habitual Criminal: The English Experience', *Michigan Law Review*, 1980, 78(8):1,371.
113. Hansard, vol. 19, col. 1,352, 20 July 1910.
114. Hansard, vol. 21, col. 275, 8 February 1911.
115. RSC VII, p. 391.
116. Charles Whibley (uncredited), 'Musings without Method', *Blackwood's Magazine*, February 1911, CLXXXIX (MCXLIV):289.
117. Hansard, vol. 21, col. 1,900, 22 February 1911. See also: *Saturday Review*, 12 August 1911.
118. For example: according to *The Times* of 6 January 1916, 'David Davies, aged 74, the Dartmoor Shepherd' had been sentenced the previous day to six months' imprisonment for theft from an offertory-box at a church in Liverpool.
119. *Law Times: The Journal and Record of the Law and the Lawyers*, vol. CXXX, November 1910 to April 1911 (London: Office of the 'Law Times', 1911), p. 330.
120. Radzinowicz and Hood, 'Incapacitating the Habitual Criminal', p. 1,373. For details of the discussions and disputes Churchill had with respect to the matter see Baxendale, *Penal Reformer*, pp. 117–28.
121. Hansard, vol. 19, col. 1,344, 20 July 1910.
122. Hansard, vol. 174, col. 294, 8 May 1907.
123. H.E. Norman, 'Conviction and Probation: The Case Against Conviction', *Canadian Bar Review*, May 1941, XIX(5):518. Norman was the Secretary of the National Association of Probation Officers at the time of writing.
124. Sir Leon Radzinowicz, *Adventures In Criminology* (London: Routledge, 1999), p. 151.
125. Hansard, vol. 19, col. 1,344, 20 July 1910.
126. Quoted in: Baxendale, *Penal Reformer*, p. 129.
127. Quoted in: Ibid, p. 131.
128. For details see Ibid, pp. 145–53.
129. Butler, *Confident Morning*, pp. 78–9. Butler does not say if this was the occasion when Churchill and Lloyd George encountered David Davies.
130. Prince George's service record is available at the UK National Archives: ADM 196/42/244.

131. *Church Times*, 3 February 1911.
132. James Pope-Hennessy, *Queen Mary 1867–1953* (London: George Allen & Unwin, 1959), pp. 428–9. For background to the matter see also: Kenneth Rose, *King George V* (London: Weidenfeld & Nicolson, 1983), pp. 82–7.
133. Robin Callender Smith, 'The Missing Witness?: George V, Competence and Compellability and the Criminal Libel Trial of Edward Frederick Mylius', *Journal of Legal History*, August 2012, 33(2):209.
134. Quoted in: Derek Walker-Smith, *Lord Reading and his Cases: The Study of a Great Career* (New York: Macmillan Co., 1934), pp. 261–2.
135. The defendant must also have intended to publish the materials that contain the libel. See Clive Walker, 'Reforming the Crime of Libel', *New York Law School Law Review*, January 2006, 50(1):171–2.
136. Quoted in: Callender Smith, 'The Missing Witness?', pp. 221–2.
137. Troup, *The Home Office*, pp. 76–7.
138. Robin Callender Smith, *Celebrity Privacy and the Development of the Judicial Concept of Proportionality: How English Law has Balanced the Rights to Protection and Interference – Thesis Submitted in Partial fulfilment of the Requirements of the Degree of Doctor of Philosophy* (London: Queen Mary University of London Centre for Commercial Law Studies, 2014), p. 181.
139. WSC to H.H. Asquith, 26 November 1910. Note dictated by Churchill 'on the present position'. RSC CVII, P2, pp. 1, 217–18.
140. WSC to the King, 18 December 1910. Quoted in: RSC CVII, P2, p. 1,219.
141. Quoted in: Walker-Smith, *Lord Reading and his Cases*, p. 92.
142. Callender Smith, 'The Missing Witness?', p. 226.
143. https://www.bankofengland.co.uk/monetary-policy/inflation/inflation-calculator.
144. Callender Smith, 'The Missing Witness?', pp. 226–7.
145. The Marquess of Reading, *Rufus Isaacs First Marquess of Reading: By His Son* (London: Hutchinson, 1950), p. 200.
146. Callender Smith, 'The Missing Witness?', p. 237. The proceedings were reported verbatim, or virtually so, in *The Times*, 2 February 1911.
147. See Callender Smith, 'The Missing Witness?', pp. 231, 233–4.
148. Ibid, p. 239.
149. WSC to the King, 28 December 1910. RSC CVII, P2, p. 1,226.
150. Quoted in: Callender Smith, 'The Missing Witness?', pp. 240–1.
151. Ibid, p. 242.
152. Simon Diary entry for 3 February 1911. Quoted in: Ibid.
153. Reading, *Rufus Isaacs*, p. 202.
154. RSC VII, p. 422.
155. Lord Morley to WSC, 1 February 1911. Quoted in: RSC CVII, P2, p. 1,237.
156. RSC CVII, P2, pp. 1,216–38.
157. See Phil Carradice, *Nautical Training Ships: An Illustrated History* (Stroud: Amberley Publishing, 2013).
158. Roger Lane and Jenny McRonald, 'Winston Churchill and the Akbar Heswall', *Heswall & District Magazine*, October 2015, p. 24.
159. John M. McEwen, 'The National Press during the First World War: Ownership and Circulation', *Journal of Contemporary History*, July 1982, 17(3):476.
160. Neil Berry, 'Godfather of Populism: The Rabid Reign of Horatio Bottomley', *Times Literary Supplement*, 9 April 2021, no. 6158.
161. Julian Symons, *Horatio Bottomley* (Looe: House of Stratus, 2014), p. 84.
162. Lane and McRonald, 'Winston Churchill and the Akbar Heswall', p. 24.
163. Hansard, vol. 21, col. 2,171, 23 February 1911.
164. See Symons, *Horatio Bottomley*, p. 89. Julius Carlebach, *Caring for Children in Trouble* (London: Routledge, 2002), p. 83.

165. Hansard, vol. 21, col. 2,163, 23 February 1911.
166. Ibid, col. 2,173, 23 February 1911.
167. Joan Rimmer, *Yesterday's Naughty Children: Training Ship, Girls' Reformatory and Farm School: A History of the Liverpool Reformatory Association, founded in 1855* (Manchester: Neil Richardson, 1986).
168. Briggs, *Reformatory Reform*, p. 86.
169. Hansard, vol. 21, col. 2,175, 23 February 1911.
170. The Churchill–Bottomley correspondence can be found in the Home Office Correspondence file at Churchill College, Cambridge: CHAR 12/3/19 – 24 Oct 1910; CHAR 12/3/21 – 26 Oct 1910; CHAR 12/3/22 – 27 Oct 1910; CHAR 12/3/26-29 – 01 Nov 1910; CHAR 12/3/30 – 02 Nov 1910; CHAR 12/3/31 – 03 Nov 1910; CHAR 12/3/32 – 02 Nov 1910; CHAR 12/3/36 – 05 Nov 1910.
171. Never, surely, has Hartley's immortal aphorism – 'The past is a foreign country: they do things differently there' – been more apposite. L.P. Hartley, *The Go-Between* (London: Hamish Hamilton, 1953), p. 9.
172. His most notable work being: C.F.G. Masterman, *The Condition of England* (London: Methuen & Co., 1909).
173. Symons, *Horatio Bottomley*, p. 90.
174. Carlebach, *Caring for Children*, p. 84.
175. C.F.G. Masterman, *Heswall Nautical School: Report of inquiry by Mr C.F.G. Masterman, MP, Under Secretary of State for the Home Department, into charges made concerning the management of the Heswall Nautical School, 1911* (London: HMSO, 1911), p. 10.
176. Hansard, vol. 21, col. 2,170, 23 February 1911.
177. Ibid, col. 2,176, 23 February 1911.
178. Quoted in: Carlebach, *Caring for Children*, p. 84.
179. Hansard, vol. 21, col. 2,171, 23 February 1911.
180. For details see Symons, *Horatio Bottomley*, pp. 90–1.
181. WSC to the King, 24 February 1911. RSC CVII, P2, p. 1,051.
182. Hansard, vol. 21, cols 2,199–200, 23 February 1911.
183. Reformatory and Industrial schools dealt with different categories of children. Reformatory schools were for those who had been convicted of some offence. Industrial schools existed for vulnerable children who had, in modern parlance, been taken into care, and trained them in an effort to keep them away from crime. The regimes in both were essentially similar.
184. Barry Godfrey, Pamela Cox, Heather Shore and Zoe Alker, *Young Criminal Lives: Life Courses and Life Chances from 1850* (Oxford: Oxford University Press, 2017), p. 98. Victor Bailey, *Delinquency and Citizenship: Reclaiming the Young Offender 1914–48* (Oxford: Clarendon Press, 1987), p. 48.
185. Briggs, *Reformatory Reform*, p. vii.
186. Clive Ponting, *Churchill* (London: Sinclair-Stevenson, 1994).
187. Symons, *Horatio Bottomley*, p. 91.

Chapter 6: Mrs Pankhurst's Army of Amazons

1. Owen, *Tempestuous Journey*, p. 159.
2. Hansard, vol. 22, col. 1,836, 10 March 1911.
3. Martin Pugh, *The Pankhursts* (London: Allen Lane, 2001), p. 207.
4. Book II of her memoirs is entitled 'Four Years of Peaceful Militancy'. Emmeline Pankhurst, *My Own Story* (London: Eveleigh Nash, 1914), pp. 81–202.
5. Dame Christabel Pankhurst and Lord Pethick-Lawrence (ed.), *Unshackled: The Story of How We Won the Vote* (London: Hutchinson, 1959), p. 153. The manuscript for this book was found among Christabel Pankhurst's possessions following her death in 1958 and had apparently been written about twenty years previously.
6. Sophia A. van Wingerden, *The Women's Suffrage Movement in Britain, 1866–1928* (London: Palgrave Macmillan, 1999), p. 118. The breakdown by party was: 16 Liberals, 10 Conservatives,

1 Unionist, 5 Irish Nationalists and 4 Labour. 'Conciliation Committee for Woman Suffrage', RSC CVII, P3, pp. 1,429–30.

7. Constance Rover, *Women's Suffrage and Party Politics in Britain, 1866–1914* (London: Routledge & Kegan Paul, 1967), p. 181.

8. Leslie Parker Hume, *The National Union of Women's Suffrage Societies 1897–1914* (Abingdon: Routledge, 2016), p. 69.

9. Roy Hattersley, *David Lloyd George: The Great Outsider* (London: Abacus, 2012), p. 236.

10. For the restricted franchise as it applied to men, see Chapter 1.

11. Richard A. Cosgrove, *The Rule of Law: Albert Venn Dicey, Victorian Jurist* (Chapel Hill, NC: University of North Carolina Press, 1980), p. 293.

12. Albert Venn Dicey, 'Woman Suffrage', in Edith M. Phelps (Comp.), *Selected Articles on Woman Suffrage* (Minneapolis, MN: The H.W. Wilson Company, 1910), pp. 281–2, 283.

13. The 1869 Municipal Franchise Act (Local Government Act) gave the vote to unmarried female rate-payers in terms of local elections, but they were still precluded from standing in them. John Garrard, *Democratisation in Britain: Elites, Civil Society and Reform Since 1800* (Houndsmills: Palgrave, 2002), p. 76. This restriction was eased somewhat in 1894 with the passing of the Local Government Act 1894, which allowed women to serve on parish and district councils. It was the Qualification of Women (County and Town Councils) Act of 1907 which expanded upon the provision, entitling women, so long as they were ratepayers, to be elected to County and Borough Councils. Richard Keen, Richard Cracknell and Max Bolton, *Women in Parliament and Government: House of Commons Briefing Paper SN01250* (London: House of Commons Library Research Service, 2018), p. 10.

14. RSC CVII, P3, p. 1,433.

15. Ibid, p. 1,431.

16. By individual MPs, rather than by the Government.

17. RSC CVII, P3, p. 1,431.

18. H.N. Brailsford to WSC, 13 April 1910. RSC CVII, P3, p. 1,427.

19. WSC to H.N. Brailsford, 19 April 1910. RSC VII, pp. 395–6.

20. Augustine Birrell (Chief Secretary for Ireland), George Barnes (Leader of the Labour Party) and Arthur Henderson (Barnes' predecessor as Labour Leader).

21. 'Circular Sent to All MPs', RSC CVII, P3, p. 1,430.

22. Betty Balfour (ed.), *Letters of Constance Lytton* (London: William Heinemann, 1925), p. xi.

23. Lady Constance Lytton and Jane Warton, Spinster, *Prison & Prisoners: Some Personal Experiences* (London: William Heinemann, 1914), pp. 1–2.

24. Ibid, p. 9.

25. Lyndsey Jenkins, *Lady Constance Lytton: Aristocrat, Suffragette, Martyr* (London: Biteback Publishing, 2015), pp. 147–8. Lytton and Warton, *Prison & Prisoners*, p. 309.

26. Lytton and Warton, *Prison & Prisoners*, p. 268.

27. Ibid, p. 269.

28. Dr Helen Pankhurst, 'Foreword' to Lyndsey Jenkins, *Lady Constance Lytton*, p. i.

29. UK National Archives, HO 144/1054/187986. 'Prisons and Prisoners – Other: Treatment of Lady Constance Lytton, Suffragette', 1910–1912.

30. Described as such by Churchill. RSC CVII, P2, p. 1,449.

31. Lord Lytton to WSC, Private, 18 March 1910. Churchill Archives Centre, CHAR 12/2/21.

32. Diary entry for 2 April 1910 in Blunt, *My Diaries*, p. 297.

33. G. Glover Alexander, *The Administration of Justice in Criminal Matters (in England and Wales)* (Cambridge: Cambridge University Press, 1915), p. 167.

34. Victor Bailey, 'English Prisons, Penal Culture, and the Abatement of Imprisonment, 1895–1922', *Journal of British Studies*, July 1997, 36(3):294.

35. Hansard, vol. 15, col. 178, 15 March 1910.

36. Viscount Gladstone to WSC, 16 March 1910. RSC CVII, P2, p. 1,157.

37. RSC CVII, P2, p. 1,157.

38. Minute by WSC for Sir E. Troup, 28 February 1910. RSC CVII, P2. pp. 1,153–4.
39. Minute by Sir E. Troup, 4 March 1910. RSC CVII, P2, pp. 1,154–5.
40. C.P. Scott to WSC, March 1910. Churchill Archives Centre, CHAR 12/2/14.
41. Hansard, 'Parliamentary Franchise (Women)', vol. 17, cols 1,203–7, 14 June 1910.
42. Pease diary entry, 15 June 1910. Quoted in Sandra Stanley Holton, *Feminism and Democracy: Women's Suffrage and Reform Politics in Britain, 1900–1918* (Cambridge: Cambridge University Press, 2002), p. 168, n. 81. Pease was Chancellor of the Duchy of Lancaster.
43. 'The word "suffragette" was invented by the *Daily Mail* as a term of abuse, taken up by the *Daily Mirror* because it sounded young and irrepressible and then accepted by the women themselves. History made it the noun which denoted violent intentions.' Hattersley, *David Lloyd George*, p. 236.
44. See Hume, *The National Union*.
45. Wingerden, *The Women's Suffrage Movement*, p. 120.
46. Memorandum by WSC, 19 July 1910. RSC CVII, P2, p. 1,449. See also: RSC VII, p. 396.
47. Lord Lytton to WSC, 6 June 1910. RSC CVII, P2, p. 1,435. 'Pamela' was Lytton's wife, and thus the Countess of Lytton, who as Pamela Plowden had been Churchill's 'first great love'. Despite her refusing his proposal of marriage they remained lifelong friends. Mary Soames (ed.), *Speaking for Themselves: The Personal Letters of Winston and Clementine Churchill* (London: Black Swan, 1999), p. 5.
48. H.N. Brailsford to WSC, 8 July 1910. RSC CVII, P2, pp. 1,435–6.
49. Lucy Masterman, *C.F.G. Masterman: A Biography* (London: Nicholson & Watson, 1939), p. 166.
50. Churchill's speech, unless otherwise stated, is taken from: Hansard, vol. 19, cols 220–8, 12 July 1910.
51. This is an almost verbatim quote from an undated memorandum by Masterman. In it he states that he has 'consulted Mr Baines, the Legal Adviser to the L[ocal] G[overnment] B[oard] about the occupation question. He says the question is difficult, but his personal opinion is that a husband could create votes for his wife or daughters by *letting* to them any property of the value of £10. Thus he might let his wife the stables or any separate building: it is even possible that different parts of the same house could be treated as separate tenements & votes conferred on daughters in respect of the rooms they occupied. But this last point is more doubtful . . .'. C.F.G. Masterman to WSC, no date. Quoted in: RSC CVII, P2, pp. 1,455–6.
52. Hansard, vol. 19, col. 305, 12 July 1910.
53. E. Sylvia Pankhurst, *The Suffragette: The History of The Women's Militant Suffrage Movement 1905–1910* (New York: Sturgis & Walton, 1911), p. 497.
54. Hansard, vol. 19, col. 256, 12 July 1910.
55. H.N. Brailsford to WSC, 12 July 1910. RSC CVII, P2, pp. 1,436–7.
56. Memorandum by WSC, 19 July 1910. RSC CVII, P2, pp. 1,447–54.
57. Memorandum by WSC, 19 July 1910. RSC CVII, P2, pp. 1,447–8.
58. Memorandum by WSC, 19 July 1910. RSC CVII, P2, p. 1,453.
59. Pankhurst, *The Suffragette*, p. 133.
60. 'Explanatory Memorandum' by the Conciliation Committee. RSC CVII, P2, p. 1,433.
61. Mary Soames, *Clementine Churchill: The Biography of a Marriage* (New York: Houghton Mifflin, 2003), pp. 69, 100.
62. Quoted in: Toye, *Lloyd George and Churchill*, p. 78.
63. Pankhurst, *My Own Story*, p. 177.
64. Pankhurst, *The Suffragette*, p. 500.
65. On the other hand, Christabel Pankhurst, writing many years later, laid the responsibility at the feet of Sir Edward Grey: 'when questioned as to the autumn facilities, he definitely refused them and would give no promise for the next or any other year': Pankhurst and Pethick-Lawrence, *Unshackled*, p. 164. Her biographer dates this announcement as occurring on 12 November after the Albert Hall meeting. Purvis, *Christabel Pankhurst*, p. 91.
66. Pankhurst, *The Suffragette*, p. 501.

67. For numbers see Lucinda Hawksley, *March, Women, March* (London: Andre Deutsch, 2015), p. 164; Caroline Morrell, *'Black Friday' and Violence Against Women in the Suffragette Movement* (London: Women's Research and Resources Centre, 1981), p. 32; Pankhurst and Pethick-Lawrence, *Unshackled*, p. 164; Pankhurst, *The Suffragette*, p. 502.

68. Sylvia Pankhurst, 'Miss Sylvia Pankhurst's Account', *Votes for Women*, Friday, 25 November 1910, IV(142):121.

69. As well as men from A Whitehall, there were contingents from: B Chelsea; E Holborn; M Southwark; R Greenwich; S Hampstead; V Wandsworth; W Clapham; and Y Highgate divisions. C.J. Bearman, 'The legend of Black Friday', *Historical Research*, November 2010, 83(222):702.

70. 'South Wales Coal Strike (Use of Police)', 24 November 1910. House of Commons.' Rhodes James, *Complete Speeches*, p. 1,614.

71. UK National Archives, MEPO 3/203. Suffragettes: Complaints against Police, 1911. 'Memorandum by Sir Edward Henry, Commissioner of the Metropolitan Police', 8 February 1911, pp. 1–2.

72. Taken by Victor Consolé of London News Agency. Katherine E. Kelly, 'Seeing Through Spectacles: The Woman Suffrage Movement and London Newspapers, 1906–13', *European Journal of Women's Studies*, 2004, 11(3):328.

73. *Daily Mirror*, 19 November 1910.

74. Antonia Raeburn, *The Militant Suffragettes* (London: Michael Joseph, 1973), p. 105.

75. Elizabeth Crawford, *The Women's Suffrage Movement: A Reference Guide 1866–1928* (London: University College London [UCL] Press), pp. 759–60.

76. 'The End of the Truce: Deputation to Westminster, Friday, November 18, Accounts of Eye-witnesses. Miss Sylvia Pankhurst's Account', *Votes for Women*, 25 November 1910, IV(142):121.

77. A 'statement' sent by 'Mrs Saul Solomon [Georgiana Margaret Solomon] to Mr Winston Churchill, Secretary of State for the Home Office' on 17 December 1910. Quoted in: 'Black Friday', *Votes for Women*, Friday, 6 January 1911, IV(148):230.

78. Hansard, vol. 22, cols 1,834W–5W, 10 March 1911.

79. *The Times*, 19 November 1910.

80. For examples, see Morrell, *'Black Friday'*, pp. 33–42.

81. David Mitchell, *Queen Christabel: A Biography of Christabel Pankhurst* (London: MacDonald & Jane's, 1977), p. 160.

82. Pankhurst, *My Own Story*, pp. 182–3.

83. Pankhurst and Pethick-Lawrence, *Unshackled*, p. 166.

84. *The Times*, 18 November 1910.

85. 'How Mrs Pankhurst Views it', *Cardiff Times and South Wales Weekly News*, 26 November 1910.

86. 'Mr Churchill and the Suffragists', *The Times*, 21 November 1910.

87. RSC VII, pp. 399–400.

88. See for example: Andrew Rosen, *Rise Up, Women!: The Militant Campaign of the Women's Social and Political Union 1903–1914* (Abingdon: Routledge, 2013), p. 139. Diane Atkinson, *Votes for Women* (Cambridge: Cambridge University Press, 1988), p. 30.

89. WSC to Sir Edward Henry, 22 November 1910. Quoted in: RSC CVII, P2, p. 1,457.

90. Sir Edward Henry to WSC, 22 November 1910. UK National Archives, HO 144/1106/200455.

91. Purvis, *Christabel Pankhurst*, p. 151.

92. Owen, *Tempestuous Journey*, p. 159.

93. *The Times*, 23 November 1910.

94. But denied admission on the grounds that as a married woman she had no status in law, and so could not be a fellow of a society incorporated by charter. Joan Mason, 'Hertha Ayrton (1854–1923) and the Admission of Women to the Royal Society of London', *Notes and Records of the Royal Society of London*, July 1991, 45(2):209.

95. Evelyn Sharp, *Hertha Ayrton 1854–1923: A Memoir* (London: Edward Arnold & Co., 1926), p. 323.

96. *Daily Mail*, 23 November 1910.
97. Reports in *The Times* and *Daily Chronicle*, 23 November 1910.
98. Journal entry for 24 November 1910. Thomas James Cobden-Sanderson, *The Journals of Thomas James Cobden-Sanderson 1879–1922: vol. II* (London: Richard Cobden-Sanderson, 1926), pp. 171–2.
99. *Weekly Mail*, 26 November 1910.
100. RSC VII, p. 400.
101. *Weekly Mail*, 26 November 1910.
102. *New York Times*, 23 November 1910.
103. 'West End Riots. Wild Scenes. Attack on Mr Birrell', *Daily News*, 23 November 1910.
104. *Daily News*, 23 November 1910.
105. Letter to Alfred Hawkins from Alice Hawkins, 22 November 1910. Newark Museum, Leicester. Quoted in: Richard Whitmore, *Membership, Policy and Strategy of the Women's Social and Political Union in Leicester and the East Midlands 1907–1914: A Thesis Submitted in Partial Fulfilment of the Requirements of De Montfort University for the Degree of Doctor of Philosophy* (Leicester: Unpublished: 2000), p. 175.
106. For example, see Harold L. Smith, *The British Women's Suffrage Campaign 1866–1928* (Abingdon: Routledge, 2007), p. 50.
107. Recruits received training in crowd control and the like, but mostly learned from more experienced colleagues 'on the job'. Thus they inevitably imbibed the culture pertaining in the area they served, which was reflected in the way they interacted with the public. See Haia Shpayer-Makov, *The Making of a Policeman: A Social History of a Labour Force in Metropolitan London 1829–1914* (Aldershot: Ashgate, 2002).
108. Pankhurst and Pethick-Lawrence, *Unshackled*, p. 169.
109. 'Chief Magistrate's Protest', *Weekly Mail*, 26 November 1910.
110. Ibid.
111. H.H. Asquith to WSC, 23 November 1910. RSC CVII, P2, p. 1,457. Birrell later refused to press charges. Augustine Birrell to WSC, 21 February 1911. RSC CVII, P2, p. 1,468.
112. Hansard, vol. 20, cols 367–8, 24 November 1910.
113. The Secretary was the executive head of the Post Office, reporting to the Postmaster General.
114. Angela V. John, 'Men, Manners and Militancy: Literary Men and Women's Suffrage', in Angela V. John and Claire Eustance (eds), *The Men's Share?: Masculinities, Male Support and Women's Suffrage in Britain, 1890–1920* (Abingdon: Routledge, 2013), p. 88.
115. RSC CVII, P2, p. 1,462.
116. Ibid, p. 1,458.
117. Ibid, p. 1,464.
118. RSC VII, p. 400.
119. Hugh Arthur Franklin, 'Why I Struck at Mr Churchill', *Votes for Women*, 9 December 1910, IV(144):162.
120. This clipping is at the Churchill Archives Centre, CHAR 12/3/49.
121. Sir John Simon to WSC, 14 December 1910. RSC CVII, P2, p. 1,467.
122. Sir Charles Mathews to WSC, 1 December 1910. RSC CVII, P2, pp. 1,464–5.
123. 'Deputation to Mr Churchill', *The Common Cause, The Organ of the National Union of Women's Suffrage Societies*, 8 December 1910, II(87):573.
124. Diane Atkinson, *Rise Up Women! The Remarkable Lives of the Suffragettes* (London: Bloomsbury Publishing, 2018), p. 440.
125. Mary Henderson, *Ethel Moorhead: Dundee's Rowdiest Suffragette* (Privately published, 2020). Available online at: https://ethelmoorhead.org.uk/chapter-3-votes-for-women/. Leah Leneman, *A Guid Cause: The Women's Suffrage Movement in Scotland* (Edinburgh: Mercat, 1995), p. 98. For biographical details of Ethel Moorhead, see Leah Leneman, *Martyrs in Our Midst: Dundee, Perth and the Forcible Feeding of Suffragettes* (Dundee: Abertay Historical Society, 1993), pp. 15–20.
126. Winston S. Churchill, *Thoughts and Adventures* (London: Thornton Butterworth, 1932), p. 159.

127. Hansard, vol. 21, col. 452, 9 February 1911.
128. Jessie Murray and H.N. Brailsford, *The Treatment of the Women's Deputations by the Metropolitan Police: Copy of Evidence collected by Dr Jessie Murray and Mr H.N. Brailsford, and forwarded to the Home Office by the Conciliation Committee for Women Suffrage, in support of its Demand for a Public Enquiry* (London: Woman's Press, 1911).
129. Hansard, vol. 22, col. 267, 1 March 1911.
130. Ibid, cols 267–8, 1 March 1911.
131. Ibid, col. 1,834, 10 March 1911.
132. Ibid.
133. Ibid, col. 1,835, 10 March 1911.
134. *The Times*, 2 March 1911. RSC CVII, P2, p. 1,469.
135. Sir Edward Troup to Sir Charles Mathews, 4 March 1911. RSC CVII, P2, p. 1,468.
136. Purvis, *Christabel Pankhurst*, p. 95.
137. See Ian Christopher Fletcher, '"A Star Chamber of the Twentieth Century": Suffragettes, Liberals, and the 1908 "Rush the Commons" Case', *Journal of British Studies*, October 1996, 35(4). See also: F.W. Pethick Lawrence, *The Trial of the Suffragette Leaders* (London: Woman's Press, 1909).
138. Mrs Saul Solomon to the editor of *The Times*, 3 March 1911. RSC CVII, P2, pp. 1,469–70. Her four-page letter of 17 December was printed in *Votes for Women* on 6 January 1911, and later published in pamphlet form.
139. Ellis Griffith to WSC, 22 March 1911. Churchill Archives Centre, CHAR 12/9/119. The answer survives as an annotation by Edward Marsh.
140. Morrell, '*Black Friday*', p. 6.
141. Ray Strachey, *The Cause: A Short History of the Women's Movement in Great Britain* (London: Bell & Sons, 1928), p. 312. For a biography of Strachey see Jennifer Holmes, *A Working Woman: The Remarkable Life of Ray Strachey* (Kibworth Beauchamp: Matador, 2019).
142. Quoted in: Fern Riddell, *Death in Ten Minutes: Kitty Marion: Activist, Arsonist, Suffragette* (London: Hodder & Stoughton, 2018), Kindle edition, locs 1541–8.
143. Pankhurst, *The Suffragette*, p. 142.
144. For brutality, corruption and abuses of power in the Metropolitan Police at the time see Sarah Wise, 'A Few Bad Apples', *History Today*, August 2020, 70(8).
145. Wingerden, *The Women's Suffrage Movement*, p. 123.
146. In legal terms, an unsupported statement that rests solely on the authority of the individual who makes it.
147. Robert Cecil, 'The Women and the Police', *The Times*, 24 March 1911.
148. Crawford, *The Women's Suffrage Movement*, p. 560.
149. Pankhurst and Pethick-Lawrence, *Unshackled*, p. 176.
150. Hansard, vol. 25, col. 807, 5 May 1911.
151. Pankhurst and Pethick-Lawrence, *Unshackled*, p. 177.
152. Hansard, vol. 26, col. 703, 29 May 1911.
153. The Coronation of King George V and Queen Mary.
154. Pankhurst and Pethick-Lawrence, *Unshackled*, p. 181.
155. Asquith to Lytton, *The Times*, 17 June 1911.
156. Bertha Mason, *The Story of the Women's Suffrage Movement* (London: Sherratt & Hughes, 1912), p. 92. For biographical details of Bertha Mason see Crawford, *The Women's Suffrage Movement*, p. 389.
157. Pankhurst, *My Own Story*, p. 196.
158. Dangerfield, *Strange Death*, p. 156.
159. Pankhurst, *My Own Story*, pp. 197, 202. See also: Purvis, *Christabel Pankhurst*, p. 172. The 'Official Organ' of the WSPU acknowledged 'militancy on an unprecedented scale', in a piece entitled 'The Women's Revolution – Reign of Terror – Fire and Bombs', *The Suffragette*, 11 April 1913.

160. Riddell, *Death in Ten Minutes*, Loc. 62.

161. Diary entry, 6 February 1912. Lord Riddell [George Riddell], *More Pages*, p. 36.

162. Hume, *The National Union*, p. 109.

163. University of Southampton, Special Collections, Manuscript collections, Mountbatten database. MB1/T. Papers of Prince Louis of Battenberg: Naval and Personal Papers, 1868–1921, 1962–79. MB1/T39/Naval Papers/378. 'Account by Admiral Prince Louis of Battenberg of the statement made to him by Sir Francis Hopwood, Additional Civil Lord of the Admiralty, about the quarrel between Lord Fisher and Churchill which led to their resignations in 1915, 24 June 1916.'

Chapter 7: A Whiff of Cordite

1. Troup, 'The Functions and Organization of the Home Office', p. 127.

2. Hansard, vol. 5, col. 5, 21 February 1910. The King's Speech.

3. *The Times*, 7 May 1910.

4. D.C. Somervell, *The Reign of King George the Fifth: An English Chronicle* (London: Faber & Faber, 1935), p. 19.

5. Basically, the minister with responsibility for governing Ireland.

6. Probably the best account of this 'Attempt at Compromise' is Chapter IX of Jenkins, *Mr Balfour's Poodle*, pp. 149–72. See also Chapter IV of John D. Fair, *British Interparty Conferences: Study of the Procedure of Conciliation in British Politics 1867–1921* (Oxford: Clarendon Press, 1980), pp. 77–102.

7. Lord Newton, *Lord Lansdowne: A Biography* (London: Macmillan & Co., 1929), p. 396.

8. Robert James Scally, *The Origins of the Lloyd George Coalition: The Politics of Social Imperialism, 1900–1918* (Princeton, NJ: Princeton University Press, 1975), p. 202.

9. Grigg, *Lloyd George: The People's Champion*, p. 206.

10. Masterman, *C.F.G. Masterman*, pp. 172–3.

11. Ibid, p. 165.

12. David Powell, *British Politics, 1910–1935: The Crisis of the Party System* (Abingdon: Routledge, 2004), p. 51.

13. David Lloyd George, *War Memoirs: vol. I* (London: Ivor Nicholson & Watson, 1933), p. 37.

14. WSC to the King, 22 November 1910. RSC CVII, P2, p. 1,027.

15. Winston S. Churchill, *To the Electors of Dundee: 23rd November 1910* (Dundee: John Leng & Co., 1910).

16. It was to be the last election held over several days.

17. *Morning Post*, 19 December 1910.

18. Colin Rogers, *The Battle of Stepney: The Sidney Street Siege: Its Causes and Consequences* (London: Robert Hale, 1981), p. 66.

19. Samantha L. Bird, *Stepney: Profile of a London Borough from the Outbreak of the First World War to the Festival of Britain, 1914–1951* (Newcastle upon Tyne: Cambridge Scholars Publishing, 2011), p. 3.

20. Supposedly a 1905 editorial in the *Manchester Evening Chronicle*. Quoted in: Ed Mynott, 'Nationalism, Racism and Immigration Control: From Anti-Racism to Anti-Capitalism', in Steve Cohen, Beth Humphries and Ed Mynott (eds), *From Immigration Controls to Welfare Controls* (Abingdon: Routledge, 2002), p. 14.

21. Geoffrey Barton, *The Tottenham Outrage and Walthamstow Tram Chase: The Most Spectacular Hot Pursuit in History* (Sherfield on Loddon: Waterside Press, 2017).

22. *Globe*, 25 January 1909.

23. *Daily Mirror*, 25 January 1909.

24. *Morning Post*, 23 December 1910.

25. *The Times*, 23 December 1910.

26. See Table 1.20 in Craig, *British Electoral Facts*, p. 20.

27. Wensley, *Forty Years of Scotland Yard*, pp. 165–6.

28. Mike Waldren, *The Siege of Sidney Street* (March: PFOA – Police Firearms Officers Association, 2013), p. 7. This work reproduces many primary sources and, all in all, is probably the best available account of the affair.

29. Churchill, *Thoughts and Adventures*, pp. 43–4.

30. The example referred to was Lord Louis Mountbatten. See Keith Kyle, *Suez: Britain's End of Empire in the Middle East* (London: I.B. Taurus, 2011), p. 136.

31. An unsent letter, 'WSC to The Coroner, London', 10 January 1911, and an 'Inquest Pamphlet on Sidney Street Case (Examined 18 January 1911)' can be found in: RSC CVII, P2, pp. 1,240–1, 1,242–4.

32. Churchill, *Thoughts and Adventures*, p. 44.

33. Simon Webb, *The Analogue Revolution: Communication Technology, 1901–1914* (Barnsley: Pen & Sword, 2018), Kindle Edition, Locs 291–6.

34. Hugh Martin, *Battle: The Life Story of Winston S. Churchill Prime Minister: Study of a Genius* (London: Victor Gollancz, 1941), pp. 70–1.

35. A deleted paragraph from the unsent letter 'WSC to The Coroner, London', 10 January 1911. RSC CVII, P2, p. 1,241, n. 3.

36. Waldren, *Siege*, p. 12.

37. 'Inquest on the Bodies of Two Unknown Men found at 100, Sidney Street, Mile End (after a conflagration), one known as "Joseph" and the other known as Fritz or Fritz Svarrs. Depositions taken on the 6th, 9th, and 18th days of January, 1911, before Wynne E. Baxter, Coroner for County of London.' Churchill College, p. 27. Copy in the Churchill Archives Centre, CHAR 12/11/3, 18 January 1911.

38. WSC to H.H. Asquith, 3 January 1911. RSC CVII, P2, pp. 1,032–3.

39. Waldren, *Siege*, p. 14.

40. For example: Peter de Mendelssohn, *The Age of Churchill: Heritage and Adventure 1874–1911* (London: Thames & Hudson, 1961), p. 591.

41. Philip Ruff, *A Towering Flame: The Life & Times of the Elusive Latvian Anarchist Peter the Painter* (London: Breviary Stuff Publications, 2019).

42. Quoted in: Rogers, *The Battle of Stepney*, p. 133.

43. Charles and Lucy were holidaying with Lloyd George at Nice.

44. Masterman, *C.F.G. Masterman*, p. 184. For reasons unexplained, she always rendered Churchill quotes phonetically, thus emphasising his slight speech impediment.

45. Hansard, vol. 21, col. 56, 6 February 1911.

46. Churchill, *Thoughts and Adventures*, p. 48.

47. Ibid, p. 44.

48. Masterman, *C.F.G. Masterman*, p. 154.

49. Howard Cox and Simon Mowatt, *Revolutions from Grub Street: A History of Magazine Publishing in Britain* (Oxford: Oxford University Press, 2014), p. 46.

50. John Grigg, *Lloyd George: War Leader, 1916–1918* (London: Faber & Faber, 2011), p. 216.

51. At that time Lloyd George and Churchill were particularly close: 'I think Mr Churchill was the only one of LG's friends who called him "David".' Frances, Countess Lloyd-George of Dwyfor, in the 'Introduction' to Malcolm Thomson with the collaboration of Frances, Countess Lloyd-George of Dwyfor, *David Lloyd George: The Official Biography* (London: Hutchinson, 1948), p. 17.

52. J.M. McEwen (ed. and Intro.), *The Riddell Diaries 1908–1923* (London: Athlone Press, 1986), p. 55.

53. WSC to H.H. Asquith, 3 January 1911. RSC CVII, P2, pp. 1,032–3.

54. Sir Arthur Bigge to WSC, 5 January 1911. RSC CVII, P2, p. 1,230.

55. *The Times*, 5 January 1911.

56. Pellew, 'The Home Office and the Aliens Act', p. 381.

57. Memorandum by WSC, 19 January 1911. RSC CVII, P2, p. 1,244.

58. The First Reading is the first stage of a Bill's passage through the House of Commons. Usually a formality, it takes place without debate.

59. Hansard, vol. 24, cols 623–9, 18 April 1911.
60. WSC to the King, 19 April 1911. RSC CVII, P2, p. 1,066.
61. Hansard, vol. 32, col. 1,160, 4 December 1911.
62. David Cesarani, 'An Alien Concept? The Continuity of Anti-Alienism in British Society before 1940', in David Cesarani and Tony Kushner (eds), *The Internment of Aliens in Twentieth Century Britain* (Abingdon: Routledge, 1993), p. 33.
63. Pellew, 'The Home Office and the Aliens Act', p. 382.
64. J.A. Spender and Cyril Asquith, *Life of Herbert Henry Asquith, Lord Oxford and Asquith: vol. I* (London: Hutchinson & Co., 1932), p. 297.
65. Jane Ridley, *George V: Never a Dull Moment* (London: Chatto & Windus, 2021), p. 248. A full account of the matter can be found in the same book, pp. 161–5.
66. Bates, *H.H. Asquith*, p. 66.
67. Jenkins, *Mr Balfour's Poodle*, p. 197.
68. A 'money bill' was one certificated as such by the Speaker of the House of Commons, and a clause in the Bill stated: 'Any certificate of the Speaker ... given under this Act shall be conclusive for all purposes, and shall not be questioned in any court of law.' See H.J. Hanham (ed.), *The Nineteenth-Century Constitution 1815–1914: Documents and Commentary* (Cambridge: Cambridge University Press, 1969), p. 199.
69. https://publications.parliament.uk/pa/ld200506/ldselect/ldconst/141/14104.htm.
70. Jenkins, *Mr Balfour's Poodle*, p. 198.
71. Hansard, vol. 25, col. 1,769, 15 May 1911.
72. Ibid, col. 1,776, 15 May 1911.
73. Spender and Asquith, *Life of Herbert Henry Asquith*, p. 309.
74. Cabinet Minute to the King, 14 July 1911. Spender and Asquith, *Life of Herbert Henry Asquith*, p. 310.
75. Balfour to Lansdowne, 27 December 1910. Newton, *Lord Lansdowne*, pp. 407–8.
76. Balfour to Lansdowne, 27 December 1910. Newton, *Lord Lansdowne*, p. 408.
77. 'Memorandum of a Conversation at the Marlborough Club', 10 January 1911. Oliver, Viscount Esher (ed.), *Journals and Letters of Reginald Viscount Esher: vol. 3 1910–1915* (London: Ivor Nicholson & Watson, 1938), p. 40.
78. Ridley, *George V*, pp. 162–3. A full account of the matter can be found on pp. 161–5.
79. 'Note of Conversation with the King, at Windsor Castle', 27 January 1911. Newton, *Lord Lansdowne*, pp. 410–11.
80. Jenkins, *Mr Balfour's Poodle*, p. 196.
81. Ibid, p. 194.
82. Margot Asquith, *The Autobiography of Margot Asquith: vol. II* (London: Thornton Butterworth, 1922), p. 144.
83. Grigg, *Lloyd George: The People's Champion*, p. 285. '[H]e was struck with a touch of serious throat trouble. His voice was threatened': Harold Spender, *The Prime Minister: Life and Times of David Lloyd George* (New York: George H. Doran, 1920), p. 166.
84. WSC to H.H. Asquith, 3 January 1911. RSC CVII, P2, pp. 1,031.
85. To HM the King [from Viscount Esher], 5 July 1911. Oliver, Viscount Esher, *Journals and Letters*, p. 55.
86. Blanche E.C. Dugdale, *Arthur James Balfour: First Earl of Balfour: vol. II 1906–1930* (New York: G.P. Putnam's Sons, 1937), pp. 42–3.
87. Jenkins, *Mr Balfour's Poodle*, p. 216.
88. Dugdale, *Arthur James Balfour*, p. 43.
89. Jenkins, *Mr Balfour's Poodle*, p. 216, n. 1.
90. Dugdale, *Arthur James Balfour*, p. 43.
91. The title of Chapter XII of Jenkins, *Mr Balfour's Poodle*, pp. 213–42.
92. Ibid, p. 216.
93. Newton, *Lord Lansdowne*, p. 417.

94. 'Memorandum – Lord Lansdowne', 19 July 1911. Newton, *Lord Lansdowne*, pp. 418–19.
95. Hansard, vol. 9, col. 572, 20 July 1911.
96. Ibid, col. 579, 20 July 1911.
97. Ibid, col. 586, 20 July 1911.
98. Newton, *Lord Lansdowne*, p. 419. Jenkins says that 'it was at the suggestion of the Palace that the Prime Minister's letters were despatched. Jenkins, *Mr Balfour's Poodle*, p. 220.
99. Asquith to Mr Balfour and Lord Lansdowne, 20 July 1911. Spender and Asquith, *Life of Herbert Henry Asquith*, pp. 312–13.
100. Churchill, *Lord Derby, King of Lancashire*, p. 118.
101. Bates, *H.H. Asquith*, p. 67.
102. Hansard, vol. 28, col. 1,467, 24 July 1911.
103. Conservative MP for Oxford University: youngest child of the 3rd Marquess of Salisbury, and Churchill's best man at his wedding.
104. WSC to the King, 24 July 1911. Quoted in RSC CVII, P2, p. 1,101.
105. Hansard, vol. 28, col. 1,476, 24 July 1911.
106. WSC to the King, 24 July 1911. RSC CVII, P2, p. 1,102.
107. Hansard, vol. 28, col. 1,484, 24 July 1911.
108. WSC to the King, 26 July 1911, RSC CVII, P2, p. 1,103.
109. Hansard, vol. 29, cols 905–12, 7 August 1911.
110. Hansard, vol. 9, cols 815–78, 8 August 1911.
111. Barry Winetrobe and Janet Seaton, *Confidence Motions: Research Paper 95/19* (London: House of Commons Library, 1995), p. 17.
112. RSC VII, p. 458.
113. Hansard, vol. 29, col. 972, 8 August 1911.
114. Ibid, col. 992, 8 August 1911.
115. Ibid, col. 988, 8 August 1911.
116. Ibid.
117. Winston Spencer Churchill, *Lord Randolph Churchill: vol. II* (London: Macmillan & Co., 1906), p. 65.
118. Hansard, vol. 29, col. 990, 8 August 1911. Churchill returned to this theme in his letter to the King reporting the day's business: 'Lord Hugh Cecil spoke well as did Sir Edward Carson: but threats of riot and violence are not suited to the occasion nor to the position of those who used them.' WSC to the King, 9 August 1911. RSC CVII, P2, p. 1,110.
119. Hansard, vol. 29, col. 1,020, 8 August 1911.
120. Hansard, vol. 9, col. 1,000, 10 August 1911.
121. The hardliners were dubbed 'ditchers' who had pledged to 'die in a ditch' rather than give in. Their opponents were termed 'hedgers'. See Jenkins, *Mr Balfour's Poodle*, p. 222, n. 1.
122. Hansard, vol. 9, col. 1,059, 10 August 1911.
123. George Wyndham to his sister Madeline, 27 August 1911. Guy Wyndham (Comp.), *Letters of George Wyndham: vol. II* (Edinburgh: Privately Printed, 1915), p. 473.
124. *Daily Mail*, 11 August 1911.
125. Balfour (Hotel Ritz, Paris) to Lady Elcho, 10 August 1911. Dugdale, *Arthur James Balfour*, p. 83.
126. Diary entry by J.S. Sandars, undated beyond 'just before Balfour went to Gastein early in August'. Dugdale, *Arthur James Balfour*, p. 85.
127. During the 1865 General Election, and before inheriting his title, he had posed the matter thus: 'The question is, whether England shall be governed by property and intelligence, or by numbers. Those who prefer the first alternative will vote for the Conservative candidate: those who prefer the last will vote for the Liberal. There is no middle term between the two. It is the great controversy of modern society, the great issue upon which the hopes of freedom, and order, and civilisation depend.' Lord Robert Cecil, 'The Six year old Parliament. London, 1865', *Quarterly Review*, July 1865, 118(235):295.

128. WSC to the King, 11 August 1911. RSC CVII, P2, p. 1,113.
129. Ibid.
130. Yann Béliard, 'Introduction: Revisiting the Great Labour Unrest, 1911–1914', *Labour History Review*, April 2014, 79(1):1.

Chapter 8: 'a dim spectre of revolution'

1. Leon Trotsky, Alan Clinton (ed.) and Richard Chappell (ed.), *Leon Trotsky: Collected Writings and Speeches on Britain: vol. 2* (London: New Park Publications, 1974), p. 8.
2. Ben Tillett, *Is the Parliamentary Labour Party a Failure?* (London: Twentieth Century Press, 1908), p. 14.
3. Quoted in Lord Askwith, *Industrial Problems and Disputes* (London: John Murray, 1920), p. 145.
4. Roland V. Sires, 'Labor Unrest in England, 1910–1914', *Journal of Economic History*, September 1955, 15(3):246.
5. Board of Trade (Department of Labour Statistics), *Sixteenth Abstract of Labour Statistics of the United Kingdom* (London: HMSO, 1913), pp. x–xi, 88–9. For the number of days lost to strikes during that period see pp. 160–1 of the same publication.
6. Philip, Viscount Snowden, *An Autobiography: vol. One 1864–1919* (London: Ivor Nicholson & Watson, 1934), p. 235.
7. Masterman, *The Condition of England*, p. 111.
8. Ibid, p. 303.
9. Sires, 'Labor Unrest', p. 247.
10. Askwith, *Industrial Problems and Disputes*, p. 148.
11. Ken Coates and Tony Topham (eds), *Workers' Control: A Book of Readings and Witnesses for Workers' Control* (London: Panther, 1970), p. xxviii.
12. This would be achieved by 'direct action and the general strike leading to workers' control over the economy and society'. Bob Holton, *British Syndicalism 1900–1914: Myths and Realities* (London: Pluto Press, 1976), p. 17.
13. Philip Snowden, *Socialism and Syndicalism* (London: Collins, 1913), p. 205.
14. Holton, *British Syndicalism*, p. 29.
15. Sires, 'Labor Unrest', p. 248.
16. Jonathan Schneer, *Ben Tillett: Portrait of a Labour Leader* (Beckenham: Croom Helm, 1982), p. 2.
17. Holton, *British Syndicalism*, p. 92.
18. Tillett, *Is the Parliamentary Labour Party a Failure?*, p. 11.
19. Matt Vaughan Wilson, 'The 1911 Waterfront Strikes in Glasgow: Trade Unions and Rank-and-File Militancy in the Labour Unrest of 1910–1914', *International Review of Social History*, August 2008, 53(2):264.
20. Askwith, *Industrial Problems and Disputes*, p. 148. Vaughan Wilson, 'The 1911 Waterfront Strikes in Glasgow', p. 264.
21. Askwith, *Industrial Problems and Disputes*, p. 149.
22. Ibid.
23. *Manchester Guardian*, 20 June 1911. Also quoted, in part, in Edmund and Ruth Frow, *The General Strike in Salford in 1911* (Salford: Working Class Movement Library, 1990), p. 9.
24. H.W. Lee, *The Great Strike Movement of 1911 and its Lessons* (London: Twentieth Century Press, 1912), p. 1.
25. Neil Evans, 'A Tidal Wave of Impatience': the Cardiff General Strike of 1911, in Geraint H. Jenkins and J. Beverley Smith (eds), *Politics and Society in Wales 1840–1922: Essays in Honour of Ieuan Gwynedd Jones* (Cardiff: University of Wales Press, 1988), p. 136.
26. Vaughan Wilson, 'The 1911 Waterfront Strikes in Glasgow', p. 278.
27. Ibid, p. 279.
28. H.R. Hikins, 'The Liverpool General Transport Strike, 1911', in J.J. Bagley and James Murphy (Hon. Eds), *Transactions of the Historic Society of Lancashire and Cheshire for the Year 1961: vol. 113* (Liverpool: Historic Society of Lancashire and Cheshire, 1962), p. 172.

29. Hikins, 'The Liverpool General Transport Strike, 1911', p. 172.
30. Tom Mann, *Tom Mann's Memoirs* (London: Labour Publishing Company, 1923), p. 259.
31. Hikins, 'The Liverpool General Transport Strike, 1911', p. 176.
32. Frow and Frow, *The General Strike in Salford*, p. 11.
33. Vaughan Wilson, 'The 1911 Waterfront Strikes in Glasgow', p. 283.
34. Robert Griffiths, 'Cardiff Cigar Workers and the "Feminine Strike" of 1911', *Our History*, May 2012, 4:6. For information on Tupper, who claimed to have been an officer and to have won the Victoria Cross amongst many other (unlikely) things, see Edward Tupper, *Seamen's Torch: The Life Story of Captain Edward Tupper, National Union of Seamen* (London: Hutchinson & Co., 1938). Campbell Balfour, 'Captain Tupper and the 1911 Seamen's Strike in Cardiff', *Morgannwg: Transactions of the Glamorgan Local History Society*, 1970, XIV.
35. Lee, *The Great Strike Movement*, p. 3.
36. Griffiths, 'Cardiff Cigar Workers', p. 8.
37. Morgan, *Conflict and Order*, p. 50. Balfour, 'Captain Tupper', p. 66.
38. Keith Brooker, *The Hull Strikes of 1911* (Beverley: East Yorkshire Local History Society, 1979), p. 16.
39. A.A. Clarke, *The Policemen of Hull: The Story of Hull Police Force, 1836 to 1974* (Beverley: Hutton Press, 1992), p. 85.
40. Reckitt & Sons Ltd, makers of household products such as Brasso metal polish and Robin Starch.
41. Quoted in Clarke, *The Policemen of Hull*, p. 85.
42. 'Riots at Hull: Landsmen join Seamen: Police Charge the Mob: A Serious Situation', *Sydney Morning Herald*, 30 June 1911.
43. Macready, *Annals*, p. 160.
44. Askwith, *Industrial Problems and Disputes*, p. 151.
45. Ibid, p. 154.
46. Macready, *Annals*, p. 161.
47. Balfour, 'Captain Tupper', pp. 73–4.
48. Askwith, *Industrial Problems and Disputes*, p. 154.
49. G.R. Askwith to WSC, 23 July 1911. RSC CVII, P2, pp. 1,263–8.
50. UK National Archives, CAB 37/107/70. 'The Present Unrest in the Labour World. Printed or circulated in 1911 June 25' [sic. The covering letter is clearly dated 25 July].
51. Ibid, p. 1.
52. Ibid, p. 4.
53. 14 June 1911 was when most men came out.
54. UK National Archives, CAB 37/107/70, pp. 4–5.
55. Ibid, p. 12.
56. Ibid. Annotation to the Covering Letter.
57. RSC VII, p. 379.
58. Memorandum by WSC, late July 1911. RSC CVII, P2, pp. 1,263–4.
59. Pope-Hennessey records Asquith telling Lord Crewe that one letter from Churchill was 'A typical missive, born of froth out of foam.' James Pope-Hennessey, *Lord Crewe 1858–1945: The Likeness of a Liberal* (London: Constable & Co., 1955), p. 67.
60. Spender and Asquith, *Life of Herbert Henry Asquith*, p. 350.
61. *Report on Strikes and Lock-outs and of Conciliation and Arbitration Boards in the United Kingdom in 1911, with Comparative Statistics for 1902–1910* [Command Paper 6472] (London: HMSO, 1912), p. 24.
62. Hikins, 'The Liverpool General Transport Strike, 1911', p. 185.
63. Ibid, p. 187.
64. Home Office to Head Constable, Liverpool, 9 August 1911. RSC CVII, P2, p. 1,268.
65. Home Office to Head Constable, Liverpool, 10 August 1911. RSC CVII, P2, p. 1,268.
66. Head Constable to Home Office, 12 August 1911. UK National Archives, HO 45/10656/212470. 'STRIKES: Liverpool Railway Strike 1911.'

67. Hikins, 'The Liverpool General Transport Strike, 1911', p. 188.

68. Hansard, vol. 29, col. 1,359, 10 August 1911.

69. *Employment of Military during Railway Strike: Correspondence between the Home Office and Local Authorities during the Railway Strike in August 1911* (London, HMSO, 1911). Quoted in: RSC CVII, P2, p. 1,269.

70. Hikins, 'The Liverpool General Transport Strike, 1911', p. 188.

71. *Liverpool Daily Post*, 14 August 1911; *Liverpool Echo*, 14 August 1911.

72. Letter from Thomas Shelmerdine, Corporation Surveyor, 9 August 1911. Quoted in: Mann, *Tom Mann's Memoirs*, p. 266.

73. Fred Bower, *Rolling Stonemason: An Autobiography* (London: Jonathan Cape, 1936), p. 210.

74. Ibid, p. 211.

75. John Belchem, *Irish, Catholic and Scouse: The History of the Liverpool-Irish, 1800–1939* (Liverpool: Liverpool University Press, 2007), p. 195.

76. Bower, *Rolling Stonemason*, p. 211.

77. Lee, *The Great Strike Movement*, p. 6.

78. S.M. Hutchinson. 'City of Liverpool: Public Warning', 14 August 1911.

79. WSC to the King, 14 August 1911. RSC CVII, P2, pp. 1,268–9.

80. WSC to the King, 14 August 1911. RSC CVII, P2, p. 1,269. Macready records orders being prepared on 10 August for bringing 25,000 troops into London. Macready, *Annals*, p. 162.

81. Hansard, vol. 29, cols 1547–8, 14 August 1911.

82. *Employment of Military during Railway Strike* ...; RSC CVII, P2, p. 1,269.

83. Hikins, 'The Liverpool General Transport Strike, 1911', p. 192.

84. The Chief Constable of Birkenhead Borough police was Walter Stocks Davies, a former officer in the Royal Irish Constabulary. *Justice of the Peace, and County, Borough, Poor Law Union, and Parish Law Recorder*, 12 October 1912, LXXVI(41):487.

85. Lord Mayor of Liverpool and Mayor of Birkenhead to WSC, 15 August 1911. RSC CVII, P2, p. 1,269.

86. Sir Edward Troup to Lord Mayor of Liverpool, 16 August 1911. RSC CVII, P2, p. 1,273.

87. WSC to Lord Mayor of Liverpool, 16 August 1911. RSC CVII, P2, p. 1,273.

88. Churchill Archives Centre, Churchill College, Cambridge. CHAR 12/12/68-72, 17 August 1911. Report from the Chief Constable of Liverpool, including notification that *Antrim* had arrived at the Mersey. *Jane's Fighting Ships of World War I* (London: Studio Editions, 1990), p. 53.

89. Steve Peak, *Troops in Strikes: Military Intervention in Industrial Disputes* (London: Cobden Trust, 1984), p. 29.

90. Later Sir Philip Gibbs. Gibbs was a prolific author. See Gibbs, Sir Philip Armand Hamilton (1877–1962) in the Oxford Dictionary of National Biography: https://www.oxforddnb.com/view/10.1093/ref:odnb/9780198614128.001.0001/odnb-9780198614128-e-33387?docPos=2.

91. Philip Gibbs, *Adventures in Journalism* (London: Harper & Brothers, 1923), pp. 212–13.

92. Later Dame Margaret Isabel Cole, writer, poet and politician. See Betty D. Vernon, *Margaret Cole 1893–1980: A Political Biography* (London: Croom Helm, 1986).

93. Margaret Cole, *Growing Up Into Revolution* (London: Longmans, Green, 1949), pp. 34–5.

94. Hikins, 'The Liverpool General Transport Strike, 1911', p. 191. Hikins was able to interview participants in the strike action, one being Mr S. Constantine of the then Mersey Quay and Railway Carters' Union. Mr Constantine recalled 'that the two men killed were a Protestant and a Catholic, and that this fact and the attendance of both sides at the two funerals was said to have done much to unite the movement'. Hikins, 'The Liverpool General Transport Strike, 1911', p. 191, n. 23.

95. Churchill, *Lord Derby, King of Lancashire*.

96. Lord Derby to WSC, 15 August 1911. Quoted in: RSC CVII, P2, pp. 1,274–5.

97. Hansard, vol. 29, cols 1,755–6, 15 August 1911.

98. The Hampshire Yeomanry were, in 1911, classed as carabiniers (mounted infantry). Army Museums Ogilby Trust, *Year of the Yeomanry: 1794–1994* (Salisbury: Army Museums Ogilby Trust, 1994), p. 72.

99. Hansard, vol. 29, col. 1,875, 15 August 1911.

100. Ibid, vol. 21, col. 240, 7 February 1911.

101. The King to WSC, 16 August 1911. Quoted in RSC CVII, P2, p. 1,274.

102. For the Russian Revolution of that year see Abraham Ascher, *The Revolution of 1905: A Short History* (Stanford, CA: Stanford University Press, 2004).

103. WSC to the King, 17 August 1911. Quoted in: RSC CVII, P2, pp. 1,276–7.

104. Which three unions were to amalgamate in 1913 to form the National Union of Railwaymen (NUR). See Philip S. Bagwell, *The Railwaymen: The History of the National Union of Railwaymen* (London: George Allen & Unwin, 1963).

105. J.R. Raynes, *Engines and Men: The History of the Associated Society of Locomotive Engineers and Firemen* (Leeds: Goodall & Suddick, 1921), p. 147.

106. W. Tetley Stephenson, 'The Railway Conciliation Scheme, 1907', *Economic Journal*, December 1911, 21(84):506.

107. *Railway News, Finance and Joint-Stock Companies Journal*, 9 November 1907.

108. Raynes, *Engines and Men*, p. 147.

109. 'For twenty-five years [from 1898], Sir Almeric FitzRoy was Clerk of the Privy Council in London and thus saw much of the British Constitution from the inside, and especially of the Executive.' Philip Whitwell Wilson, 'Review: Dramatic Victorians', *North American Review*, December 1925–February 1926, 222(829):341.

110. Diary entry for 18 August 1911. Sir Almeric Fitzroy, *Memoirs: vol. II* (London: Hutchinson & Co., 1925), pp. 461–2.

111. Spender and Asquith, *Life of Herbert Henry Asquith*, p. 350.

112. Bates, *H.H. Asquith*, p. 74.

113. W. Watkin Davies, *Lloyd George 1863–1914* (London: Constable & Co., 1939), p. 393.

114. Edward Troup, Letter to Chief Constables, 17 August 1911. RSC CVII, P2, p. 1,278.

115. WSC to Mayor of Birkenhead, 19 August 1911. RSC CVII, P2, p. 1,285. See also: *Report on Strikes and Lock-outs . . .* , p. 40.

116. Macready, *Annals*, p. 163.

117. Childs, *Episodes and Reflections*, p. 98.

118. Macready, *Annals*, p. 163.

119. Brian Benjamin, *Send the Gunboats up the Mersey* (Liverpool: Brian Benjamin, 2019), p. 27.

120. Mayor of Birkenhead to WSC, 19 August 1911. RSC CVII, P2, p. 1,285.

121. Mayor of Birkenhead to Sir Edward Troup, 19 August 1911. RSC CVII, P2, p. 1,286.

122. Butler, *Confident Morning*, p. 101.

123. WSC to the King, 19 August 1911. RSC CVII, P2, p. 1,287.

124. Butler, *Confident Morning*, p. 101.

125. Macready, *Annals*, pp. 163–4.

126. Butler, *Confident Morning*, p. 101.

127. Quoted in Michael Shelden, *Young Titan: The Making of Winston Churchill* (New York: Simon & Schuster Paperbacks, 2014), p. 252.

128. Quoted in Deian Hopkin, 'The Llanelli Riots, 1911', *Welsh History Review Cylchgrawn Hanes Cymru*, December 1983, 11(4):495. Unless otherwise stated, this section is derived from Hopkin's account.

129. Ibid, pp. 492–3.

130. See John Edwards, *Remembrance of a Riot: The Story of the Llanelli Railway Strike Riots of 1911* (Llanelli: Llanelli Borough Council, 1988).

131. Colin Holmes, 'The Tredegar Riots of 1911: Anti-Jewish Disturbances in South Wales', *Welsh History Review Cylchgrawn Hanes Cymru*, December 1982, 11(2):220.

132. A.G. Gardiner, *Prophets, Priests and Kings* (London: Alston Rivers, 1908), p. 154.

133. Hattersley, *David Lloyd George*, p. 307.
134. Letter from Austen Chamberlain to Mary Endicott Chamberlain, 1 March 1912. Sir Austen Chamberlain, *Politics From Inside: An Epistolary Chronicle 1906–1914* (London: Cassell & Co., 1936), p. 437.
135. Raynes, *Engines and Men*, pp. 150–1.
136. WSC to Mayor of Birkenhead, 1 a.m., 20 August 1911. RSC CVII, P2, p. 1,288.
137. Hikins, 'The Liverpool General Transport Strike, 1911', p. 195.
138. Ibid.
139. Hattersley, *David Lloyd George*, p. 308.
140. Roy Jenkins, *Asquith: Portrait of a Man and an Era* (New York: Chilmark Press, 1964), p. 234.
141. Diary entry for 22 August 1911. Fitzroy, *Memoirs*, p. 462.
142. H.H. Asquith to Chancellor of the Exchequer, 20 August 1911. UK Parliament, Parliamentary Archives, GB-061, LG/C/6/11/9.
143. Alexander Murray [Liberal Chief Whip] to Chancellor of the Exchequer, 20 August 1911. UK Parliament, Parliamentary Archives, GB-061, LG/C/5/6/1. Telegram quoting the King's message.
144. Troup, *The Home Office*, p. 188.
145. Masterman, *C.F.G. Masterman*, pp. 207–8.
146. Ibid, p. 208.
147. Another, later, Winston Churchill was to write in his 'filial yet objective biography' of Randolph Churchill that his grandfather's 'tenure at the Home Office is ... frequently associated with the violent and turbulent events taking place at the time: the Siege of Sidney Street and the Tonypandy riots'. Winston S. Churchill, *His Father's Son: The Life of Randolph Churchill* (London: Weidenfeld & Nicolson, 1996), p. 1.
148. WSC to the King, 1 a.m., 20 August 1911. RSC CVII, P2, p. 1,289.
149. Quoted in Weinberger, *Keeping the Peace?*, p. 107, n. 11. See also Toye, *Lloyd George and Churchill*, p. 87.
150. As one newspaper put it vis-à-vis Liverpool, but with wider application: 'So long as Liverpool continues to inflict on a large proportion of its workers not only dire poverty but the soul and body destroying system of casual labour, so long will you have a Liverpool mob whose flash point (as someone aptly expressed it) is low.' *London Daily News*, Thursday, 24 August 1911.
151. The Home Secretary is recorded as opining, in June 1911, that Lloyd George was 'the greatest political genius of the day', possessing 'more political insight than any other statesman'. Lord Riddell [George Riddell], *More Pages*, pp. 18–19.
152. *Report on Strikes and Lock-outs . . .* , p. 7, n.
153. One of Lloyd George's posthumous biographers, Frank Owen, who very likely knew her to some degree given they were both Liberal parliamentary candidates at the 1929 general election, described their relationship: 'When the House rose in July, 1910, for the long summer adjournment, Lloyd George went off with the Mastermans on a motor tour, via Bavaria, to Italy. "He was an extraordinarily attractive and, at times, extraordinarily provoking travelling companion", wrote Lucy Masterman in her diary, herself an interesting and provoking woman.' [Owen, *Tempestuous Journey*, p. 194]. He was actually misquoting her concerning Lloyd George. What she had written was: 'Charlie [Masterman] went abroad with Lloyd George for about a fortnight at the end of this summer. He said he was an extraordinarily attractive and, at times, an extraordinarily provoking travelling companion.' [Masterman, *C.F.G. Masterman*, p. 169]. His assessment of her is, though, undoubtedly valid.
154. See Bentley Brinkerhoff Gilbert, Review of: '*Eric Hopkins, Charles Masterman (1873–1927), Politician and Journalist: The Splendid Failure* (Lewiston, NY: Edward Mellen Press, 1999)', *Albion: A Quarterly Journal Concerned with British Studies*, Winter 2000, 32(4):684. Jenkins, *Asquith*, p. 190.
155. Grigg, *Lloyd George: The People's Champion*, p. 376.
156. Hattersley, *David Lloyd George*, p. 286.

157. Mendelssohn, *The Age of Churchill*, p. 321.
158. Hansard, vol. 29, col. 2,284, 22 August 1911.
159. Lansbury was speaking about a particular instance which had occurred in Poplar. According to his account, the local authority had subsequently 'ordered the soldiers out, and they had to go out'. The principle obviously applied more widely. Hansard, vol. 29, col. 2,285, 22 August 1911.
160. Ibid.
161. Ibid.
162. Ibid, col. 2,286, 22 August 1911.
163. Ibid.
164. Ibid.
165. Ibid, col. 2,291, 22 August 1911.
166. Ibid, col. 2,296, 22 August 1911.
167. Ibid, col. 2,297, 22 August 1911.
168. Ibid.
169. Ibid, cols 2,298–9, 22 August 1911.
170. Ibid, cols 2,312–13, 22 August 1911.
171. Ibid, cols 2,313–24, 22 August 1911.
172. Ibid, col. 2,325, 22 August 1911.
173. RSC VII, p. 380.
174. Hansard, vol. 29, col. 2,327, 22 August 1911.
175. Ibid, col. 2,328, 22 August 1911.
176. Ibid, col. 2,331, 22 August 1911.
177. Morgan, *Conflict and Order*, p. 46.
178. 'The Book of the Month: What a Revolution is Like: A Prophetical Forecast by Mr Winston Churchill', *Review of Reviews for Australasia*, November 1911.
179. Jonathan Rose, *The Literary Churchill: Author, Reader, Actor* (New Haven, CT: Yale University Press, 2014). Kindle edition, Loc. 1620.
180. WSC to Lady Randolph, 24 August 1897. Randolph S. Churchill, *Winston S. Churchill 1874–1965: vol. I Companion Part 2 1896–1900* (London: Heinemann, 1967), p. 779.
181. A.G. Gardiner, *Pillars of Society* (London: James Nisbet & Co., 1913), p. 153.
182. Hardie's weekly column in the *Merthyr Pioneer*, 2 September 1911.
183. Shelden, *Young Titan*, p. 252.
184. Gardiner, *Pillars of Society*, p. 154.
185. Trotsky, Clinton and Chappell, *Leon Trotsky: Collected Writings and Speeches*, p. 8.
186. Edith K. Harper, *Stead: The Man: Personal Reminiscences* (London: William Rider & Son, 1918), p. 214.
187. 'Cause and Effect', *Referee*, 20 August 1911.
188. *Morning Post*, 14 August 1911.
189. Masterman, *C.F.G. Masterman*, p. 206.
190. Gardiner, *Prophets, Priests and Kings*, p. 106.
191. *Review of Reviews*, November 1911.
192. Diary entry (undated) for November 1911, in McEwen, *Riddell Diaries*, p. 25. There is also a slightly different published version of this entry, which does not change the overall meaning: 'During the recent strikes Winston had a difficult job which caused him much anxiety. He was freely criticised by the Press and certain of his colleagues. The situation weighed upon him, and obviously he was very unhappy at the Home Office. Nevertheless, like all public men, he frequently alleged that, being concentrated on his job, he was not concerned with his critics.' 'November 1911', in Lord Riddell, *More Pages*, p. 24.
193. Paul Addison, 'Churchill and Social Reform', in Blake and Louis, *Churchill*, p. 78.
194. Robert Rhodes James, *Churchill: a Study in Failure, 1900–1939* (London: Weidenfeld & Nicolson, 1970), p. 39.
195. Bonham Carter, *Winston Churchill as I Knew Him*, p. 197.

196. Gardiner, *Pillars of Society*, p. 158.
197. Attributed to Harold Macmillan, Prime Minister January 1957–October 1963.
198. Diary entry for 18 August 1911. Fitzroy, *Memoirs*, pp. 461–2.

Chapter 9: As Dead as Queen Anne

1. Churchill, *Thoughts and Adventures*, p. 87.
2. Harold D. Lasswell, *Propaganda Technique in the World War* (New York: Peter Smith, 1927), p. 192. Lasswell was quoting Kennedy Jones, a close associate of Alfred Harmsworth/Lord Northcliffe for many years. See Kennedy Jones, *Fleet Street and Downing Street* (London: Hutchinson, 1920), p. 198.
3. Erskine Childers, *The Riddle of the Sands: A Record of Secret Service* (London: Smith, Elder & Co., 1903). Childers' life and death encompass several 'Boy's Own' elements. See for example Leonard Piper, *Dangerous Waters: The Life and Death of Erskine Childers* (London: Hambledon Continuum, 2003); Jim Ring, *Erskine Childers* (London: Faber & Faber, 1997); Andrew Boyle, *The Riddle of Erskine Childers: A Biography* (London: Hutchinson, 1977).
4. A film starring Michael York, Jenny Agutter and Simon MacCorkindale appeared in 1979: https://www.imdb.com/title/tt0079808/.
5. Danny Laurie-Fletcher, *British Invasion and Spy Literature, 1871–1918: Historical Perspectives on Contemporary Society* (London: Palgrave Macmillan, 2019), p. 13.
6. William Le Queux, *The Great War in England in 1897* (London: Tower Publishing Company, 1894).
7. Asa Briggs and Peter Burke, *A Social History of the Media: from Gutenberg to the Internet* (Cambridge: Polity Press, 2005), p. 181.
8. Laurie-Fletcher, *British Invasion and Spy Literature*, p. 15.
9. Adrian Addison, *Mail Men: The Unauthorized Story of the Daily Mail – The Paper That Divided and Conquered Britain* (London: Atlantic Books, 2017), p. 44. Joel H. Wiener, *The Americanization of the British Press, 1830s–1914: Speed in the Age of Transatlantic Journalism* (London: Palgrave Macmillan, 2011), p. 198.
10. Their relationship in that context went back to 1893, when Harmsworth's first newspaper, *Answers*, serialized Le Queux's *The Great War in England in 1897*. David Stafford, *The Silent Game: The Real World of Imaginary Spies* (London: Lume Books, 2020), Kindle edition, Loc. 421.
11. He had been created 'Baron Northcliffe of the Isle of Thanet in the county of Kent', in 1906. *London Gazette*, 5 January 1906.
12. Roger T. Stearn, 'The Mysterious Mr Le Queux: War Novelist, Defence Publicist and Counter-spy', *Soldiers of the Queen*, September 1992, 70:14.
13. Hansard, vol. 157, col. 187, 14 May 1906.
14. Ibid, col. 188, 14 May 1906.
15. Rhodri Jeffreys-Jones, *In Spies We Trust: The Story of Western Intelligence* (Oxford: Oxford University Press, 2013), p. 14.
16. Laurie-Fletcher, *British Invasion and Spy Literature*, p. 64.
17. William Le Queux, *The Invasion of 1910 With a Full Account of the Siege of London: Naval Chapters by H.W. Wilson and an Introductory Letter by Field-Marshal Earl Roberts* (London: Eveleigh Nash, 1906), p. viii.
18. Cecil D. Eby, *The Road to Armageddon: The Martial Spirit in English Popular Literature* (Durham, NC: Duke University Press, 1987), p. 35.
19. Le Queux, *Invasion of 1910*, p. 403.
20. The total German population in England and Wales has been calculated, using census records, at 53,324 in 1911. Included in this figure were Jews who had left Germany to 'escape from the indignities of German anti-Semitism'. See 'Table 1.1. German population of England and Wales, 1861–1911', in Panikos Panayi, *The Enemy in our Midst: Germans in Britain during the First World War* (London: Bloomsbury, 2014), Kindle edition, Locs 290, 307.
21. 'Article XII – The German Peril', *Quarterly Review*, July 1908, 209(416):295–6.

22. Nicholas Hiley, 'The Failure of British Counter-Espionage against Germany, 1907–1914', *Historical Journal*, December 1985, 28(4):844.

23. Thomas Boghardt, *Spies of the Kaiser: German Covert Operations in Great Britain During the First World War Era* (Houndsmills: Palgrave Macmillan, 2004), p. 30.

24. Christopher Andrew, *The Defence of the Realm: The Authorized History of MI5* (London: Allen Lane, 2009), pp. 7–8.

25. Ibid, pp. 4–5.

26. Matthew S. Seligmann, *Spies in Uniform: British Military and Naval Intelligence on the Eve of the First World War* (Oxford: Oxford University Press, 2006), p. 8.

27. Christened Albert Edward Wilfred von Gleichen, he was of royal German descent. 'Count Gleichen, who, as the son of Prince Victor of Hohenlohe-Langenburg, was not just of blue blood, but technically at least, was a member of a German princely house. He was also a cousin of both the Kaiser and Edward VII, who was, in addition, his godfather.' Seligmann, *Spies in Uniform*, p. 54.

28. Alan Judd, *The Quest for C: Sir Mansfield Cumming and the Founding of the British Secret Service* (London: Harper Collins, 1999), p. 71.

29. Anthony Verrier, *Through the Looking Glass: British Foreign Policy in an Age of Illusions* (London: Jonathan Cape, 1983), p. 20.

30. Formed in 1883 as the Special (Irish) Branch in an effort to counter Irish terrorism as embodied in the Fenian dynamite campaign of 1880–1885. Niall Whelehan, *The Dynamiters: Irish Nationalism and Political Violence in the Wider World 1867–1900* (Cambridge: Cambridge University Press, 2012). Ray Wilson and Ian Adams, *Special Branch: A History: 1883–2006* (London: Biteback, 2015). Rupert Allason, *The Branch: A History of the Metropolitan Police Special Branch 1883–1983* (London: Secker & Warburg, 1983).

31. For Melville see Andrew Cook, *M: MI5's First Spymaster* (Stroud: History Press, 2006).

32. Andrew, *Defence of the Realm*, p. 5.

33. Ibid, pp. 6, 7.

34. Ibid, p. 8.

35. Ibid, p. 7.

36. Balfour had been instrumental in the creation of the Committee of Imperial Defence in 1904, the rationale behind it being to reinforce coordination of foreign and defence policy or, in Balfour's own words: 'to survey as a whole the strategic needs of the Empire, to deal with the complicated questions which are all essential in that general problem, and to revise from time to time their own previous decisions so that the Cabinet shall always be informed and always have at its disposal information upon these important points'. W.J. McDermott, 'The Immediate Origins of the Committee of Imperial Defence: A Reappraisal', *Canadian Journal of History*, published online 5 May 2016, 7(3):253.

37. Hansard, vol. 8, cols 1,387–8, 29 July 1909.

38. The 'Haldane Reforms' posited the formation of an 'Expeditionary Force of six large divisions and one cavalry division – 160,000 men in 72 battalions'. Edward M. Spiers, 'Haldane's Reform of the Regular Army: Scope for Revision', *British Journal of International Studies*, April 1980, 6(1):74.

39. Andrew, *Defence of the Realm*, p. 14.

40. Major General Sir Frederick Maurice, *Haldane, 1856–1915: The Life of Viscount Haldane of Cloan* (London: Faber & Faber, 1937), p. 256.

41. Hiley, 'The Failure of British Counter-Espionage', p. 844, n. 49.

42. Ibid, p. 845. UK National Archives, CAB 16/8. Foreign Espionage in the United Kingdom: Report and Proceedings, 1909.

43. Quoted in Christopher Andrew, 'Governments and Secret Services: A Historical Perspective', *International Journal*, Spring 1979, 34(2):177.

44. Lord Hankey, *The Supreme Command 1914–1918: vol. One* (London: George Allen & Unwin, 1961), p. 116.

45. Journal entry for 30 March 1909. In Maurice V. Brett (ed.), *Journals and Letters of Reginald Viscount Esher: vol. 2 1903–1910* (London: Ivor Nicholson & Watson, MCMXXXIV [1934]), p. 379. An 'arras' is a curtain or wall hanging concealing an alcove.

46. Hankey, *Supreme Command*, p. 116.

47. See Andrew Vincent, 'German Philosophy and British Public Policy: Richard Burdon Haldane in Theory and Practice', *Journal of the History of Ideas*, January 2007, 68(1).

48. Andrew, *Defence of the Realm*, p. 19.

49. See UK National Archives, CAB 16/232. 'Conclusions of the sub-committee requested to consider the setting up of a secret service bureau', 1909.

50. Andrew, *Defence of the Realm*, pp. 26–7.

51. UK National Archives, KV1/9. 'Kell's Bureau six-monthly progress reports, 1909–1914.' 'April 1910–October 1910: General Report on the work done during the six months ending October 1910', 17 November 1910, p. 9.

52. RSC VII, p. 312.

53. Ibid, p. 196. Lady Leonie Leslie, née Jerome, was the youngest of his mother's two younger sisters.

54. WSC to his wife, 15 September 1909. RSC CVII, P2, pp. 910–11.

55. WSC to his wife, 15 September 1909. RSC CVII, P2, p. 911.

56. WSC to his wife, 19 September 1909. RSC CVII, P2, p. 913.

57. Theobald von Bethmann Hollweg had been appointed Chancellor of the German Reich by the Kaiser on 14 July 1909. He is generally considered to have attempted to pursue policies of moderation.

58. Covering Minute of the report, 3 November 1909. WSC WC (1923), p. 40; WSC WC (1938), pp. 25–6.

59. Andrew, *Defence of the Realm*, p. 20.

60. William Le Queux, *England's Peril: A Novel* (London: F.V. White & Co., 1899), p. 106. As Morgan put it nearly a century later: 'Britain's governors have long been foremost among the world's protected species. A shroud of secrecy ... has long insulated its politicians from the inquiries of journalists, historians, or simply the voters.' Kenneth O. Morgan, book review of: 'John F. Naylor, *A Man and an Institution: Sir Maurice Hankey, the Cabinet Secretariat and the Custody of Cabinet Secrecy* (Cambridge: Cambridge University Press, 1984)', *Journal of Modern History*, June 1986, 58(2):553.

61. David Stafford, *Churchill and Secret Service* (London: Abacus, 2000), pp. 33, 404, n. 5.

62. His diary entries include: 'It is dreadful to think that we have such men in the cabinet as Winston Churchill and Lloyd George. The one a half-bred American politician, the other a silly sentimental Celt.' They, in particular, were pouring 'torrents of scurrilous and socialist oratory ... upon the country'. Toye, *Lloyd George and Churchill*, p. 73; Addison, *Unexpected Hero*, p. 46.

63. Stafford, *Churchill and Secret Service*, p. 34.

64. Addison, *Unexpected Hero*, p. 46.

65. Stafford, *Churchill and Secret Service*, p. 34.

66. UK National Archives, KV1/9, Kell's Bureau six-monthly progress reports, 1909–1914. 'April 1910–October 1910: General Report on the work done during the six months ending October 1910', 17 November 1910, p. 7.

67. Stafford, *Churchill and Secret Service*, p. 43.

68. Ewart to Churchill, 27 April 1910. Andrew, *Defence of the Realm*, pp. 29–30, 870, n. 9.

69. E. Marsh (Home Office) to Chief Constables of England and Wales, 28 April 1910. Andrew, *Defence of the Realm*, pp. 30, 870, n. 10.

70. UK National Archives, KV 1/10. 'KV 1 Kell's Diary', 1 June 1910–28 July 1911, p. 2. Diary entry for 2 June 1910.

71. Ibid, pp. 3–4. Diary entry for 7 June 1910.

72. Ibid, p. 4. Diary entry for 8 June 1910. The Scottish Office was created in 1885. The post of Secretary of State for Scotland was held by Lord Pentland from 10 December 1905 to 13 February

1912. See Lady Pentland, *The Right Honourable John Sinclair, Lord Pentland, GGSI: A Memoir* (London: Methuen & Co., 1928).

73. UK National Archives, KV 1/10. 'KV 1 Kell's Diary', 1 June 1910–28 July 1911, p. 6. Diary entry for 15 June 1910.

74. Ibid, pp. 9–10.

75. Stafford, *Churchill and Secret Service*, p. 9.

76. UK National Archives, KV 1/10. 'KV 1 Kell's Diary', 1 June 1910–28 July 1911, pp. 41, 42. Diary entries for 31 October and 3 November 1910.

77. Ibid, p. 48. Diary entry for 9 December 1910. A point raised by Major Hugh Lang of East Sussex Constabulary.

78. Ibid, p. 54. Diary entry for 19 January 1911.

79. That question being 'so complex that no definite conclusion could be formulated'. The matter was not readdressed until 1912. UK National Archives, CAB 38/23/4. 'Standing Sub-Committee of the Committee of Imperial Defence. Enquiry regarding Press and Postal Censorship in Time of War. Reports and Proceedings. Enquiry Regarding Postal Censorship in Time of War or Impending War', February 1913, p. 1.

80. The Secretary was the executive head of the Post Office, reporting to the Postmaster General.

81. UK National Archives, CAB 38/23/4, p. 5. 'Minutes of First Meeting, July 11 1910.'

82. Ibid, p. 7. 'Appendix I: Memorandum by the General Staff.'

83. Ibid, p. 5. 'Minutes of First Meeting, July 11 1910.'

84. 'Historically, the Home Secretary had the power to issue warrants authorising interceptions of post and there are numerous instances in the 17th and 18th centuries of intercepted mail being used as evidence in criminal trials.' https://justice.org.uk/intercept-evidence/. See also Julie M. Flavell, 'Government Interception of Letters from America and the Quest for Colonial Opinion in 1775', *William and Mary Quarterly*, April 2001, 58(2). However, it was only with the Interception of Communications Act 1985 (IOCA) that interception of communications, whether by post or telephone, was placed on a statutory basis for the first time. https://www.cyber-rights.org/interception/ioca.pdf.

85. UK National Archives, CAB 38/23/4, p. 5. 'Minutes of First Meeting, July 11 1910.'

86. Ibid, p. 6.

87. Andrew, *Defence of the Realm*, pp. 36–7.

88. WSC WC (1923), p. 52; WSC WC (1938), p. 36.

89. For a detailed study of the affair see Geoffrey Barraclough, *From Agadir to Armageddon: Anatomy of a Crisis* (New York: Holmes & Meier, 1982). Also Ima C. Barlow, *The Agadir Crisis* (Hamden CT: Archon Books, 1971).

90. John Charmley, *Splendid Isolation?: Britain and the Balance of Power 1874–1914* (London: Hodder & Stoughton, 1999), p. 250.

91. Hew Strachan, *The First World War: vol. I: To Arms* (Oxford: Oxford University Press, 2003), p. 26.

92. WSC WC (1923), p. 50; WSC WC (1938), p. 34.

93. WSC to his wife, 3 July 1911. RSC CVII, P2, p. 1,095.

94. At that time, no records whatsoever were kept of Cabinet discussions or decisions. Only when Lloyd George became Prime Minister in December 1916 was a formal mechanism put in place to take minutes, record decisions, etc. Then the secretariat of the Committee for Imperial Defence, under Hankey, became the nucleus of a new Cabinet Office. https://www.nationalarchives.gov.uk/cabinetpapers/cabinet-gov/development-cabinet-government.htm.

95. WSC to his wife, 5 July 1911. Quoted in RSC VII, p. 522.

96. RSC VII, p. 523.

97. Memorandum by WSC, undated. RSC CVII, P2, p. 1,105.

98. RSC VII, p. 523.

99. M.L. Dockrill, 'British Policy During the Agadir Crisis of 1911', in F.H. Hinsley (ed.), *British Foreign Policy Under Sir Edward Grey* (Cambridge: Cambridge University Press, 1977), p. 276.

100. David Lloyd George, David Lloyd George, *War Memoirs of David Lloyd George: Two Volume Edition* (London: Odhams Press, 1938), vol. I, p. 26.
101. Dockrill, 'British Policy During the Agadir Crisis', p. 279.
102. UK National Archives, KV 1/10. 'KV 1 Kell's Diary', 1 June 1910–28 July 1911, pp. 56. Diary entry for 24 February 1911. The name of the informant was redacted, though given the other information divulged on the German battleships *Rheinland* and *Posen* it may have been Hector Bywater, the Secret Service Bureau's 'most prolific source'. Andrew Boyd, *British Naval Intelligence through the Twentieth Century* (Barnsley: Seaforth, 2020), pp. 71–2.
103. WSC WC (1923), pp. 50–1; WSC WC (1938), p. 35.
104. WSC WC (1923), p. 51; WSC WC (1938), p. 35.
105. Diary entry (undated) for August 1911, in McEwen, *Riddell Diaries*, p. 24.
106. WSC WC (1923), pp. 50–1; WSC WC (1938), p. 35.
107. Even Clive Ponting in his fiercely unsympathetic biography points out that: 'Throughout his life colleagues and friends were impressed by the intensity and variety of Churchill's activities and by his enormous capacity for work ...'. Ponting, *Churchill*, p. 19.
108. WSC WC (1923), pp. 52–3; WSC WC (1938), p. 36.
109. *London Gazette*, 2 August 1910. Randolph Churchill argues that: 'Largely under the tuition of Henry Wilson ... alertness to the German menace had quickened in him.'
110. Viscount Grey of Fallodon, *Twenty Five Years 1892–1916: vol. I* (New York: Frederick A. Stokes, MCMXXV[1925]), p. 229.
111. Strachan, *The First World War*, pp. 26–7. For a full biography see Keith Jeffery, *Field Marshal Sir Henry Wilson: A Political Soldier* (Oxford: Oxford University Press, 2006).
112. 'Military Aspects of the Continental Problem: Memorandum by Mr Churchill', 13 August 1911. WSC WC (1923), pp. 60–4; WSC WC (1938), pp. 42–6.
113. RSC VII, p. 528.
114. WSC WC (1923), p. 63; WSC WC (1938), p. 45.
115. RSC VII, p. 528.
116. Diary entry for 10 August 1911. Major General Sir C.E. Callwell, *Field Marshal Sir Henry Wilson: His Life and Diaries: vol. I* (London: Cassell & Co., 1927), p. 99.
117. Charmley, *Splendid Isolation?*, p. 325.
118. John W. Coogan and Peter F. Coogan, 'The British Cabinet and the Anglo-French Staff Talks, 1905–1914: Who Knew What and When Did He Know It?', *Journal of British Studies*, January 1985, 24(1):117–18.
119. Ibid, p. 128.
120. WSC WC (1923), p. 205; WSC WC (1938), p. 165.
121. Diary entry for 8 November 1918 in: Trevor Wilson (ed.), *The Political Diaries of C.P. Scott 1911–1928* (Ithaca, NY: Cornell University Press, 1970), p. 328.
122. David Lloyd George, *War Memoirs of David Lloyd George: Two Volume Edition* (London; Odhams Press, 1938) Volume I. p. 28.
123. A.J.P. Taylor, *The Struggle for Mastery in Europe 1848–1915* (Oxford: Oxford University Press, 1954), pp. 436–7.
124. William Cecil, Lord Burghley, was chief adviser to Queen Elizabeth I for most of her reign (1558–1603), and an ancestor of Robert Gascoyne-Cecil, 3rd Marquess of Salisbury and three-times Prime Minister.
125. King of England, Ireland and Scotland, 1689–1702.
126. John Churchill, 1st Duke of Marlborough, 1650–1722. Famed as victor of the battles of Blenheim (1704), Ramillies (1706), Oudenarde (1708) and Malplaquet (1709), and an ancestor of Winston S. Churchill.
127. William Pitt the Elder, 1st Earl of Chatham, the leader of Britain in the Seven Years' War (1756–63).
128. William Pitt the Younger, Prime Minister of Great Britain 1783–1801; Prime Minister of the United Kingdom January–March 1801 and then again 1804–06.

129. The Military Correspondent of *The Times* [Charles à Court Repington], 'Statecraft and Strategy', *The Times*, 10, 12, 27 June and 8 July 1908. Reproduced in *The Foundations of Reform* (London: Simpkin, Marshall & Co., 1908), pp. 156–7.

130. Coogan and Coogan, 'The British Cabinet', pp. 114–15.

131. Maurice, *Haldane, 1856–1915*, p. 280. According to McKenna's biographer, Haldane proposed this meeting at a dinner with Asquith, Grey, Churchill and McKenna on 14 August 1911. Farr, *Reginald McKenna*, p. 211.

132. Hankey to McKenna, 15 August 1911. Keith Wilson, 'Hankey's Appendix: Some Admiralty Manoeuvres During and After the Agadir Crisis, 1911', *War in History*, March 1994, 1(1):84, 85–6. Hankey's papers relating to the issue at hand can be found at Churchill College, Cambridge. Churchill Archives Centre, GBR/0014/HNKY 7/3. 'Papers on transport of an Expeditionary Force to France, 1909–1911.'

133. Arthur J. Marder, *From the Dreadnought to Scapa Flow: The Royal Navy in the Fisher Era 1904–1919: The Road to War 1904–1914* (Barnsley: Seaforth, 2013), p. 388.

134. 'Memorandum of Meeting held on July 20, 1911, between General Dubail and General Wilson', Document Number 640. In G.P. Gooch and Harold Temperley (eds), *British Documents on the Origins of the War 1898–1914: vol. VII: The Agadir Crisis* (London: HMSO, 1932), p. 629.

135. Jeffery, *Field Marshal Sir Henry Wilson*, p. 97.

136. In attendance: Politicians: Asquith (in the chair), Lloyd George, Grey, Churchill, McKenna and Haldane. Army: Henry Wilson, General Sir John French (Inspector General of the Forces), Field Marshal Sir William Nicholson (Chief of the Imperial General Staff) and Major General Sir Archibald Murray (Director of Military Training). Navy: Rear Admiral Alexander Bethell (Director of Naval Intelligence) and Admiral of the Fleet Sir Arthur Wilson (First Sea Lord of the Admiralty). Secretary: Rear Admiral Sir Charles Ottley. See UK National Archives, CAB 38/19/49. 'Minutes of 114th Meeting [of the CID]. (Action to be taken in the event of intervention in a European war: Appreciation of the military situation on the outbreak of a Franco-German war: Naval criticism of the General Staff proposals: Admiralty policy on the outbreak of war', 23 August 1911', p. 1.

137. WSC WC (1923), p. 56; WSC WC (1938), p. 39.

138. UK National Archives, CAB 38/15/15. 'Report of the Sub-Committee of the Committee of Imperial Defence on the Military Needs of the Empire', 24 July 1909.

139. UK National Archives, CAB 38/19/49. 'Minutes of 114th Meeting [of the CID]. (Action to be taken in the event of intervention in a European war: Appreciation of the military situation on the outbreak of a Franco-German war: Naval criticism of the General Staff proposals: Admiralty policy on the outbreak of war.) 23 August 1911, pp. 1–2.

140. Ibid, p. 2.

141. Ibid.

142. Ibid, pp. 2–4.

143. WSC WC (1923), pp. 56–8; WSC WC (1938), pp. 39–41.

144. Jeffery, *Field Marshal Sir Henry Wilson*, pp. 83–4.

145. Thomas Jones, *Lloyd George* (Cambridge, MA: Harvard University Press, 1951), p. 138.

146. For a positive view see David Morgan-Owen, 'Cooked up in the Dinner Hour? Sir Arthur Wilson's War Plan, Reconsidered', *English Historical Review*, August 2015, 130(545):865–906.

147. UK National Archives, CAB 38/19/49, p. 10.

148. Ibid, p. 11.

149. Richard Hough, *First Sea Lord: An Authorised Biography of Admiral Lord Fisher* (London: Severn House, 1977), p. 168.

150. As he was to explain it in 1913: 'I see no way of stopping this except catching them in shoal water at the mouths of their own rivers ... I think that the advent of the submarine is the reason which makes the close blockade absolutely necessary ... the principal danger [to the British battle fleet] is the submarine which will get out.' Nicholas A. Lambert, *Sir John Fisher's Naval Revolution* (Columbia, SC: University of South Carolina Press, 2002), p. 208.

151. UK National Archives, CAB 38/19/49, p. 12.
152. Ibid.
153. Ibid, p. 14.
154. Ibid, pp. 11–12.
155. Admiral of the Fleet Sir A.K. Wilson, 'Remarks on the War Plans, May 1907', in P.K. Kemp (ed.), *The Papers of Admiral Sir John Fisher: vol. II* (London: Navy Records Society, 1964), p. 459.
156. UK National Archives, CAB 38/19/49, pp. 12–13.
157. 'For the first two decades of the twentieth century he was the most influential military writer in the country. On questions of defence he was unmatched as a critic and communicator.' A.J.A. Morris, *Reporting the First World War: Charles Repington, 'The Times' and the Great War, 1914–1918* (Cambridge: Cambridge University Press, 2015), p. xi. 'Repington wielded astonishing influence and was called the "23rd member of the cabinet, very much more powerful than many of the 22 others".' 'Voices from the front: Times correspondents. Charles à Court Repington', *The Times*, 10 November 2018.
158. For the amphibious attacks or 'raids' on Rochefort in 1757 and on St Malo and Cherbourg in 1758, see Daniel Baugh, *The Global Seven Years War 1754–1763: Britain and France in a Great Power Contest* (Abingdon: Routledge, 2014), pp. 262–70, 306–10. W. Kent Hackmann, 'The British Raid on Rochefort, 1757', *Mariner's Mirror*, 1978, 64(3):263–75.
159. Repington, *The Foundations of Reform*, p. 186.
160. UK National Archives, CAB 38/19/49, p. 13.
161. WSC WC (1923), p. 59; WSC WC (1938), p. 41.
162. Hankey, *Supreme Command*, p. 82.
163. Hankey to Fisher, 24 August 1911. Wilson, 'Hankey's Appendix', pp. 86–7.
164. Hankey, *Supreme Command*.
165. Hankey to Fisher, 24 August 1911. Wilson, 'Hankey's Appendix', p. 81.
166. Diary entry for 1 November 1911. Farr, *Reginald McKenna*, p. 212.
167. Mr Churchill to Sir Edward Grey, 30 August 1911. WSC WC (1923), pp. 55–6; WSC WC (1938), p. 47.
168. Asquith to Haldane, 31 August 1911. Samuel R. Williamson Jr, *The Politics of Grand Strategy: Britain and France Prepare for War, 1904–1914* (Cambridge, MA: Harvard University Press, 1969), p. 193.
169. Richard Burdon Haldane, *An Autobiography* (London: Hodder & Stoughton, MCMXXIX [1929]), pp. 227–8.
170. Haldane to Asquith, undated [September 1911?]. Maurice, *Haldane, 1856–1915*, pp. 283–4.
171. WSC to Lloyd George, 14 September 1911. Stephen Roskill, *Hankey: Man of Secrets: vol. I 1877–1918* (London: Collins, 1970), p. 102.
172. Cloan House, Auchterarder, Perthshire.
173. Archerfield House, Dirleton, East Lothian.
174. Haldane, *Autobiography*, p. 228.
175. WSC WC (1923), p. 56; WSC WC (1938), p. 39.
176. Undated entry for 'November 1911' [probably 4 November] in Riddell, *More Pages*, p. 25.
177. H.H. Asquith to Violet Asquith, 24 August 1911. Bonham Carter and Pottle, *Lantern Slides*, p. 282.
178. Diary entry for 7 March 1915. McEwen, *Riddell Diaries*, p. 102.
179. 'In the autumn of 1911 Mr McKenna and Mr Churchill, at my request, exchanged the offices of Home Secretary and First Lord of the Admiralty.' Oxford and Asquith, *Fifty Years*, p. 109.
180. Haldane, *Autobiography*, p. 230.
181. WSC WC (1923), p. 67; WSC WC (1938), p. 49.
182. WSC WC (1923), pp. 67–8; WSC WC (1938), p. 49.
183. The King had ennobled him as 'Viscount Haldane of Cloan in the County of Perth' on 27 March 1911. *London Gazette*, 28 March 1911.
184. Haldane, *Autobiography*, p. 230.

185. Ibid, pp. 230–1.
186. Diary entry, 1 October 1911. Bonham Carter and Pottle, *Lantern Slides*, p. 285. Edward Marsh, his private secretary, confirmed that he did throw himself into the job. He informed his good friend Dorothy Gladstone, wife of the former Home Secretary, at the end of November that: 'Sundays are no longer my own … We have made a new commandment, "The seventh day is the Sabbath of the First Lord, on it thou shalt do all manner of work."' Edward Marsh to Lady Gladstone, 30 November 1911. Quoted in Christopher Hassall, *Edward Marsh Patron of the Arts: A Biography* (London: Longmans, Green & Co., 1959), p. 175.
187. Bonham Carter and Pottle, *Lantern Slides*, p. 284.
188. Lady Randolph to WSC, 1 October 1911. RSC CVII, P2, p. 1,294.
189. Churchill Archives Centre, Churchill College, Cambridge, CHAR 1/392/3. Letter from Lady Randolph Churchill (Glenmuick House, Ballater, Scotland) to WSC, 28 September 1911.
190. Italy declared war on the Ottoman Empire on 29 September. See Charles Stephenson, *A Box of Sand: The Italo-Ottoman War 1911–1912: The First Land, Sea and Air War* (Ticehurst: Tattered Flag, 2014).
191. Lady Randolph to WSC, 1 October 1911. RSC CVII, P2, p. 1,294.
192. Churchill to Nicolson (from Balmoral), 26 September 1911. UK National Archives, FO 800/350. Nicolson, Sir Arthur, Miscellaneous Correspondence, 1911, 4:77.
193. Churchill to Nicolson (from Archerfield), 29 September 1911. UK National Archives, FO 800/350, p. 80.
194. H.H. Asquith to Reginald McKenna, 10 October 1911. Stephen McKenna, *Reginald McKenna 1863–1943: A Memoir* (London: Eyre & Spottiswoode, 1948), p. 113.
195. Farr, *Reginald McKenna*, p. 216.
196. For the 'Navy Scare of 1909' see Marder, *From the Dreadnought to Scapa Flow*, pp. 151–85.
197. Fisher to Edward VII, 3 January 1909. Arthur J. Marder (ed.), *Fear God and Dread Nought: The Correspondence of Admiral of the Fleet Lord Fisher of Kilverstone: vol. II: Years of Power, 1904–1914* (London: Jonathan Cape, 1956), p. 220.
198. WSC WC (1923), p. 37; WSC WC (1938), p. 24.
199. Farr, *Reginald McKenna*, p. 216.
200. A point made by Otte. See T.G. Otte, *Statesmen of Europe: A Life of Sir Edward Grey* (London: Allen Lane, 2020), p. 435.
201. Spender and Asquith, *Life of Herbert Henry Asquith*, p. 347.
202. Grey to McKenna, 11 October 1911. Farr, *Reginald McKenna*, p. 216. McKenna, *Reginald McKenna 1863–1943*, p. 113.
203. He had been operated on for a badly inflamed appendix, which had been close to bursting, in November 1910. This was, at that time, a major operation, and he was still not fully recovered a year later. Farr, *Reginald McKenna*, p. 196.
204. Asquith to McKenna, 15 October 1911. Farr, *Reginald McKenna*, p. 216.
205. McKenna to Asquith, 17 October 1911. Asquith to McKenna, 18 October 1911. Farr, *Reginald McKenna*, p. 216.
206. Farr, *Reginald McKenna*, p. 217.
207. Reginald McKenna, 'Minute of a conversation at Archerfield, Friday, 20 October 1911'. Extract. Farr, *Reginald McKenna*, p. 217. The full text of the Minute can be found in Marder, *From the Dreadnought to Scapa Flow*, pp. 250–1.
208. Farr, *Reginald McKenna*, pp. 217–18.
209. Margot Asquith. Diary entry for 13 November 1911. Farr, *Reginald McKenna*, p. 218.
210. Lord Riddell diary entry for 22 May 1915. Quoted in Bentley Brinkerhoff Gilbert, *David Lloyd George: A Political Life: Organizer of Victory 1912–1916* (Columbus, OH: Ohio State University Press, 1992), p. 203.
211. Journal entry, 20 March 1909. Brett, *Journals and Letters*, p. 378.
212. Farr, *Reginald McKenna*, p. 161.
213. Lucy Masterman. Diary entry, 26 June 1912. Masterman, *C.F.G. Masterman*, p. 234.

214. Diary entry for 14 April 1915. McEwen, *Riddell Diaries*, p. 106.
215. Farr, *Reginald McKenna*, p. 219.
216. H.H. Asquith to Lord Crewe, 7 October 1911. RSC CVII, P2, p. 1,295.
217. McKenna to Fisher, 5 November 1911. Farr, *Reginald McKenna*, p. 218.
218. Nor the previous day, when he had written to his wife from Balmoral. WSC to his wife, 24 September 1911. RSC VII, p. 529.
219. WSC WC (1923), p. 70; WSC WC (1938), p. 51.

Chapter 10: 'Home Secretaries never do have an easy time'

1. Home Secretary Reginald McKenna, 29 September 1913. Farr, *Reginald McKenna*, p. 223.
2. Robert Rhodes James, 'The Enigma', in James W. Muller (ed.), *Churchill as Peacemaker* (Cambridge: Cambridge University Press, 2002), p. 6.
3. Margaret Thatcher, *The Downing Street Years* (London: Harper Collins, 1995), p. 307.
4. Charmley, *The End of Glory*, p. 67.
5. Sir Martin Gilbert, 'Foreword' to Alan S. Baxendale, *Winston Leonard Spencer-Churchill: Penal Reformer* (Bern: Peter Lang, 2009), p. vii.
6. 'While public opinion is now a crucial consideration in the formulation of penal policy, this was not always the case. Post-war penal policy development was restricted to the strategies of the educated few in Westminster and Whitehall, protected from the glare of media or public scrutiny. This private, elitist way of working started to dissipate from the 1980s onwards, as a consequence of the increasingly populist (vote-winning) policies espoused by both the Conservative and Labour parties.' Gemma Birkett, *Media, Politics and Penal Reform: Influencing Women's Punishment* (London: Palgrave Macmillan, 2017), p. 24.
7. Hansard, vol. 19, col. 1,354, 20 July 1910.
8. RSC VII, pp. 320–1.
9. Richard Allen Solloway, 'Neo-Malthusians, Eugenists, and the Declining Birth-Rate in England, 1900–1918', *Albion: A Quarterly Journal Concerned with British Studies*, Autumn 1978, 10(3):264.
10. UK National Archives, HO 144/1098/197900.
11. John Macnicol, 'Eugenics and the Campaign for Voluntary Sterilization in Britain Between the Wars', *Social History of Medicine*, August 1989, 2(2):149–50.
12. Butler, *Confident Morning*, p. 78.
13. RSC VII, p. 386.
14. Mobilisation would have involved calling up the reserves.
15. Hansard, vol. 29, col. 2,284, 22 August 1911.
16. Eunan O'Halpin, 'British Government and Society in the Twentieth Century', *Historical Journal*, September 1985, 28(3):762.
17. Thatcher, *Downing Street Years*, p. 307.
18. Bayley makes an interesting observation, with wider applicability than his context: 'police are immediately identified with law. In many respects they are more important than law, for they implement its strictures and decide when it is to be applied. Whether government is by men or by law depends to a marked extent on the nature of the police.' David H. Bayley, *Police and Political Development in India* (Princeton, NJ: Princeton University Press, 1969), p. 15.
19. Chief Magistrate Sir Albert de Rutzen at Bow Street police court. 'Chief Magistrate's Protest,' *Weekly Mail*, 26 November 1910.
20. 'Deeds, not words, was to be our permanent motto.' Pankhurst, *My Own Story*, p. 38.
21. WSC to the Master of Elibank, 18 December 1911. Quoted in Randolph S. Churchill, *Winston S. Churchill 1874–1965: vol. II Companion Part 3 1911–1914* (London: Heinemann, 1969), p. 1,473.
22. Paul Addison, 'Churchill and Social Reform', in Blake and Louis, *Churchill*, p. 78.
23. Janet Maslin, 'What Befits a Leader in Hard Times? An Intimate Knowledge of Insanity': review of Ghaemi, *A First-Rate Madness* in *New York Times*, 11 August 2011. https://www.nytimes.com/2011/08/11/books/a-first-rate-madness-by-nassir-ghaemi-review.html.
24. Moran, *Winston Churchill*, p. 167, footnote.

25. Churchill's Assistant Private Secretary 1940–1941, 1943–1945 and Joint Principal Private Secretary 1951–1955.

26. Lord Normanbrook, John Colville, John Martin, Ian Jacob, Lord Bridges, Leslie Rowan and John Wheeler-Bennett (eds), *Action this Day, Working with Churchill: Memoirs* (New York: St Martin's Press, 1969), p. 116.

27. Anthony M. Daniels and J. Allister Vale, 'Did Sir Winston Churchill Suffer From the "Black Dog"?', *Journal of the Royal Society of Medicine*, November 2018, 111(11):405. Vale and Scadding, *Winston Churchill's Illnesses*, Kindle edition, Loc. 9625.

28. Ghaemi, *A First-Rate Madness*, p. 34.

29. 'November 1911', in Riddell, *More Pages*, p. 24.

30. WSC to CSC, 27 October 1909. Quoted in Soames, *Speaking for Themselves*, p. 35.

31. David Lough, *No More Champagne: Churchill and His Money* (London: Head of Zeus, 2015), Kindle edition, Loc. 91.

32. Ibid, Loc. 1602.

33. Ibid, Locs 133–43, 1501.

34. https://www.bankofengland.co.uk/monetary-policy/inflation/inflation-calculator.

35. For an exhaustive account of the matter see Vale and Scadding, 'Did Churchill Suffer from the "Black Dog"?', ch. 30. See also: https://openhistorysociety.org/members-articles/how-churchills-mind-worked-by-paul-addison/#_edn1.

36. Rhodes James, 'Enigma', 6.

37. Ibid.

38. John Colville, *The Fringes of Power: Downing Street Diaries 1939–1955* (London: Hodder & Stoughton, 1985), p. 128. Also quoted in: Rhodes James, 'Enigma', p. 10.

39. Richard Shannon, *The Crisis of Imperialism 1865–1915* (London: Paladin, 1986), p. 403. Egerton goes further, arguing that: 'Lloyd George was never the captive of liberal ideology, or any other'. George W. Egerton, 'The Lloyd George "War Memoirs": A Study in the Politics of Memory', *Journal of Modern History*, March 1988, 60(1):91.

40. Shannon, *Crisis*, p. 403.

41. Jenkins, *Churchill*, pp. 273–6. Martin Gilbert, *Churchill: A Life* (London: Heinemann, 1991), pp. 316–20.

42. Alexander Mackintosh, *From Gladstone to Lloyd George: Parliament in Peace and War* (London: Hodder & Stoughton, 1921), p. 229.

43. David Lloyd George, *War Memoirs of David Lloyd George: vol. III* (London: Ivor Nicholson & Watson, 1934), pp. 1,069–70. David Lloyd George, *War Memoirs of David Lloyd George: vol. II* (London: Odhams Press, 1938), p. 637. Lloyd George's *War Memoirs* were originally published in six volumes: two each in the years 1933, 1934 and 1936 respectively. In 1938 a two-volume edition appeared. The latter was the best-selling, and therefore the best known and most widely available version, so reference has been made to it as well as the original volume.

44. He is supposed to have said, apropos his change of party, that: 'Anyone can rat, but it takes a certain kind of ingenuity to re-rat.'

45. Jenkins, *Churchill*, p. 465.

46. Quoted in: Charmley, *The End of Glory*, p. 282.

47. Clare Griffiths, 'Broken Promises and the Remaking of Political Trust: Debating Reconstruction in Britain During the Second World War', in David Thackeray and Richard Toye (eds), *Electoral Pledges in Britain since 1918: The Politics of Promises* (Cham, Switzerland: Springer Nature, 2020), pp. 96–7.

48. Hattersley, *David Lloyd George*, p. 616.

49. Egerton, 'The Lloyd George "War Memoirs"', p. 62. Hattersley, *David Lloyd George*, p. 619.

50. Terraine, *Business in Great Waters*, p. 72.

51. Otte describes them as 'mendacious even by the low standards of that genre [of wartime memoirs] in general and of their author in particular'. T.G. Otte, *July Crisis: The World's Descent into War, Summer 1914* (Cambridge: Cambridge University Press, 2014), p. 144. Barnett labels them a

'monumental work of mendacious self-praise'. Correlli Barnett, *The Lords of War: Supreme Leadership from Lincoln to Churchill* (Barnsley: Praetorian Press, 2013), p. 99.

52. Andrew Suttie, *Rewriting the First World War: Lloyd George, Politics and Strategy 1914–1918* (London: Palgrave Macmillan, 2005), p. 12.
53. Egerton, 'The Lloyd George "War Memoirs"', p. 85.
54. Suttie, *Rewriting the First World War*, p. 203.
55. Review in the *Times Literary Supplement*, 19 October 1933. Egerton, 'The Lloyd George "War Memoirs"', p. 82.
56. No doubt a reference to his published works on various military campaigns, memoranda such as 'Military Aspects of the Continental Problem', and his performance as First Lord of the Admiralty.
57. Lloyd George, *War Memoirs* (1934), p. 1,067; (1938), pp. 635–6.
58. Ibid, p. 1,068; (1938), p. 636.
59. Ibid, p. 1,069; (1938), p. 637.
60. Churchill's assessments of Lloyd George, as earlier revealed in *The World Crisis*, were complimentary and dwelt on his 'qualities, energy and resolution'. Winston S. Churchill, *The World Crisis 1916–1918: vol. III Part I* (London: Thornton Butterworth, 1927), pp. 256–7; Winston S. Churchill, *The World Crisis 1911–1918: vol. II* (London: Odhams Press, 1938), pp. 1,145–6.
61. It may be apocryphal. See David G. Stern, 'Heraclitus' and Wittgenstein's River Images: Stepping Twice into the Same River', *Monist*, October 1991, 74(4):579–80.
62. Farr, *Reginald McKenna*, p. 233.
63. The 'Prisoners (Temporary Discharge for Ill Health) Act 1913'. This allowed for the early release of prisoners who were so weakened by hunger striking that they were at risk of death. They were to be recalled to prison once their health was recovered, where the process would begin again.
64. Farr, *Reginald McKenna*, p. 240
65. Barbara Winslow, *Sylvia Pankhurst: Sexual Politics and Political Activism* (London: Verso, 2021), p. 49. Also quoted in Dangerfield, *Strange Death*, p. 196.
66. Home Secretary Reginald McKenna, 29 September 1913. Farr, *Reginald McKenna*, p. 223.
67. Rodney Brazier, *Ministers of the Crown* (Oxford: Clarendon Press, 1997), p. 169. As Noel Annan was to phrase it: 'the Home Office had become the graveyard of several political reputations'. Hansard, vol. 581, col. 678, 9 July 1997.

Bibliography

Newspapers and Journals

Aberdare Leader
British Medical Journal
Cambrian
Cambrian News
Cardiff Times
Church Times
Crediton Chronicle & North Devon Gazette
Daily Canadian
Daily Mail
Daily Mirror
Daily News
Daily Telegraph
Edinburgh Review
Evening Express and Evening Mail
Examiner (Tasmania)
Globe
Industrial Worker
Journal (Newcastle, England)
Journal of Mental Science
Justice of the Peace, and County, Borough, Poor Law
   Union, and Parish Law Recorder
Law Society Gazette
Law Times: The Journal and Record of the Law
   and the Lawyers
Liverpool Daily Post
Liverpool Echo
Llan a'r Dywysogaeth, Y (The Church and the
   Principality)
London Daily News
London Evening News

London Gazette
Los Angeles Herald
Manchester Evening Chronicle
Manchester Guardian
Merthyr Express
Merthyr Pioneer
Morning Post
National Review
New York Times
Police Gazette
Quarterly Review
Railway News, Finance and Joint-Stock Companies
   Journal
Referee
Review of Reviews
Rhondda Leader
Saturday Review
South Wales Daily News
South Wales Daily Post
South Wales Journal of Commerce
South Wales Weekly News
Spectator
Sydney Morning Herald
The Times (London)
Wanganui Herald
Weekly Mail
Welshman
Western Mail
Western Times

Documents, Diaries, Reports, etc.

Blunt, Wilfrid Scawen. *My Diaries: Being a Personal Narrative of Events, 1888–1914: Part Two 1900 to 1914* (London: Martin Secker, 1920).

Board of Trade (Department of Labour Statistics), *Sixteenth Abstract of Labour Statistics of The United Kingdom* (London: HMSO, 1913).

Bodleian Archives & Manuscripts. Miscellaneous letters to Asquith or his private secretaries, 1909–1910. MS. Asquith 12.

Bonham Carter, Mark and Pottle, Mark (eds). *Lantern Slides: The Diaries and Letters of Violet Bonham Carter* (London: Wiedenfeld & Nicolson, 1996).

Brett, Maurice V. (ed.). *Journals and Letters of Reginald Viscount Esher: Vol. 2 1903–1910* (London: Ivor Nicholson & Watson, MCMXXXIV [1934]).

Callwell, Major General Sir C.G. *Field-Marshal Sir Henry Wilson: His Life and Diaries: Vol. I* (London: Cassell & Co., 1927).

Churchill College, Cambridge. Churchill Archives Centre. CHAR 12. Home Office. Documents pertaining to Churchill's tenure as Home Secretary.

Churchill College, Cambridge. Churchill Archives Centre. GBR/0014/HNKY 7/3. 'Papers on transport of an Expeditionary Force to France, 1909–1911'.

Churchill, Randolph S. *Winston S. Churchill 1874–1965: Vol. I Companion Part 2 1896–1900* (London: Heinemann, 1967).

Churchill, Randolph S. *Winston S. Churchill 1874–1965: Vol. II Companion Part I 1901–1907* (London: Heinemann, 1969).

Churchill, Randolph S. *Winston S. Churchill 1874–1965: Vol. II Companion Part 2 1907–1911* (London: Heinemann, 1969).

Cobden-Sanderson, Thomas James. *The Journals of Thomas James Cobden-Sanderson 1879–1922: Vol. II* (London: Richard Cobden-Sanderson, 1926).

Craig, F.W.S. (Comp. and ed.). *British Electoral Facts, 1832–1987* (Dartmouth: Parliamentary Research Services, 1989).

Gooch, G.P. and Temperley, Harold (eds). *British Documents on the Origins of the War 1898–1914: Vol. VII: The Agadir Crisis* (London: HMSO, 1932).

Great Britain Prison Commission, *Report of the Commissioners of Prisons and Directors of Convict Prisons 1903–4* (London: HMSO, 1904).

Hansard. Parliamentary Debates. Available online, though not all volumes have been transcribed as yet (https://hansard.parliament.uk/).

HMSO. *Minutes of Proceedings of The Colonial Conference, 1907* (London: HMSO, 1907).

Home Office. *Colliery Strike Disturbances in South Wales: Correspondence and Report. November, 1910* (London: HMSO, 1911).

Home Office. *Employment of Military during Railway Strike: Correspondence between the Home Office and Local Authorities during the Railway Strike in August 1911* (London, HMSO, 1911).

Kemp, P.K. (ed.). *The Papers of Admiral Sir John Fisher: Vol. II* (London: Navy Records Society, 1964).

McEwen, J.M. (ed. and Intro.). *The Riddell Diaries 1908–1923* (London: Athlone Press, 1986).

Marder, Arthur J. (ed.). *Fear God and Dread Nought: The Correspondence of Admiral of the Fleet Lord Fisher of Kilverstone: Vol. II: Years of Power, 1904–1914* (London: Jonathan Cape, 1956).

Marrot, H.V. *The Life and Letters of John Galsworthy* (London: William Heinemann, 1935).

Masterman, C.F.G. *Heswall Nautical School: Report of inquiry by Mr C.F.G. Masterman, MP, Under Secretary of State for the Home Department, into charges made concerning the management of the Heswall Nautical School, 1911* (London: HMSO, 1911).

Report of the Royal Commission on the Care and Control of the Feeble-Minded: Vol. VIII (London: HMSO, 1908).

Report of the Select Committee on Employment of Military in Cases of Disturbances. 16 July 1908. Parliamentary Paper 236 (London: HMSO, 1908).

Report on Strikes and Lock-outs and of Conciliation and Arbitration Boards in the United Kingdom in 1911, with Comparative Statistics for 1902–1910 [Command Paper 6472] (London: HMSO, 1912).

Rhodes James, Robert (ed.). *Winston S. Churchill: His Complete Speeches 1897–1963. Vol. II: 1908–1913* (New York: Chelsea House/R.R. Bowker 1974).

Riddell, Lord [George Riddell]. *More Pages From My Diary 1908–1914* (London: Country Life, 1934).

Ruxton, Ian (transcriber, annotator, and indexer). *Sir Ernest Satow's Private Letters to W.G. Aston and F.V. Dickins: The Correspondence of a Pioneer Japanologist from 1870 to 1918* (Morrisville, NC: Lulu Press, 2008).

Soames, Mary (ed.). *Speaking for Themselves: The Personal Letters of Winston and Clementine Churchill* (London: Black Swan, 1999).

UK National Archives, ADM 196/42/244. Prince of Wales later King George V, George Frederick Ernest Albert.

UK National Archives, CAB 16/8. Foreign Espionage in the United Kingdom: Report and Proceedings. 1909.

UK National Archives, CAB 16/232. 'Conclusions of the sub-committee requested to consider the setting up of a secret service bureau.' 1909.

UK National Archives, CAB 24/89/85. Memorandum by Mr Churchill. 'Condiditon of Cyprus'.

UK National Archives, CAB 37/107/70. 'The Present Unrest in the Labour World. Printed or circulated in 1911 June 25' [sic. The covering letter is clearly dated 25 July].

UK National Archives, CAB 37/108/189. 'The Feeble Minded – A Social Danger'.

UK National Archives, CAB 38/15/15. 'Report of the Sub-Committee of the Committee of Imperial Defence on the Military Needs of the Empire', 24 July 1909.

UK National Archives, CAB 38/19/49. 'Minutes of 114th Meeting [of the CID]. (Action to be taken in the event of intervention in a European war; Appreciation of the military situation on the outbreak of a Franco-German war; Naval criticism of the General Staff proposals; Admiralty policy on the outbreak of war.) 23 August 1911.

UK National Archives, CAB 38/23/4. 'Standing Sub-Committee of the Committee of Imperial Defence. Enquiry regarding Press and Postal Censorship in Time of War. Reports and Proceedings. Enquiry Regarding Postal Censorship in Time of War or Impending War.' February 1913.

UK National Archives, FO 800/350. Nicolson, Sir Arthur. Miscellaneous Correspondence Vol. 4. 1911.

UK National Archives, HO 45/10608/192905/22. Strikes: Strike at Newport Docks.

UK National Archives, HO 45/10656/212470. 'STRIKES: Liverpool Railway Strike 1911'.

UK National Archives, HO 144/1054/187986. 'Prisons and Prisoners – Other: Treatment of Lady Constance Lytton, Suffragette'. 1910–1912.

UK National Archives, HO 144/1085/193548. PRISONS AND PRISONERS – OTHER: Treatment of weakminded prisoners. Proposals by the Secretary of State (Mr. Winston Churchill). 1910.

UK National Archives, HO 144/1088/194663. 'CRIMINAL: Expert opinions on the question of sterilisation; CRIMINAL.

UK National Archives, HO 144/1098/197900. 'CRIMINAL: Sterilization of the mentally degenerate'.

UK National Archives, HO 144/1551/199768. DISTURBANCES: South Wales miners' strike (Tonypandy riots).

UK National Archives, KV 1/9. 'Kell's Bureau six-monthly progress reports. 1909–1914.' 'April 1910–October 1910; General Report on the work done during the six months ending October 1910' 17 November 1910.

UK National Archives, KV 1/10. 'KV 1 Kell's Diary.' 1 June 1910 – 28 July 1911.

UK National Archives, MEPO 3/203. Suffragettes: Complaints against Police. 1911. 'Memorandum by Sir Edward Henry, Commissioner of the Metropolitan Police'. 8 February 1911.

UK National Archives, PCOM 7/38. 'Departmental Committee on Prisons, 1895: The "Gladstone Committee" – report and minutes of evidence.' 1894–1895.

UK National Archives, PCOM 7/279. 'Standing Order (New Series), No. 10. 30 July 1897.

UK Parliament, Parliamentary Archives, GB-061. LG/C.

University of Southampton, Special Collections, Manuscript collections, Mountbatten database MB1/T. Papers of Prince Louis of Battenberg: Naval and Personal Papers, 1868–1921, 1962–79; MB1/T39/Naval Papers/378.

Wilson, Trevor (ed.). *The Political Diaries of C.P. Scott 1911–1928* (Ithaca, NY: Cornell University Press, 1970).

Wyndham, Guy (Comp.). *Letters of George Wyndham: Vol. II* (Edinburgh: Privately Printed, 1915).

Books, Articles etc.

Abinger, Edward. *Forty Years at The Bar: Being the Memoirs of Edward Abinger, Barrister of The Inner Temple* (London: Hutchinson & Co., 1930).

Adams, R.J.Q. *Balfour: The Last Grandee* (London: Thistle, 2013) Kindle edition.

Addison, Adrian. *Mail Men: The Unauthorized Story of the Daily Mail – The Paper That Divided and Conquered Britain* (London: Atlantic Books, 2017).

Addison, Paul. 'The Political Beliefs of Winston Churchill' in *Transactions of the Royal Historical Society*, 1980, 30.

Addison, Paul. 'Churchill and Social Reform' in Robert Blake and Wm Roger Louis (eds), *Churchill* (Oxford: Clarendon Press, 2002), p. 78.

Addison, Paul. *Churchill: The Unexpected Hero* (Oxford: Oxford University Press, 2005).

Alexander, G. Glover. *The Administration of Justice in Criminal Matters (in England and Wales)* (Cambridge: Cambridge University Press, 1915).

Allason, Rupert. *The Branch: A History of the Metropolitan Police Special Branch 1883–1983* (London: Secker & Warburg, 1983).

Andrew, Christopher. 'Governments and Secret Services: A Historical Perspective' in *International Journal*, Spring 1979, 34(2).

Andrew, Christopher. *The Defence of the Realm: The Authorized History of MI5* (London: Allen Lane, 2009).

Anon. 'Deputation to Mr Churchill' in *Common Cause, The Organ of the National Union of Women's Suffrage Societies*, 8 December 1910, II(87).

Anon. 'The Book of The Month: What a Revolution is Like: A Prophetical Forecast by Mr Winston Churchill.' In *Review of Reviews for Australasia*, November 1911.

Anon. 'The Man at the Wheel' in *Seaman: The Official Organ of The National Sailors' & Firemen's Union*, 29 May 1914, 1(42) [New Series].

Archibald, W.F.A., Greenhalgh, J.H. and Roberts, James. *The Metropolitan Police Guide, Being a Compendium of the Law Affecting the Metropolitan Police* (London: HMSO, 1922).

Army Museums Ogilby Trust, *Year of the Yeomanry: 1794–1994* (Salisbury: Army Museums Ogilby Trust, 1994), p. 72.

Arnot, R. Page. *South Wales Miners Glowyr De Cymru: A History of the South Wales Miners Federation (1898–1914)* (London: George Allen & Unwin, 1967).

Ascher, Abraham. *The Revolution of 1905: A Short History* (Stanford, CA: Stanford University Press, 2004).

Ashworth, Andrew and Zedner, Lucia. *Preventive Justice* (Oxford: Oxford University Press, 2014).

Askwith, Lord. *Industrial Problems and Disputes* (London: John Murray, 1920).

Asquith, Margot. *The Autobiography of Margot Asquith: Vol. II* (London: Thornton Butterworth, 1922).

Atkinson, Diane. *Votes for Women* (Cambridge: Cambridge University Press, 1988).

Atkinson, Diane. *Rise Up Women! The Remarkable Lives of the Suffragettes* (London: Bloomsbury Publishing, 2018).

Austin, Douglas. *Churchill and Malta: A Special Relationship* (Stroud: Spellmount, 2014).

Bagwell, Philip S. *The Railwaymen: The History of The National Union of Railwaymen* (London: George Allen & Unwin, 1963).

Bailey, Victor. *Delinquency and Citizenship: Reclaiming the Young Offender 1914–48* (Oxford: Clarendon Press, 1987).

Bailey, Victor. 'English Prisons, Penal Culture, and the Abatement of Imprisonment, 1895–1922' in *Journal of British Studies*, July 1997, 36(3).

Baimbridge, Mark and Darcy, Darren. 'MPs' Pay 1911–1996: Myths and Realities' in *Politics*, 1999, 19(2).

Bale, Islwyn. *Through Seven Reigns: A History of the Newport Police Force 1836–1959* (Pontypool: Hughes, 1960).

Balfour, Betty (ed.). *Letters of Constance Lytton* (London: William Heinemann, 1925).

Balfour, Campbell. 'Captain Tupper and the 1911 Seamen's Strike in Cardiff' in *Morgannwg: Transactions of the Glamorgan Local History Society*, 1970, XIV.

Barclay, Martin. '"The Slaves of the Lamp": The Aberdare Miners' Strike 1910' in *Llafur: The Journal of the Society for the Study of Welsh Labour History*. Summer 1978, 2(3).

Barker, R.J. *Christ in the Valley of Unemployment* (London: Hodder & Stoughton, 1936).

Barlow, Ima C. *The Agadir Crisis* (Hamden CT: Archon Books, 1971).

Barnett, Correlli. *The Lords of War: Supreme Leadership from Lincoln to Churchill* (Barnsley: Praetorian Press, 2013).

Barraclough, Geoffrey. *From Agadir to Armageddon: Anatomy of a Crisis* (New York: Holmes & Meier, 1982).

Barton, Geoffrey. *The Tottenham Outrage and Walthamstow Tram Chase: The Most Spectacular Hot Pursuit in History* (Sherfield on Loddon: Waterside Press, 2017).

Bates, Stephen. *H.H. Asquith* (London: Haus, 2006).

Baugh, Daniel. *The Global Seven Years War 1754–1763: Britain and France in a Great Power Contest* (Abingdon: Routledge, 2014).

Baxendale, Alan S. *Winston Leonard Spencer-Churchill: Penal Reformer* (Bern: Peter Lang, 2009).

Bayley, David H. *Police and Political Development in India* (Princeton, NJ: Princeton University Press, 1969).

Bearman, C.J. 'The legend of Black Friday' in *Historical Research*, November 2010, 83(222).

Belchem, John. *Irish, Catholic and Scouse: The History of the Liverpool-Irish, 1800–1939* (Liverpool: Liverpool University Press, 2007).

Béliard, Yann. 'Introduction: Revisiting the Great Labour Unrest, 1911–1914' in *Labour History Review*, April 2014, 79(1).

Benjamin, Brian. *Send the Gunboats up the Mersey* (Liverpool: Brian Benjamin, 2019).

Berry, Neil. 'Godfather of Populism: The Rabid Reign of Horatio Bottomley in *Times Literary Supplement*, 9 April 2021, no. 6158.

Bird, Samantha L. *Stepney: Profile of a London Borough from the Outbreak of the First World War to the Festival of Britain, 1914–1951* (Newcastle upon Tyne: Cambridge Scholars Publishing, 2011).

Birkett, Gemma. *Media, Politics and Penal Reform: Influencing Women's Punishment* (London: Palgrave Macmillan, 2017).

Blacker, C.P. *Eugenics: Galton and After* (London: Gerald Duckworth & Co., 1952).

Blake, John D. *Civil Disorder in Britain, 1910–39: The Roles of Civil Government and Military Authority* (University of Sussex: D. Phil. Thesis, 1979).

Blewett, Neal. *The Peers, The Parties and The People: The British General Elections of 1910* (London: Palgrave Macmillan, 1972).

Boghardt, Thomas. *Spies of the Kaiser: German Covert Operations in Great Britain During the First World War Era* (Houndsmills: Palgrave Macmillan, 2004).

Bonham Carter, Violet. *Winston Churchill as I Knew Him* (London: Eyre & Spottiswoode & Collins, 1965). Published in the US as: *Winston Churchill: An Intimate Portrait* (New York: Konecky & Konecky, 1965).

Boothby, Lord. *Boothby: Recollections of a Rebel* (London: Hutchinson, 1978).

Bower, Fred. *Rolling Stonemason: An Autobiography* (London: Jonathan Cape, 1936).

Boyd, Andrew. *British Naval Intelligence through the Twentieth Century* (Barnsley: Seaforth, 2020).

Boyer, George R. *The Winding Road to the Welfare State: Economic Insecurity and Social Welfare Policy in Britain* (Princeton, NJ: Princeton University Press, 2019).

Boyle, Andrew. *The Riddle of Erskine Childers: A Biography* (London: Hutchinson, 1977).

Bramwell, B.S. 'Galton's "Hereditary Genius" and the Three Following Generations since 1869' in *Eugenics Review*, January 1948, 39(4).

Brazier, Rodney. *Ministers of the Crown* (Oxford: Clarendon Press, 1997).

Breitman, Richard. *Official Secrets: What the Nazis Planned, What the British and Americans Knew* (London: Allen Lane, 1999).

Briggs, Asa and Burke, Peter. *A Social History of the Media: from Gutenberg to the Internet* (Cambridge: Polity Press, 2005).

Briggs, Isaac G. *Reformatory Reform* (London: Longmans, Green & Co., 1924).

Brooker, Keith. *The Hull Strikes of 1911* (Beverley: East Yorkshire Local History Society, 1979).

Brown, Alyson. *English Society and the Prison: Time, Culture and Politics in the Development of the Modern Prison, 1850–1920* (Woodbridge: Boydell Press, 2003).

Bruce, Steve. *Politics and Religion in the United Kingdom* (Abingdon: Routledge, 2012).

Buczacki, Stefan. *My Darling Mr Asquith: The Extraordinary Life and Times of Venetia Stanley* (London: Cato & Clarke, 2016).

Burnett, Brigadier General Charles. *The Memoirs of the 18th (Queen Mary's Own) Royal Hussars, 1906–1922: Including Operations in the Great War* (Winchester: Warren & Son, 1926).

Butler, David and Butler Gareth. *Twentieth-Century British Political Facts 1900–2000* (Houndmills: Palgrave Macmillan, 2000).

Butler, Harold. *Confident Morning* (London: Faber & Faber, 1950).

Cain, Peter. 'Political Economy in Edwardian England: The Tariff-Reform Controversy' in Alan O'Day (ed.), *The Edwardian Age: Conflict and stability, 1900–1914* (London: Macmillan, 1979).

Callender Smith, Robin. 'The Missing Witness?: George V, Competence and Compellability and the Criminal Libel Trial of Edward Frederick Mylius' in *Journal of Legal History*, August 2012, 33(2).

Callender Smith, Robin. *Celebrity Privacy and the Development of the Judicial Concept of Proportionality: How English Law has Balanced the Rights to Protection and Interference – Thesis Submitted in Partial fulfilment of the Requirements of the Degree of Doctor of Philosophy* (London: Queen Mary University of London Centre for Commercial Law Studies, 2014).

Campbell, John. *Roy Jenkins: A Well-Rounded Life* (London: Jonathan Cape, 2014).

Carlebach, Julius. *Caring for Children in Trouble* (London: Routledge, 2002).

Carradice, Phil. *Nautical Training Ships: An Illustrated History* (Stroud: Amberley Publishing, 2013).

Cecil, Lord Robert. 'The Six year old Parliament. London, 1865' in *Quarterly Review*, July 1865, 118(235).

Cesarani, David. 'The Anti-Jewish Career of Sir William Joynson-Hicks, Cabinet Minister' in *Journal of Contemporary History*, July 1989, 24(3).

Cesarani, David. 'An Alien Concept? The Continuity of Anti-Alienism in British Society before 1940' in David Cesarani and Tony Kushner (eds), *The Internment of Aliens in Twentieth Century Britain* (Abingdon: Routledge, 1993).

Chamberlain, Sir Austen. *Politics From Inside: An Epistolary Chronicle 1906–1914* (London: Cassell & Co., 1936).

Charmley, John. *Churchill: The End of Glory – A Political Biography* (London: Hodder & Stoughton, 1993).

Charmley, John. *Splendid Isolation?: Britain and the Balance of Power 1874–1914* (London: Hodder & Stoughton, 1999).

Childers, Erskine. *The Riddle of the Sands: A Record of Secret Service* (London: Smith, Elder & Co., 1903).

Childs, Major General Sir Wyndham. *Episodes and Reflections: Being Some Records from the Life of Major-General Sir Wyndham Childs, KCMG, KBE, CB, One Time Second Lieut., 2nd Volunteer Battalion, the Duke of Cornwall's Light Infantry* (London: Cassell & Co., 1930).

Churchill, Randolph S. *Lord Derby, King of Lancashire: The Official Life of Edward, Seventeenth Earl of Derby, 1865–1948* (London: Heinemann, 1959).

Churchill, Randolph S. *Winston S. Churchill Vol. II: Young Statesman 1901–1914* (London: Heinemann, 1967).

Churchill, Winston S. [grandson]. *His Father's Son: The Life of Randolph Churchill* (London: Weidenfeld & Nicolson, 1996).

Churchill, Winston S. *The Story of The Malakand Field Force: An Episode of Frontier War* (London: Longmans Green, 1898).

Churchill, Winston S. *The River War* in two Vols (London: Longmans Green, 1899).

Churchill, Winston S. *Savrola* (New York: Longmans Green, 1899).

Churchill, Winston S. *Ian Hamilton's March* (New York: Longmans, Green, 1900).

Churchill, Winston S. *London to Ladysmith via Pretoria* (New York: Longmans, Green, 1900).

Churchill, Winston Spencer. *Mr Brodrick's Army* (London: Arthur L. Humphreys, 1903).

Churchill, Winston S. *Mr Winston Churchill on the Aliens Bill: A Letter Addressed to a Manchester Correspondent: Leaflet 2006* (London: Liberal Publication Department, 1904).

Churchill, Winston S. *For Free Trade* (London: Arthur L. Humphreys, 1906).

Churchill, Winston Spencer, *Lord Randolph Churchill* (London: Macmillan, 1906).

Churchill, Winston S. *For Liberalism and Free Trade, Principal Speeches of the Rt. Hon. Winston S. Churchill, MP during the campaign in Dundee, May 1908* (Dundee: John Leng, 1908 and London: 186 Fleet St., 1908).

Churchill, Winston Spencer. *My African Journey* (London: Hodder & Stoughton, 1908).

Churchill, Winston S. *Liberalism and The Social Problem* (London: Hodder & Stoughton, 1909).

Churchill, Winston S. *To the Electors of Dundee: 23rd November 1910* (Dundee: John Leng & Co., 1910).

Churchill, Winston S. *The People's Rights* (London: Hodder & Stoughton, 1910).

Churchill, Winston S. *The World Crisis 1915: Vol. II* (London: Thornton Butterworth, 1923).

Churchill, Winston S. *The World Crisis 1916–1918: Vol. III Part I* (London: Thornton Butterworth, 1927).

Churchill, Winston S. *Thoughts and Adventures* (London: Thornton Butterworth, 1932).

Churchill, Winston S. *The World Crisis 1911–1918: Vol. II* (London: Odhams Press, 1938).

Churchill, Winston S. *Great Contemporaries* (London: Reprint Society, 1941).

Churchill, Winston S. *The Second World War: Vol. Two: Their Finest Hour* (London: Reprint Society, 1951).

Churchill, Winston S. *My Early Life: A Roving Commission* (London: Mandarin, 1991).

Clarke, A.A. *The Policemen of Hull: The Story of Hull Police Force, 1836 to 1974* (Beverley: Hutton Press, 1992).

Clarke, P.F. 'The Electoral Position of the Liberal and Labour parties, 1910–1914' in *English Historical Review*, October 1975, XC(CCCLVII).

Coates, Ken and Topham, Tony (eds). *Workers' Control: A Book of Readings and Witnesses for Workers' Control* (London: Panther, 1970).

Cole, Margaret. *Growing Up Into Revolution* (London: Longmans, Green, 1949).

Colville, John. *The Fringes of Power: Downing Street Diaries 1939–1955* (London: Hodder & Stoughton, 1985).

Conservative and Liberal Unionist Organisations, National Unionist Association of. *The Constitutional Year Book for 1899* (London: Conservative Central Office, 1899).

Coogan, John W. and Coogan, Peter F. 'The British Cabinet and the Anglo-French Staff Talks, 1905–1914: Who Knew What and When Did He Know It?' in *Journal of British Studies*, January 1985, 24(1).

Cook, Andrew. *M: MI5's First Spymaster* (Stroud: History Press, 2006).

Cook, Chris. *The Routledge Companion to Britain in the Nineteenth Century, 1815–1914* (Abingdon: Routledge, 2005).

Cosgrove, Richard A. *The Rule of Law: Albert Venn Dicey, Victorian Jurist* (Chapel Hill, NC: University of North Carolina Press, 1980).

Cox, Howard and Mowatt, Simon. *Revolutions from Grub Street: A History of Magazine Publishing in Britain* (Oxford: Oxford University Press, 2014).

Crawford, Elizabeth. *The Women's Suffrage Movement: A Reference Guide 1866–1928* (London: University College London [UCL] Press).

Crewe, Marquess of. *Lord Rosebery: Vol. II* (London: John Murray, 1931).

Crichton, Michael. 'Appendix I: Why Politicized Science is Dangerous' in Crichton, Michael. *State of Fear* (London: Harper Collins, 2004).

Cronin, James E. 'Strikes and Power in Britain, 1870–1920' in *International Review of Social History*, 1987, 32(2).

Cross, Rupert. *Punishment, Prison and The Public: An Assessment of Penal Reform in Twentieth Century England by an Armchair Penologist* (London: Stevens & Sons, 1971).

Cubitt, Eliza. *Arthur Morrison and the East End: The Legacy of Slum Fictions* (Abingdon: Routledge, 2019).

Daily Mail. *The Ghastly Blunders of The War: A Guide to the Report of the Royal Commission on the South African War, 1899–1900* (London: Daily Mail, No date (*c.*1903).

Dangerfield, George. *The Strange Death of Liberal England* (London: Constable, 1936).

Daniels, Anthony M. and Vale, J. Allister. 'Did Sir Winston Churchill Suffer From the 'Black Dog'?' in *Journal of the Royal Society of Medicine*, November 2018, 111(11).

Darwin, Charles. *The Descent Of Man, and Selection in Relation to Sex: In Two Vols – Vol I* (New York: D. Appleton & Co., 1872)

David Lloyd George, *War Memoirs of David Lloyd George: Two Vol. Edition* (London: Odhams Press, 1938).

David Lloyd George, *War Memoirs of David Lloyd George: Vol. III* (London: Ivor Nicholson & Watson, 1934).

Davidson, Roger. 'Social Conflict and Social Administration: The Conciliation Act in British Industrial Relations' in Smout, T.C. (ed.). *The Search for Wealth and Stability: Essays in Economic and Social History presented to M.W. Flinn* (London: Macmillan, 1979).

Davies, Rhys. *Print of a Hare's Foot: An Autobiographical Beginning* (London: Heinemann, 1969).

Davies, Rhys. *Ram with Red Horns* (Bridgend: Seren, 1996).

Davies, T. Alban. 'Impressions of Life in the Rhondda Valley' in in K.S. Hopkins (ed.), *Rhondda: Past and Future* (Ferndale: Rhondda Borough Council, 1975).

Davies, W. Watkin. *Lloyd George 1863–1914* (London: Constable & Co., 1939).

Devlin, The Honourable Sir Patrick. *Trial by Jury* (London: Stevens & Sons, 1956).

Dicey, Albert Venn. 'Woman Suffrage' in Edith M. Phelps (Comp.), *Selected Articles on Woman Suffrage* (Minneapolis, MN: H.W. Wilson Co., 1910).

Dixon, James Main. *Dictionary of Idiomatic English Phrases* (London: T. Nelson & Sons, 1891).

Docherty, James C. and van der Velden, Sjaak. *Historical Dictionary of Organized Labor* (Plymouth: Scarecrow, 2012).

Dockrill, M.L. 'British Policy During the Agadir Crisis of 1911' in F.H. Hinsley (ed.), *British Foreign Policy Under Sir Edward Grey* (Cambridge: Cambridge University Press, 1977).

Dockter, Warren. 'The Influence of a Poet: Wilfrid S. Blunt and the Churchills' in *Journal of Historical Biography*, Autumn 2011, 10.

Donkin, H. (Sir Horatio Bryan). 'Thoughts on Ignorance and Quackery' in *British Medical Journal*, 9 October 1880, 2(1032).

Douglas, Roy. *The History of the Liberal Party 1895–1970* (London: Sidgwick & Jackson, 1971).

Dowding, Keith. 'Government at the Centre' in Patrick Dunleavy, Andrew Gamble, Ian Holliday, and Gillian Peele, *Developments in British Politics 4* (Houndsmills: Macmillan, 1993).

Doyle, Arthur Conan. *His Last Bow: Some Reminiscences of Sherlock Holmes* (London: John Murray, 1917).

Du Cane, Colonel Sir Edmund F. *The Punishment And Prevention of Crime* (London: Macmillan And Co., 1885).

Dugdale, Blanche E.C. *Arthur James Balfour: First Earl of Balfour: Vol. II 1906–1930* (New York: G.P. Putnam's Sons, 1937)

Dundee Social Union, *Report upon Housing and Industrial Conditions and Medical Inspection of School Children* (Dundee: John Leng, 1905).

Eby, Cecil D. *The Road to Armageddon: The Martial Spirit in English Popular Literature* (Durham, NC: Duke University Press, 1987).

Eddleston, John J. *The Encyclopaedia of Executions* (London: John Blake, 2002).

Eddleston, John J. *The Murder of John Alexander Dickman: The Newcastle Train Murder 1910* (Sussex: Bibliofile Publishers, 2012).

Edwards, John. *Remembrance of a Riot: The Story of the Llanelli Railway Strike Riots of 1911* (Lanelli: Llanelli Borough Council, 1988).

Edwards, Ness. *The History of the South Wales Miners' Federation: Vol. I* (London: Lawrence & Wishart, 1938).

Egerton, George W. 'The Lloyd George 'War Memoirs': A Study in the Politics of Memory' in *Journal of Modern History*, March 1988, 60(1).

Egremont, Max. *Balfour: A Life of Arthur James Balfour* (London: Collins, 1980).

Ellis, John. *Diary of a Hangman* (London: True Crime Library, 1996).

Emsley, Clive. *The English Police: A Political and Social History* (Abingdon: Routledge, 2014).

Esher, Oliver, Viscount (ed.). *Journals and Letters of Reginald Viscount Esher: Vol. 3 1910–1915* (London: Ivor Nicholson & Watson, 1938).

Evans, David. *Labour Strife in the South Wales Coalfield: A Historical and Critical Record of the Mid-Rhondda, Aberdare Valley and other Strikes* (Cardiff: Educational Publishing, 1911).

Evans, David. 'The Captain of Industry' in Margaret Haig Mackworth [née Thomas, 2nd Viscountess Rhondda], *D.A. Thomas Viscount Rhondda: By his Daughter and Others* (London: Longmans, Green, 1921).

Evans, E.W. *Mabon: A Study in Trade Union Leadership* (Cardiff: University of Wales Press, 1959).

Evans, Neil. 'A Tidal Wave of Impatience': the Cardiff General Strike of 1911, in Geraint H. Jenkins & J. Beverley Smith (eds) *Politics and Society in Wales 1840–1922: Essays in Honour of Ieuan Gwynedd Jones* (Cardiff: University of Wales Press, 1988).

Fair, John D. *British Interparty Conferences: Study of the Procedure of Conciliation in British Politics 1867–1921* (Oxford: Clarendon Press, 1980).

Fairfield, Letitia. *The Case Against Sterilisation* (London: Catholic Truth Society, 1934).

Farmer, Ann. *By Their Fruits: Eugenics, Population Control, and the Abortion Campaign* (Washington, DC: Catholic University of America Press, 2008).

Farr, Martin. *Reginald McKenna: Financier among Statesmen, 1863–1916* (Abingdon: Routledge, 2008).

Felstead, S. Theodore. *In Search of Sensation: Being Thirty Tears of a London Journalist's Life* (London: Robert Hale, 1945).

Fennell, Phil. *Treatment Without Consent: Law, Psychiatry and the Treatment of Mentally Disordered People Since 1845* (London: Routledge, 1996).

Fischel, Jack R. *Historical Dictionary of the Holocaust* (Lanham, MD: Rowman & Littlefield, 2020)

Fitzroy, Sir Almeric. *Memoirs: Vol. II* (London: Hutchinson & Co., 1925).

Flavell, Julie M. 'Government Interception of Letters from America and the Quest for Colonial Opinion in 1775' in *William and Mary Quarterly*, April 2001, 58(2).

Fletcher, Ian Christopher. '"A Star Chamber of the Twentieth Century": Suffragettes, Liberals, and the 1908 "Rush the Commons" Case' in *Journal of British Studies*, October 1996, 35(4).

Fludernik, Monika. *Metaphors of Confinement: The Prison in Fact, Fiction, and Fantasy* (Oxford: Oxford University Press, 2019).

Foster, R.F. *Lord Randolph Churchill: A Political Life* (Oxford: Clarendon, 1981).

Francis, Hywel and Smith, David. *The Fed: A History of the South Wales Miners in the Twentieth Century* (London: Lawrence & Wishart, 1980).

Franklin, Hugh Arthur. 'Why I Struck at Mr Churchill' in *Votes for Women*, 9 December 1910, IV(144).

Fraser, Sir Hugh. *The Representation of The People Act, 1918 with Explanatory Notes* (London: Sweet and Maxwell, 1918).

Fraser, W. Hamish. 'The Labour Party in Scotland' in Brown K.D. (ed.). *The First Labour Party 1906–1914* (Abingdon: Routledge, 2019).

Frow, Edmund and Frow, Ruth. *The General Strike in Salford in 1911* (Salford: Working Class Movement Library, 1990).

Galsworthy, John. *Justice: A Tragedy in Four Acts* (London: Duckworth, 1911).

Galton, Francis. *Hereditary Genius: An Inquiry into its Laws and Consequences* (London: Macmillan & Co., 1869).

Galton, Francis. *English Men of Science: Their Nature and Nurture* (New York: D. Appleton & Co., 1875).

Galton, Francis. *Memories of My Life* (London: Methuen & Co., 1908).

Galton, Francis. 'Eugenics: Its Definition, Scope and Aims' in Sir Francis Galton, *Essays in Eugenics* (London: Eugenics Education Society, 1909).

Galton, Francis. 'The Possible Improvement of the Human Breed Under the Existing Conditions of Law and Sentiment' in Sir Francis Galton, *Essays in Eugenics* (London: Eugenics Education Society, 1909).

Galton, Francis. 'Segregation' in Mrs Walter Slater, *The Problem of the Feeble Minded: an Abstract of the Report of the Royal Commission on the Care and Control of the Feeble Minded* (London: P.S. King & Son, 1909).

Gardiner, A.G. *Prophets, Priests and Kings* (London: Alston Rivers, 1908).

Gardiner, A.G. *Pillars of Society* (London: James Nisbet & Co., 1913).

Garrard, John. *Democratisation in Britain: Elites, Civil Society and Reform Since 1800* (Houndsmills: Palgrave, 2002).

Garvin, J.L. *The Life of Joseph Chamberlain Vol. III: 1895–1900, Empire and World Policy* (London: Macmillan & Co., 1934).

Geary, Roger. *Policing Industrial Disputes: 1893 to 1985* (Cambridge: Cambridge University Press, 1985).

George, W.R.P. *Lloyd George: Backbencher* (Llandysul: Gomer Press, 1983).

Ghaemi, Nassir. *A First-Rate Madness: Uncovering the Links Between Leadership and Mental Illness* (New York: Penguin Press, 2011).

Gibbs, Philip. *Adventures in Journalism* (London: Harper & Brothers, 1923).

Gilbert, Bentley Brinkerhoff. *David Lloyd George: A Political Life: Organizer of Victory 1912–1916* (Columbus, OH: Ohio State University Press, 1992).

Gilbert, Bentley Brinkerhoff. Review of: '*Eric Hopkins, Charles Masterman (1873–1927), Politician and Journalist: The Splendid Failure* (Lewiston, NY: Edward Mellen Press, 1999)' in *Albion: A Quarterly Journal Concerned with British Studies*, Winter 2000, 32(4).

Gilbert, Martin. *Prophet of Truth: Winston S. Churchill 1922–1939* (London: Minerva, 1990).

Gilbert, Martin *In Search of Churchill: A Historian's Journey* (London: HarperCollins, 1995).

Gillham, Nicholas Wright. *A Life of Sir Francis Galton: From African Exploration to the Birth of Eugenics* (New York: Oxford University Press, 2001).

Gindin, James. *John Galsworthy's Life and Art: An Alien's Fortress* (London: Palgrave Macmillan, 1987).

Godfrey, Barry, Cox, Pamela, Shore, Heather and Alker, Zoe. *Young Criminal Lives: Life Courses and Life Chances from 1850* (Oxford: Oxford University Press, 2017).

Grey of Fallodon, Viscount [Sir Edward Grey]. *Twenty Five Years 1892–1916: Vol. I* (New York: Frederick A. Stokes, MCMXXV[1925]).

Griffiths, Clare. 'Broken Promises and the Remaking of Political Trust: Debating Reconstruction in Britain During the Second World War' in David Thackeray and Richard Toye (eds), *Electoral Pledges in Britain since 1918: The Politics of Promises* (Cham, Switzerland: Springer Nature, 2020).

Griffiths, Richard. *The Entrepreneurial Society of the Rhondda Valleys, 1840–1920: Power and Influence in the Porth-Pontypridd Region* (Cardiff: University of Wales Press, 2010).

Griffiths, Robert. 'Cardiff Cigar Workers and the 'Feminine Strike' of 1911' in *Our History*, May 2012, 4.

Grigg, John. *Lloyd George: The People's Champion 1902–1911* (London: Methuen, 1991).

Grigg, John. 'Churchill and Lloyd George' in Blake, Robert and Louis, Wm Roger (eds), *Churchill* (Oxford: Clarendon, 1993).

Grigg, John. *Lloyd George: War Leader, 1916–1918* (London: Faber & Faber, 2011).

Gugliotta, Angela. '"Dr. Sharp with His Little Knife": Therapeutic and Punitive Origins of Eugenic Vasectomy – Indiana, 1892–1921' in *Journal of the History of Medicine and Allied Sciences*, October 1998, 53(4).

Hackmann, W. Kent. 'The British Raid on Rochefort, 1757' in *Mariner's Mirror*, 1978, 64(3).

Haffner, Sebastian and Brown, John (Trans.), *Churchill* (London: Haus, 2003).

Hainsworth, John. *The Llanfyllin Union Workhouse: A Short History* (Llanfyllin: The Llanfyllin Dolydd Building Preservation Trust, 2004).

Haldane, Richard Burdon. *An Autobiography* (London, Hodder & Stoughton, MCMXXIX [1929]).

Hamlin, Alexandra and Oakes, Peter. 'Reflections on Deinstitutionalization in the United Kingdom' in *Journal of Policy and Practice in Intellectual Disabilities*, March 2008, 5(1).

Hanham, H.J. (ed.). *The Nineteenth-Century Constitution 1815–1914: Documents and Commentary* (Cambridge: CAmbridge University Press, 1969).

Hankey, Lord. *The Supreme Command 1914–1918: Vol. One* (London: George Allen & Unwin, 1961).

Harley, C. Knick. 'Trade: Discovery, Mercantilism and Technology' in Roderick Floud and Paul Johnson (eds), *The Cambridge Economic History of Modern Britain Vol. I: Industrialisation, 1700–1860* (Cambridge: Cambridge University Press, 2004).

Harling, Philip. 'The Trouble with Convicts: From Transportation to Penal Servitude, 1840–67' in *Journal of British Studies*, January 2014, 53(1).

Harper, Edith K. *Stead: The Man: Personal Reminiscences* (London: William Rider & Son, 1918).

Harrison, Elaine (ed.). *Office-Holders in Modern Britain: Vol. 10: Officials of Royal Commissions of Inquiry 1870–1939* (London: University of London, 1995).

Hassall, Christopher. *Edward Marsh Patron of the Arts: A Biography* (London: Longmans, Green & Co., 1959).

Hattersley, Roy. *David Lloyd George: The Great Outsider* (London: Abacus, 2012).

Havighurst, Alfred F. *Radical Journalist: H.W. Massingham (1860–1924)* (Cambridge: Cambridge University Press, 1974).

Hawksley, Lucinda. *March, Women, March* (London: Andre Deutsch, 2015).

Heath, Alison. *The Life of George Ranken Askwith, 1861–1942* (Abingdon: Routledge, 2016).

Henderson, Mary. *Ethel Moorhead: Dundee's Rowdiest Suffragette* (No place: Privately published, 2020).

Hikins, H.R. 'The Liverpool General Transport Strike, 1911' in J.J. Bagley and James Murphy (hon. eds), *Transactions of The Historic Society of Lancashire and Cheshire For The Year 1961: Vol. 113* (Liverpool: Historic Society of Lancashire and Cheshire, 1962).

Hiley, Nicholas. 'The Failure of British Counter-Espionage against Germany, 1907–1914' in *Historical Journal*, December 1985, 28(4).

Hobhouse, Stephen and Brockway, A. Fenner (eds). *English Prisons Today: Being the Report of the Prison System Enquiry Committee* (London: Longmans, Green & Co., 1922).

Holmes, Colin. 'The Tredegar Riots of 1911: Anti-Jewish Disturbances in South Wales' in *Welsh History Review Cylchgrawn Hanes Cymru*, December 1982, 11(2).

Holmes, Jennifer. *A Working Woman: The Remarkable Life of Ray Strachey* (Kibworth Beauchamp: Matador, 2019).

Holton, Bob. *British Syndicalism 1900–1914: Myths and Realities* (London: Pluto Press, 1976).

Holton, Sandra Stanley. *Feminism and Democracy: Women's Suffrage and Reform Politics in Britain, 1900–1918* (Cambridge: Cambridge University Press, 2002).

Hopkin, Deian. 'The Llanelli Riots, 1911' in *Welsh History Review Cylchgrawn Hanes Cymru*, December 1983, 11(4).

Houdini, *A Magician Among The Spirits* (London: Harper & Brothers, 1924).

Hough, Richard. *First Sea Lord: An Authorised Biography of Admiral Lord Fisher* (London: Severn House, 1977).

Howard, Anthony. *RAB: The Life of R.A. Butler* (London: Jonathan Cape, 1986).

Hume, Leslie Parker. *The National Union of Women's Suffrage Societies 1897–1914* (Abingdon: Routledge, 2016).

Hyam, Ronald. *Elgin and Churchill at the Colonial Office 1905–1908: The Watershed of the Empire-Commonwealth* (London: MacMillan, 1968).

Inge, The Rev W.R. MA, DD. 'The Religious Aspect of the Problem' in Mrs. Walter Slater, *The Problem of the Feeble Minded: an Abstract of the Report of the Royal Commission on the Care and Control of the Feeble Minded* (London: P.S. King & Son, 1909).

Jane's Fighting Ships of World War I (London: Studio Editions, 1990).

Jeffery, Keith. *Field Marshal Sir Henry Wilson: A Political Soldier* (Oxford: Oxford University Press, 2006).

Jeffrey, Douglas. 'Riddles, Mysteries, Enigmas' in *Finest Hour: Magazine of The International Churchill Society*, May 2013, 142.

Jeffreys-Jones, Rhodri. *In Spies We Trust: The Story of Western Intelligence* (Oxford: Oxford University Press, 2013).

Jenkins, Lyndsey. *Lady Constance Lytton: Aristocrat, Suffragette, Martyr* (London: Biteback Publishing, 2015).

Jenkins, Roy. *Asquith: Portrait of a Man and an Era* (New York: Chilmark Press, 1964).

Jenkins, Roy. *Mr Balfour's Poodle: People v Peers* (London: Papermac, 1999).

Jenkins, Roy. *Churchill* (London: Macmillan, 2001).

John, Angela V. 'Men, Manners and Militancy: Literary Men and Women's Suffrage' in Angela V. John and Claire Eustance (eds), *The Men's Share?: Masculinities, Male Support and Women's Suffrage in Britain, 1890–1920* (Abingdon: Routledge, 2013) p. 88.

Jones, D.J.V. 'The New Police, Crime and People in England and Wales, 1829–1888' in *Transactions of the Royal Historical Society*, 1983, 33.

Jones, Gareth Elwyn. *People, Protest and Politics: Case Studies in Twentieth Century Wales* (Llandysul: Gwasg Gomer, 1987).

Jones, Greta. *Social Hygiene in Twentieth-Century Britain* (London: Croom Helm, 1986).

Jones, Kennedy. *Fleet Street and Downing Street* (London: Hutchinson, 1920).

Jones, Thomas. *Lloyd George* (Cambridge, MA: Harvard University Press, 1951).

Judd, Alan. *The Quest for C: Sir Mansfield Cumming and the Founding of the British Secret Service* (London: Harper Collins, 1999).

Keen, Richard, Cracknell, Richard and Bolton, Max. *Women in Parliament and Government: House of Commons Briefing Paper SN01250* (London: House of Commons Library Research Service, 2018).

Kelly, Katherine E. 'Seeing Through Spectacles: The Woman Suffrage Movement and London Newspapers, 1906–13' in *European Journal of Women's Studies*, 2004, 11(3).

Kelly's Directory of Monmouthshire and South Wales: 1914 (London: Kelly's Directories, 1914).

Kevles, Daniel J. *In the Name of Eugenics: Genetics and the Uses of Human Heredity* (Cambridge, MA: Harvard University Press, 1999).

King, Brian. *Rediscovered Dundee* (Kibworth Beauchamp: Matador, 2020).

King, Desmond. *In The Name of Liberalism: Illiberal Social Policy in the United States and Britain* (Oxford: Oxford University Press, 1999).

Kipling, Rudyard. *The Collected Poems of . . .* (Ware: Wordsworth Editions, 1994).

Kirby, Dick. *Whitechapel's Sherlock Holmes: The Casebook of Fred Wensley OBE KPM Victorian Crime Buster* (Barnsley: Pen & Sword, 2015) Kindle Edition.

Kirby, M.W. *The Decline of British Economic Power since 1870* (Abingdon: Routledge, 2014).

Kyle, Keith. *Suez: Britain's End of Empire in the Middle East* (London: I.B. Taurus, 2011).

Lambert, Nicholas A. *Sir John Fisher's Naval Revolution* (Columbia, SC: University of South Carolina Press, 2002).

Lane, Roger and McRonald, Jenny. 'Winston Churchill and the Akbar Heswall' in *Heswall & District Magazine*, October 2015.

Langworth, Richard M. *A Connoisseur's Guide to the Books of Sir Winston Churchill* (London: Brassey's, 1998).

Lasswell, Harold D. *Propaganda Technique in the World War* (New York: Peter Smith, 1927).

Laurie-Fletcher, Danny. *British Invasion and Spy Literature, 1871–1918: Historical Perspectives on Contemporary Society* (London: Palgrave Macmillan, 2019).

Le Queux, William. *The Great War in England in 1897* (London: Tower Publishing Co., 1894).

Le Queux, William. *England's Peril: A Novel* (London: F.V. White & Co., 1899).

Le Queux, William. *The Invasion of 1910 With a Full Account of The Siege of London: Naval Chapters by H.W. Wilson and an Introductory Letter by Field-Marshal Earl Roberts* (London: Eveleigh Nash, 1906).

Lee, Geoffrey. *The People's Budget: An Edwardian Tragedy* (London: Shepheard-Walwyn, 2008).

Lee, H.W. *The Great Strike Movement of 1911 and its Lessons* (London: Twentieth Century Press, 1912).

Leneman, Leah. *Martyrs in Our Midst: Dundee, Perth and the Forcible Feeding of Suffragettes* (Dundee: Abertay Historical Society, 1993).

Leneman, Leah. *A Guid Cause: The Women's Suffrage Movement in Scotland* (Edinburgh: Mercat, 1995)

Leng, Philip J. *The Welsh Dockers* (Ormskirk: Hesketh, 1981).

Leslie, Shane (Comp.). *Sir Evelyn Ruggles-Brise: A Memoir of the Founder of Borstal* (London: John Murray, 1938).

Lewis, E.D. 'Population Change and Social Life, 1860–1914' in K.S. Hopkins (ed.), *Rhondda: Past and Future* (Ferndale: Rhondda Borough Council, 1975).

Lloyd George, David. *War Memoirs: Vol. I* (London: Ivor Nicholson & Watson, 1933).

Lloyd George, Earl [Richard Lloyd George]. *My Father, Lloyd George* (New York: Crown, 1960).

Long, The Right Honourable Viscount Long of Wraxall, FRS [Walter Long]. *Memories* (London: Hutchinson, 1923).

Lough, David. *No More Champagne: Churchill and His Money* (London: Head of Zeus, 2015) Kindle edition.

Low, Valentine. 'Tonypandy: The Miners' Strike that Blighted Churchill's Career' in *The Times*, 14 February 2019.

Lytton, Lady Constance and Warton, Jane Spinster. *Prison & Prisoners: Some Personal Experiences* (London: William Heinemann, 1914).

Macaulay, Thomas Babington. *Reviews, Essays, and Poems Including Essays from 'The Edinburgh Review', Lays of Ancient Rome, and Miscellaneous Writings in Prose and Verse* (London: Ward, Lock, 1890).

McDermott, W.J. 'The Immediate Origins of the Committee of Imperial Defence: A Reappraisal' in *Canadian Journal of History*, May 2016, 7(3).

McEwen, John M. 'Tonypandy: Churchill's Albatross' in *Queen's Quarterly: A Canadian Review*, Spring 1971, 78.

McEwen, John M. 'The National Press during the First World War: Ownership and Circulation' in *Journal of Contemporary History*, July 1982, 17(3).

McKenna, Stephen. *Reginald McKenna 1863–1943: A Memoir* (London: Eyre & Spottiswoode, 1948).

MacKenzie, Donald. 'Review of Eugenics and Politics in Britain, 1900–1914 by G.R. Searle' in *British Journal for the History of Science*, March 1978, 11(1).

MacKenzie, Donald. 'Karl Pearson and the Professional Middle Class' in *Annals of Science*, 1979, 36(2).

Mackintosh, Alexander. *Joseph Chamberlain: An Honest Biography* (London: Hodder & Stoughton, 1906).

Mackintosh, Alexander. *From Gladstone to Lloyd George: Parliament in Peace and War* (London: Hodder & Stoughton, 1921).

Macnicol, John. 'Eugenics and the Campaign for Voluntary Sterilization in Britain Between the Wars' in *Social History of Medicine*, August 1989, 2(2).

Macready, General The Rt. Hon. Sir Nevil. *Annals of An Active Life: Vol. I* (London: Hutchinson, 1924).

Maddox, David and Evans, Gwyn. *The Tonypandy Riots 1910–1911* (Bridgend: Mid Glamorgan County Council Education Department, 1992).

Mann, Tom. *Tom Mann's Memoirs* (London: Labour Publishing Co., 1923).

Marder, Arthur J. *From the Dreadnought to Scapa Flow: The Royal Navy in the Fisher Era 1904–1919: The Road to War 1904–1914* (Barnsley: Seaforth, 2013).

Marsh, Edward. *A Number of People: A Book of Reminiscences* (London: William Heinemann, 1939).

Martin, Hugh. *Battle: The Life Story of Winston S. Churchill Prime Minister: Study of a Genius* (London: Victor Gollancz, 1941).

Mason, Bertha. *The Story of the Women's Suffrage Movement* (London: Sherratt & Hughes, 1912).

Mason, Joan. 'Hertha Ayrton (1854–1923) and the Admission of Women to the Royal Society of London' in *Notes and Records of the Royal Society of London*, July 1991, 45(2).

Masterman, C.F.G. *The Condition of England* (London: Methuen & Co., 1909).

Masterman, Lucy. *C.F.G. Masterman: A Biography* (London, Nicholson &. Watson, 1939).

Maurice, Major General Sir Frederick. *Haldane, 1856–1915: The Life of Viscount Haldane of Cloan* (London: Faber & Faber, 1937).

Mazumdar, Pauline. *Eugenics, Human Genetics and Human Failings: The Eugenics Society, its Sources and its Critics in Britain* (London: Routledge, 1992).

Mendelssohn, Peter de. *The Age of Churchill: Heritage and Adventure 1874–1911* (London: Thames & Hudson, 1961) p. 591.

Menzies, Mrs Stuart (Amy Charlotte Menzies *née* Bewicke). *Modern Men of Mark: The Romantic Stories of Lord Armstrong, Sir Richard Burbidge, Lord Leverhulme, Lord Northcliffe, Sir Joseph Lyons, Sir Joseph Pease, Lord Rhondda and Others* (London: Herbert Jenkins, 1921).

Mitchell, David. *Queen Christabel: A Biography of Christabel Pankhurst* (London: MacDonald & Jane's, 1977).

Moore, James. *Good Breeding: Science and Society in a Darwinian Age* (Milton Keynes: Open University, 2001).

Moran, Lord. *Winston Churchill: The Struggle for Survival 1940–1965* (London: Constable & Co., 1966).

Morgan, J. Vyrnwy. *The Welsh Religious Revival 1904–5: A Retrospect and a Criticism* (London: Chapman & Hall, 1909).

Morgan, J. Vyrnwy. *Life of Viscount Rhondda* (London: H.R. Allenson, 1918).

Morgan, Jane. *Conflict and Order: The Police and Labour Disputes in England and Wales, 1900–1939* (Oxford: Clarendon Press, 1987).

Morgan, Jane. 'Police and Labour in the age of Lindsay, 1910–1936' in *Llafur: Cymdeithas Hanes Pobl Cymreig – Welsh People's History Society*, 1988, 5(1).

Morgan, Kenneth O. 'Review of *Mabon: A Study in Trade Union Leadership*' in *Cymdeithas Hanes Lleol Morgannwg – Transactions of the Glamorgan Local History Society*, 1960, IV.

Morgan, Kenneth O. Book review of: 'John F. Naylor, *A Man and an Institution: Sir Maurice Hankey, the Cabinet Secretariat and the Custody of Cabinet Secrecy* (Cambridge: Cambridge University Press, 1984)' in *Journal of Modern History*, June 1986, 58(2).

Morgan, Kenneth O. *Wales in British Politics, 1868–1922* (Cardiff: University of Wales Press, 1991).

Morgan, Kenneth O. 'Lloyd George and Germany' in *Historical Journal*, September 1996, 39(3).

Morgan, Ted. *Churchill: Young Man in a Hurry, 1874–1915* (New York: Simon & Schuster, 1982).

Morgan-Owen, David. 'Cooked up in the Dinner Hour? Sir Arthur Wilson's War Plan, Reconsidered' in *English Historical Review*, August 2015, 130(545).

Morrell, Caroline. *'Black Friday' and Violence Against Women in the Suffragette Movement* (London: Women's Research & Resources Centre, 1981).

Morris, A.J.A. *Reporting the First World War: Charles Repington, 'The Times' and the Great War, 1914–1918* (Cambridge: Cambridge University Press, 2015).

Morris, Homer Lawrence. *Parliamentary Franchise Reform in England from 1885 to 1918* (London: P.S. King & Son, 1921).

Moulton, H. Fletcher (ed.). *Trial of Steinie Morrison* (London: William Hodge & Co., 1922)

Murray, Jessie and Brailsford, H.N. *The Treatment of the Women's Deputations by the Metropolitan Police: Copy of Evidence collected by Dr Jessie Murray and Mr H.N. Brailsford, and forwarded to the Home Office by the Conciliation Committee for Women Suffrage, in support of its Demand for a Public Enquiry* (London: Woman's Press, 1911).

Mynott, Ed. 'Nationalism, Racism and Immigration Control: From Anti-Racism to Anti-Capitalism' in Steve Cohen, Beth Humphries, and Ed Mynott, *From Immigration Controls to Welfare Controls* (Abingdon: Routledge, 2002).

Nellis, Mike. 'John Galsworthy's Justice' in *British Journal of Criminology*, Winter 1996, 36(1).

Neville, Robert G. 'The Yorkshire Miners and the 1893 Lockout: The Featherstone "Massacre"' in *International Review of Social History*, 1976, 21(3).

Newman, Anne. 'Dundee's Grand Old Man' in *Journal of Liberal History*, Spring 2005, 46.

Newton, Lord. *Lord Lansdowne: A Biography* (London: Macmillan & Co., 1929).

Nicolson, James Badenach. *Analysis of Recent Statutes Affecting Parliamentary Elections in Scotland, With Appendix Containing the Statutes, and a Digest of Recent Decisions of the Registration Appeal Court* (Edinburgh: Bell & Bradfute, 1885).

Norman, H.E. 'Conviction and Probation: The Case Against Conviction' in *Canadian Bar Review*, May 1941, XIX(5).

Normanbrook, Lord, Colville, John, Martin, John, Jacob, Ian, Bridges, Lord, Rowan, Leslie and Wheeler-Bennett, John (ed.). *Action this Day, Working with Churchill: Memoirs* (New York: St Martin's Press, 1969).

O'Brien, Anthony Mor (ed.). *The Autobiography of Edmund Stonelake* (Bridgend: Mid Glamorgan County Council, 1981).

O'Brien, Anthony Mor. 'Churchill and the Tonypandy Riots' in *Welsh History Review – Cylchgrawn Hanes Cymru*, June 1994, 17(1).

O'Halpin, Eunan. 'British Government and Society in the Twentieth Century' in *Historical Journal*, September 1985, 28(3).

Ostrogorski, M. and Clarke, Frederick (Trans.). *Democracy and The Organization of Political Parties: Vol. I* (London: Macmillan & Co., 1902).

Otte, T.G. *July Crisis: The World's Descent into War, Summer 1914* (Cambridge: Cambridge University Press, 2014).

Otte, T.G. *Statesmen of Europe: A Life of Sir Edward Grey* (London: Allen Lane, 2020).

Otte, T.G. and Readman, Paul (eds), *By-Elections in British Politics, 1832–1914* (Woodbridge: Boydell Press, 2013).

Owen, Frank. *Tempestuous Journey: Lloyd George His Life and Times* (London: Hutchinson, 1954).

Oxford and Asquith, Earl of, *Fifty Years of Parliament: Vol. II* (London: Cassell, 1926).

Pakenham, Thomas. *The Boer War* (London: Futura, 1988).

Panayi, Panikos. *The Enemy in our Midst: Germans in Britain during the First World War* (London: Bloomsbury, 2014) Kindle edition.

Pankhurst, Dame Christabel, and Pethick-Lawrence, Lord (ed.). *Unshackled: The Story of How We Won the Vote* (London: Hutchinson, 1959).

Pankhurst, E. Sylvia. *The Suffragette: The History of The Women's Militant Suffrage Movement 1905–1910* (New York: Sturgis & Walton, 1911).

Pankhurst, Emmeline. *My Own Story* (London: Eveleigh Nash, 1914) pp. 81–202.

Pankhurst, Sylvia. 'The End of the Truce: Deputation to Westminster, Friday, November 18, Accounts of Eye-witnesses. Miss Sylvia Pankhurst's Account' in *Votes for Women*, 25 November 1910, IV(142).

Parker, Geoffrey. 'The Etiquette of Atrocity: The Laws of War in Early Modern Europe' in Geoffrey Parker (ed.), *Empire, War and Faith in Early Modern Europe* (London: Allen Lane, 2002).

Parkinson, Henry. *A Primer of Social Science* (London: P.S. King, 1920).

Paterson, Tony. *Churchill: A Seat for Life* (Dundee: David Winter, 1980).

Peak, Steve. *Troops in Strikes: Military Intervention in Industrial Disputes* (London: Cobden Trust, 1984).

Pellew, Jill. 'The Home Office and the Aliens Act, 1905' in *Historical Journal*, June 1989, 32(2).

Pelling, Henry. *Winston Churchill* (London: Book Club Associates, 1974).

Pelling, Henry. 'Churchill and the Labour Movement' in Robert Blake and Wm Roger Louis (eds), *Churchill* (Oxford: Clarendon, 1993).

Pentland, Lady. *The Right Honourable John Sinclair, Lord Pentland, GGSI: A Memoir* (London: Methuen & Co., 1928).

Pethick Lawrence, F.W. *The Trial of the Suffragette Leaders* (London: Woman's Press, 1909).

Philip Whitwell Wilson, 'Review: Dramatic Victorians' in *North American Review*, December 1925–February 1926, 222(829)

Piper, Leonard. *Dangerous Waters: The Life and Death of Erskine Childers* (London: Hambledon Continuum, 2003).

Ponting, Clive. *Churchill* (London: Sinclair-Stevenson, 1994).

Pope-Hennessey, James. *Lord Crewe 1858–1945: The Likeness of a Liberal* (London: Constable & Co., 1955).

Pope-Hennessy, James. *Queen Mary 1867–1953* (London: George Allen & Unwin, 1959).

Porritt, Edward. 'Barriers Against Democracy in the British Electoral System' in *Political Science Quarterly*, March 1911, 26(1).

Porter, Bernard. *The Origins of the Vigilant State: The London Metropolitan Police Special Branch before the First World War* (Woodbridge: Boydell Press, 1991).

Porter, Dorothy. '"Enemies of the Race" Biologism, Environmentalism, and Public Health in Edwardian England' in *Victorian Studies*, Winter 1991, 34(2).

Porter, Theodore M. *Karl Pearson: The Scientific Life in a Statistical Age* (Princeton, NJ: Princeton University Press, 2004).

Powell, David. 'The New Liberalism and the Rise of Labour, 1886–1906' in *Historical Journal*, June 1986, 29(2).

Powell, David. *British Politics, 1910–1935: The Crisis of the Party System* (Abingdon: Routledge, 2004).

Powell Dyffryn Steam Coal Company, The. *The Powell Dyffryn Steam Coal Co., Ltd. 1864–1914* (Cardiff: Business Statistics, 1914).

Powell, L.H. *The Shipping Federation: A History of the First Sixty Years 1890–1950* (London: Shipping Federation 1950).

Price, Richard. *An Imperial War and the British Working Class: Working-Class Attitudes and Reactions to the Boer War 1899–1902* (London: Routledge & Kegan Paul, 1972).

Priestley, J.B. *The Edwardians* (London: Sphere, 1972).

Prys-Williams, Barbara. 'Rhys Davies as Autobiographer: Hare or Houdini?' in Meic Stephens (ed.), *Rhys Davies: Decoding the Hare: Critical Essays to Mark the Centenary of the Writer's Birth* (Cardiff: University Of Wales, 2001).

Pugh, Martin. *The Pankhursts* (London: Allen Lane, 2001).

Pugh, Martin. '"Queen Anne is Dead": The Abolition of Ministerial By-Elections, 1867–1926' in *Parliamentary History*, 2002, 21(3).

Purvis, June. *Emmeline Pankhurst: A Biography* (Abingdon: Routledge, 2002).

Purvis, June. *Christabel Pankhurst: A Biography* (Abingdon: Routledge, 2018).

Quinault, R.E. 'Lord Randolph Churchill and Tory Democracy, 1880–1885' in *Historical Journal*, March 1979, 22(1).

Quinton, R.F. *The Modern Prison Curriculum: A General Review of Our Penal System* (London: Macmillan & Co., 1912).

Radzinowicz, L. 'The Persistent Offender' in *Cambridge Law Journal*, March 1939, 7(1).

Radzinowicz, Sir Leon. *Adventures in Criminology* (London: Routledge, 1999).

Radzinowicz, Sir Leon and Hood, Roger. 'Incapacitating the Habitual Criminal: The English Experience' in *Michigan Law Review*, 1980, 78(8).

Raeburn, Antonia. *The Militant Suffragettes* (London: Michael Joseph, 1973).

Rasor, Eugene L. *Arthur James Balfour, 1848–1930: Historiography and Annotated Bibliography* (Westport, CT: Greenwood Press, 1998).

Raynes, J.R. *Engines and Men: The History of the Associated Society of Locomotive Engineers and Firemen* (Leeds: Goodall & Suddick, 1921).

Reading, The Marquess of. *Rufus Isaacs First Marquess of Reading: By His Son* (London: Hutchinson, 1950).

Reckless, Walter C. *The Crime Problem* (New York: Appleton-Century-Crofts, 1961).

Rempel, Richard A. *Unionists Divided: Arthur Balfour, Joseph Chamberlain and the Unionist Free Traders* (Newton Abbot: David & Charles, 1972).

Repington, Charles à Court. Writing as 'The Military Correspondent of *The Times*', *The Foundations of Reform* (London: Simpkin, Marshall & Co., 1908).

Rhodes James, Robert. 'The Enigma' in James W. Muller (ed.), *Churchill as Peacemaker* (Cambridge: Cambridge University Press, 2002).

Rhodes James, Robert. *Churchill: a Study in Failure, 1900–1939* (London: Weidenfeld & Nicolson, 1970).

Rhodes James, Robert. *Rosebery: A Biography of Archibald Philip, Fifth Earl of Rosebery* (London: Macmillan, 1964).

Riddell, Fern. *Death in Ten Minutes: Kitty Marion: Activist, Arsonist, Suffragette* (London: Hodder & Stoughton, 2018) Kindle edition.

Ridley, Jane. *George V: Never a Dull Moment* (London: Chatto & Windus, 2021).

Riley, Sam G. (ed.). *Consumer Magazines of the British Isles* (Westport, CT: Greenwood Press, 1993).

Rimmer, Joan. *Yesterday's Naughty Children: Training Ship, Girls' Reformatory and Farm School: A History of the Liverpool Reformatory Association, founded in 1855* (Manchester: Neil Richardson, 1986).

Ring, Jim. *Erskine Childers* (London: Faber & Faber, 1997).

Roberts, Christopher. *The British Courts and Extra-territoriality in Japan, 1859–1899* (Leiden: Global Oriental, Boston).

Rogers, Colin. *The Battle of Stepney: The Sidney Street Siege: Its Causes and Consequences* (London: Robert Hale, 1981).

Rose, Jonathan. *The Literary Churchill: Author, Reader, Actor* (New Haven, CT: Yale University Press, 2014). Kindle edition.

Rose, Kenneth. *King George V* (London: Weidenfeld & Nicolson, 1983).

Rose, Norman. *Churchill: An Unruly Life* (London: Touchstone, 1998).

Rosen, Andrew. *Rise Up, Women!: The Militant Campaign of the Women's Social and Political Union 1903–1914* (Abingdon: Routledge, 2013).

Rosenbaum, S. 'The General Election of January, 1910, and the Bearing of the Results on Some Problems of Representation' in the *Journal of the Royal Statistical Society*, May 1910, 73(5).

Roskill, Stephen. *Hankey: Man of Secrets: Vol. I 1877–1918* (London: Collins, 1970).

Rover, Constance. *Women's Suffrage and Party Politics in Britain, 1866–1914* (London: Routledge & Kegan Paul, 1967).

Rowan-Hamilton, S.O. (ed.). *Trial of John Alexander Dickman* (London: Butterworth & Co., 1914).

Rubinstein, William D. 'The Liberal Government, 1910–14: A 'General Crisis'?' in William D. Rubinstein, *Twentieth-Century Britain: A Political History* (Houndmills: Palgrave Macmillan, 2003).

Ruff, Philip. *A Towering Flame: The Life & Times of the Elusive Latvian Anarchist Peter the Painter* (London: Breviary Stuff Publications, 2019).

Ruggles-Brise, Sir Evelyn. *The English Prison System* (London: Macmillan, 1921).

Sandys, Celia. *Churchill Wanted Dead or Alive* (London: Harper Collins, 1999).

Saville, John. 'Trade Unions and Free Labour: The Background to the Taff Vale Decision' in Asa Briggs and John Saville (eds), *Essays in Labour History in Memory of G.D.H. Cole 25 September 1889–14 January 1959* (London: Palgrave Macmillan, 1967).

Scally, Robert James. *The Origins of the Lloyd George Coalition: The Politics of Social Imperialism, 1900–1918* (Princeton, NJ: Princeton University Press, 1975).

Schneer, Jonathan. *Ben Tillett: Portrait of a Labour Leader* (Beckenham: Croom Helm, 1982).

Searle, G.R. *Eugenics and Politics in Britain 1900–1914* (Leyden: Noordhoff International Publishing, 1976).

Searle, G.R. 'Eugenics and Class' in Charles Webster (ed.), *Biology, Medicine and Society 1840–1940* (Cambridge: Cambridge University Press, 1981).

Searle, G.R. *A New England? Peace and War 1886–1918* (Oxford: Oxford University Press, 2004).

Seligmann, Matthew S. *Spies in Uniform: British Military and Naval Intelligence on the Eve of the First World War* (Oxford: Oxford University Press, 2006)

Seymour, Charles. *Electoral Reform in England and Wales: The Development and Operation of the Parliamentary Franchise, 1832–1885* (London: Humphrey Milford Oxford University Press, MDCCCCXV [1915]).

Shannon, Richard. *The Crisis of Imperialism 1865–1915* (London: Paladin, 1986).

Sharp, Evelyn. *Hertha Ayrton 1854–1923: A Memoir* (London: Edward Arnold & Co., 1926).

Shaw, [George] Bernard. *Three Plays for Puritans: The Devil's Disciple, Caesar and Cleopatra, & Captain Brassbound's Conversion* (London: Grant Richards, 1901).

Shelden, Michael. *Young Titan: The Making of Winston Churchill* (New York: Simon & Schuster Paperbacks, 2014).

Shpayer-Makov, Haia. *The Making of a Policeman: A Social History of a Labour Force in Metropolitan London 1829–1914* (Aldershot: Ashgate, 2002).

Sires, Roland V. 'Labor Unrest in England, 1910–1914' in *Journal of Economic History*, September 1955,15(3).

Smith, Dai. *Wales: A Question for History* (Bridgend: Seren, 1999).

Smith, David. 'Tonypandy 1910: Definitions of Community' in *Past & Present*, May 1980, 87.

Smith, David. 'From Riots to Revolt: Tonypandy and The Miners' Next Step' in Trevor Herbert and Gareth Elwyn Jones (eds), *Wales 1880–1914* (Cardiff: University of Wales Press, 1988).

Smith, Harold L. *The British Women's Suffrage Campaign 1866–1928* (Abingdon: Routledge, 2007).

Snowden, Philip. *Socialism and Syndicalism* (London: Collins, 1913).

Snowden, Philip, Viscount. *An Autobiography: Vol. One 1864–1919* (London: Ivor Nicholson & Watson, 1934).

Soames, Mary. *Clementine Churchill: The Biography of a Marriage* (New York: Houghton Mifflin, 2003).

Soloway, Richard A. *Demography and Degeneration: Eugenics and the Declining Birthrate in Twentieth-century Britain* (Chapel Hill, NC: University of North Carolina Press, 1995).

Soloway, Richard Allen. 'Neo-Malthusians, Eugenists, and the Declining Birth-Rate in England, 1900–1918' in *Albion: A Quarterly Journal Concerned with British Studies*, Autumn 1978, 10(3).

Somervell, D.C. *The Reign of King George the Fifth: An English Chronicle* (London: Faber & Faber, 1935).

Spender, Harold. *The Prime Minister: Life and Times of David Lloyd George* (New York: George H. Doran, 1920).

Spender, J.A. *The Life of The Right Hon Sir Henry Campbell-Bannerman, GCB: Vol. II* (London: Hodder & Stoughton, 1923).

Spender, J.A. and Asquith, Cyril. *Life of Herbert Henry Asquith, Lord Oxford and Asquith: Vol. I* (London: Hutchinson & Co., 1932).

Spiers, Edward M. 'Haldane's Reform of the Regular Army: Scope for Revision' in *British Journal of International Studies*, April 1980, 6(1).

Stafford, David. *Churchill and Secret Service* (London: Abacus, 2000).

Stafford, David. *The Silent Game: The Real World of Imaginary Spies* (London: Lume Books, 2020) Kindle edition.

Standage, Tom. *The Victorian Internet: The Remarkable Story of the Telegraph and the Nineteenth Century's On-Line Pioneers* (London: Phoenix, 1999).

Stearn, Roger T. 'The Mysterious Mr Le Queux: War Novelist, Defence Publicist and Counterspy' in *Soldiers of the Queen*, September 1992, 70.

Stephenson, Charles. *A Box of Sand: The Italo-Ottoman War 1911–1912: The First Land Sea and Air War* (Ticehurst: Tattered Flag, 2014).

Stephenson, W. Tetley. 'The Railway Conciliation Scheme, 1907' in *Economic Journal*, December 1911, 21(84).

Stern, David G. 'Heraclitus' and Wittgenstein's River Images: Stepping Twice into the Same River', in *The Monist*, October 1991, 74(4).

Stickler, Paul. *The Murder That Defeated Whitechapel's Sherlock Holmes: At Mrs Ridgley's Corner* (Barnsley: Pen & Sword, 2018).

Stokoe, John. 'The Shipping Federation' in *Bulletin: Journal of The Liverpool Nautical Research Society*, June 2013, 57(1).

Strachan, Hew. *The First World War: Vol. I: To Arms* (Oxford: Oxford University Press, 2003).

Strachey, Ray. *The Cause: A Short History of the Women's Movement in Great Britain* (London: Bell and Sons, 1928).

Suttie, Andrew. *Rewriting the First World War: Lloyd George, Politics and Strategy 1914–1918* (London: Palgrave Macmillan, 2005).

Symons, Julian. *Horatio Bottomley* (Looe: House of Stratus, 2014).

Tanner, Duncan. 'The Parliamentary Electoral System, the 'Fourth' Reform Act and the Rise of Labour in England and Wales' in *Bulletin of the Institute of Historical Research*, November 1983, 56(134).

Tanner, Jakob. 'Eugenics before 1945' in *Journal of Modern European History/Zeitschrift für moderne europäische Geschichte/Revue d'histoire européenne contemporaine*, 2012, 10(4).

Taylor, A.J.P. *The Struggle for Mastery in Europe 1848–1915* (Oxford: Oxford University Press, 1954).

Terraine, John. *Business in Great Waters: The U-Boat Wars 1916–1945* (London: Mandarin, 1990).

Thatcher, Margaret. *The Downing Street Years* (London: Harper Collins, 1995).

Thompson, Andrew S. 'Tariff Reform: An Imperial Strategy, 1903–1913' in *Historical Journal*, December 1997, 40(4).

Thompson, Larry V. '*Lebensborn* and the Eugenics Policy of the Reichsführer-SS' in *Central European History*, March 1971, 4(1).

Thomson, Sir Basil. *The Scene Changes: An Autobiography* (London: Collins, 1939).

Thomson, Malcolm with the collaboration of Frances, Countess Lloyd-George of Dwyfor. *David Lloyd George: The Official Biography* (London: Hutchinson, 1948).

Thurlow, Richard C. *The Secret State: British Internal Security in the Twentieth Century* (Oxford: Blackwell, 1994).

Tillett, Ben. *Is the Parliamentary Labour Party a Failure?* (London: Twentieth Century Press, 1908).

Tollefson, Harold. *Policing Islam: The British Occupation of Egypt and the Anglo-Egyptian Struggle Over Control of the Police, 1882–1914* (Westport, CT: Greenwood Press, 1999).

Tomlinson, Jim. *Dundee and the Empire: 'Juteopolis' 1850–1939* (Edinburgh: Edinburgh University Press, 2014).

Townshend, Charles. "One Man Whom You Can Hang If Necessary': The Discreet Charm of Nevil Macready' in John B. Hattendorf and Malcolm H. Murfett (eds), *Limitations Of Military Power: Essays Presented To Professor Norman Gibbs on his Eightieth Birthday* (Houndmills: Palgrave Macmillan, 1990).

Toye, Richard. *Lloyd George and Churchill: Rivals for Greatness* (London: Pan Books, 2008).

Trotsky, Leon, Clinton, Alan (ed.) and Chappell, Richard (ed.). *Leon Trotsky: Collected Writings and Speeches on Britain: Vol. 2* (London: New Park Publications, 1974).

Troup, Sir Edward. *The Home Office* (London: G.P. Putnam's Sons, 1925).

Troup, Sir Edward. 'The Functions and Organization of the Home Office' in *Public Administration: Journal of the Institute of Public Administration*, 1926, IV.

Tupper, Edward. *Seamen's Torch: The Life Story of Captain Edward Tupper, National Union of Seamen* (London: Hutchinson & Co., 1938).

Vale, Allister and Scadding, John. *Winston Churchill's Illnesses, 1886–1965* (Barnsley: Frontline Books, 2020) Kindle edition.

van Wingerden, Sophia A. *The Women's Suffrage Movement in Britain, 1866–1928* (London: Palgrave Macmillan, 1999).

Vernon, Betty D. *Margaret Cole 1893–1980: A Political Biography* (London: Croom Helm, 1986).

Verrier, Anthony. *Through the Looking Glass: British Foreign Policy in an Age of Illusions* (London: Jonathan Cape, 1983).

Vincent, Andrew. 'German Philosophy and British Public Policy: Richard Burdon Haldane in Theory and Practice' in *Journal of the History of Ideas*, January 2007, 68(1).

Vincent, John (ed.). *The Crawford Papers: The Journals of David Lindsay, Twenty-Seventh Earl of Crawford and Tenth Earl of Balcarres, 1871–1940, During the Years 1892 To 1940* (Manchester: Manchester University Press, 1984).

Waldren, Mike. *The Siege of Sidney Street* (March: PFOA – Police Firearms Officers Association, 2013).

Walker, Clive. 'Reforming the Crime of Libel' in *New York Law School Law Review*, January 2006, 50(1).

Walker-Smith, Derek. *Lord Reading and his Cases: The Study of a Great Career* (New York: Macmillan Co., 1934).

Warwick, Paul. 'Did Britain Change? An Inquiry into the Causes of National Decline' in *Journal of Contemporary History*, January 1985, 20(1).

Watson, Katherine D. *Poisoned Lives: English Poisoners and Their Victims* (London: Hambledon Continuum, 2004).

Webb, Simon. *The Analogue Revolution: Communication Technology, 1901–1914* (Barnsley: Pen & Sword, 2018) Kindle Edition.

Weinberger, Barbara. *Keeping the Peace?: Policing Strikes in Britain 1906–1926* (Oxford: Berg, 1991).

Wensley, Frederick Porter. *Forty Years of Scotland Yard: The Record of a Lifetime's Service in the Criminal Investigation Department* (Garden City, NY: Doubleday, Doran & Co., 1931).

Whelehan, Niall. *The Dynamiters: Irish Nationalism and Political Violence in the Wider World 1867–1900* (Cambridge: Cambridge University Press, 2012).

Whetham, William Cecil Dampier and Whetham, Catherine Durning. *The Family and the Nation: A Study in Natural Inheritance and Social Responsibility* (London: Longmans, Green & Co., 1909).

Whibley, Charles. 'Musings without Method' in *Blackwood's Magazine*, February 1911, CLXXXIX(MCXLIV).

Whitmore, Richard. *Membership, Policy and Strategy of the Women's Social and Political Union in Leicester and the East Midlands 1907–1914: A Thesis Submitted in Partial Fulfilment of the Requirements of De Montfort University for the Degree of Doctor of Philosophy* (Leicester: Unpublished, 2000).

Whittington-Egan, Molly. *Murder on the Bluff: The Carew Poisoning Case* (Glasgow: Neil Wilson Publishing, 2012).

Wiener, Joel H. *The Americanization of the British Press, 1830s–1914: Speed in the Age of Transatlantic Journalism* (London: Palgrave Macmillan, 2011).

Wilkinson, Richard. *Lloyd George: Statesman or Scoundrel* (London: I.B. Tauris, 2018).

Williams, John. *Was Wales Industrialised?: Essays in Modern Welsh History* (Llandysul: Gwasg Gomer, 1995).

Williamson, Samuel R. Jr. *The Politics of Grand Strategy: Britain and France Prepare for War, 1904–1914* (Cambridge, MA: Harvard University Press, 1969).

Wilson, Matt Vaughan. 'The 1911 Waterfront Strikes in Glasgow: Trade Unions and Rank-and-File Militancy in the Labour Unrest of 1910–1914' in *International Review of Social History*, August 2008, 53(2).

Wilson, Ray and Adams, Ian. *Special Branch: A History: 1883–2006* (London: Biteback 2015).

Winetrobe, Barry and Seaton, Janet. *Confidence Motions: Research Paper 95/19* (London: House of Commons Library, 1995).

Winslow, Barbara. *Sylvia Pankhurst: Sexual Politics and Political Activism* (London: Verso, 2021).

Wise, Sarah. 'A Few Bad Apples' in *History Today*, August 2020, 70(8).

Wodehouse, P.G. *Mr Mulliner Speaking* (London: Herbert Jenkins, 1921) pp. 167–8.

Young, Paul. *The Mid and the Mush: Mid Rhondda Ground and its Football Team* (Treorchy: Paul Young, 2003).

Internet

Addison, Paul. *How Churchill's Mind Worked* at: https://openhistorysociety.org/members-articles/how-churchills-mind-worked-by-paul-addison/#_edn1

Annis, Geoffrey and Radcliffe, John. 'Notes on The City of Brass' at: http://www.kiplingsociety.co.uk/rg_cityofbrass1.htm

Anonymous, 'The Man at the Wheel' in *Seaman: The Official Organ of The National Sailors' & Firemen's Union* at: https://wdc.contentdm.oclc.org/digital/collection/tav/id/5194

Bank of England. Inflation Calculator at: https://www.bankofengland.co.uk/monetary-policy/inflation/inflation-calculator

Brazier, Rodney. The Parliament Acts at: https://publications.parliament.uk/pa/ld200506/ldselect/ldconst/141/14104.htm

Census, 1911 at: https://www.1911census.org.uk/ http://www.census.nationalarchives.ie/

Davies, Rhys. The Rhys Davies Trust at: http://www.rhysdaviestrust.org/

Galton, Francis. 'Hereditary Talent and Character' at https://galton.org/essays/1860-1869/galton-1865-hereditary-talent.pdf

Gibbs, Sir Philip Armand Hamilton (1877–1962) in the Oxford Dictionary of National Biography at: https://www.oxforddnb.com/view/10.1093/ref:odnb/9780198614128.001.0001/odnb-9780198614128-e-33387?docPos=2

Harrison, Elaine (ed.). 'List of commissions and officials: 1900-1909' in *Office-Holders in Modern Britain: Vol. 10, Officials of Royal Commissions of Inquiry 1870-1939* at: https://www.british-history.ac.uk/office-holders/vol10/pp42-57#h3-0018

Henderson, Mary. *Ethel Moorhead: Dundee's Rowdiest Suffragette* at: https://ethelmoorhead.org.uk/chapter-3-votes-for-women/

Jeffrey, Douglas. 'Riddles, Mysteries, Enigmas' *in Finest Hour: Magazine of The International Churchill Society* at: Online edition at: https://winstonchurchill.org/publications/finest-hour/finest-hour-142/riddles-mysteries-enigmas-10/

Justice, *Intercept Evidence* at: https://justice.org.uk/intercept-evidence/

Maslin, Janet. Review of Nassir Ghaemi, *A First-Rate Madness: Uncovering the Links Between Leadership and Mental Illness* at: https://www.nytimes.com/2011/08/11/books/a-first-rate-madness-by-nassir-ghaemi-review.html

National Records of Scotland website at: https://www.nrscotland.gov.uk/

Riddle of the Sands film. Information at: https://www.imdb.com/title/tt0079808/

Secretary of State for the Home Department, *Interception of Communications in the United Kingdom: A Consultation Paper*. June 1999 at https://www.cyber-rights.org/interception/ioca.pdf

UK Government, 'Prevention of Crime Act 1908' at: https://www.legislation.gov.uk/ukpga/1908/59/section/10/enacted

UK National Archives, *The Cabinet Papers: Development of Cabinet Government* at: https://www.nationalarchives.gov.uk/cabinetpapers/cabinet-gov/development-cabinet-government.htm

Williams, David. 'Thomas, Sir Daniel (Lleufer) (1863–1940), stipendiary magistrate' in *Y Bywgraf-fiadur Cymreig Dictionary of Welsh Biography*. https://biography.wales/article/s-THOM-LLE-1863

Wilson, Bee. 'A Little Talk in Downing St'; review of Stefan Buczacki, 'My Darling Mr Asquith: The Extraordinary Life and Times of Venetia Stanley' in *London Review of Books* at: https://www.lrb.co.uk/the-paper/v38/n22/bee-wilson/a-little-talk-in-downing-st.

Index